Election Management Bodies in East Africa

A comparative study of the contribution of electoral commissions to the strengthening of democracy

A review by AfriMAP
and the
Open Society Initiative for Eastern Africa

Alexander B Makulilo
Eugène Ntaganda
Francis Ang'ila Aywa
Margaret Sekaggya
Patrick Osodo

OPEN SOCIETY
FOUNDATIONS

Published by African Minds on behalf of
Open Society Foundations
224 West 57th Street
New York, NY 10019
www.opensocietyfoundations.org

African Minds
4 Eccleston Place, Somerset West, 7130, Cape Town, South Africa
info@africanminds.org.za
www.africanminds.org.za

ISBN:
978-1-920677-97-8 Print
978-1-928331-17-9 e-Book
978-1-928331-18-6 e-Pub

Copies of this book are available for free download at www.africanminds.org.za

ORDERS
To order printed copies from Africa, please contact:
African Minds
Email: info@africanminds.org.za
To order printed copies from outside Africa, please contact:
African Books Collective
PO Box 721, Oxford OX1 9EN, UK
Email: orders@africanbookscollective.com

Contents

List of tables and figures

List of boxes

Abbreviations and acronyms

ACDEG	African Charter on Democracy, Elections and Governance
ACE	Administration and Cost of Elections
ACHPR	African Charter on Human and Peoples' Rights
ADC-Ikibiri	*Alliance Démocratique pour le Changement* (Democratic Alliance for Change)
AEMO	African Elected Members Organisation
AfriCOG	Africa Centre for Open Governance
AfriMAP	Africa Governance Monitoring and Advocacy Project
AMNUT	All Muslim Nationalist Union of Tanganyika
ANC	African National Congress
APP	Akamba Peoples' Party
APRM	African Peer Review Mechanism
APRODH	*Association Burundaise pour la Protection des Droits Humains et des Personnes Détenues*
APROSOMA	*Association pour la Promotion Sociale des Masses* (Association for Social Promotion of the Masses)
ASP	Afro-Shirazi Party
AU	African Union
BIF	Burundi Francs
BNUB	United Nations Bureau in Burundi
BVR	biometric voter registration
CCA	Commission for the Constituent Assembly
CCEDU	Citizen's Coalition for Electoral Democracy in Uganda
CCM	*Chama Cha Mapinduzi* (Party of the Revolution)
CECI	Municipal Independent Electoral Commission
CENI	*Commission Electorale Nationale Indépendante* (National Independent Electoral Commission)
CEO	chief executive officer
CEPI	*Commission électorale provinciale indépendante* (Provincial Independent Electoral Commission)

CHADEMA	*Chama cha Demokrasia na Maendeleo* (Party for Democracy and Progress)
CNC	National Communication Council
CNDD	*Conseil National Pour la Défense de la Démocratie* (National Council for the Defence of Democracy)
CNDD-FDD	*Conseil National Pour la Défense de la Démocratie – Forces de Défense de la Démocratie* (National Council for the Defence of Democracy – Democracy Defence Forces)
COSOME	*Coalition de la Société Civile pour le Monitoring Electoral* (Coalition for the Monitoring and Observation of Elections)
CP	Conservative Party
CPP	Coast People's Party
CRC	Constitutional Review Commission
CSEOM	Rwandan Civil Society Election Observation Mission
CSO	civil society organisation
CUF	Civic United Front
Danida	Danish International Development Agency
DP	Democratic Party
DPP	Director of Public Prosecutions
EAC	East African Community
EACC	Ethics and Anti-Corruption Authority
EACEOM	East African Community Electoral Observer Mission
EACFEM	East African Community Forum of Electoral Commissions
EAMWS	East African Muslim Welfare Society
EC	Electoral Commission
ECK	Electoral Commission of Kenya
ECT	Electoral Commission of Tanzania
EISA	Electoral Institute for Sustainable Democracy in Africa
ELOG	Election Observation Group
EMB	election management body
ESF	Electoral Stakeholders Forum
ESP	Election Support Programme
EU	European Union
EUR	Euro
EVID	*electronic voter identification device*
FAR	*Forces armées rwandaises*
FDC	Forum for Democratic Change
FDU Inkingi	*Forces Démocratiques Unifiées*
FNL-Palipehutu	*Forces nationales de libération*
FPR	*Front Patriotique Rwandais*

FRODEBU	*Front pour la Démocratie au Burundi*
GDP	gross domestic product
GNU	government of national unity
GTBE	*Gouvernement de transition à base élargie*
HRW	Human Rights Watch
IDEA	International Institute for Democracy and Electoral Assistance
IEBC	Independent Electoral and Boundaries Commission
IEC	Interim Electoral Commission
IFES	International Foundation for Electoral Systems
IIBRC	Interim Independent Boundaries Review Commission
IIEC	Interim Independent Electoral Commission
IPC	Inter-Party Cooperation
IPPG	Inter-Parties Parliamentary Group
IREC	Independent Review Commission of the 2007 Elections
JEEMA	Justice Forum
JLOS	Justice, Law and Order Sector
JWCEP	Judiciary Working Committee on Election Preparations
KADU	Kenya African Democratic Union
KANU	Kenya African National Union
KPS	Kenya Prisons Service
KPU	Kenya People's Union
Ksh	Kenya Shillings
KWS	Kenya Wildlife Service
KY	*Kabaka Yekka*
LDGL	*Ligue des Droits de personnes des Grands Lacs*
LEGCO	Legislative Council
MDR	*Mouvement Démocratique Républicain* (Democratic Republican Movement)
MHC	Media High Council
MP	Member of Parliament
MRC	*Mouvement pour la Réhabilitation des Citoyens* (Movement for the Rehabilitation of Citizens)
MRND	*Mouvement Révolutionnaire National pour le Développement* (National Revolutionary Movement for Development)
MRNDD	*Mouvement Républicain National pour la Démocratie et le Développement* (National Republican Movement for Democracy and Development)
MSD	*Mouvement pour la solidarité et la démocratie* (Movement for Solidarity and Democracy)
NARC	National Rainbow Coalition
NCCR-Mageuzi	National Convention for Construction and Reform-Mageuzi

NCF	National Consultative Forum
NCFP	National Consultative Forum of Political Organisations
NEC	National Electoral Commission
NEMU	National Elections Monitoring Unit
NGO	non-governmental organisation
NHRC	National Human Rights Commission
NIEC	National Independent Electoral Commission
NIS	National Intelligence Service
NORDEM	Norwegian Resource Bank for Democracy and Human Rights
NPR	National Party of Rwanda
	(*Parti National du Rwanda*)
NPUA	Nyanza Province African Union
NRC	National Resistance Council
NRM	National Resistance Movement
NUDIPU	National Union of Disabled Persons in Uganda
NURC	National Unity and Reconciliation Commission (Rwanda)
NYS	National Youth Service
OAU	Organisation of African Unity
ODM	Orange Democratic Movement
OLUCOME	Organisation on the Control of Economic Embezzlement
ORINFOR	Rwanda Bureau for Information and Broadcasting
OSIEA	Open Society Initiative for Eastern Africa
PACAM	Joint Action Plan for Support to the Media
PACE	*Projet d'Appui au Processus Electoral*
	(Electoral Cycle Support Project)
PARENA	*Parti pour la Reconstruction Nationale*
	(Party for National Reconstruction)
Parmehutu	*Parti de l'émancipation du peuple Hutu*
PDC	*Parti démocratique Chrétien* (Christian Democratic Party)
PDI	*Parti démocratique idéal* (Ideal Democratic Party)
PDI	*Parti Démocratique islamique*
PDP	People's Development Party
PL	*Parti libéral* (Liberal Party)
POER	*Programme d'Observatoire des Elections au Rwanda*
PP	*Parti du Peuple*
PPC	*Parti du Progrès et de la Concorde*
	(Party for Progress and Concord)
PPD	*Pacte de Défense du Peuple*
	(Pact for Peoples' Defence)
PPDT	*Political Parties Disputes Tribunal*
PPLC	Political Parties Liaison Committee

PPP	People's Progressive Party
PRP	*Parti pour la Réconciliation du Peuple*
PRV	Principal Register of Voters
PSD	*Parti social démocrate*
	(Social Democratic Party)
PS-Imberakuri	*Parti Social Imberakuri*
	(Social Party Imberakuri)
PSP	*Parti de la solidarité et du progrès*
	(Solidarity and Progress Party)
PSR	*Parti Socialiste Rwandais*
	(Rwandan Socialist Party)
PV	minutes (*procès-verbaux*)
PVF1	minutes of the organisation of operations in the polling station
PVF2	minutes of the results of the ballot count
PVT	parallel vote tabulation
RADDES	*Ralliement pour la Démocratie et le Développement Economique et Social*
RADER	*Rassemblement Démocratique Rwandais*
	(Rwandese Democratic Rally)
RBA	Rwanda Broadcasting Agency
RCSP	Rwanda Civil Society Platform
REDET	Research and Education for Democracy in Tanzania
RPA	Rwandan Patriotic Army
RPB	*Rassemblement Populaire du Burundi*
RPF	Rwandan Patriotic Front
	(also *Front Patriotique Rwandais*, FPR)
RPP	Registrar of Political Parties
RTV	Rwanda Television
RURA	Rwanda Utility Regulatory Authority
RWF	Rwanda Francs
SADC	Southern African Development Community
TAMWA	Tanzania Media Women's Association
TANU	Tanganyika African National Union
TEMCO	Tanzania Election Monitoring Committee
TLP	Tanzania Labour Party
Tsh	Tanzania Shillings
UBC	Uganda Broadcasting Corporation
UDP	United Democratic Party
UDPR	*Union Démocratique du Peuple Rwandais*
	(Democratic Union of the Rwandan People)
UFA	Uganda Federal Alliance
UGX	Uganda Shillings

UHRC	Uganda Human Rights Commission
UN	United Nations
UNAMIR	United Nations Assistance Mission for Rwanda
UNAR	*Union Nationale Rwandaise*
UNDP	United Nations Development Programme
UNLF	Uganda National Liberation Front
UPC	Uganda People's Congress
UPD	*Union pour la Patrie et la Démocratie*
	(Union for the Fatherland and for Democracy)
UPR	*Union populaire pour la République*
UPRONA	*Union pour le Progrès National*
URT	United Republic of Tanzania
USD	United States dollars
UTP	United Tanganyika Party
ZEC	Zanzibar Electoral Commission
ZLSC	Zanzibar Legal Services Centre
ZNP	Zanzibar Nationalist Party
ZPPP	Zanzibar and Pemba Peoples Party
ZRC	Zanzibar Revolutionary Council

Preface

Electoral management bodies (EMBs) have become a keystone of the process of democratisation in the countries of East Africa. Their composition, mandate and activities have attracted increasing public attention. In some countries, EMBs and the rules of the electoral game are the focus of passionate interest and debate each time elections come around. In others, the debates around EMBs are semi-permanent and attract attention even outside the electoral cycle. The lack of a clear understanding of the issues at stake in the design of these bodies has often led to the generation of more heat than light, while leading to proposals that do not address actual challenges.

This report responds to the evident need for more knowledge about an institution that occupies an increasingly important place in the political process in East Africa. It is an in-depth study of EMBs in five countries of East Africa – Burundi, Kenya, Rwanda, Tanzania and Uganda – based on documentary research and detailed interviews in each country.

Each of the country studies explores in detail the following:
- The extent to which the EMBs fulfil their responsibilities;
- The degree to which they are independent of the executive;
- The effectiveness of their performance; and
- Their contribution to the improvement of the quality of elections and consequently the quality of democracy in each country, as well as the systems for adjudicating electoral disputes.

The study situates EMBs in their broader context, taking account of their status as a product of the struggle for democracy, their anchorage in the constitutional traditions of each society, their place in the history of political reform and their interaction with the other institutions of each country.

As institutions that apply the rules governing elections, EMBs are at the heart of discussion and practice on the critical question of effective citizen participation in the public affairs of their countries. EMBs independent of government under various guises have emerged in some countries of the region, or are the subject of serious reforms. Consequently, the way in which they are established and the effectiveness of their operations have continued to preoccupy those who advocate competitive elections, while reforms to EMBs have taken centre stage in more general political reforms. The demand – achieved in some cases – by citizens, political actors and members of the governing class to have the right to oversee the functioning of these bodies is a measure of the critical role that they play in translating the principles of transparency in democratic government into reality. Yet, often this oversight goes no further than the adoption of the formal rules for the composition and mandate of the EMB. The issues that make the real difference to the independence and effectiveness of the EMB, beyond the level of formal guarantees, are left unexamined. As a result, the ordinary citizen, and all the other protagonists in the political contest, often have a limited knowledge of the impact that the formal structures of the EMB have or could have on the quality of democracy in the countries concerned.

This study comes at an opportune moment for discussions of electoral reform. Its aim is to compare theory and practice of electoral management in countries with different traditions and political cultures. From this point of view, the study offers an overview of the socio-historical, institutional, and political context, allowing a deeper understanding of EMBs in East Africa. Thus, the study provides a detailed account of the current situation, opening up the debate on the bodies charged with the management of elections in the countries concerned, and offering citizens, political actors, governments and international institutions an evaluation of the issues at stake. It also recommends necessary reforms. The study aims to be a tool to increase understanding of the institutions and procedures governing elections and to encourage reforms in the management, oversight and credibility of the electoral process, to strengthen election observation, and to improve the management of electoral disputes.

Methodology

The idea of carrying out a critical study of electoral management bodies (EMBs) and to evaluate their role in the organisation of credible elections in East Africa came from a series of consultations carried out from mid-2009 by AfriMAP, the Africa Governance Monitoring and Advocacy Project, now a part of the Africa Regional Office (AFRO) of the Open Society Foundations.

This East African study drew inspiration and benefited a great deal from the experience and input from a similar West African study. In August 2009, AfriMAP co-organised, with the Open Society Initiative for West Africa (OSIWA) and the Council for the Development of Social Science Research in Africa (CODESRIA), a consultative workshop on elections and the role of civil society in West Africa. The meeting concluded that a systematic study of the institutional framework for the organisation of elections in comparative perspective would allow an examination of the reasons for the weaknesses of EMBs and give decision-makers and activists a tool for reforming electoral practice based on reliable research. Drawing on the recommendations of this consultative meeting, AfriMAP commissioned a comparative study of EMBs in six countries in West Africa, published in 2011.

Individual country research for the East African study was carried out by the authors on the basis of documentary research, field trips to and validation meetings in the country concerned in 2012 and 2013. In each country, the researchers interviewed leading players in the management of elections, including representatives of the EMBs and other relevant government bodies, the United Nations Development Program governance programmes, development partners, political parties and civil society. The information presented in this report aims to be up to date as of August 2013.

Field research, a review of literature and interviews were used to generate analytical reports addressing a range of aspects related to the functioning of EMBs, among them:

- The history and politics shaping their founding;
- The legal and institutional frameworks established to guide their operations;
- Their mandate and functions;
- Their independence; and
- How they function and relate with other agencies to deliver free, fair and transparent elections.

Data and information for the research were drawn from in-depth interviews with institutions and opinion leaders involved with elections in each country, individual and focus group discussions with ordinary citizens, and from an extensive review of literature on electoral history, the conduct and management of elections, as well as the constitutional, legal and institutional bases guiding them.

Face-to-face qualitative interviews with officials and representatives of the EMBs, the various national political parties, and CSOs involved in elections, media owners and practitioners, as well as international election observer missions were also conducted.

Several validation workshops were convened between April 2013 and September 2013 to discuss the draft reports. Adjustments were thereafter incorporated to accommodate a range of updates to the legal framework, as well as the outcomes of elections that had just been concluded.

Acknowledgements

This volume benefited from the support and participation of the following persons, whom we thank for their contribution: Shamshad Rehmatullah, then Programme Officer, Open Society Initiative for Eastern Africa (OSIEA) Tanzania Programme; Deus Rweyemamu, then Programme Assistant, OSIEA Tanzania Programme; Mugambi Kiai, then Programme Manager, OSIEA Kenya Programme; Richard Mugisha, Programme officer, OSIEA Uganda Programme; Jackie Kintu, Programme Assistant OSIEA Uganda Programme; Josephine Ihuthia, Programme Assistant, OSF's Africa Regional Office (AFRO); Myra Karani, Executive Assistant, OSIEA Director's Office; Chris Abuor, Intern OSIEA Kenya Programme.

Heartfelt appreciation to the *Coalition de la Société Civile pour le Monitoring Electoral* (COSOME), Burundi, under the leadership of JM Kavumbagu and Justine Nkurunzisa, for organising and leading the validation meeting for the Burundi chapter. Appreciation to Bronwen Manby, then Senior Programme Adviser with AFRO, and Jeggan Grey-Johnson, Programme Officer, AFRO, who read and commented on several chapters. Special thanks to Pascal Kambale, Senior Programme Adviser, Research and Advocacy, AFRO, who read and commented on the complete study and made a substantial contribution to its final version. None of the validation meetings could have been organised without the help of Mary Wandia, then Programme Officer OSIEA/AFRO, who also gave important support for our field research by programming and coordinating the visits of the authors to the five countries, as well as commenting on several chapters. The study was edited by Kwamchetsi Makokha.

The country chapters were researched and written by:

Alexander B. Makulilo: Dr Alexander B Makulilo is a lecturer in the Department of Political Science and Public Administration, University of Dar es Salaam, Tanzania.

Eugène Ntaganda: Eugène Ntaganda is a governance researcher who earned a Masters degree in international law from the University of Montreal in Canada in 1999. He has been an executive director of the Centre for Conflict Management, a policy research centre based at the University of Rwanda. He holds dual citizenship in Rwanda and Canada.

Francis A. Aywa: Francis Aywa is a lawyer with more than 15 years of experience in democracy and governance work. He has extensively conducted elections research and managed election observation missions. In 2008, he served as a member of the Independent Review Commission, established to inquire into all aspects of the general election held on 27 December 2007 in Kenya with particular emphasis on the presidential election. He is currently Chief of Party of the State University of New York's Kenya Parliamentary Support Programme.

Margaret Sekaggya: Margaret Sekaggya was appointed UN Special Rapporteur on the situation of human rights defenders in 2008. She has worked with the governments of Uganda and Zambia, as well as the United Nations, and taught law in various institutions. She has worked in the judiciary and was appointed a Judge of the High Court of Uganda. She was chairperson of the Coordination Committee of the Africa National Human Rights Institutions, the chairperson of the Ugandan Human Rights Commission and the chairperson of the Commonwealth National Human Rights Institution Forum.

Patrick Osodo: Patrick Osodo is an organisational development, governance and human rights professional with more than 20 years progressive experience in development management. He has held various senior programme management positions and worked extensively in consulting roles with a number of national and international non-governmental and governmental development organisations.

Introduction

Elections are one of the most important activities that draw on direct citizen participation in democratic processes in East Africa, and their management is increasingly generating impassioned debate. The bodies that manage and conduct elections are, therefore, coming under intense citizen and stakeholder scrutiny for the manner in which they are composed, how they organise and perform their mandates, and the outcomes they achieve.

Within the next two years, all the five East African countries will be in the grip of presidential and legislative elections, starting with Burundi and Tanzania in 2015, Uganda in 2016 and Kenya and Rwanda in 2017 and 2018. Although each of the East African nations has an elections management body dedicated to the delivery of democratic, transparent, free and fair elections, many of them are still in their early stages of development. They are all products of ongoing reforms initiated in the aftermath of violent disputes over elections.

Although changes to constitutions and the laws in these countries have sought to make election management bodies (EMBs) independent and, therefore, more inclined to deliver free, fair and credible elections, the results have not always been clearly articulated. Beyond formal guarantees of independence in constitutions and in the law, there are many issues that determine the impartiality of EMBs and which affect their ability to facilitate the aggregation and free expression of the will of the people. These shortcomings negatively impact democracy.

This volume is a compendium of five country reports jointly commissioned in June 2012 by the Open Society Foundation's Africa Regional Office (AFRO) and the Open Society Initiative for Eastern Africa (OSIEA). It is a comparative analysis of EMBs in the five East African countries – Burundi, Kenya, Rwanda, Tanzania and Uganda – and their respective contribution to the quality of citizens' participation in public affairs.

An introductory overview brings together the common strands in the evolving narrative of the growth of EMBs in East Africa, from their colonial history to the constitutional and legal reforms that gave birth to them. It highlights the similarities and differences between these bodies, as well as the common challenges they face in their structures and operations.

Each of the country reports seeks to respond to the need for more knowledge about EMBs as institutions at the centre of critical political processes in East Africa. Each report examines the political context of the country under study, the legal infrastructure under which EMBs are created and run, and the performance of the entire gamut of election activities, from registration of voters to supervision of political actors, civic education, the management of voting and results announcement, and the resolution of disputes.

The reports are the product of longitudinal assessments of the management of elections in Burundi, Kenya, Rwanda, Tanzania and Uganda, with particular emphasis on each country's EMB. They analyse the development of each country's EMB over time, evaluating its strength and performance based on indices that are comparable to other similar bodies in the region. Some countries, like Kenya, have had root-and-branch reforms that have replaced erstwhile EMBs, while others, like Tanzania, have been more gradual in embracing change. Burundi, Rwanda and Uganda, which emerged from civil war, chose to install new institutions. These standards provide a benchmark for assessing the composition, management and performance of EMBs in the region. Each country report explores in detail the extent to which EMBs effectively fulfil their mandates, the degree to which they are independent, and their contribution to improving the quality of democracy.

The studies provide an important context within which to review the evolution of EMBs in ongoing discussions about transforming the state through constitutional and legal reform. They aim to enhance the public's understanding of EMBs, as well as to embolden citizens to demand reforms that would strengthen election observation and oversight, enhance transparency in the management of elections, and improve the resolution of electoral disputes.

1

Overview

A. Introduction

Since the return of multi-party politics in Kenya, Tanzania and Uganda during the second wave of democratisation in the 1990s, and the subsequent signing of the Rwanda and Burundi peace accords, electoral competition has become an important barometer of the health of democracy in East Africa. The Draft East African Community Protocol on Democracy and Good Governance commits member countries 'to entrench the culture of observance of human rights, adherence to the principles of democracy, regular, transparent, free and fair elections conducted by independent and impartial national electoral management bodies (EMBs) as a preventive measure against instability and conflicts within the region'. In Article 7(1) of the Draft Protocol, partner states commit themselves to the principle that the exercise of public authority emanates from the will of the people through regular, transparent, free and fair elections. They further undertake to develop policies and mechanisms for harmonised regional benchmarks to conduct regular, transparent, free, fair and credible elections in line with internationally accepted standards.

Efforts to consolidate and entrench democracy in the five East African countries have focused heavily on reforming EMBs into midwives of free and fair political competition. The status, powers and functions of electoral commissions have constituted a significant portion of national debates about reforming politics through constitutional review. Contestations over the fairness of elections have generated some of the most violent conflicts witnessed in the region. Reforms in the political system over the past two decades have been incremental and largely focused on enhancing the credibility of the arbiters in electoral contests.

Among the reforms introduced in the last 20 years to consolidate the re-emergence of the practice of democracy, those aimed at improving electoral management have generated the most passionate debates. One of the general traits of the reforms introduced in this area is the effort to reinforce or initiate mechanisms to insulate electoral management from the normal administrative responsibilities of the executive. As a result, all the countries in East Africa have created EMBs designed to be free of executive control. The emergence of constitutionally and statutorily independent EMBs has necessitated that they be equipped with competent personnel and equipment, as well as rules and procedures to facilitate their work. However, our studies show that constitutional and statutory guarantees of independence do not always produce the intended results.

B. Models of EMBs

There are different models of EMBs. Pastor provides a broad understanding based on five models:[1]

- Election office within the government;
- Election office within a government ministry but supervised by a judicial body;
- An independent election commission composed of experts and directly accountable to Parliament;
- A multi-party election commission composed of representatives of the political parties; and
- A non-partisan electoral commission composed of distinguished individuals from a list proposed by the President and legislature, reduced by a veto of the political parties, and selected by a group of judges for a ten-year term.

Pastor's classification is based on the composition of the commission. Frequently cited International Institute for Democracy and Electoral Assistance (IDEA) work has categorised these models based on whether they are governmental or independent, or comprising both characteristics,[2] and has emerged with three models:

- The independent model;
- The government model; and
- The mixed model.

The categorisation of these models is based on a number of attributes, i.e. institutional arrangement, implementation, formal accountability, powers, composition, term of office and budget. These characteristics are the basis for the assessment of EMBs across the international organisations, as well as within the academic community.[3]

---

1   Pastor, R (1999) 'The Role of Electoral Administration in Democratic Transitions: Implications for Policy and Research', *Democratisation* 6(4): 1–27.
2   International IDEA (2006) *Electoral Management Design: International IDEA Handbook*, IDEA, Stockholm.
3   See Elklit, J & Reynolds, A (2002) 'The Impact of Election Administration on the Legitimacy of Emerging Democracies', *Commonwealth and Comparative Politics* 40(2): 86–119; ECF (2008) 'Principles and Guidelines on the Independence of Election Management Bodies (EMBs) in the SADC Region', adopted by the Annual General Conference August 2007, Luanda Angola; ECF & EISA (2004) 'Principles for Election Management, Monitoring and Observation in the SADC Region', EISA, Auckland Park Johannesburg, SA; Makulilo, A (2009) 'Independent Electoral Commission in Tanzania: A False Debate', *Representation* 45: 435–453; Makulilo, A (2011) 'The Zanzibar Electoral Commission and its Feckless Independence', *Journal of Third World Studies* 28(1): 263–283; Mozaffar, S (2002) 'Patterns of Electoral Governance in Africa's Emerging Democracies', *International Political Review* 23(1): 85–101; UNDP [UN Development Programme] (1997) *Reconceptualising Governance*, New York, UNDP.

Various election stakeholders have not been concerned with whether or not these EMBs are independent, governmental or mixed but rather with whether or not they adhere to the principles of impartiality, transparency and integrity.[4] However, as a prerequisite for countries in transition to democracy, in order to achieve that ultimate end, there should be a degree of autonomy from the state.[5] The state or other actors can have a negative influence on the EMB to the extent that it fails to act impartially regardless of its model, or it can be as a result of perceptions.[6] Justice should not only be done, but it should be seen to be done.[7]

The independent model of electoral commissions, which is common to East Africa, is not located in any government ministry or within the executive branch. It is, instead, an independent body established constitutionally. Normatively, this model is important in ensuring impartiality of the EMB as it is not under the executive or subject to the control of a government ministry.[8] On the one hand, it faces operational constraints due to limited independence, unclear mandates and inadequate resources unless democratically designed.[9] On the other hand, it may lack political influence, which could impede the effective performance of its functions and acquisition of sufficient funding.[10]

The question of membership of the commission is often critical and central. IDEA[11] describes a multi-party electoral commission as the best model in the countries that have experienced difficult transitions to multi-party democracy. In such societies, public servants are likely to have been largely discredited as electoral policy-makers because of a history of being agents of the authoritarian former ruling party.[12] However, such a proposition is subject to criticism because despite having a multi-party electoral commission; the state can still exert its control on the commission and hence undermine its independence.[13]

4   Martini, M (2013) *EMBs and Their Composition*, Transparency International.
5   Birch, S (2007) 'Electoral Management Bodies and the Electoral Integrity: Evidence from Eastern Europe and the Former Soviet Union', accessed 13 November 2013; Eisenstadt, T (2004) 'Catching the State off Guard: Electoral Courts, Campaign Finance, and Mexico's Separation of State and Ruling Party', *Party Politics* 10(6): 723–45; Elklit, J & Reynolds, A (2002) 'The Impact of Election Administration on the Legitimacy of Emerging Democracies', *Commonwealth and Comparative Politics* 40(2): 86–119.
6   Pastor, R (1999) 'The Role of Electoral Administration in Democratic Transitions: Implications for Policy and Research', *Democratisation* 6(4): 1–27; Seifu, T (2012) 'Causes of Electoral Violence: Lessons from the May 2005 Election of Ethiopia', Thesis submitted in partial fulfilment for the award of Master of Philosophy in Peace and Conflict Transformation, University of Tromso, Norway.
7   *R vs Sussex Justices, Ex parte McCarthy* ([1924] [1923] All ER Rep 233)
8   Mozaffar, S & Schedler, A (2002) 'The Comparative Study of Electoral Governance – An Introduction', *International Political Science Review* 23(2): 5–27.
9   Carter, E & Farrell, D (2009) 'Electoral Systems and Election Management', in L Larry, D Niemi & P Norris (eds) *Comparing Democracies*, London, Sage.
10   López-Pintor, R (2000) *Electoral Management Bodies as Institutions of Governance*, New York, Bureau for Development Policy, UNDP, www.undp.org/governance/docs/Elections-Pub-EMBbook.pdf.
11   IDEA (2006) *Electoral Management Design: International IDEA Handbook*, IDEA, Stockholm.
12   Pastor (1999) 'The Role of Electoral Administration', op. cit.; IDEA (2006) *Electoral Management Design: International IDEA Handbook*, IDEA, Stockholm.
13   Garber, L (1994) 'Election Commissions: Responsibilities and Composition', paper presented at the NDI-sponsored African Election Colloquium, Victoria Falls, Zimbabwe, November 1994.

Pastor[14] considers multi-party electoral commissions ineffective in the following cases:

- When there are too many parties in Parliament, the commission becomes unworkable as the commissioners from different political parties cannot reach a consensus.
- When there are just two political parties, the commission has the possibility of becoming polarised unless it has a non-partisan chairperson.

In Zanzibar, for instance, the main opposition party, the Civic United Front (CUF), has consistently complained of electoral fraud and rigging. This is despite the fact that it is represented in the electoral commission. This can result from how members are obtained, as well as the chief of the commission, the budget and the security of tenure.[15]

On the other hand, there is support for expert member commissions comprising judges of High Courts.[16] Using experts in commissions has an advantage over using members with political party affiliations. However, it depends on who these experts are accountable to – a Parliament or a president? Also their tenure, whether permanent or at the discretion of their appointing authority, is important. With these factors, consideration of the impartiality, independence and integrity of the EMB can be understood.

Moreover, the issue of fiscal resources is critical. In order to carry out electoral functions and day-to-day activities, EMBs need adequate financial resources. EMBs' independence and impartiality can be jeopardised by lack of sufficient resources to carry out their activities.[17] This can result from two factors: lack of adequate funds, especially in developing countries, and deliberate action by government intent on limiting independence.[18] It is from this view that the international and regional standards provide that EMBs should have special votes in the national budget, just like other departments of the government.[19]

Most of the countries in East Africa have taken a similar approach in the creation of EMBs, with mixed results for increased citizen participation in democratic processes and governance. The choices that each country has taken have largely been shaped by its history, going back to the colonial era and its political inheritance at independence.

---

14 Pastor (1999) 'The Role of Electoral Administration', op. cit.
15 ECF & EISA (2004) 'Principles for Election Management, Monitoring and Observation in the SADC Region', EISA, Johannesburg; IDEA (2006) *Electoral Management Design*, op. cit.
16 Hartlyn, J, McCoy, J & Mustillo, T (2008) 'Electoral Governance Matters: Explaining the Quality of Elections in Contemporary Latin America', *Comparative Political Studies* 41(1): 73–98.
17 IDEA (1998) *Code of Conduct: Ethical and Professional Administration of Elections*, Stockholm, IDEA.
18 Hounkpe, M & Fall, I (2011) *Electoral Commissions in West Africa: A Comparative Study*, 2nd edn, Friedrich-Ebert-Stiftung, Abuja, Nigeria.
19 UNDP (1997) *Reconceptualising Governance*, New York, UNDP; IDEA (2006) *Electoral Management Design*, op. cit.

C. Colonial legacy

The five East African countries have held elections since their independence from Britain, in the case of Kenya, Tanzania and Uganda, and Belgian tutelage, in the case of Burundi and Rwanda. Their initial experiences with election administration at the sunset of the colonial era greatly influenced the context within which political competition for power was pursued. In an attempt to moderate the internal tensions generated by the introduction of party politics, semi-autonomous elections commissions were established. Additionally, because of the special colonial status for Rwanda and Burundi, the 1961 elections were conducted by Belgian colonial authorities but supervised by representatives of the United Nations (UN) Commission for Rwanda-Urundi.

After independence, the electoral commissions were systematically emasculated and only began to make a comeback with the return of multi-party political competition, whose clamour included the creation of a level playing field and impartial election management and arbitration. More or less autonomous electoral commissions have thus evolved as a tradition in Kenya, Uganda and Tanzania, with Burundi and Rwanda fashioning new independent commissions after the Arusha peace accords.

D. Violence and election management reforms

The consequences of political violence on elections management reforms have followed two opposite directions in the region. In some cases, political violence has triggered or consolidated major reforms in the management of elections, while in others, violence has hampered or delayed reforms. While important reforms of EMBs have been effected as a result of, or a direct response to, political violence in Burundi, Kenya and Uganda, decades of stability marked by an absence of major political violence can be said to have been among the reasons for a weak EMB in Tanzania. In Rwanda, on the other hand, the government has put in place specific policies aimed at preventing political violence of the scale of the 1994 Genocide. Such policies usually translate into deliberate efforts to suppress any source of social tension in the country, including in the way elections are managed and conducted. As a result, the EMB in Rwanda has been designed to preoccupy itself more with easing or preventing election-related political tensions than ensuring the delivery of free and fair elections.

Constitutional review in Uganda and Kenya, coming after violent conflict stemming from failed elections, ushered in a new breed of independent electoral commissions. In Burundi, which emerged from conflict by adopting the Arusha peace accords, the constitutional architecture for electoral commissions was a natural consequence of the push to create stable institutions that were more representative of the nation's ethnic and gender diversity. The anarchy that characterised Uganda after the overthrow of Idi Amin and two other military regimes, the turbulence accompanying the clamour for multi-party politics in Kenya and the violence that erupted in the aftermath of the disputed 2007 elections, as well as the genocide in Rwanda and the conflict in Burundi, altogether appear to have fuelled faster reforms in the EMBs of these countries. Similarly, the contestations over elections in Zanzibar have yielded some changes to its EMB. In mainland Tanzania, where there has not been a transition in the ruling party since independence in 1962, the evolution of the National Elections Commission has remained unhurried and the executive continues to play a significant role in the management of elections. The ongoing drafting of the Constitution in Tanzania is expected to deliver reforms in the EMBs for the mainland and Zanzibar.

E. Membership of EMBs and the appointment of commissioners

Although the EMBs in the region are anchored in each country's Constitution, the institutional design varies from one nation to the next.

Kenya has probably the most elaborate process of identifying and selecting the commissioners, as clearly laid out in the Constitution and the law establishing the Independent Electoral and Boundaries Commission (the IEBC). An independent selection panel proposed by the President, the Judicial Service Commission and the Ethics and Anti-Corruption Commission, among others, and vetted and approved by the National Assembly, publicly advertises for the positions of chairperson and commissioners. It proceeds to shortlist and interview applicants publicly and presents to the President a list of three candidates qualified for the post of chairperson of the commission and 13 persons qualified for the posts of commissioners. Out of this list, the President nominates and sends back to the National Assembly for vetting and approval one person for appointment as chairperson of the commission and eight persons for appointment as commissioners. Upon approval, the Speaker of the National Assembly forwards the final list to the President for appointment. The institutional framework for Kenya's the IEBC creates an executive board of nine commissioners (with the chairman as a first among equals) to operate the organisation, and a secretariat that manages the day-to-day administrative functions. Commissioners are appointed for a single term of six years and are not eligible for re-appointment.

In Uganda, the President appoints seven members of the Electoral Commission with the approval of Parliament. The members work full time and are supported by a secretariat headed by the secretary, who is assisted by directors, managers and staff at lower levels.

Burundi's seven electoral commission members are appointed after approval by a three-fourths majority in the National Assembly and the Senate. The most influential political groups represented in Parliament and in the government, therefore, have a voice in the approval of commissioners.

In Rwanda, the seven-member Council of Commissioners is appointed through an order prepared by the Cabinet and signed by the President. It is not clear how the commissioners are identified and selected. The Cabinet then presents a list of seven nominees to the Senate for further scrutiny and approval. Two of the seven commissioners must be lawyers and, in line with the Constitution, at least 30% of them must be women. Once approved, the names of the nominees are sent back to the Cabinet. A presidential order is then prepared and signed by the President to appoint them. The Council of Commissioners in Rwanda is not a full-time organ. Once appointed, members continue with their ordinary duties. During elections, commissioners convene meetings whenever necessary. The Council of Commissioners is supported by a technical executive secretariat in managing the commission's day-to-day functioning. The national secretariat maintains a pool of experienced coordinators and volunteers who manage elections at polling centres at cell and sector levels.

Commissioners of the National Elections Commission (NEC) in Tanzania and the director of elections are appointed by the President. The Zanzibar Elections Commission (ZEC) has seven commissioners, whose chairman is appointed by the President of Zanzibar. Two commissioners are appointed by the President on the recommendation of the Second Vice-President, who is the head of government in the House of Representatives. Two other commissioners are appointed by the President on the recommendation of the leader of the opposition in the House of Representatives. Another member is appointed from among the judges of the High Court, and the last member is appointed by the President as he sees fit. Commissioners are appointed for a period of five years and can be removed for reason of illness or failure to perform their tasks properly. The President also appoints the Director of the ZEC, who heads the permanent secretariat. Unlike the NEC, which relies on civil servants, the ZEC has offices down to the district level.

Three trends emerge from the various institutional models. On one end of the spectrum is the model of partisan membership followed in Burundi, where electoral commission members are appointed by parties represented in Parliament to maintain the political equilibrium sought under the Arusha Accord. On the other end of the spectrum, Kenya applies a model that favours technical expertise and the appointment process is designed to shield electoral commissioners from political interference. Rwanda, Tanzania and Uganda occupy the middle of the spectrum. While members of electoral commissions in the three countries are independent professionals on paper, their appointment by the President using his discretionary powers – and in some cases on the basis of selection criteria only known by him – can have a negative impact on their independence and professional integrity. However, the contrast between the professional management of the 2005 elections in Burundi and the technically questionable management of the 2013 elections in Kenya seems to indicate that technical expertise doesn't favour one model over the others.

F. Independence and effectiveness

The constitutions of all five East African states guarantee the independence of their EMBs and free them from the direction or control of any person or body. Yet, the independence of EMBs remains one of the most contested issues in election administration in the region. Since the resumption of plural politics in East Africa, EMBs have been the object of deep-seated mistrust for their real or perceived lack of political independence. Public trust in the electoral system has consequently been eroded over time, with the perception of their independence and impartiality at its nadir despite apparent legal guarantees of freedom from political interference.

While many EMBs in the region have demonstrated an increasingly high level of organisational capacity in handling elections, opinion is still divided on their independence, capacity and ability to deliver free, fair and transparent elections. The system for appointment and removal of commissioners has not assuaged anxieties about independence from the executive. In particular, concerns have been raised over the over-weening influence of presidents in the appointment of commissioners. In Tanzania and Burundi, for example, while election commissions can claim that their constitutions legally protect their independence and autonomy, there are low selection thresholds for the President to use as the appointing authority. In Kenya, commissioners are appointed in a competitive process and have security of tenure. The EMB has the latitude to hire its own professional staff and, as a constitutional commission, it also has operational independence. Even then, this has not eliminated opportunities for political horse-trading, because the names of nominated commissioners must be approved by the National Assembly. In the other countries, political parties play a role in the nomination of commissioners, which again presents problems if the legislature is dominated by one party or coalition, such as in Rwanda and Tanzania. In Uganda, many political groups strongly believe that the electoral commission is not independent and does not reflect the diversity expected in a multi-party system. In particular, there were concerns relating to the system for appointments to the electoral commission, credibility and security of tenure for commissioners, among other concerns.

Members of the electoral commissions can be removed from office by the President for physical and mental incapacity, misconduct or misbehaviour and incompetence, although in Kenya, the process involves the National Assembly. It has been argued that this affects their independence.

The interface between EMBs and other constitutional and statutory agencies presents interesting checks on their independence. Since EMBs are creatures of their respective constitutions, they are subject to parliamentary oversight, especially regarding their vetting, funding and budget, which can introduce political bias. The absence of secure, guaranteed funding for EMBs is of particular concern: financial and logistical dependence on the executive has undermined effective completion of critical electoral activities in Burundi and Kenya.

The electoral commissions' decisional independence over electoral operations and determination of boundaries appears secure, but their decisions are subject to judicial review in the courts – with the sole exception of Tanzania, where the Constitution states that, 'No court is allowed to inquire into the election of a presidential candidate who is declared by the National Electoral Commission (NEC) to have been duly elected', or into any matter done by the NEC in discharging its duties.

In Rwanda and Tanzania, the electoral commissions rely heavily on government administrative cadres, while in Burundi great use is made of volunteers whose political neutrality has repeatedly come into question. In Zanzibar, employees of the state invite the influence of regional and district commissioners, who wield considerable arbitrary powers and often interfere with some of the decisions of the Zanzibar Electoral Commission.

G. Common challenges to electoral management

EMBs in the five countries, whatever their level of independence, face similar challenges. All electoral commissions face challenges in updating the national voters' registers, resulting in disenfranchisement of some voters. They have also confronted challenges in the demarcation of constituencies, oversight of political parties and candidates, and ensuring equal access to public media.

Political party regulation

Political party regulation continues to present a challenge for all EMBs in the region. Although many EMBs are past the initial difficulties experienced in managing multi-party electoral contests through the creation of laws and adoption of codes of conduct, political hygiene is still low and poorly policed. Elections are still dominated by incumbent political parties. The pre-election campaign period is characterised by tension, uneven access to public media and suppression of plural, competitive ideas because of parties zoning off areas. Continuing weaknesses in enforcing electoral law, or a lack of political will to enforce it, have raised doubts about the EMBs' capacity to deal with law-breaking by diverse electoral role players. Enforcement of nomination procedures is also somewhat hampered by overlapping mandates with other dispute resolution agencies. Further, EMB investigation and prosecution output from previous elections, compared to the number of allegations of malfeasance, is wanting.

National voters' registers

All EMBs face challenges in maintaining a permanent and credible national register of voters. The reluctance or failure to deploy technological investments in the electoral process has raised legitimacy questions about the accuracy of outcomes and therefore the legitimacy of the political leadership in office. In Burundi, the electoral commission has transmitted directives verbally, without providing written records, thus depriving political party representatives of the opportunity to verify the fairness of the electoral process. The imprecision of the modalities of transmission and consolidation of results has given rise to uncertainty and undermined electoral transparency.

Voter education

The delivery of civic and voter education is still inadequate. There is no comprehensive legal framework or syllabus for the participatory development and delivery of civic and electoral education. Civil society organisations (CSOs)and other stakeholders participate in civic education only at the discretion of the EMBs. As a result, a comprehensive civil society programme for civic and electoral education has not evolved.

Voting

Voting, vote counting and declaration of results have been marred by controversy – particularly where opposition parties are strong, with fears of attempted manipulation of results. In highly contested constituencies, crowds have often massed around vote tallying stations waiting for results to be announced, resulting in confrontations when the police attempted to disperse them.

Electoral transparency continues to present a challenge for all EMBs in the region. Transparency and accountability questions on results persist, thus undermining the credibility and trust of EMBs.

Funding

Electoral management in all the East African countries faces serious budgetary constraints. There are delays in the disbursement of funds meant for elections activities, thus undermining plans for staff recruitment or equipment purchases. Although financial independence of EMBs is implied in the provisions of the constitutions that create them, national treasuries habitually try to moderate their estimates long before they get to the National Assembly.

Donors have continued to support critical activities and to bridge funding shortfalls in priority areas, such as voter education, technical assistance and change management in all five countries. Most donor contributions to elections pass through a basket fund where they pool their resources to create a project. Donors do not always honour their pledges in full –sometimes because of recipients' inability to meet aid conditions.

The cost of elections and the proper management of finances is a major issue across all EMBs. Cost-saving measures such as using government officials and volunteers as returning officers have undermined trust in the electoral commissions, thus presenting them with a dilemma between reducing costs and losing credibility. Important questions have been raised about the cost of each vote and the need reduce the cost of elections, even as EMBs seek to acquire expensive technological solutions.

Disputes

Electoral disputes present a special challenge. The institutions responsible for electoral litigation remain unclear across the five countries. Where they exist, there is still lack of clarity on processes for electoral litigation that are not widely known to the public or the political actors.

Kenya has the most detailed rules of procedure for electoral litigation. The Constitution allows seven days between the declaration of presidential election results and the filing of a petition in the Supreme Court, and 14 days for the judges to deliver a decision. This time limit, however, while met in the disputed 2013 Kenya presidential elections, was considered too short by contesting parties to allow a comprehensive examination of the issues in question. For the other election petitions, the Kenya Constitution allows 28 days after publication of results to file a petition.

H. EMBs and the East African Community

All five electoral commissions have collaborative relationships with the African Union (AU) and regional bodies such as the Southern African Development Community (SADC), of which Tanzania is a member, and the East African Community (EAC). These regional bodies are expected to be influenced by the African Charter on Democracy, Elections and Governance. Tanzania has, however, not yet ratified the AU Charter. All five EMBs are members of the East African Community Electoral Observer Mission (EACEOM) and the East African Community Forum of Electoral Commissions (EACFEM).

The EAC has a forum for heads of national electoral commissions, which meets regularly and has made contributions to the East African Community Draft Protocol on Democracy and Good Governance. The draft protocol addresses the issues of democracy and democratisation processes in Article 7. Matters on institutionalisation of democracy, democratisation processes and good governance are addressed in great detail in Article 7(3). The first priority is given to establishing independent and well-funded EMBs, managed by members transparently appointed on the basis of merit, gender equity and professionalism. Other matters include democratic elections and peaceful transfer-of-power mechanisms, political parties and parliamentary accountability, as well as the harmonisation of regional benchmarks for conducting free, fair and credible elections.

Whereas EMBs are members of the regional bodies, strengthening election management depends on individual governments. There is no evidence of pressure from the regional organisations for improvements in the EMBs in the partner countries.

The aim of EACFEM is to build stronger EMBs in the region through greater collaboration, peer learning and exchange of ideas and best practices. Representatives of each EMB have participated as observers and have shared their experiences in different regional elections. In reciprocation, individual EMBs have invited other electoral bodies to monitor elections and share their experience. Some of them, notably from Rwanda and Tanzania, are also active in ongoing processes in their countries to ratify and adopt the East African Protocol on Good Governance and were part of the efforts to negotiate and adopt the East African Principles on Elections Observation and Evaluation. The protocol has specific pillars on democracy and democratisation, while the principles offer guidance on structure, methodology, timeframe and reporting on elections observation and on the code of conduct for election observers.

I. Conclusion

Elections play an important role in shaping the political destiny of countries in East Africa, not only because of the legitimacy they confer on the political leadership, but also as a peaceful way of resolving competition and differences. The management of elections, which decide development and governance priorities and outcomes, therefore acquires a critical importance. The institutions that bear the responsibility for conducting elections have become the focus of scrutiny, monitoring and reform to enable citizens to have a greater say in how their governments are run. Many reforms have created competent and professional bodies and have focused on the need to give the EMBs greater legal and institutional independence, but the reports in this volume demonstrate that constitutional and legal guarantees of independence still leave gaps that could hobble the performance of EMBs in increasing public participation in democratic processes. More attention needs to be given to securing the technical independence of EMBs in delivering on their mandates.

J. Options for reforming electoral management

Policy-makers in the five East African nations need to strengthen the legal framework for elections. All pending reforms and revisions of laws to streamline operations and improve other aspects of elections should be promptly concluded.

Independence

- Across the board, parliaments need to pass laws that respond to anxieties about the appointment and removal of the members of electoral commissions in order to secure their independence and financial autonomy. It is recommended that the process of selecting candidates be open and transparent, and that the criteria for selection be based on high levels of professional competence and integrity. Even where such a process is based on compromise, it still needs to be open and transparent. Candidates need to be interviewed and screened by an independent technical team, and a gender-balanced list should be presented to the National Assembly for confirmation before appointment.
- Parliaments should, additionally, secure the administrative and managerial autonomy of EMBs to enable them to perform their duties effectively.

- There is also a need to adequately define the limits of the responsibilities and substantive jurisdiction of electoral officials.
- Governments should embrace comprehensive reforms that separate the ruling parties from the state to ensure free and fair elections. The use of government administrative cadres in the running of elections undermines the independence of EMBs. As a rule, titular government officials should not be involved in managing elections.
- Greater focus must be placed on rules for access to public media, the use of state resources during election campaigns, term limits for the office of President, and time limits for the declaration of parliamentary election results.
- Precise and clear criteria should guide electoral commissions in the exercise of their power of co-optation, rectification of imbalances in electoral registers and nomination for special seats.
- Governments should also consider streamlining and increasing funding for political parties in order to include an operational budget.
- EMBs in each country should lead discussions on critical constitutional and legal reforms necessary for the further improvement of elections in areas such as access to public media, voter education and the creation of realistic election calendars that are easier to manage logistically.

Voters' registers

- All electoral commissions should maintain accurate, credible and accessible national voters' registers and ensure continuous updating of the roll. Where such an electoral roll has proven its quality and credibility, it should be maintained with continuous improvement to make the necessary corrections.
- In Burundi and Zanzibar, there is a need to review requirements that could disenfranchise populations on the basis of income or residency.
- Political parties and their representatives should be fully involved in updating the electoral roll to enhance its transparency and to eliminate any suspicion of fraud.
- Ultimately, all EMBs need to move towards establishing computerised and integrated voter registration rolls.

Enhancing efficiency

- A system-wide organisational assessment of EMBs' institutional structures, work-flows and ability to discharge their mandate should inform the critical capacity investments that are required to make them more effective.
- Staff needs to be trained to act in accordance with the law, to be impartial at all times, and to comprehensively and competently deal with electoral crime.
- EMBs should enhance their adjudication mechanisms by strengthening and establishing complaints desks in all districts and at the national level to handle election-related complaints.

- Electoral commissions should also establish and strengthen liaison committees at the national and local level, comprising representatives of the police, the EMB and competing political parties.
- Electoral commissions should comprehensively perform their roles and use their constitutional and statutory powers to ensure that elections are conducted in compliance with the law.
- EMBs should organise their work better and share responsibilities.
- EMBs need to develop manuals to clarify roles between commissioners and technical staff to minimise conflicts and management paralysis.
- Training programmes for senior officials should be initiated to make them more efficient, notably on logistics, data management and communication, both internally and externally.
- Commissions also need to review their procurement and hiring systems to address all integrity concerns. Commissions should strengthen their internal audit functions, with a view to consistently bring down the cost of elections and institutionalise election audits and evaluations in order to learn from all their electoral exercises.

Election results management
- EMBs need to establish transparency requirements throughout the entire results audit trail and make the information publicly available by using technology. Adequate resources should be allocated, well in advance, for the drafting of results management protocols to ensure transparency, particularly in relation to the rapid publication of the election results in every polling station.
- Polling-station-level data should be available electronically in easily accessible formats.
- Future electoral laws should guarantee greater transparency in results management, notably the publication of complete results for each polling station during the announcement of provisional results.
- All EMBs should invest in robust public communication strategies and mobilise resources for their implementation to manage public expectations and improve stakeholder relations. There is a need for electoral commissions in the region to reach out to the entire cross-section of electoral role players and constructively discuss how they can improve their effectiveness.
- Post-election audits would enable commissions to answer important questions about the previous election and gain insights into how to improve future performance.
- They should make customer satisfaction surveys a routine part of their service delivery through diverse mechanisms such as an interactive website and exit surveys for critical processes like voter registration and other areas of service provision.

Civic and voter education

- States should take measures to ensure that all citizens with basic primary education understand each country's democracy and how to participate in it, including by voting. In the short to medium term, states should adequately fund the provision of targeted voter education for diverse stakeholder groups in partnership with civil society and other civic education providers.
- EMBs should provide leadership in the development of a national curriculum, set standards for voter education and monitor its provision.
- Electoral commissions should work in partnership with CSOs and other stakeholders to provide comprehensive and continuous civic education.
- All electoral stakeholders need to remain vigilant and relentlessly continue the long journey to free and fair elections.
- CSOs should build their capacity to observe elections, including electronically, and to be able to observe the whole electoral process including the pre-election and post-election period. It may be necessary to consider establishing an independent monitoring system to audit the whole electoral process from beginning to end.
- Electoral commissions should work closely with political parties to expand their role in offering civic and political education in line with their mandate.

Management of disputes

- Greater clarity is required in the management of election disputes. Although there is value in endowing EMBs with power to resolve lower-level disputes, there is an equal need to make provision for courts of law to be the final arbiters.
- A rational training programme for judicial officers should be planned, organised and implemented well before the elections by drawing from the experiences within the region.
- There should be clear and simple rules of procedure for electoral litigation that facilitate appeals from the political parties to the electoral commission, and ultimately to the courts. Litigation needs to be conducted promptly and judgment delivered within a specified short period so as to avoid creating a governance vacuum.
- Where EMBs are involved in dispute resolution, they should strengthen their internal capacity to investigate and prosecute election offences and enhance inter-agency coordination with the police and prosecution agencies to ensure strict compliance with the electoral law.
- Further, EMBs should have the power to ensure that the political parties competing in elections respect electoral laws, comply with registration requirements and adhere to campaign finance rules and codes of conduct.

Regional and stakeholder collaboration

- Relations between regional EMBs need to be enhanced in order to strengthen capacity to implement agreed-upon standards, as well as lobby governments for support. The objective of such collaboration and cooperation should be to consistently benchmark EMBs with the best regional and global standards in electoral practice and to further regional and global electoral democracy practices.

- It is imperative to launch advocacy campaigns aimed at speeding up the process of ratifying the East African Draft Protocol on Good Governance and educating the public on its content and meaning, along with those of the East African Principles for Elections Observation, Monitoring and Evaluation.

- Efforts aimed at further expanding civic and democratic spaces for East African citizens should be supported by deepening the role of the media and promoting initiatives that bring together regional civil societies, publics and political groups in joint analyses, researches, debates and sharing of relevant experiences.

- EMBs need to improve their relations with donors, particularly those involved in elections support, to facilitate the financing of activities related to elections, including the provision of voter and civic education.

- Donors should honour their pledges adequately and on time to allow EMBs time to prepare for the management of elections. Donors should also adequately support CSOs to provide civic and voter education.

2

Burundi

Eugène Ntaganda

A. Summary

The Burundi Peace and Reconciliation Accord signed in Arusha, Tanzania, in August 2000 (Arusha Accord), marked a major turning point in the country's political history. It was also the beginning of a new era in Burundi's electoral management processes. Negotiated to end the bloody civil war that broke out in 1993 after the assassination of Melchior Ndadaye, the first democratically elected President, the Arusha Accord attempted to resolve recurring ethnic tensions and political violence – two problems that had undermined Burundi's national cohesion since its independence in 1962. The Arusha negotiations had identified the need to organise successful elections with broad majority acceptance of the results and end the cycle of exclusion based on identity as permanent solutions to the country's problems.

Besides the universally recognised functions assigned to elections, the Arusha negotiations had assigned an extra responsibility to the Burundi process as a response to national historical circumstances, namely to guarantee the representation of all the ethnic groups in the country. The Electoral Code, which was drafted after the Arusha Accord, grants the National Independent Electoral Commission (NIEC or CENI – *Commission Electorale Nationale Indépendante*) specific powers, including those of implementing the 'rectification of imbalances' and 'co-optation' required to ensure that the political parties' lists for MPs resulted in 60% Hutu representation and 40% Hutu, with women constituting a minimum of 30% of the whole. Partly because of the ambiguities in the criteria, the NIEC fulfils these requirements in a totally arbitrary manner.

Burundi legislation provides a sufficiently strong base for the management of free and fair elections in conformity with the relevant international and regional standards. The elections organised in 2005 and 2010 presented the first test of the effectiveness of the new electoral regulations drafted under the Arusha Accord framework. The training of officials was one of the major successes recorded during the 2010 elections and explains the excellent work done at the vast majority of polling stations. The quality of this training should be maintained and, indeed, improved, for future elections.

Nevertheless, the 2005 and 2010 elections exposed major challenges in elections management in Burundi. Although some of these challenges are external to the NIEC, the commission needs to take them into account, anticipate them and integrate them into its planning, as they have a considerable influence on how elections are managed. For example, in 2005, the consensus of political groups on the rules of the electoral process facilitated the organisation of the elections in a peaceful climate, whereas its absence in 2010 contributed to the poor management of the process.

Other challenges are internal in nature and emanate from weaknesses that the NIEC must rectify. Among these is the fact that the NIEC too often resorted to verbal messages to transmit directives that were crucial to conducting a transparent process. The absence of written directives deprived political party representatives of the opportunity to verify the fairness of the entire electoral process. Likewise, the NIEC has often failed in its obligation to compensate for the lack of clarity on some procedures of the Electoral Code, for instance the imprecision of the modalities of transmission and consolidation of the results, which gives rise to uncertainty contrary to electoral transparency. The NIEC needs to provide the political party representatives with copies of the minutes (*procès-verbaux* or 'PV') from the polling stations as well as those of the consolidated results at the community and provincial levels, with statistical data to facilitate the reconstitution and accurate accounting of the elections.

Burundi's electoral system is undermined by numerous defects, which seriously erode its credibility. Three of these defects deserve to be highlighted and urgently rectified:

- The use of multiple ballots;
- A restrictive electoral calendar; and
- The equivocal management of election-related disputes.

Burundi was unwilling to make the transition to a single ballot in 2010. It is still using the multiple ballot system, that is, a different ballot for each candidate. This method gives rise to three negative consequences:

- Increased opportunities for electoral fraud;
- More complicated logistical arrangements due to the sometimes inconceivably great number of ballots to be transported; and
- The higher costs involved.

The single ballot is less susceptible to fraud, easier to check and less costly.

In effect, the adoption of a single ballot would also eliminate the obligation of double counting set out by Article 62 of the Electoral Code, under which even the unused ballots placed in black envelopes have to be counted. This operation, adopted to reduce distrust among electoral actors, makes the work of the polling station officials far more arduous, consumes a lot of time and diminishes the overall quality of the work. Likewise, the elections cycle dictates a hectic electoral marathon with the successive organisation of municipal, presidential, legislative and senatorial, as well as district elections. Five elections (six in the event of a second presidential round) within a period of less than four months makes the electoral cycle particularly complex and some NIEC activities difficult to plan.

Fortunately, the participants at the meeting held in March 2013 in Kayanza under the auspices of the UN Bureau in Burundi (BNUB) and the Burundian government agreed on the need to change to a single ballot and to relax the electoral calendar by staggering the various processes. This was later taken up and included in the Bill amending the Electoral Code, which was passed by the National Assembly in April 2014. The Bill is yet to be passed by the Senate before it is signed into law by the President. It is important that these steps are completed before the 2015 electoral cycle.

The management of electoral disputes is beset with numerous uncertainties that undermine the transparency and credibility of elections. The regulations governing the mechanisms for dealing with electoral disputes and the institutions responsible for this litigation are unclear under the law. Electoral litigation is based on a complex mechanism of complaints and appeals, little known to the public or political actors. Electoral litigation has never been followed up by effective action and some complaints have often been declared inadmissible for lack of tangible evidence.

In effect, the Electoral Code sets out that the provincial electoral commissions (*Commission électorale provinciale indépendante*, CEPI) should preside over the petitions lodged at the end of the voter registration period and the district and municipal elections, while the Constitutional Court deals with the petitions presented in the context of legislative and presidential elections and referenda. The CEPI is, however, prevented from dealing competently with disputes by the fact that its members lack the qualifications to do so. Moreover, the 2010 elections experience has shown that the CEPI or its members are implicated in most of the disputes that it is supposed to deal with, which makes it at once judge and defendant. Finally, the CEPI is far too involved in other administrative and logistical duties assigned to it by the Code to really have time to deal efficiently with electoral disputes.

The current review of the Electoral Code has been launched in a timely manner to allow for its conclusion before the next electoral cycle scheduled for 2015. This review should be as inclusive as possible and should take into account the need to strengthen the independence of the NIEC by granting it administrative and managerial autonomy. In order to achieve this, the new Electoral Code must sever all ties between the NIEC and the Ministry of the Interior. The Electoral Code should also spell out the role of the electoral litigation mechanism more clearly by defining the responsibilities assigned specifically to the NIEC, the CEPIs and the Constitutional Court. In view of its originality and political significance, the NIEC's power in ensuring respect for ethnic representation should be exercised with maximum transparency and probity. It is important to set out provisions that reduce the risks of arbitrary action by the NIEC in exercising its prerogative of ethnic re-adjustment and co-optation for party lists. The criteria used by the NIEC to effect co-optation and re-adjustment of imbalances need to be clarified, known in advance, and communicated to all the interested parties at the time of use.

B. Historical and political context

Burundi is one of the few nation-states in Africa. It was a kingdom prior to its colonisation, first by Germany from 1890, then by Belgium under successive mandate systems of the League of Nations from 1919, and later under the tutelage of the UN from 1945.

The elections organised by the Belgian colonial administration on 18 September 1961 were to determine the course of the political history of post-independence Burundi. These elections pitted two major forces against each other. On the one side was the 'Common Front', a coalition of parties brought together for the most part by the colonial administration and favourable to the idea of a deferred independence, negotiated with the Belgian tutelage; on the other, UPRONA (*Union pour le Progrès National*) and its allies, led by Prince Louis Rwagasore, the son of the *Mwami* (king), favoured immediate independence. Following UPRONA's landslide victory, Prince Rwagasore was assassinated by a Greek mercenary in the pay of the colonial administration. This assassination marked the beginning of a series of political assassinations – including that of a Prime Minister in 1965 and of a former *Mwami* in 1972 – that punctuated the country's political life, particularly during elections.

Two of these assassinations left deep marks in the collective psyche of Burundi and justify the trauma that traditionally accompanies elections in the country. These were the 1961 assassination of the victor in the newly independent state's first elections, Louis Rwagasore, and that of the winner of the first democratic and pluralist elections, Melchior Ndadaye, in 1993. The recurring political violence in Burundi constitutes both the cause and consequence of worsening ethnic tensions and justifies a profound mistrust of electoral processes.

Political development

Pre-colonial Burundi was a feudal society consisting of more than 200 clans. The political structure had a king (*Mwami*) at its peak, who belonged to none of these clans, but came from one of the four dynasties that succeeded each other in turn at the head of the monarchy: the Batare, Bezi, Bataga and Bambutsa dynasties. It was a king from the Bezi dynasty, Mwami Mwezi Gisabo, who ruled at the start of the German colonisation in 1889; Mwami Mwambutsa Bangiricenge, who ruled when the country achieved independence in 1962, came from the Bambutsa dynasty. The ruling class from the four dynasties constituted the Batwa, the Bahutu, the Batutsi and the Baganwa. In effect, according to anthropologists, the dynasty in Burundi 'was not Tutsi but Baganwa, originating from the South East'[20] and 'the Baganwa constituted a special category in that it controlled the political organisation and power'.[21]

German colonisation, which began at the end of the 19th century, completely transformed this politico-social structure of Burundian society. From 1889, the German colonial administration organised an ethnic census, which served to categorise the population, no longer on the basis of clan membership, but henceforth between Hutu and Tutsi. Those household heads who owned fewer than ten cows were considered to be Hutu, whereas those who had more than ten cows were categorised as Tutsi. The Twa pygmy population was considered far too insignificant numerically to warrant their counting. It was this 1889 census, the only one which had ever been organised on the basis of ethnicity, that implemented the ethnic-based distribution of the Burundian population (84% of Bahutu, 14% of Batutsi and 1% of Batwa) long considered valuable, even in the post-independence years.[22]

One of the main features of Belgian colonisation was the system of indirect rule inherited from German colonisation and institutionalised in 1925.[23] The principle of indirect rule was founded on the maintenance of and respect for local institutions, and the idea that power remains in the hands of the Mwami, whom the resident colonial administrator served as Advisor or Tutor. The limitations of this indirect rule are, however, clearly marked out by one of the Belgian administrators in Burundi, P Ryckmans, according to whom the traditional chiefs 'should submit to European control for the good of the country, control which was to be sometimes painful to them'.[24] By favouring the traditional chiefs, all categorised as Tutsi, the system of indirect rule also institutionalised the rift between the two communities by establishing ethnic origin as the sole criterion for the administrative identification of persons.

Elections, political parties and ethnic divisions

The first electoral experiment in Burundi was during the transition from colonial administration to independence. In effect, just before independence, the Belgian tutelage organised two major elections at the national level: municipal elections in 1960 and legislative elections in 1961.[25] These elections were, above all, characterised by animosity between the political parties with nationalist convictions grouped together under the leadership of UPRONA, and those that called for a controlled transition to independence under the banner of the 'Common Front', which grouped together the *Parti*

20   Ghislain, J (1970) *La Féodalité au Burundi*, Académie royale des Sciences d'Outre-Mer, N.S., XXXVI-3, Bruxelles.
21   Ntahombaye, P (2005)'Ethnicité et citoyenneté au Burundi', *The African Anthropologist* 12(1): 52.
22   Nsengimana, A, 'Mémoire de la guerre de 1914–1918 en Afrique Orientale Allemande', témoignage disponible sur le site du service interreligieux *Souffle et chemins*, www.souffle-et-chemins.fr/index.php?option=com_content&task=view&id=34&Itemid=2, accessed 20 February 2013.
23   Pursuant to the Law of 21 August 1925 on the Government of Rwanda-Urundi.
24   Cited by Gahama, J (1983) *Le Burundi sous administration belge*, Karthala, Paris, p. 62.
25   See Deslaurier, C (2002) 'Un monde politique en mutation: le Burundi à la veille de l'indépendance (1956–1961)', Doctoral Thesis, University of Paris I-Panthéon-Sorbonne, p. 391.

démocratique chrétien (PDC), the *Parti du Peuple* (PP) and the *Union populaire pour la République* (UPR).[26] In view of Burundi's special colonial status, the 1961 elections were also supervised by representatives of the UN Commission for Rwanda-Urundi.

On the eve of independence, Burundi had about 27 political parties of variable importance. Very few were as strongly established as the charismatic Prince Louis Rwagasore's separatist UPRONA party. At the end of the September 1961 legislative elections, despite the hostility of the Belgian tutelage, UPRONA obtained an overwhelming majority of 90% of the votes. It won 58 out of the 64 seats being contested, while the remaining six were won by the Common Front, seen as close to the Belgian tutelage circles.[27] The Belgian colonial elite could not stomach this crushing defeat and set about to undermine the ongoing decolonisation process. On 13 October 1961, a few weeks after his victory in the legislative elections, Prince Rwagasore was assassinated. There then followed a ferocious succession race between his various close collaborators who broke up into two groups: 'Moderates', largely made up of Hutus, and 'Progressives', comprising a majority of Tutsis. For the first time, these clashes took on a pronounced ethnic tone.

After independence on 1 July 1962, these internal tensions within UPRONA led to the brutal assassination of Hutu Prime Minister Pierre Ngendadumwe on 15 January 1965. During this period, a Hutu ethnic revolution in neighbouring Rwanda led to mass killings of Tutsis. This gave rise to paranoia within Burundi's Tutsi political elite and strengthened the sentiment within the Hutu political elite that the majority (ethnic Hutu formed 85% of the population according to several estimates) should have the right to govern the country.[28]

During the 1965 elections, UPRONA, although divided and in the grip of a succession war, won the majority of the seats, obtaining 63.6% of the votes (21 out of 33 parliamentary seats). A political party materialised from the identity conflict, and having based its campaign on the mobilisation of ethnic solidarity, it won ten seats while the independents gained two. For the first time, the Hutu UPRONA MPs were in the majority. The Mwami was not happy with this ethnic configuration of parliamentary seats. He subsequently dissolved Parliament on 3 March 1965 and appointed his Cousin Ganwa Muhirwa as Prime Minister. Muhirwa's legitimacy, in the eyes of the Hutu political elite, was questionable. An assassination attempt on Mwami Mwambutsa Bangiricenge failed, resulting in the arrest and execution of 60 persons suspected of having tried to orchestrate it. The Mwami, who was not endowed with leadership qualities, was an ineffective unifier and incapable of rallying the political elites round to a common vision of the country. He went into exile abroad and abdicated his throne to the young Prince Charles Ndiseye in July 1966.

---

26   See Deslaurier (2002), op. cit., p. 392.
27   See Guay, A (2009–2010) 'Histoire des élections au Burundi', Thesis for the Diploma of Master in History, University of Pau and the Adour countries, www.ifra-nairobi.net.
28   See in particular Niyongabo, C (2008) *Le phénomène identitaire au Burundi et son impact sur les élections de 2005*, University of Bujumbura, p. 53.

The Chief of Staff, Captain Michel Micombero, who had quelled the 1965 attacks against the royal palace, took over power on 28 November 1966 and established the first Republic in Burundi. Under this regime, power became militarised, followed by the establishment of a single party, UPRONA, as the sole mechanism for accessing power. The one-party system thus institutionalised sought to exploit electoral practices to legitimise a usurped power acquired through a *coup d'état*. Following the ethnic tensions generated by the events of 1965, the new rulers felt that competitive democracy and its corollary, free and fair elections, were the cause of identity conflicts in Burundi.

This regime, founded on the force of arms, would in turn be overthrown by a young officer, Jean Baptiste Bagaza, on 1 November 1976. In 1981, Bagaza had a new Constitution drafted which, submitted to a referendum, was approved by more than 99.28% with 94.3% of voters participating. In 1983, like his predecessor, he organised presidential and legislative elections under the leadership of the single party, UPRONA. He stood as the sole candidate while other aspirants were discouraged from submitting their candidature by means of a full array of ploys ranging from intimidation, conscience buyout and demonisation to the point of repressing any desire to seek a mandate. For the legislative elections, the names were shortlisted by the single party on the basis of an equivocal, arbitrary and secret procedure.[29] At the end of the presidential elections, Bagaza was elected by 99.66% of the voters with 97% turnout.

From the Charter of National Unity to the Arusha Accords

In 1988, the regime of the President Pierre Buyoya, who had overthrown Jean-Baptiste Bagaza in September 1987, was confronted with new inter-ethnic massacres followed by police repression. For the first time, it recognised the imperative to establish an all-encompassing national dialogue to deal with problems linked to ethnic identity in Burundi and their impact on the stability of national institutions.

President Buyoya, therefore, set up a 'National Commission Responsible for Studying the Issue of National Unity' comprising Hutu and Tutsi commissioners who criss-crossed the country gathering the views and opinions of the population on the ethnic issue in Burundi. The commission's report declares that Burundi 'in fact constitutes a sole ethnic group' even though it is characterised by a 'multidimensional homogeneity'.[30] The commission also drafted a Charter of National Unity, a series of institutional measures and constitutional instructions intended to solve the problem linked to ethnic identity and exclusion based on ethnic differences. The charter,

---

29 Guay (2009–2010), op. cit., p. 54. During the validation workshop of this report held in July 2013 in Bujumbura, one of the participants, Isidore Hakisimana, former minister and member of the single party elected during the legislative elections organised on the basis of this logic, contested this interpretation and insisted on the fact that these elections were transparent in that the candidates chose to present themselves before an Electoral College.
30 Vandeginste, S (2006) 'Théorie consociative et partage du pouvoir au Burundi', in F Reyntjens & S Marysse (eds), *L'Afrique des Grands Lacs: Annuaire 2005–2006*, L'Harmattan, p. 181.

submitted to a peoples' referendum, was approved in February 1991 by a majority of 89.77% of the votes cast.[31]

There ensued a rapid series of reforms for a major democratic consensus in Burundi. In March 1992, a new Constitution establishing a multi-party system was adopted by more than 90.42% of the votes. It signalled the end of the domination by UPRONA, which had to submit to electoral competition. On the eve of the 1993 elections there were about 12 political parties, three of which had a genuine national and popular base – UPRONA, FRODEBU (*Front pour la* Démocratie au *Burundi*) and the PRP (*Parti pour la Réconciliation du Peuple*). Several elections, presidential and legislative, were held under the supervision of an Electoral Commission set up by an UPRONA-dominated government.

During the presidential election, Pierre Buyoya stood under the banner of UPRONA, Melchior Ndadaye stood under that of FRODEBU and Pierre Claver Sendegeya under that of the PRP. To UPRONA's surprise Melchior Ndadaye won the presidential election by an overwhelming majority of 64.75% while the UPRONA candidate, Pierre Buyoya, obtained only 32.39% of the vote. The participation rate of 97.3% for this election was considered to be historic.

In the legislative elections, voter participation fell to about 91% because of calls for boycott by some leaders of the UPRONA. For the legislative elections, five parties fielded candidates: UPRONA, FRODEBU, the PRP, the *Ralliement pour la Démocratie et le Développement Economique et Social* (RADDES)and the *Rassemblement Populaire du Burundi* (RPB). Overall, 744 candidates contested 81 vacant seats.[32] Once again, FRODEBU won a resounding victory of 72.55%, whereas UPRONA had to settle for 20.43% of the votes. As regards seats, FRODEBU obtained 65 seats and UPRONA 16 out of 81. In ethnic terms, the new National Assembly comprised 85% Hutu and 15% Tutsi members.

Determined to torpedo the engaged process, a political party attempted a *coup d'état* in an effort to stem the changes that followed these elections. Finally, on the night of 21 October 1993, the newly elected president was assassinated. Some of his close collaborators were also killed. There followed a long period of political instability, genocide and chronic war, which was to last 15 years until the end of the hostilities of the last rebel movement, the *Forces nationales de libération* (FNL)-Palipehutu.[33]

---

31 Well before the existence of the Arusha Accords, the Charter of National Unity was considered as the founder law of the official recognition of the ethnic factor and the first attempt at institutional mitigation of the rifts emanating from the ethnic reality in Burundi; see F Reyntjens (1992) 'L'ingénierie de l'unité nationale: Quelques singularités de la constitution burundaise de 1992', *Politique africaine* 47: 141–146.

32 See Palmans, E (2005) 'Médias et élections au Burundi: l'expérience de 1993 et perspectives pour 2005', in F Reyntjens & S Marysse (eds), *L'Afrique des Grands Lacs: Annuaire 2005–2006*, L'Harmattan, p. 35.

33 This movement agreed to end the hostilities in April 2008 following the more or less bloody attacks on the City of Bujumbura which produced a shockwave within the urban population that had started to taste the positive effects of peace with the signing of the Arusha Accord.

Arusha Accords, new Constitution and the 2005 elections

In 2000, the parties to the Burundi conflict finally signed an inclusive global accord in Arusha, first under the aegis of the mediator, Tanzanian President Mwalimu Julius Nyerere, and later under the moderation of South Africa.[34] The Arusha Peace and Reconciliation Accord set out, in particular, a 36-month transition period during which the two major political parties, UPRONA and FRODEBU, were to hold power on a rotational basis. After this period, the government was to tackle the task of organising a general election.

Under the Arusha Accord, the parties undertook to introduce ethnic quotas in all the institutions of the country, in particular, the army, the police, the government, the National Assembly and the Senate, as well as the various committees established by the Accord and the Constitution that was to be its offshoot. It was agreed that each institution would comprise 40% Tutsi and 60% Hutu. However, the Accord made a point of separating political from technical posts. The quotas related, therefore, solely to political posts. Concerning the technical posts, the Accord advocated consideration of the gender dimension and ethnic and regional diversity. The quota system was of capital importance for the 2005 elections. The Electoral Commission was, in effect, constitutionally bound to ensure that the lists presented by the political parties respected the quotas established by the Arusha Accord and to effect co-optation if there was need for it.

It was within this climate of dialogue and political détente that the 2005 elections were held. The Constitution was adopted by referendum in 2005 with 92.4% of voters participating.[35] In 2005, several polls were organised: municipal, legislative, senatorial, district and presidential elections.

The legislative elections were a major point of interest, as the first presidential election was to be held on the basis of indirect suffrage. In effect, the President of the Republic was to be elected by Parliament with a two-thirds majority of the members present. It was, therefore, evident that the candidate of the political party with the greatest number of seats in Parliament had the greater chance of winning the presidential election. Six political parties presented candidates on the basis of a voting procedure of lists based on proportional representation:

- *Conseil National Pour la Défense de la Démocratie – Forces de Défense de la Démocratie* (National Council for the Defence of Democracy – Democracy Defence Forces) (CNDD-FDD);
- UPRONA;
- FRODEBU;
- *Conseil National Pour la Défense de la Démocratie* (National Council for the Defence of Democracy) (CNDD);

---

34   In November 2003, the rebel movement CNDD-FDD (National Council for the Defence of Democracy – Democracy Defence Forces) in turn signed the Global Peace and Reconciliation Accord.

35   See COSOME (2005) *Rapport synthèse du déroulement des élections, December 2005*, Bujumbura, p. 22; see also www.cosome.bi.

- *Mouvement pour la Réhabilitation des Citoyens* (Movement for the Rehabilitation of Citizens) (MRC); and
- *Parti pour la Reconstruction Nationale* (Party for National Reconstruction) (PARENA).

Altogether 3,225 candidates entered the lists. At the end of this ballot, the CNDD-FDD won 55% of the seats, FRODEBU obtained 25%, UPRONA 8%, the CNDD 4% and PARENA and the MRC barely gained 2.7% and 2.3%, respectively. After co-optation, the CNDD-FDD obtained 64 seats, FRODEBU 30 seats, UPRONA 15, the CNDD four and PARENA and the MRC two each. During the presidential election by indirect suffrage, the CNDD-FDD candidate, Pierre Nkurunzisa, received 93% of the vote.[36]

The controversial 2010 elections

In 2010, for the first time, Burundi organised a presidential election by universal suffrage. It was an opportunity to consolidate the achievements of a peace acquired with great difficulty during the negotiations of the Arusha Accord in 2000.

The enactment of the 2009 Electoral Code was the subject of an all-inclusive parliamentary debate. The recruitment of the members of the Electoral Commission was also subjected to consultations and negotiation between the different political parties participating in the government, namely FRODEBU and UPRONA. The electoral cycle for that year comprised five ballots:
- May 24 – municipal elections;
- June 28 – presidential elections;
- July 23 – legislative elections;
- July 28 – senatorial elections; and
- September 7 – district elections.

For the municipal elections, seven political parties had presented candidates:
- CNDD-FDD;
- FNL;
- UPRONA;
- FRODEBU;
- *Mouvement pour la solidarité et la démocratie* (Movement for Solidarity and Democracy) (MSD);
- *Union pour la Patrie et la Démocratie* (Union for the Fatherland and for Democracy) (UPD); and
- CNDD.

---

36   See Guay (2009–2010), op. cit., p. 89.

The CNDD-FDD obtained 64% of the vote, the FNL received14%, UPRONA 6%, FRO-DEBU 5%, the MSD 3%, the UPD 2% and the CNDD1%. These results were immediately contested by the opposition parties, which called for the annulment of the vote and the replacement of the Electoral Commission for alleged large-scale fraud.[37] They joined forces within the *Alliance Démocratique pour le Changement* (Democratic Alliance for Change)(ADC-Ikibiri), comprising the FNL, the MSD, the UPD and the CNDD. Only UPRONA and FRODEBU-Nyakuri[38] remained in the running. The latter two withdrew from the race in favour of other elections, which were programmed during this marathon of elections.

It was within this tense environment that the presidential elections were held. The withdrawal of the principal opposition parties was testimony to the loss of confidence in the Electoral Commission, which was accused of bias and open support for the ruling party.[39] On this basis, therefore, Pierre Nkurunzisa, the sole candidate of the CNDD-FDD for the presidential elections, unsurprisingly scored an overwhelming victory with a total of 91.62% of the vote and a voter participation rate of 76.98%. This reduced voter participation was also due to the calls for a boycott of the elections by the ADC-Ikibiri parties, which had been widely respected in the provinces where they obtained a comfortable majority, for example, in the city of Bujumbura, in greater Bujumbura and in Bururi.

The legislative elections took place in an equally tense environment, with opposition parties being harassed by the security forces. According to the human rights association *Association Burundaise pour la Protection des Droits Humains et des Personnes Détenues* (APRODH), 294 persons were arrested during this period.[40] However, three political parties fielded candidates during the election. They were the CNDD-FDD, UPRONA and FRODEBU-Nyakuri. Once again, the CNDD-FDD won the elections with 81.19% of the votes, UPRONA obtained barely 11.06%, and FRODEBU-Nyakuri 3.24%. The new National Assembly had 106 vacant seats. After co-optation, the configuration of the Parliament confirmed the CNDD-FDD's predominance. It had 81 members, UPRONA 17 and FRODEBU-Nyakuri five.[41] In ethnic terms, Parliament comprised 60% Hutu and 40% Tutsi. The representation of women was also guaranteed, thanks to the co-optation system: women's representation was about 32%, meaning that out of 106 MPs, 34 were women.

---

37 See UNDP (2011) *Report of the Electoral Cycle Support Project* Projet d'appui au Processus Electoral *(PACE) in Burundi*, Bujumbura, p. 45.
38 A FRODEBU splinter group, known officially as 'Sahwanya FRODEBU Nyakuri iragi rya Ndadaye' (or just 'FRODEBU-Nyakuri', meaning 'the genuine FRODEBU').
39 See the ADC-Ikibiri Declaration on the Municipal Elections, Press Release, 15 June 2010, Bujumbura.
40 APRODH (2010) *Report on the Monitoring of Human Rights During the 2010 Elections*, Bujumbura, p. 18.
41 European Union Election Observation Mission (2010) *Burundi: Rapport Final: Elections communales, présidentielle, législatives, sénatoriales et collinaires*, eeas.europa.eu/eueom/pdf/missions/final-report-burundi-2010_fr.pdf.

Electing district councillors

The electoral marathon that started on 24 May2010 was to end with the district elections scheduled for 7 September 2010, the second such elections in the history of Burundi. Altogether 38,000 candidates were on the ballot in the 2,639 hills or districts of Burundi, each of which was to have five councillors. The record of those who had previously served in the administration at district level in the preceding five years was to be a benchmark for selecting men and women who could help citizens live in peace and security and to develop their country and families.

A ballot different from the others

Whereas the district councillors are elected by direct universal suffrage like the municipal councillors, the President and MPs, the district elections different from the other ballots in three main aspects:

- Firstly, 'the candidates are independent and are, in principle, apolitical.' Without denying that the candidates may have their own political convictions, National Independent Electoral Commission spokesperson Prosper Ntahorwamiye stressed that 'the law prohibits them from declaring their affiliation to any political party while on the campaign trail.' Concerning the penalty set out by law for this offence, he declined to give more details since such a case had not yet arisen.

- Secondly, 'there would only be one ballot and one ballot box for these elections.' In effect, Prosper Ntahorwamiye explained, voters were expected to list three names of individuals for which they wished to vote, whereas in the other ballots the candidates' names figured on closed lists. The five candidates winning the greatest number of votes would constitute the District Council. In the event of a tie in the votes, the oldest candidate would be chosen; where they were of the same gender, the one whose gender was least represented would be chosen. The law does not make provision for any solution where the candidates are of the same age and gender: 'Should the situation arise either a drawing of lots will be considered or a choice made on the basis of the alphabetic order of their names,' Ntahorwamiye added.

- Thirdly, there are no quotas based on gender or ethnicity for these elections. Votes are cast taking into consideration the composition of the inhabitants of the hill or district: 'It is possible to find a hill with only one ethnic group; for this reason the issue of quotas has not been taken into account for this ballot.' However, Burundi is in any case growing towards recognition for the candidates' competence and not their ethnic group or gender. Also, the results of the district elections are forwarded to the Independent Municipal Electoral Commission (CECI) and in the event of any irregularity or fraud, the complainants should report to the Independent Provincial Electoral Commission (CEPI), which makes a final ruling.

The role of district councillors

District councillors are grassroots administrators who monitor and find solutions to the problems that citizens under their jurisdiction experience on a daily basis. These elected officials transmit the peoples' grievances to the relevant authority. They are bound to implement a local policy that requires the participation of the population. Underscoring the important role district councillors play, the political scientist Siméon Barumwete notes that they participate in the decision-making process, in the realisation of development activities and the safeguarding of social peace within the hill or district. He points out that in collaboration with the *Bashingantahe*,[42] the district councillors arbitrate, mediate, reconcile and settle disputes among neighbours. They also give opinions on all issues affecting the hill or district.

SOURCE:
Mbarisa Ntore (Pool of Burundian Journalists' Newsletter gathered to cover the 2010 elections) 33.

C. The National Independent Electoral Commission

Burundi's electoral management system is established along the lines of similar bodies in most francophone countries. Although initially the prerogative of the government in the immediate post-independence period, the management of elections was undertaken more or less professionally by officials in the Ministry of the Interior, even though each public service was biased in favour of UPRONA, which had led the struggle for independence. Following the 1966 *coup d'état* and the establishment of the military regime, elections were reduced to a ritual intended to give a semblance of legitimacy to the military dictatorship. With the restoration of a multi-party system in the early 1990s came calls for the creation of a specific institution independent of the government to manage elections. The Electoral Commissiont hat was established progressed slowly to become more independent and professional. Its greatest transformation took place following the 2000 Arusha Accord, which granted it specific powers, including that of ensuring that elections never culminated in the exclusion of one ethnic group for the benefit of another.

Development of EMBs in Burundi

The elections held in 1961 on the eve of independence were organised by the colonial administration under the supervision of the UN Commission for Rwanda-Urundi.[43]

---

42   'The ancient institution of *bashingantahe* in Burundi is made up of elders, people of irreproachable morality. It presided over the judicial organization of the country at all levels and played the role of check and balance on power, ensuring that arbitrary judgement and lack of justice were curbed.' Naniwe-Kaburahe, A (2008) 'The institution of bashingantahe in Burundi', in *Traditional Justice and Reconciliation after Violent Conflict: Learning from African Experiences*, International IDEA, Strömsborg, www.idea.int/publications/traditional_justice/upload/Chapter_6_The_institution_of_bashingantahe_in_Burundi.pdf, accessed 24 June 2014.

43   See Guay (2009–2010), op. cit., p. 45.

The Trusteeship Administration organised the elections under the Ministry for Local Government. Thus, it can be said to have been far from neutral, independent and unbiased, particularly since the Administration had openly voiced its hostility towards the political parties that campaigned for 'immediate independence', and instead favoured the politicians who advocated a deferred independence.

During the three post-independence decades, elections were organised within the framework of the one-party system established in 1966. They were organised by the Ministry for Local Government, which was a department within the single-party government and therefore satisfied none of the criteria – independence, neutrality and impartiality – required for free, fair and transparent elections.

It was only with the return of a multi-party system and the 1992 Constitution that freer and more democratic elections could be organised. Electoral management was then entrusted to a National Electoral Commission (NEC) comprising 45 members nominated by all the registered political parties and by the members of civil society. The provincial electoral commissions were chaired by judges.

It would appear that this NEC was highly politicised and had to submit to immense pressure from the political parties that had established it. Moreover, close links existed between the NEC and local government institutions, since it was the municipal officers appointed by the government who recruited the officers responsible for voter registration. Provincial governors, who were themselves answerable to the executive, appointed the officers for polling stations.[44] The 1993 NEC had no managerial autonomy because it was placed under the supervision of the Ministry of the Interior, on which it depended for material and operational resources. Furthermore, its independence was somewhat undermined by its temporary nature and the limited mandate of its members. Despite these constraints, the 1993 elections managed by the NEC were adjudged free, peaceful, fair and transparent.[45]

The legitimacy of the National Independent Electoral Commission (NIEC)springs mainly from the Second Protocol of the Arusha Accord, whose Article 5 sets out the establishment of an electoral commission with the responsibility of guaranteeing the integrity, freedom, impartiality and independence of the electoral process, as well as the establishment of a Constitutional Court, responsible, in particular, for ruling on the regularity of presidential and legislative elections and referenda. The first version of the NIEC had been established in 2004 as a 'temporary bureau' responsible for the material preparation of the elections.[46] This NIEC comprised five members, all selected from civil society. None of these appointed members had the required expertise in electoral matters apart from the chairman, who was a member of the NEC during the 1993 elections. The commission was empowered to draft and adopt its Rules of Procedure but

---

44   European Union Election Observation Mission (2005) Report of the European Commission's Election
       Observation Mission, Bujumbura, p. 25.
45   Palmans (2005), op. cit., p. 49.
46   Decree No. 103 of 5 August 2004.

was obliged to submit them to the Minister of the Interior for final endorsement, a sign of very limited autonomy. Moreover, the temporary nature of this institution restricted its independence even more in the proper execution of its mandate. It was only in 2009 that the government, following broad consultations with the political parties, considered establishing a permanent NIEC comprising five members with a neutral President and Vice-President and three other members nominated by the political parties within the current government, namely the CNDD-FDD, UPRONA and FRODEBU.

Legal framework

Burundi is a member of the East African Community (EAC), which seeks to create and strengthen a sub-regional area in which stable democracies prevail and the nations are economically prosperous. Burundi has also committed to respecting and upholding the principles of the African Charter on Good Governance, Democracy and Elections. The 2005 Burundi Constitution, in its Article 89, stipulates that 'a National, Independent Electoral Commission guarantees the freedom, impartiality and independence of the electoral process.'[47] The current Electoral Code – enacted in 2005 and amended in 2009[48]– reiterates this provision, specifying that 'its missions, its composition, its organisation and its functions are determined by specific provisions.'[49]

Under its current form, the NIEC is directly governed by Decree No. 100/76 of 12 March 2012 on the Organisation and Functioning of the National Independent Electoral Commission, as well as by the NIEC's Rules of Procedure. The 2012 Decree, which had been voted for in anticipation of the 2015 general election, is the result of a review of Decree No. 100/22 of 20 February 2009 on the Organisation and Functioning of the National Independent Electoral Commission. The 2012 Decree effected a few important amendments to the old provisions. These amendments related to the competence of the NIEC members, decentralised branches to effect appointments, and the duration of their term of office (Articles 17 and 19 of the old Decree, as well as the addition of a new Article 23).

These instruments contain the essence of the legal provisions applicable to the elections. Other enactments, which contain provisions governing the elections, consist of:

- Law No. 1/02 of 25 January 2010 effecting the review of the Law No. 1/016 of 20 April 2005 on the organisation of local government;
- Law No. 1/16 of 10 September 2011 on the review of the Law No. 1/006 of 26 June 2003 on the organisation and functioning of political parties;
- Law No. 1/025 of 27 November 2003 governing the Media in Burundi;

---

47 Law No. 1/10 of 18 March 2005 on the Constitution of the Republic of Burundi.
48 Law No. 1/22 of 18 September 2009 on the review of Law No. 1/015 of 20 April 2005 on the Electoral Code.
49 Electoral Code, Article 3.

- Law No. 01/18 of 25 September 2009 governing the organisation and functioning of the National Communication Council and Organic Statute No. 1/018 of 19 December 2002 on the organisation and functioning of the Constitutional Court.

Article 31 of the Electoral Code stipulates that 'the candidates and the political parties may use the state media for their electoral campaign.' It adds that 'the National Communication Council guarantees equal access to the state media for all candidates.' Article 284 of the Constitution sets out that 'the National Communication Council (CNC) will safeguard the freedom of audio-visual and written communication in respect for the law, public law and order, and public decency' and in this respect it has 'decisional power particularly in matters of respect for and promotion of press freedom and equal access to the public media for the various political, social, economic and cultural convictions.' Article 286 specifies that 'the members of the CNC are appointed by the President of the Republic in consultation with the Vice-President of the Republic.' The CNC is, therefore, dependent on the executive, which may compromise its independence with regard to the President's original party.

Structure, organisation and functioning of the NIEC

The NIEC comprises the Bureau, the Provincial Independent Electoral Commissions, the Municipal Independent Electoral Commissions and Commissioners' Offices.

The Bureau

The Bureau is the NIEC's supervisory and national coordination body and comprises five members:
- A President;
- A Vice-President;
- A Commissioner responsible for electoral operations, logistics and legal matters;
- A Commissioner responsible for administration and financial matters; and
- A Commissioner responsible for electoral education and for communication issues.[50]

The members are appointed for a five-year non-renewable term. They work full-time in the NIEC. Pursuant to Article 8 of the Decree on the organisation and functioning of the NIEC, a presidential decree spells out their working conditions, status and rank.

The Bureau is supported by the appropriate technical departments, subdivided into as many divisions as required. These departments are under departmental heads who

---

50   Article 90 of the Constitution and Decree on the Organisation and Functioning of the NIEC. Decree No. 100/22 of 20 February 2009 as well as that of 2012 set out at the time that, 'are Members of the Commission, the President, the Vice-President and three Commissioners ...'

are supervised and coordinated by an Executive Secretary. The Executive Secretary takes part in the meetings of the Bureau in an advisory capacity. He implements the decisions taken by the Bureau and is responsible for all the activities relating to the preparation and conduct of the electoral process. The President of the NIEC is also assisted by a Principal Private Secretary, of the rank of Head of Department.[51]

Each Commissioner's Office has three departments:

- The departments of Electoral Operations, Electoral Logistics and Legal Affairs fall under the supervision of the commissioner responsible for electoral operations, logistics and legal affairs.
- The Finances, Administration and Computer Science Departments fall under the office of the commissioner responsible for administration and finance.
- The Civic Education, Information and Communication, Interpreting and Translation departments fall under the office of the commissioner responsible for civic education and communication.[52]

Provincial Independent Electoral Commissions

The Provincial Independent Electoral Commissions (CEPIs) were established by the NIEC Order of 12 November 2009 in each of the country's 17 provinces for a one-year term.[53]

The CEPIs have the following powers and responsibilities:

- To receive appeals relating to matters of enrolment (Article 22, 23, 24 CE);
- To receive appeals against the composition of polling stations (Article 40 CE);
- To issue special cards to political party representatives (Article 41 CE);
- To receive the minutes on the closure of the enrolment (Article 12 CE);
- To receive the minutes on vote counting (Article 71 CE); and
- To announce the provisional results of the municipal elections and to receive appeals (Article 72 and 75 CE).

Municipal Independent Electoral Commissions

The Municipal Independent Electoral Commissions (CECIs) were established by the CEPI Order of 2 December 2009 in each of the country's 129 districts for a one-year term.[33]

The CECIs have the following powers and responsibilities:

- To designate registration bureaux (Article 12 CE);
- To prepare the minutes on the closure of registration (Article 18 CE);
- To determine places for bill-posting (Article 27 CE);
- To designate the members of polling stations (Article 40 CE); and
- To announce the provisional results of district elections (Article 74 CE).

---

51   Article 24 of the Rules of Procedure.
52   See the NIEC Website, www.NIECburundi.bi/Organisation-missions-et.
53   Article 16 Order No. 100/22 of 20 February 2009.

Polling staff

For the 2010 elections, the NIEC and the International Foundation for Electoral Systems (IFES) trained polling staff with assistance from the UN Development Fund's 2010 Electoral Cycle Support Project (PACE). A large number of polling staff were recruited by the NIEC and trained by the IFES – enrolment officers and their supervisors, polling station officials, and electoral administration officials at the national, provincial and district levels, notably those in charge of reception and storage equipment.

Vacancies were announced on radio stations and advertised in the most widely read newspapers in Burundi. The recruitment had to adhere to the criteria of ethnic, regional, political and gender diversity, as required in the appointment of public service officials in Burundi. The technical criteria were, however, rather rudimentary, since the only qualification required in some cases was a high school certificate or technical diploma.

Although 24 training sessions were organised between 2009 and 2010 in a capacity-building exercise, there was very little time for the assimilation of skills learnt and their application to real cases in the field.[54] The planning of training sessions was hurried, with the likelihood that teaching aids were inadequate, despite IFES' proven experience in capacity-building. The NIEC also organised retreats for the evaluation of the training sessions between October and November 2010. There is no official report on the conclusions from this self-assessment to capture lessons from the exercise.

In 2010, the NIEC again had to resort to the use of temporary staff to accomplish its tasks. It recruited 15,790 census officers, 792 keyboarding officials, 20 filing staff, 28 officers for its computing section, 36 technical validation officers, 3,302 billposting officers and 542 supervisors, as well as 8,845 officials for the distribution of election materials, and 34,845 polling station staff.[55]

Powers and functions of the NIEC

Article 91 of the Constitution sets out the general responsibilities of the NIEC:

a) To organise elections at the national, municipal and district levels;

b) To ensure that these elections are free, fair and transparent;

c) To announce the provisional results of the elections within a time limit defined by the law;

d) To promulgate the arrangements, the code of conduct and the technical details including the placement of the polling stations and the time these should open;

---

54 See NIEC (2010) *General Report on the 2010 Elections*, Bujumbura, p. 53; see in particular the annex on the training calendar on p. 111.

55 See NIEC (2010) *General Report on the 2010 Elections*, op. cit., p. 34.

e) To listen to complaints pertaining to respect for electoral rules and take necessary action on them. The rulings of the Commission cannot be appealed;

f) To ensure, by applying the appropriate regulations, that electoral campaigns are not carried out in a manner to incite ethnic violence or in any other manner that contravenes the present Constitution;

g) To guarantee respect for the provisions of the present Constitution pertaining to multi-ethnicity and gender, and to hear and determine disputes in this regard.

Paragraphs (a) to (d) grant exclusive power to the NIEC to organise elections; paragraphs (e) and (f) seek to ensure the proper organisation of campaigns and to sanction any breach of the Electoral Code, while (g) takes into account Burundi's peculiarities by granting the commission a specific power to ensure the representation of various ethnic groups, as well as the equality of women.

Organising elections

Article 38 of the Electoral Code stipulates that the NIEC shall directly supervise voting operations at the national level and, with the assistance of the CEPIs and the CECIs, at the provincial, municipal and district levels. Article 130 also grants the NIEC the power to ascertain the eligibility of candidates for the legislative elections. The commission additionally verifies the eligibility of candidates to the presidential election. The CEPIs receive the minutes on the closure of the registration of voters (Article 12 CE) and determine appeals arising from the exercise (Article 22, 23, 24 CE). Article 71 of the Electoral Code mandates the CEPIs (as well as the NIEC and the candidate representatives) to receive the minutes on the counting of ballots, which testify to the accuracy of the election results. Articles 72 and 75 recognise the CEPIs as the chief agents of the municipal elections. They prepare the provisional results, deal with all related appeals and announce the final results.

Pursuant to Articles 74 and 180, in the case of district elections, the relevant CECI counts the votes and makes a provisional announcement of the results. Appeals are addressed to the CEPI, which makes a final determination on them. In the municipal council elections, the CEPI counts the ballots and announces the provisional results. Appeals are addressed to the same CEPI, which makes a final ruling. Articles 72 to 75 grant the CEPI powers to authenticate the district and municipal election results. They have the responsibility to declare the results, as well as hear appeals against these results, which creates a conflict of interest.

The CECIs can designate registration bureaux (Article 12 CE) and are mandated to prepare the minutes on the closure of registration (Article 18 CE). Article 27 stipulates that CECIs allocate specially reserved slots to candidates in the election for campaign bill-posting. Article 171 states that 'the responsibilities devolved to the CEPI by the present law are exercised by the CECI' in district elections. Under Article 172, the CECIs, in collaboration with the district electoral bureaux, organise electoral meetings where the candidates introduce themselves to the public and present their manifesto. This type of electoral campaigning was an innovation of the 2010 elections. The electorate is invited to participate in these public debates by billboards posted in public places like markets ,as well as letters to churches. Candidates are given 5–20 minutes to present their manifestos. This type of debate is neither set out in the Electoral Code nor organised for the legislative, presidential and senatorial elections. Several sources say that this exercise was highly successful in the 2010 elections.[56]

Article 40 of the Electoral Code stipulates that an electoral bureau comprising a president, two assessors and two deputies be designated by the CECI for each polling station. Article 70 requires that on completion of the counting, 'the President of the Bureau reads out the results aloud. These are then entered in the minutes, which are closed by the signature of the bureau members.' The management of the results is highly sensitive. The NIEC has been criticised for lacking transparency in this regard. Where the legal provisions regarding this issue are not adopted, the NIEC has a responsibility to draft a clear protocol of results management, defining the role and competencies of the data processing centre, and ensuring that the results from each polling station are accessible to all (voters, political parties, candidates, observers, etc.) simultaneously with the announcement of the provisional results.

Safeguarding campaigns and sanctioning offenders

The NIEC is obligated to ensure 'that the electoral campaigns are not carried out in a manner to incite ethnic violence or in any other manner that contravenes the present Constitution.' However, this power is neither specified nor detailed in the Electoral Code, even where it grants the National Communication Council power to regulate equal access to state media.[57] In the event of breaches during a campaign, including the use of state assets, insults or false accusations, or even violence, the NIEC refers the matter to the security forces. It should be noted that the members of the CEPIs and the CECIs have powers similar to those of judicial police officers, which NIEC commissioners do not have. The rules governing the electoral campaign do not, therefore, clearly delineate the institutions responsible for implementing the provisions outlined in the Electoral Code regarding the campaign.

The Electoral Code lists offences before or after the election and the sanctions for each in Articles 221–237. In any case, the Electoral Code does not spell out the procedure to be followed when such offences are reported. Moreover, judges have admitted that they lack a proper mastery of these offences' constitutive elements. The UN Integrated Bureau in Burundi (BINUB) produced a Manual on Electoral Transgressions and their

---

56   European Union Election Observation Mission (2010), op. cit., p. 28.
57   In Articles 25–35 of the Electoral Code.

Investigation for the benefit of 600 judges at all levels of the courts, and ran training workshops to disseminate it.[58]

The Electoral Commission can annul results for district and municipal polls – without possibility of appeal – in the event of irregularities. In the event of disagreement during a presidential or legislative election beyond the deadline fixed by the NIEC, the Constitutional Court would be seized of the request to annul the election. The NIEC can only annul municipal and district elections.[59] This discretionary power is open to abuse and arbitrary decisions, since NIEC's rulings in this respect are not appealable. In the event that there is an annulment, the NIEC has five days to organise new elections or by-elections.

The legal framework does not give the NIEC effective means of imposing sanctions without seeking the cooperation of the police force, the prosecutor's office or the public service – in which the various offenders hold senior positions. It should be noted that only the presidents of the polling stations – and not the NIEC commissioners – have the powers of judicial police officers.[60]

Guaranteeing ethnic balance

The Constitution and the Electoral Code give the NIEC important responsibilities in ensuring ethnic balance in Burundi. After legislative elections, the NIEC must ensure that the composition of the National Assembly and the Senate reflects the major ethnic groups in proportion to their population size. Article 108 of the Electoral Code stipulates that should the parliamentarians' election results not guarantee the required balance in ethnic representation (60% Hutu, 40% Tutsi, with 30% being women), the NIEC must rectify this imbalance. Co-optation is carried out in consultation with the political parties concerned. The NIEC also co-opts three MPs from the Twa ethnic group. In the event of any dispute between the NIEC and the party concerned, the commission has the last word. Dissatisfied parties can appeal to the Constitutional Court to review decisions regarding legislative and senatorial elections.

The NIEC also has the power to co-opt senators in line with Article 141 of the Electoral Code. If the senatorial elections do not deliver the gender balance required by the Constitution (a minimum of 30% women), the NIEC, in consultation with the parties concerned, co-opts members to rectify the imbalance.

At the local authority level, the NIEC guarantees respect for ethnic balance within the municipal councils and the municipal public service corps. The Constitution stipulates that the NIEC is responsible for 'ensuring that the municipal councils generally reflect the ethnic diversity of their electorate'.[61] If this is not achieved through the ballot, the NIEC must implement it through co-optation. The NIEC is also required to supervise

---

58   European Union Election Observation Mission (2010), op. cit.
59   Article 65 of the Electoral Code.
60   Ibid., Article 44.
61   Article 266 of the Constitution.

the appointment of municipal staff by the councils to ensure the balance established by the Constitution. None of the country's major ethnic groups can have more than 67% representation within the public service corps, since these proportions are calculated on a national basis. In other words, no single ethnic group should control more than 67% of the 130 districts that make up the country.

The NIEC has the power to prescribe co-optation if a municipal council does not reflect the electorate's ethnic and gender diversity (a minimum of 30% of women),to rectify the perceived imbalance.[62] The NIEC can co-opt an individual from the Twa ethnic group wherever s/he appears on the political parties' electoral lists but is not elected. According to Article 191 of the Electoral Code, the NIEC, in consultation with the parties represented in the municipal councils, adjudicates on the appointment of municipal public servants to ensure that no ethnic group has more than 67% representation within this corps at the national level, as well as to guarantee gender balance.

Ethnic representation and the role of the NIEC in the 2005 elections

Where legislative elections are concerned, proportionality constitutes a fundamental principle for each electoral constituency. Thus, it is rectified differently in the Constitution and in the Electoral Code. First of all it is set out that, overall, the National Assembly should have a minimum of 100 members, comprising 60% Hutu and 40% Tutsi, of which 30%must be women. To 'orient' the results in the desired direction, it is also required that, on the closed lists presented for the elections, *'out of every three candidates registered in succession on a list, only two can belong to the same ethnic group, and at least one out of four should be a woman.'*[63] This provision in fact also governs the diversification (from the ethnic and gender viewpoints) of the total number of elected parliamentarians coming from the same party. Finally, the Constitution also sets out that three MPs coming from the Twa ethnic group should be co-opted.[64] The result of the 4 July 2005 legislative elections did not conform to the quotas required by the Constitution, forcing the NIEC to co-opt members to rectify the situation. Apart from the three Twa members, the CNDD-FDD, FRODEBU and UPRONA parties all have five co-opted MPs.

Parliament comprises two chambers: the National Assembly and the Senate. The senators were elected on 29 July 2005 by indirect suffrage. In effect, the Senate, which is required to approve the appointments of provincial governors and some senior judges, among other responsibilities, is composed of two delegates drawn from each province and elected by an Electoral College comprising members of the municipal councils in the province. The two must originate from different ethnic communities and be elected through clear-cut

---

62   Article 181 of the Electoral Code.
63   Article 168 of the Constitution, Article 118 of the Electoral Code.
64   Article 164 of the Constitution, Article 118 of the Electoral Code.

balloting.[65] Besides the co-optation of the three Twa senators and former heads of state, the Constitution regulates the Hutu and Tutsi parity within the Senate. Ethnic parity in no way guarantees the representation of the different parties: out of the 34 elected senators, 30 belong to the CNDD-FDD. After the elections, eight women were co-opted into the Senate by the NIEC to meet the 30% threshold set out in the Electoral Code.[66] This co-optation somewhat reduced the CNDD-FDD's overwhelming majority in the Senate. In co-opting women senators, the Electoral Code allocates each party that obtained 5% of the votes an equal number of supplementary seats. Thus, the CNDD-FDD, FRODEBU, UPRONA and the CNDD have two co-opted women senators each.

SOURCE:
Vandeginste,S (2006) 'Théorie consociative et partage du pouvoir au Burundi', in F Reyntjens and S Marysse (eds), *L'Afrique des Grands Lacs: Annuaire 2005–2006*, L'Harmattan, pp. 188–193.

Independence of the NIEC

In principle, the independence of the NIEC is guaranteed by the manner in which its members are appointed, as well as their security of tenure. The President's role in appointing NIEC members is nonetheless overweening and prejudices the commission's independence. The commission's managerial autonomy is also compromised by its financial dependence on the government. The manner in which the NIEC is financed, in particular the control mechanisms on the management of the resources provided, also undermines its independence.

Window dressing autonomy

As an independent institution, the NIEC does not fall under the administrative tutelage of any republican institution. Articles 89 and 90 of the Constitution, as well as Article 3 of the Electoral Code, stipulate that the NIEC is an independent institution. Decree 2012 on the Organisation and Functioning of the National Independent Electoral Commission (identical to that of 2009) stipulates in Article 3 that the NIEC enjoys organic and financial management autonomy.

However, the second paragraph of the same Article stipulates that the commission 'gives an account of its management in a report addressed to the President of the Republic, and copied to the minister responsible for Local Government, as well as the President of the Audit Department'. It should be noted here that this relates solely to the report on financial management. According to the Decree on the organisation of the NIEC, the latter has autonomy in administrative and financial management, but in practice, this autonomy is yet to be concretised despite the commission's desire for it.[67] Article 12 of the 2009 Decree stipulated that: 'During their term of office, the members

---

65   Article 6, para. 14 of the Arusha Accord; Article 180 of the Constitution.
66   Article 150 of the Constitution.
67   See Auger, A-M (2011) *Rapport d'évaluation des besoins de la CENI*, Bujumbura.

of the Commission enjoy the immunity from prosecution recognised for serving officials.'[68] This Article was repeated word for word in Decree No. 100/76 of 12 March 2012, which replaced its predecessor. The purpose of this provision is to protect the commission members from pressure that might be exerted on them to prevent them from fulfilling their mandate in total independence.[69]

Finally, Article 7 of the NIEC's Rules of Procedure sets out that 'the members of the NIEC benefit from the use of a Diplomatic Passport and of a Special Membership Card facilitating easy movement in the exercise of their duties.'

Appointment to the NIEC, the CEPI and the CECI

Commission members are 'appointed by Decree after having been separately approved beforehand by the National Assembly and the Senate by a three-fourths majority.'[70] The rationale for determining and arranging the organisation and functioning of the NIEC by decree when electoral matters fall under the law –as required by Article 159 of the Constitution–is not clear. Given the importance, delicacy and sensitivity of the responsibilities entrusted to the NIEC, its independence would have been greatly strengthened if its organisation and functioning had been set out in a specific law.

In practice, the members of the commission are pre-selected by the President in consultation with the leaders of the political parties represented in Parliament and in the government, as well as with CSOs. The President then submits the candidates for approval to the two chambers of Parliament for a vote.

In 2009, during the establishment of the commission that is currently in charge, a first team selected by the President had obtained the approval of the National Assembly but had been opposed in the Senate. The opposition parties had argued that the selected individuals did not inspire any confidence, in particular in relation to their neutrality and impartiality. The President then proposed a second revamped team, which was approved by both chambers of Parliament. The first team had been accused of being too close to the executive and the ruling party, particularly the individual who had been proposed as its head.[71] It was only on 13 March 2009 that the President issued Decree No. 100/38 appointing the five members picked by political party consensus ahead of the elections. The NIEC that was finally approved, comprised two renowned civil society members – the President and Vice-President, who had been appointed by consensus between the President of the Republic and the leaders of the parties represented in the government – and three commissioners, each proposed by one of the three political

---

68   Decrees No. 100/22 of 20 February 2009 and No. 100/76 of 12 March 2012.
69   NIEC, interview, Bujumbura, 23 August 2012.
70   Article 90 of the Constitution.
71   Antoine Kaburahe, Editor-in-Chief, *Iwacu Journal*, interview, 12 August 2012; see also ICG (2010) *Guaranteeing a Credible Electoral Process*, Africa Report No. 155.

parties represented in the government, namely the CNDD-FDD, FRODEBU[72] and UPRONA.[73] But the confidence they enjoyed was short-lived. The NIEC and its members were criticised by the parties that had just withdrawn from the electoral process following their defeat in the municipal elections, and accused of being in the pay of the CNDD-FDD executive. The parties even called for the resignation of all the commission's members.[74]

From the signing of the Arusha Accords, the spirit of dialogue on the choice of the commissioners often prevailed, in particular among the most influential political groups represented in Parliament and in the government. There is no doubt that the executive can use its influence to establish a commission favourable to it or at least one that will bend to its will. Compared to the other models that favour technical expertise at the expense of political equilibrium, the main drawback of the political parties' representative model is that the members of the commission are not always equipped to carry out and conclude significantly complex operations at the national level with only a few months to prepare. For instance, none of the commissioners appointed by the President and confirmed by the Senate had previously worked in the area of elections administration. Certainly, they had undergone training and undertaken study tours, but know-how, expertise and competence can only be acquired over time.

The members of the CEPI and CECI 'are appointed by the Commission from the next point of the hierarchy'.[75] The 2009 Decree on the organisation of the NIEC fully respected this prescription of the Electoral Code. Articles 16 and 17 of the Electoral Code in effect granted the NIEC the power to appoint the members of the CEPI, and gave to the CEPI the power of appointing the CECIs. This is what prevailed in the 2010 elections. Nonetheless, the decree establishing the NIEC enacted in 2012 grants the power of appointing the CECIs to the NIEC, in contravention of Article 38 of the Electoral Code. In Article 17, the new decree in effect withdraws the power of appointing the CECIs from the CEPI and assigns it to the NIEC.

Article 38 of the Electoral Code stipulates that the members of the CEPI and CECI 'are appointed to guarantee political neutrality and ethnic and gender balance'. Article 40 of the Electoral Code underwrites the principle of respect for political, ethnic and gender balance in the identification of polling stations by the CECI. Complaints regarding the CECI's failure to respect this principle are addressed to the CEPI, which makes a final determination. The proper interpretation of this Article allows one to deduce that if the complaints relate to the appointment of the CEPI by the NIEC, only the latter is empowered to revise its own ruling.

---

72   This relates to FRODEBU'S historical wing and not the dissident wing known as 'FRODEBU-Nyakuri iragi rya Ndadaye' (or just 'FRODEBU-Nyakuri', meaning 'the true FRODEBU'). The latter entered the government in 2005 and was removed in 2007. It re-entered government in 2010.
73   Vice-President, FRODEBU, interview, Bujumbura, 14 August 2012.
74   Statement by the President of the ADC-Ikibiri, Léonce Ngendakumana, on the municipal elections, June 2010.
75   Article 38, Electoral Code.

Tenure

The President has power to establish the terms of service for the commission members. Article 19 of the 2012 Decree on the organisation and functioning of the NIEC changed the term of the NIEC from three years, renewable, to five years non-renewable. The new Article 23 also relates to the duration of the NIEC mandate and stipulates that, 'in case of necessity the mandate of the current NIEC members can be extended for a period not exceeding six months', which was not provided for in the 2009 Decree. The term of office for the members of the CEPI and the CECI is one year. At the end of this mandate, the provincial and municipal commissions are reduced to light structures. The members of the NIEC and its branches perform their duties as permanent staff for the duration of their term in office.[76]

The legislation in force does not specify the circumstances under which the appointing authority can dismiss members of the NIEC before the expiry of their term, such as incompetence or failure to carry out their duties. The only provision relating to the end of mandate is Article 8 of the NIEC Rules of Procedure, which sets out that 'the mandate of a member of the NIEC shall end on resignation, disablement or death', or 'where the Commissioner is a candidate for an election supervised by the NIEC'.

D. Funding of elections

Elections management in Burundi faces serious budgetary constraints. One of its most worrisome aspects relates to delays in the disbursement of funds meant for the NIEC. For instance, the NIEC did not receive its operational budget for the 2010 electoral cycle until several months after its establishment. The disbursement commenced only seven months before the elections, and even then, it was too late to enable it to effectively plan the recruitment of support staff or purchase equipment and furniture for offices provided by the state. The fact that the NIEC has to request funds required for its operations from the Ministry of the Interior, whereas the UNDP chooses to make some payments directly to the commission, also erodes its independence.

The government's limited financial contribution

The contribution of the Burundi Government to the 2010 elections was very limited, totalling 9.7 billion BIF (approximately USD 60 million). This budget was intended to cover operating costs, namely allowances for NIEC commissioners and staff, those of its branches and elections-related security.

As will be shown later, the state's contribution remains inadequate in view of the high costs of electoral operations and the donors' contributions. This raises the issue of the cost of free and transparent elections for countries that have limited resources, and

---

76 Article 1 of the 2009 Decree stipulates: 'The Commission exercises its responsibilities on a permanent standing'. Likewise, Article 19 of the same Decree sets out that, 'On their appointment, the members of the Commission work in it full-time'.

which are faced with competing social requirements (health, education, agriculture, poverty alleviation, and so on).

Some have even proposed requesting the private sector to finance elections in Burundi.[77] This option should be viewed with great caution, since it is evident that the political parties and the private sector work closely together in a context where the latter is not yet developed enough to be able to slough off the state's control. This path would, therefore, entail serious risks of interference by business people in a domain that is complex and sensitive in a young democracy.

Development partners' contributions to the basket fund

The contributions by the development partners to a basket fund totalled 34.3 billion BIF (approximately USD 28 million). The largest contributor to the basket fund remains the European Union (EU), followed by Belgium, the Netherlands, Norway and Sweden.[78] The UN Development Programme (UNDP) and the UN Peace Building Fund (PBF) also made substantial contributions.

Within the context of executing elections-related activities, some payments were made by the NIEC with 'Elections Support' funds from the UNDP, following the supplementary agreements signed between the UNDP Country Director and the President of the NIEC. Other payments were made directly by the UNDP as the administrator of the basket fund. Up to July 2010, the direct purchase of goods and services by the UNDP external to the supplementary agreements totalled 10.7 billion BIF (USD 8.8 million). The amounts paid under the supplementary agreements signed between the UNDP and the NIEC totalled 14.6 billion BIF (USD 11.4 million). Included in this amount are some goods and services that were ordered and paid for by the NIEC from the funds channelled into its account by the UNDP, as indicated in each supplementary agreement.

The procedures governing acquisition of goods and services present significant problems, as do delays in making payments. These problems saw some election officials threaten to terminate their contracts with the NIEC if their outstanding salaries were not paid.[79] Should these procedures not become less cumbersome, they may give rise to reasonable suspicion that the NIEC is being controlled, thereby diminishing its independence. Then again, in relation to the basket fund of PACE, the initial deficit, despite the first budget reviews, left a major gap between urgent requirements and available funds. Just before the end of the first quarter of 2010, the available resources totalled USD 22.5 million, about 64% of the total basket fund requirement. The delay in making extra contributions available had a direct impact on scheduling equipment purchases for the organisation of the elections –given that most of the operations were

---

77   Ndayicariye, PC, NIEC President, Report of the Validation Workshop, 9 July 2013.
78   See UNDP (2011) Report of the Electoral Cycle Support Project, op. cit., p. 117.
79   Ibid.

concentrated between May and September 2010. The electoral operations therefore required funds that were not always available.[80]

Contributions outside the basket fund

Some partners made contributions outside the basket fund. Certain countries or organisations also made contributions both into and outside the basket fund. Contributions outside the basket fund were intended to finance, on an ad hoc basis, subsidiary activities in logistics, equipment acquisition and elections security payments. The amounts totalled about USD 8.5 million.[81]

Consequently, the NIEC of 2010 was independent in terms of financial management, but not so in relation to its sources of funding – although the procedures in place considerably reduced the commission's room for manoeuvre. Given that the government of Burundi was not the sole provider of funds, this made for a certain degree of independence of the NIEC in relation to the government. But the NIEC, and indeed the state, remain generally dependent on donors (from Europe and the United States), who financed the elections and maintain an evident interest in the political future of the nations benefitting from their assistance.

Audits and reports

The NIEC resources came from the state budget and donors' contributions through the basket fund, as well as from PACE. According to the decree governing the organisation and functioning of the NIEC, the commission's financial report must be submitted to the President, with a copy to the Ministry for Local Government. By August 2012, this financial report was yet to be submitted, that is two years after the end of the electoral process.[82] It is clear that NIEC's budget should be checked after the event through audit by the National Audit Department to verify the accuracy and propriety of the expenditure incurred during the exercise as described in the financial report set out by the decree governing the organisation and functioning of the NIEC. The amounts allocated indicate a checking-in principle, since the NIEC does not have control over these amounts, being simply required to manage the resources placed at its disposal by the state. The same is true for the procedures to incur expenditure. Where the NIEC is responsible for cumulative management, the harmonised procedures centralised within the Ministry of Finance constrain any room for manoeuvre, leaving only the possibility of concomitant auditing.

The PACE project was administered by a steering committee set up by the electoral commission, UNDP and the principal donors contributing to the electoral process on the basis of a project document and Letters of Comfort signed between the UNDP and

---

80 Ibid., p. 54.
81 Data reconstituted from UNDP (2011) *Report of the Electoral Cycle Support Project*, p. 118.
82 Interview with a member of the Audit Department and a senior official of the Ministry of the Interior, Bujumbura, 21 August 2012.

the NIEC. The management model constitutes direct delivery by the UNDP, which held supervisory power on the commitment and expenditure-incurring mechanisms. This was because an NIEC needs assessment report showed that the NIEC lacked the expertise to convince its partners to grant it power to commit resources and incur expenditure.[83]

E. Management of electoral disputes

Electoral litigation reposes on a rather complex complaints and appeals mechanism, which is not very well known to the public in general and politicians in particular. Electoral litigation has never been followed up by effective action and some complaints have been declared inadmissible for not being based on tangible evidence. The transparency and credibility of elections in Burundi is undermined by these uncertainties. Generally, electoral litigation has never necessitated the inclusion of complete and coherent provisions in the Electoral Code and the procedures to be followed before the Constitutional Court and the NIEC. They have also never been sufficiently disseminated or popularised before the various elections observed.[84]

The little-known principle of preclusion

In Burundi, the rules governing electoral litigation are based on the principle of preclusion. Political representatives are required to have all their duly signed comments recorded in the minutes in a space specially reserved for this purpose. Any attempt by the president of the polling station to block the recording of the political representatives' comments[85] constitutes a violation. Yet, this rule has consequences that may be detrimental to political parties seeking to lodge a complaint or appeal against the counting of results or the organisation of the elections. In effect, Article 42 of the Electoral Code states that, 'only the recorded comments are taken into consideration in support of a future request introducing an electoral litigation'. Without a record of these comments in the minutes, any appeal or complaint based on points that are not mentioned in this space is declared null and void and is, therefore, rejected or adjudged inadmissible by the CEPI.

During the municipal elections, some political parties (members of the ADC-Ikibiri) attempted to lodge a complaint even when their grievances had not been recorded in the space reserved for this purpose within the minutes. Their complaints were rejected on the grounds that they did not adhere to the provisions in Article 42.

---

83   See Auger (2011), op. cit.
84   It should be noted that the analysis of the NIEC's requirements indicated the absence of a clear, precise and coherent communication strategy. This shortcoming seriously eroded the confidence of the political stakeholders and that of the parties in the independence, impartiality, neutrality and transparency of the NIEC; see in this regard Auger (2011), op. cit.
85   See Article 42 of Law No. 1/22 of 18 September 2009 on the review of Law No. 1/015 of 20 April 2005 on the Electoral Code.

It is unclear if this legal requirement had been widely disseminated and is suffi-ciently known by all the political stakeholders. On reading some of the comments, cer-tain commissioners[86] were of the view that the requirement was not widely dissemi-nated and was little known by the main political stakeholders and their representatives. Evidently, the political stakeholders did not receive enough information on electoral litigation. International standards require, in particular, that electoral procedures be known to all political stakeholders, to political representatives and to national observ-ers at least a year in advance.[87] The Electoral Code was only promulgated in September 2009, a mere eight months before the start of an electoral race that would last five months. Neither the Electoral Commission nor the different partners of the NIEC were able to organise intensive sessions to familiarise stakeholders with the new law.

When the permanent NIEC was finally established, it lacked the human, material and financial resources to plan the training, education and communication necessary to guard against accusations by members of the ADC-Ikibiri, which considered it as 'being a stronghold of the ruling party, the CNDD-FDD'.[88] At another level, the procedure for dealing with appeals relating to municipal elections remains vague, thus eroding the credibility of the electoral process. Articles 75 and 74 of the Electoral Code stipulate that the political representatives and any other interested person may lodge appeals within four working days of the counting of votes, and the CEPI has six working days to adju-dicate. These decisions cannot be appealed. In 2010, several appeals were rejected 'for lack of detailed and tangible evidence'.[89]

Disputes over results

Different authorities adjudicate in disputes over results depending on the category of elections. Electoral litigation is, therefore, divided into two distinct categories:
- Litigation of the results of local elections (municipal and district) falls under the jurisdiction of the CEPI; while
- Litigation of national election results (presidential, legislative, senatorial and referenda) falls under the authority of the Constitutional Court.

The Electoral Code distinguishes municipal from district elections, but in relation to these two there is no right of appeal for the political representatives who consider them-selves wronged, since the rulings of the CEPIs are final.[90] Yet, the right of appeal is not only guaranteed by international law, including the international convention on civil and political rights[91] to which Burundi is a signatory, but also by Title 2 of the Constitution,[92]

---

86   See also European Union Election Observation Mission (2010), op. cit., p. 47.
87   See Wall, A et al. (2010) *Developing Electoral Management: The IDEA Manual.*
88   Interview with the Vice-President of FRODEBU, 19 August 2012.
89   See COSOME (2010) *Elections Observation Report*, www.cosome.bi/IMG/doc/r240519_resume_ex.doc.
90   Articles 74 and 75 of the Electoral Code.
91   See in particular Article 14 of the Agreement on Defence Guarantees in any Proceedings.
92   See in particular the Rights of Defence in Articles 38 and 39 of the Constitution.

which guarantees a right of appeal against any ruling. Even where the provisions of the Electoral Code pertaining to local elections litigation specify the time limit for appeals, there is no procedure at the level of the CEPIs. In effect, pre-electoral litigation has been clearly spelt out under NIEC Orders, but post-electoral litigation, which does not target electoral transgressions, remains unclear. In fact, there is no register of the complaints filed before and judgments pronounced by the CEPIs.

Nonetheless, the CEPIs are faced with major challenges:
- Most of them do not have any legal training to enable them to deal with highly sensitive electoral issues.
- Their inexperience and heavy workload during this election period compounds their inability to deal with litigation issues.
- The provisions relating to their competencies in organising elections and the adjudicator's role assigned to them creates a conflict of interest for officials, putting them in the awkward position of being at once judge and defendant.[93]

The Constitutional Court has jurisdiction to ascertain the legality of the national elections and proclaim the final results. It is also hampered by inadequate operational resources and the low technical capacity of its staff in electoral litigation. The Constitutional Court has, in effect, only one courtroom, a process registry with activities kept to a strict minimum and old equipment. Access to research tools on other countries' precedents is also limited since the Internet is reportedly non-functional within the Burundi judicial system.

The Constitutional Court does not publish its judgments, which could have provided a record of emerging jurisprudence in electoral matters. It does not have archives of cases that it dealt with during the 1993 and 2005 elections. Development partners observed on several occasions the reluctance of the national authorities and of this institution to benefit from capacity-building even where the UN Integrated Bureau, the IFES and the member states of the EU had offered to provide assistance.[94]

A balance needs to be struck between speedy actions that guarantee a useful and still relevant remedy on the one hand, and the quality of rulings, on the other, to allow the court sufficient room to pronounce a judgment and settle electoral disputes. In this context, the incoherence emerging from the time limits set out for the filing of appeals and those assigned to the Constitutional Court for a ruling, which do not always respect the good practices relative to the procedures for submission of complaints, are deplorable. The NIEC's Rules of Procedure allow the commission to 'deal with complaints from any interested party on matters of respect for electoral rules. The NIEC can be seized in writing and it has a maximum deadline of seven days to take action on it.'

---

93 Interview, UNDP, 20 August 2012; see also UNDP (2011) *Report of the Electoral Cycle Support Project*, op. cit.
94 Interview with an expert of the European Commission in Bujumbura, August 2012.

Pertaining to the announcement on the legality of the final results, the Constitutional Court was approached by the NIEC on 6 July 2010 and completed its examination of the electoral process by 8 July, whereas the initial deadline was 13 July. For such an important election,[95] it took the Constitutional Court only two days to assess the legality of the presidential election. The rapidity with which the Constitutional Court dealt with the legality of the presidential elections suggests a lack of rigour, despite the absence of major electoral interests, considering that there was only one candidate for the office of President.[96]

Moreover, the documents transmitted by the NIEC to the Constitutional Court for verifying the legality of the election did not allow for a complete check – including an audit as prescribed by the Electoral Code – since the details of the results from polling stations, as well as the minutes, were not available for examination. This lack of effective communication and the publication of the results at the polling stations somewhat undermined the image of a transparent electoral process, even if, from the point of view of neutral observers,[97] these problems could not undermine the truth in the ballot boxes.

Electoral offences

Electoral offences are set out by the Electoral Code in Articles 221 to 237. They are grouped together under two main categories:

- Transgressions committed prior to the actual poll, for instance:
  - To have oneself registered on a list under a false name or false qualifications;
  - To have oneself registered while hiding a disability set out by the Electoral Code;
  - Engaging in electoral propaganda beyond the legal duration of the campaign;
  - Engaging in propaganda during working hours while one is a public servant;
  - Using or allowing the use of the assets and resources of the state, of an institution or of a public institution for propaganda purposes; or
  - Influencing or attempt to influence the vote of one or several voters by means of gifts or donations, favours, employment in the public or private service or other benefits.
- Breaches concomitant with or posterior to the polling, for instance:
  - Possessing unused ballots;
  - Carrying or displaying any distinctive sign of a political party, of a candidate, or a list of candidates;

---

95 Interview with the President of the Constitutional Court, August 2012.
96 See Order No. 235 of 8 July 2010 relative to the legality of the presidential election in which there was only one candidate.
97 See COSOME (2010), op. cit.

- Exerting on the polling premises or the immediate surroundings by whatever means, pressure on one or several voters for the purpose of influencing their vote, of obtaining their ballots or of preventing them from voting;
- Determining or attempting to determine the vote of an elector through abuse or threats against him or by making him fear to lose his job or of being exposed to some danger to himself, to his family or to his fortune;
- Removing, adding or altering one or several ballots while having the responsibility during the elections for opening or counting the ballots that express the suffrage of the voters;
- Entering into a polling station with a visible or hidden weapon;
- Disturbing the organisation of the elections;
- Inducing one or several voters to abstain from voting by means of false news, slander, or other fraudulent manipulations; or
- Violating the secrecy of the ballot.

For each of these categories of electoral offences, there are different sanctions. For the first, the offender can receive a prison sentence of between 15 days and three years or be fined from 10,000–400,000 BIF (approximately USD 9–265). For offences in the second category, the offender can be sentenced to prison for between 15 days and ten years or a fine of 10,000–200,000 BIF (USD 9–135). Although the prison sentence appears to be heavy, the fine is very low.

The NIEC has enacted two orders listing administrative and moral sanctions over and above the criminal ones set out by the Electoral Code.[98] Despite these orders, the NIEC lacked mechanisms to enforce and implement the provisions in the law. Therefore, it was restricted to verbal condemnation without being able to take appropriate action.[99] Very few cases have been dealt with by the courts, owing to a lack of information and inadequate staff. Under these circumstances, it is difficult to know the exact number of electoral offences committed or prosecuted. Like the complaints and appeals submitted to the CEPI, there is also no register of offences. Whereas the presidents of the polling stations have the power of judicial police officers, NIEC members do not have this power under the electoral law. Coordination and collaboration with the public prosecutor's office and the police department still leaves much to be desired.[100]

A source at the Supreme Court said some 83 cases were still pending before the courts and tribunals during the 2010[101] electoral races. The outcome of these cases is still uncertain, for they concern members of political parties who argue that they are

---

98 See Judgments No. 1 of 19 July 2009 on administrative and moral sanctions and No. 18 of 3 April 2010 governing the enactment of sanctions to complement the criminal sanctions provided for by the Criminal Code.
99 Jean Marie Gasana, Political Analyst, interview, Bujumbura, 16 August 2012.
100 Interview, NIEC, Bujumbura, 13 August 2012.
101 Elie Ntungwanayo, spokesperson of the Supreme Court, Bujumbura, interview, 18 August 2012.

being harassed because of their political convictions.[102] Whatever the case, the violations committed during elections punishable by criminal convictions require that all the cases be processed to avoid discrediting the guarantees of a fair trial set out in the Constitution[103] and under the International Convention on Civil and Political Rights.[104] This evidently implies that any decision to prosecute must be taken on the basis of tangible evidence but above all 'regardless of political considerations'.

In short, during the workshop held in Kayanza in March 2013, a consensus was arrived at concerning the amendment of the rules relating to litigation. Nothing has come of the proposed amendments on the allocation of powers on litigation – whether they are to be entrusted to the ordinary courts, to specialised chambers or to an independent ad hoc commission. There is nothing to indicate the direction the Burundi legislature should take on this matter. From the time set aside for the establishment of such an institution and its effective and optimal functioning, it is not possible to see how these amendments can be operationalised by 2015, in which case it would be appropriate to design a simple system of electoral mediators as already suggested by the *Coalition de la Société Civile pour le Monitoring Electoral* (Coalition for the Monitoring and Observation of Elections, COSOME).[105]

F. A critical assessment of election management in Burundi

The management of the 2010 electoral cycle provides interesting lessons that can be used to measure the efficiency of the NIEC and its capacity to ensure respect for the Electoral Code. The NIEC and the independent media collaborated effectively in implementing civic and electoral education, which greatly contributed to a qualitative participation in the elections and to the improvement of women's representation. The NIEC nonetheless failed in its legal obligation to ensure respect for a balanced electoral campaign. The NIEC's professionalism had also been severely tested in its conduct of the technical voting operations on Election Day.

Successful civic and electoral education

In anticipation of the 2010 electoral cycle, the Action Plan of Civic and Electoral Education was validated by the NIEC, the IFES and CSOs. The NIEC used a series of media campaigns to sensitise, train and inform the population, including the use of posters, brochures, billboards, sketches, *téléradio* spots, a booklet titled 'Chronogram of the electoral process, the 2010 elections', banners, radio broadcasts, the bulletin '*Amatora meza*' (or 'good elections'), the NIEC website, a song contest for the 2010 elections, and a

---

102   Interview with a representative of the MSD, 20 August 2012.
103   Articles 38 and 39 of the Constitution.
104   Article 14 of the International Convention.
105   See recommendations proposed by Justine Nkurunzisa, President of COSOME, at the end of this report's validation workshop, September 2013.

calendar for the year 2010, in which each month carries a message in Kirundi on the elections. The *téléradio* spots had been broadcast by both the public and private media and printed in the newspapers. They reiterated the voting procedures for the presidential and district elections, and included a simulation of the voting process.

Despite a few incidents observed during the presidential election,[106] these initiatives created an environment conducive to a calm electoral competition. Generally, the Burundian voters cast their ballots peacefully during the various elections. Very few cases of violence between supporters of the different camps were observed.[107] For the candidates, the municipal elections took place in a peaceful atmosphere. However, the announcement of the election results sparked tension between the NIEC and the opposition parties that had lost the elections. This lack of confidence in the NIEC has endured to this day.[108]

Women's participation in elections

The Constitution and the Electoral Code make provision for a minimum representation of women in the country's institutions. Women should, in effect, constitute at least 30% of the elected members in Parliament and in the municipal councils. Beyond this legal requirement, the NIEC and its national and international partners embarked on a vigorous sensitisation exercise with political parties and women that resulted in the election of women beyond the quotas reserved for them. As summarised by the PACE Report:

> in 2010, the representation of women in Parliament and in the municipalities increased by 11% in comparison to 2005 … Burundi became the first country in Africa and the second in the world to have women representatives in the Senate. These results are that much more appreciable in that they were achieved without any need for co-option.[109]

Media performance during the elections

The rise in media pluralism is concomitant with the return of multi-party democracy in Burundi. Following the events in neighbouring Rwanda in 1994, several organisations defending journalism, like Reporters without Borders, undertook to sensitise and

---

106 APRODH (2010) *Report on the Monitoring of Human Rights During the 2010 Elections*, op. cit. According to this report, about 100 grenades had been thrown. Individuals had been arrested following elections-linked incidents. The headquarters of political parties had been burnt down, in particular those of the CNDD-FDD. Most of the persons arrested were genuine or so-called members of the FNL, the MSD and the UPD, all member parties of the ADC-Ikibiri.

107 See the different reports produced by the project *Amatora mu mahoro*, www.burundi.ushahidi.com.

108 During the appointment of the new NIEC team, these political parties denounced a non-consensual action by the ruling party, arguing that they had not been consulted. *Iwacu Journal*, 20 December 2012.

109 See UNDP (2011) *Report of the Electoral Cycle Support Project*, op. cit., p. 30.

train Burundian journalists on social responsibility.[110] These efforts greatly impacted the role of journalists in the resolution of the Burundian crisis. Since 2005, despite the aggressive climate prevailing during elections, the media have endeavoured to produce balanced information in a country where, according to Panos, 88.6% of households have a radio set. However, due to the lack of a market for the generation of revenue from advertising, the media are faced with a serious lack of operational resources.[111]

The Burundian media conducted themselves professionally during the 2010 elections, even though a few elements, according to some stakeholders and observers, could be improved. The Burundian media are reputed for their freedom, but they operate in a highly hostile environment marked by intimidation, arrests of journalists, and seizure of equipment.[112] In particular, the arrest on 17 July 2010 of Jean Claude Kavumbagu, Editor in Chief of Net Press, for having criticised the Burundian security forces, and that of Thierry Ndayishimiye, Editor in Chief of the *Rainbow* newspaper, on 10 August 2010 for having reported on allegations of corruption within the public water and electricity distribution company REGIDESO, illustrate that freedom of the press remains tenuous in Burundi.

One of the weaknesses of the Burundian media is its inadequacy of resources for their work, a weakness partly compensated for by foreign donors, in particular the Joint Action Plan for Support to the Media (PACAM), one of the programmes included in the PACE document.[113] This programme received about USD 498,000 from several contributor countries (with France as leader) and made possible a transparent and fair coverage of the electoral campaign, which increased awareness of the social projects of the different political parties in the electoral race.[114]

Some stakeholders also denounced a tendency by the public media to give more space to the ruling party in their broadcasts. The political subservience of the National Communication Council (CNC) – or the appearance of subservience – has seriously undermined its credibility. In particular, during the 2010 elections, the CNC had been headed by a ruling party militant who, moreover, had been registered as candidate in the municipal council elections of her native district, Mpanda.[115]

NIEC's supervision of the electoral campaign

Election observers, notably the EU's Election Observation Mission,[116] specifically deplored the fact that the NIEC had prevented the unrepresented parties in the

---

110 Frère, M-S (2012) *News and New Media in Central Africa: Challenges and Opportunities*, Open Society Foundations.
111 Interview, *Iwacu Journal*, Bujumbura, August 2012.
112 Ibid.
113 Frère (2012), op. cit.
114 Interview, Panos Institute, Bujumbura, 2010.
115 This concerns Vestine Nahimana, chairperson of the CNDD-FDD Women's League. She figured on this party's register for the municipal elections and the Senate; see European Union Election Observation Mission (2010), op. cit., p. 37.
116 Ibid.

presidential election from campaigning. In effect, on the withdrawal of one of the opposition parties, two decrees[117] had, on the basis of an erroneous interpretation of Article 29 of the Electoral Code, indeed prevented any campaign against the sole presidential candidate by prohibiting the parties that were not contesting the elections from campaigning.[118] From this point on, it became a lopsided campaign in which the population could receive no pluralist information that would have enabled it to weigh options in relation to the single candidate.[119]

The NIEC favoured continuity in the electoral process without playing the role of arbiter when disputes arose as required of it by the Electoral Code. The NIEC's poor performance in this area is also linked to the inadequate time available to examine all the complaints relating to human rights violations that occurred during the campaign and which could jeopardise the smooth running of the elections. Also, the resources made available to the NIEC were insufficient to enable it to effectively assume its role as arbiter since electoral logistics were the priority.

A number of observers reported that the officials of the ruling party had been seen moving around the voter queues offering sums of money or persuading the voters to influence their vote. According to the *Ligue des Droits de personnes des Grands Lacs* (LDGL) report, some observers had alluded to other illegal manoeuvres intended to influence the vote. LDGL cites examples illustrating the buying of consciences through the provision of various gifts, the exhibition of already filled out ballots, the tearing up in public of some ballots or the fact of certain voters remaining on the premises after voting, with the objective of influencing the vote.[120]

The NIEC's technical preparations for the elections

The voters' register

The voters' register is one of the avenues for committing electoral fraud, as the lists can be inflated in the segments of the electorate where a candidate considers that s/he has greater support. During the 2010 elections, all the observers noted that there had not been any major attempt to falsify the voters' register with the intention to commit fraud. On the contrary, everything appeared to have been done to allow the highest possible number of potential voters to be registered and to vote. First of all the NIEC had established an 'attestation of identity for voter registration' for those individuals who had no other identity card.[121] The UNDP also funded a system to help provide 900,000 free

---

117 See Decree No. 100/108 of 6 July 2010 and Decree No. 100/109 of 11 July 2010.
118 Interview, human rights activist, *Forum pour le Renforcement de la Société Civile*, 22 August 2012.
119 According to the monitoring done by APRODH, several members of the political parties that had withdrawn from the electoral race had been intimidated, arrested and had fled into exile. Such a situation results in the holding of a referendum-type unilateral campaign; see APRODH (2010) *Report on the Monitoring of Human Rights*, op. cit.
120 LDGL (2010) *Report on the Observation of the Municipal Elections of 24 May 2010*, Bujumbura, p. 7.
121 Order No. 014/NIEC of 1 February 2010.

identity cards for individuals who did not have any and who could not afford to pay for identity cards from the local government department. Furthermore, the initial registration deadline fixed for 4 February 2010 had been pushed to 9 February to enable voters who had procured proof of identity to register. This postponement resulted in deferring the posting of the provisional voters' register.

Article 57 of the Electoral Code contains a provision that limits the number of voters who can be excluded from voting for lack of personal accreditation documents to a bare minimum, in effect stipulating that the voter who holds an identification document and not his voter's card may be allowed to vote if he is registered on the voters' roll. Likewise, the voter holding his voter's card but has no identification document may be allowed to vote if he is well known by at least three members of the Electoral Bureau.

Finally, it would appear that Burundi is heading towards the use of a biometric card whose cost would be about USD 4 for per voter. For the great majority of citizens living below the poverty line in Burundi, this cost is prohibitive and constitutes a major obstacle to the exercise of their political rights in general, and to their right to vote in particular. COSOME has proposed that this cost requirement be removed for low-income voters.[122]

Discrepancies in the voters' register

The registration of voters on electoral lists was properly carried out throughout the territory by all interested parties, in particular political parties. The NIEC reported no dispute over the registration.[123] The grievances raised by the opposition political parties within the ADC-Ikibiri related to other points but not to the quality of the voters' lists.[124] Stakeholders in the opposition, however, made some allegations suggesting the rigging of lists, notably:

- Issuing of national identity cards to citizens who were below 16 years of age (school children, students) and to foreigners, as well as their registration on the roll;
- Refusal to issue national identity cards to eligible citizens;
- Refusal to issue proof of identity for electoral use to eligible citizens by claiming, for example, that insufficient forms had been sent to the NIEC;
- Obstacles and harassment against certain categories of citizens intended to deny them the documents mentioned above, in particular by demanding proof to participate in municipal activities, or an unnecessary amount of money before issuing the card;
- Illegal, biased and partial distribution of identity cards (during the night and in private or secret places);

---

122 COSOME, Recommendations formulated during the validation workshop of the study on the elections management institutions, July 2013, p. 2.
123 European Union Election Observation Mission (2010), op. cit.
124 See COSOME (2010), op. cit., p. 15.

- Issuing of several voters' cards to some citizens;
- The registration of dead or absent persons, or the use of fictitious names on the voters' list;
- Buying back of the roll registration slip; and
- Impunity of grassroots administrators who issued identity cards.

Most observers felt that these discrepancies were not sufficiently widespread to alter the results of the elections.[125]

Single ballot vs multiple ballots

Article 55 of the Electoral Code stipulates that multiple ballots be used for voting, despite the high costs involved; the 46,374,100 ballots ordered from South Africa are said to have cost about USD 733,008.[126] The opposition parties had strongly resisted the system of multiple ballots during discussions on the 2009 Electoral Code project. Their arguments had been supported by civil society and the international community.

The opponents of the multiple ballot system criticised it for giving the CNDD-FDD militants the opportunity in 2005 to threaten voters by requiring them to bring back ballots to show that they had indeed voted CNDD-FDD. This system also made for a tedious counting exercise after the opening of the ballot boxes. During the 2010 elections, the counting went from the afternoon late into the night and was only completed the following day. This discouraged some of the agents, who abandoned the exercise before the counting was completed.

The proponents of the multiple ballot system argued that it was practicable since the voters were illiterate. Voters who could not locate or tick the name of their candidate, if all the names were grouped together on a single ballot, were disadvantaged. Their opponents argued that several methods could be used, including the identification of the parties and their candidates by means of distinctive signs and symbols, drawings, logos, photographs, animal totems or objects.

The single ballot system has considerable advantages:
- It allows a rationalisation of the electoral costs, assuming that Burundi needs to gradually evolve towards a system in which the foreign contributions to the elections would be reduced in favour of an autonomous funding from the budget when the country has re-established sustained economic growth.
- It simplifies the voting procedures and vote counting.
- It is widely practiced in the neighbouring countries with the same level of illiteracy, like Rwanda. So far, it has not presented any challenge to individuals with little education since they can seek the assistance of a clerk without the secrecy of the ballot being compromised. Moreover, it is always possible to

---

125 European Union Election Observation Mission (2010), op. cit.
126 See UNDP (2011) *Report of the Electoral Cycle Support Project.*

make this category of persons vote by thumbprint on the ballot of the candidate of their choice.

The debate over a single ballot has witnessed two major developments recently. First, during the workshop organised in Kayanza in partnership with the BNUB, representatives of the main political leaders agreed on the use of a single ballot and on staggering the elections to make the electoral calendar more flexible.[127] While welcoming the agreement, COSOME, an organisation that groups together several civil society associations active in the field of elections, cautioned against the risk that a consensus on introducing a single ballot would not materialise before the 2015 elections, giving rise to doubts about the rapid implementation of such a project.[128] However, the proposal was taken up and the National Assembly formally included the single ballot system in the new electoral code Bill it passed in April 2014. COSOME's apprehensions still stand, though, as it is still not clear whether Burundi will be ready for the single ballot system for the 2015 elections. For this to happen the Senate must also pass the Bill and the President sign it into law. It is crucial that these steps be completed before the 2015 electoral cycle.

Performance on Polling Day

During the 2010 elections, several deficiencies were observed. The discrepancies that had been observed during the voting operations can be cited specifically as examples:
- Bad positioning of the polling booths, thus compromising the secrecy of the vote;
- Security forces carrying weapons while coming to cast their votes;
- Political parties' activists positioning themselves at crossroads to campaign;
- Running out of supplies before the deadline, in particular voting cards in some zones;
- Delays in opening the polling stations;
- Paucity/lack of electoral equipment, ballots in particular; and
- Suspension of voting operations due to insufficiency of ballots or disturbance caused by the voters who queued to vote.[129]

Distribution of ballots

The NIEC faced problems of inefficiency in the distribution of ballots. This situation not only indicated a lack of professionalism but also introduced creeping doubts about the reliability of the voting operations. It undermined the credibility of the elections by fuelling rumours by the opposition parties' candidates of a plan to rig the elections. The distribution of ballots therefore constituted a major challenge for the NIEC. In effect, a few hours before the municipal elections, several municipal commissions had

---

127 Pierre Claver Ndayicariye, President of the NIEC, interview, 9 July 2013.
128 Justine Nkurunzisa, President of COSOME, interview, 9 July 2013.
129 COSOME (2010) *Elections Observation Report*, op. cit.

informed the NIEC about the shortage of ballots for almost all the parties. The NIEC decided to postpone the first election by a few days to allow for ordering of extra ballots from the supplier.[130] Shortages of electoral ballots had been experienced on polling day, resulting in the suspension of operations to allow for replenishment.

Publication of election results

Several international observers noted a lack of transparency on the part of the NIEC, particularly in relation to instructions (which were communicated verbally to CEPIs and CECIs most of the time) and the publication of results (not posted up, absent from the NIEC website) and unavailability of minutes.[131] A lack of transparency in the electoral process was observed in relation to the failure by the NIEC to post the minutes of the voting operations and the election results in the polling stations, as well as in failure to deliver the minutes to political representatives. This situation bred suspicions among the voters, and in particular the political parties in the race, who debated on whether or not to accept results that may have been rigged.

At the close of voting, two types of minutes were prepared: the first gave a narrative account of the organisation of operations in the polling station (PVF1), while the second focused on the results of the ballot count (PVF2).[132] The following discrepancies observed during the counting were highlighted:
- Failure to count the ballots in the black boxes;
- The disappearance of the results;
- Minutes that had been signed before completion of the exercise;
- The departure of the political representatives before the end of the count; and
- Power outages.[133]

Securing the elections and the voters

The Electoral Code contains provisions that seek to guarantee the security of the polling stations.[134] Generally, security for the 2010 electoral process was adequately guaranteed, except for a few incidents of violence between the different youth groups affiliated to political parties, but they did not degenerate into serious conflicts. In effect, violence could have constituted a threat, especially in a country where disarmament of the

---

130 UNDP (2011) *Report of the Electoral Cycle Support Project.*
131 European Union Election Observation Mission (2010), op. cit.
132 COSOME (2010) *Elections Observation Report*, op. cit.
133 NDI (2010) *Recueil des déclarations d'observation électorale des organisations de la société civile*, Bujumbura, p. 17.
134 Voters are prohibited from entering the polling station or its surroundings with weapons or as an organised group (Article 53). Law enforcement officers cannot be stationed inside the polling station or in its immediate surroundings, except in the event of a requisition by the chairman of the polling station (Article 54). The President of the Electoral Bureau [...] guarantees the vote for the police and holds the rank of judicial police officer but with limited territorial and material competence. S/he takes note of the transgressions committed inside the polling station and its surroundings. S/he may, for the aforementioned objectives, seek assistance and a helping hand from the civilian or military authorities (Article 44).

civilian population remains unaccomplished. Nonetheless, the situation was controlled generally. The Burundi National Police was supported in this task by the officers of the National Defence Force. These officers had been deployed to the entire territory during the various elections. They had received some training beforehand to prepare them for their role during the electoral period.

Role of political party representatives

Article 41 of the Electoral Code stipulates that

> each candidate, each list of independent candidates or each independent candidate, as the case may be, has the right to check the overall electoral operations, including verification of the quality and quantity of the voting equipment from the opening of the polling station to the ballot counting.

The CEPI issues the party representatives with special cards. According to Article 43 of the Electoral Code, there is a fixed amount of money paid by the NIEC to the duly recognised political parties' representatives at the polling stations to meet all their expenses.

There were reports that some representatives had been bribed by the officials of the ruling party to abandon their watch over the counting or even to sign a blank ballot count report,[135] thus allowing the perpetrators of rigging to register false results.

Opposition parties' representatives abandoned their observation posts after spending long hours without any refreshment. In Article 43, the Electoral Code set out that political party representatives should enjoy the full benefits due to officials should they be present during the voting. None of this was implemented and only the ruling party provided refreshments for its own representatives.

Under the terms of Article 42 of the Electoral Code, copies of the minutes should be handed over to the political representatives, who must ensure that all their observations are recorded in a section reserved for this purpose. The NIEC restricted the number of PVF1 copies to four and the number of PVF2 copies to five. As a result, all the representatives of the different political parties in the race had to share the available copies between them. The failure to provide a copy of the minutes for each representative undermined the right to appeal and the principle of preclusion, which makes the prior recording of their objection in the minutes a condition for lodging a valid complaint. The political party representatives did not receive adequate training to appreciate the importance of entering their observations in the minutes.

---

135 NDI (2010) *Recueil des déclarations*, op. cit., p. 12.

Whereas the greatest responsibility for the transparency of the voting reposes in the NIEC, the political party representatives are expected to remain in their polling stations until vote counting is completed, to record any observations in the minutes, and to request a copy of these minutes. A large number of the representatives left the polling station before the completion of the vote count and the preparation of the minutes due to fatigue and delays in counting.

Generally, party representatives did not receive relevant training, and many were not informed about the principle of preclusion requiring that they raise their objections in writing while the minutes were being prepared. For purposes of transparency, it would have been desirable for civil society or observers and political parties to carry out a parallel tallying of the results as happens in numerous other countries. One of the serious consequences of the lack of transparency was the withdrawal of the competing political parties from the municipal and other elections, namely the legislative, presidential, district and senatorial elections, and their subsequent rejection of the results.

Use of the power of sanction

In 2010, only a few minor violations were punished through fines imposed by the municipal authorities and the presidents of the polling stations, or by the police. The opposition party leaders felt that by using diverse manoeuvres of obstruction and intimidation, the ruling party had won the elections even before the actual voting took place – by using all the possible means to compel the electorate to vote for it and by preventing opponents from carrying out a proper campaign.[136] The NIEC generally remained passive in the face of acts of intimidation or harassment against opposition party members, arguing that these matters were beyond its jurisdiction and should be brought before the courts, to the administration, or to the units concerned.[137]

Ethnic balance

The NIEC has succeeded in operating the co-optation mechanisms to restore balance within the ranks of the candidates. The Electoral Code and the Constitution are, however, all silent on the procedure and modalities for co-optation, leaving it entirely to the discretion of the NIEC on how this eminently political operation is to be handled. This sometimes produces tensions such as those observed during the municipal elections.[138] Co-optation remains a hazy area in which arbitrariness reigns.

---

136 Interview, Vice-President MSD, 11 August 2012.
137 NIEC, interview, 12 August 2012.
138 European Union Election Observation Mission (2010), op. cit.

Electoral Code on co-optation is incomplete

In Burundi, the elections are supplemented by a co-optation system, following a decision from the Arusha Accords. The co-optation solution addresses the minorities' feeling of exclusion from power and their desire for integration into leadership institutions, thus enabling them to put forward their views, which might have been excluded from the electoral process. This proceeds from the logic that many minorities are often victims of a form of social discrimination. This is also the case for women and the Batwa. Co-optation is also implemented where the quotas of 60% for the Hutu and 40% for the Tutsi are not met through elections. But the Electoral Code is silent on many aspects of how to deliver on co-optation.

Augustin Nkengurutse, the Executive Secretary of the NIEC, says it is lamentable that the Electoral Code is silent on co-optation within the municipal councils. In effect, a minimum of 30% of the 15 municipal council members should be women, namely 4.5 women. This figure is, therefore, rounded off to five. Another atypical example is when the NIEC was obliged to replace the member Jean-Baptiste Manwangari, elected in the Busoni municipality, in Kirundo Province, by a Twa who was on the list of the UPRONA party. The Tutsi, exceeded (reached) the quota and the Twa were not represented whereas the Electoral Code stipulates that where a Twa figures on the list but has not been elected, he should be co-opted in a bid to ensure ethnic balance. Contrary to what takes place in the National Assembly, the municipal council should not exceed 15 members, even in the event of co-optation.

The NIEC boss admits that the co-optation operated by the commission within the municipal councils had been by an amicable arrangement and recommends that legislators take the electoral commission members' suggestions into account so that in future, co-optation would be implemented in the most democratic manner possible.

SOURCE:
Jean Bosco Nzosaba, Observatory of Government Action, www.oag.bi/spip.php?article1084

Funding political parties and use of state assets

The Constitution prohibits foreign funding for political parties except under a special dispensation authorised by the law.[139] However, Articles 21 and 44 of the law governing political parties authorise the grant of funds to political parties to enable them to participate in political fora abroad, including seminars, workshops, conferences and meetings.[140] The same law stipulates that the state shall contribute to the financing of electoral campaigns with an amount to be determined, and provision shall generally be

---

139 Article 84 of the 2005 Constitution moreover stipulates that a law shall determine and organise the sources of funding for political parties.
140 See Articles 21 and 44 of Law No. 001/006 of 26 June 2003 on the organisation and functioning of political parties in Burundi.

made for this within the National Budget during the financial year in which the elections are to take place.[141]

The intention of the law is to guarantee that the political parties compete on equal terms. Although this fund existed during the 2005 elections,[142] no provision was made for it in the 2010 National Budget,[143] thus depriving most parties outside the CNDD-FDD of resources to engage in a large-scale electoral campaign. Likewise, under Article 224 of the Electoral Code, the use of state assets and resources is prohibited, with offenders risking fines between 40,000 and 200,000 BIF.[144] The political parties' code of conduct sets out in its Article 28 'that no political party, no candidate should use state resources for personal benefit'. Several organisations, however, noted numerous cases of state vehicles being used during the campaigns by public servants, including ministers and administrators, most of them members of the CNDD-FDD party.[145] The NIEC did not punish these offenders, resorting instead to public censure[146] in the case of the municipal council elections. This failure to sanction resulted from the frenetic electoral activities and the rushed organisation of the polls, leaving the NIEC with neither the time and resources, nor the technical capacity to process complaints and denunciations lodged by CSOs.

Conclusions

Viewed in comparison with the 2005 elections, the 2010 polls represented a regression from the democratic consensus and dialogue advocated in Arusha. This can be attributed largely to reasons beyond the control of the NIEC. The boycott of the elections organised by the opposition parties after the municipal polls undermined the participation necessary for legitimacy. The CNDD-FDD's strong grip on state institutions made the country a de facto one-party state, which drove development partners to support the establishment of an extra-parliamentary opposition party. There was a need to ensure that the Arusha achievements were not sacrificed in a new war in Burundi, especially when numerous politicians who felt threatened went into exile.

In applying some of its powers in only a partial, flawed and equivocal manner, the NIEC contributed to the deterioration of the political environment in the period preceding the 2010 presidential and legislative elections and thereafter. It failed to rise to the political role assigned to it under the Arusha Accords and to exercise its unique powers as an EMB. For instance, the NIEC's lack of transparency on the voting operations during the municipal elections is one of the main reasons that the opposition parties

---

141   Article 20 of the Law on Political Parties.
142   European Union Election Observation Mission (2010), op. cit., p. 34.
143   Interview with the Minister of the Interior, Bujumbura, August 2012.
144   Article 224 of the Burundian Electoral Code.
145   In its report dated 19 May 2010, the Organisation on the Control of Economic Embezzlement (OLUCOME), referred to the use of state vehicles by some ministers and municipal public servants; for the legislative elections, OLUCOME referred to 40 cases of the use of vehicles, while for the presidential elections, there were 86 cases.
146   *Iwacu Journal*, 5 May 2010.

withdrew from these and subsequent elections. The NIEC failed to re-establish contact with these parties and to express its readiness to conduct more transparent elections, which might have brought some of the parties back into the process. The vague and hazy nature of the rules for electoral dispute resolution could hardly guarantee the credibility of the elections. This constraint would have been overcome if the NIEC had a coherent and clear interpretation of these rules.

G. Pre-2015 debate on electoral reform

The inadequacies of the 2010 elections left a bitter aftertaste that prompted a national debate on the reforms to be made to the electoral system to improve its performance. In concert with technical and financial partners and more specifically the UN Operation in Burundi, the key political players have undertaken a number of initiatives drawing on the lessons learned from the elections of 2005 and 2010. One of the consultations undertaken was the Kayanza meeting of March 2013, whose goal was to facilitate dialogue and reach a national consensus on the fundamental issues for free, transparent and peaceful elections. The participants in the Kayanza meeting adopted a roadmap for the necessary reforms. However, at the same time, a proposed constitutional revision that was widely debated by the stakeholders in December 2013 was narrowly defeated in the National Assembly, thereby postponing any changes to the Constitution until after the elections of 2015. In April 2014, the National Assembly adopted a new electoral code.

National and international public opinion has saluted a Draft Electoral Bill founded on a national consensus that met with the overall satisfaction of the political actors.[147] However, as the electoral code is an organic law, the Draft Bill needs to be adopted by the Senate and enacted by the President of the Republic. It is worthwhile to point out that some of the innovations found in the draft electoral code were already included in the recommendations issued by the present study and were submitted for critical review by the participants in the study validation workshop in July 2013, which was attended by key players as well as the chairman of the NIEC.

Among these innovations, the Draft Bill introduces combined elections.[148] This provision establishes the order of the elections, with elections of MPs and communal councillors taking place first. These will be followed by the presidential election, then by the election of the Senators, and finally by the elections of hill and neighbourhood councillors. As noted in the report, and in compliance with a recommendation issued by the study, combined elections facilitate electoral operations and logistics and reduce the cost of elections.

In the second place, the Draft Bill establishes a single ballot,[149] as recommended by a number of analysts and observers, and addressed in several sections of this study.

---

147 See *Iwacu Journal*, 2 May 2014, p. 3.
148 Article 1, paragraph 2 of the Draft Bill.
149 Article 37 of the Draft Bill.

However, a number of analysts and observers have pointed out the pressing need to carry out civic education and awareness campaigns for the population, which is often illiterate, to reduce the risks for potential voters.

Thirdly, it rejects the requirement of an undergraduate degree for candidates wishing to run in the presidential elections.[150] A number of MPs have rightly pointed out that such a provision would be contrary to the spirit and the letter of Article 97 of the Constitution, which does not include this condition among the requirements for candidates in presidential elections. The provision is even contrary to Article 25 of the International Covenant on Civil and Political Rights ratified by Burundi, which lays down the principle that no one may be discriminated against on grounds of their level of education, their ethnic background or political affiliations.

In the fourth place, article 104 of the Draft Bill makes eligibility to run in any type of election conditional upon the payment of a non-refundable deposit. This deposit was the focus of heated debates on the part of political parties and players who lacked sufficient means, but the Kayanza meeting agreed that a deposit constituted a guarantee of seriousness and commitment to a major political project and a way to eliminate frivolous and joke candidates.

In the fifth place, the Draft Bill reinforces criminal sanctions based on the premise that electoral offences were not sufficiently sanctioned during the 2010 elections.[151] However, mechanisms for coordination and cooperation with security and justice organisations are not specified in the Draft Bill. Regulations and other instruments will be needed to specify how such offences may be found and by whom and how they are to be prosecuted in compliance with defence rights and the right to a fair trial. In addition to legal sanctions, the Draft Bill innovates by stipulating a certain number of administrative sanctions regarding offences against electoral rules.[152] According to some stakeholders, the powers conferred on the NIEC are contrary to Article 91, which presents a limitative list of the missions of the NIEC and does not include the ability to implement measures as sweeping as those stipulated, which are not subject to review or appeal.[153]

Finally, the Draft Bill also innovates by establishing the mandatory continuous presence of two public representatives per political party to monitor the conduct of the elections and countersign the reports in compliance with the stipulations of Article 42 of the draft code.[154] Note should be taken of the relevance of these reports in the event of electoral disputes, since only the facts stated in these reports may be examined by the CEPIs in elections supervised by the CECIs. The draft electoral code also innovates

---

150   Paragraph 6 of Article 94 of the Draft Bill was included in the consensus established among the political stakeholders during the Kayanza workshop in March 2013.
151   See Title IX of the Draft Bill.
152   See Title X of the Draft Bill.
153   Comments by MPs, *Iwacu Journal*, 2 May 2014, p. 3.
154   It should be noted that the unavailability of the reports raised suspicions of fraud and lack of transparency on the part of the NIEC during the 2010 elections.

by allowing the coverage of the costs of political party representatives responsible for observing the conduct of elections on behalf of their parties and/or candidates.

H. Recommendations

Functioning of the NIEC

- Appointments to the NIEC need to respect the rules, principles and procedures that guarantee a broad political consensus so as to secure the full credibility and authority of the commission to satisfactorily fulfil its mandate.
- Commissioners need to be recruited on the basis of specific verified competence criteria.
- The members of the NIEC need to organise their work better and share responsibilities to prevent overworking some of them.
- Support staff should be technically trained to make them effective and capable of providing quality assistance to each commissioner in his or her specific assignments.
- A training programme for senior NIEC officials should be initiated to make them more efficient, notably on logistics, data management (e.g. Microsoft Excel) and internal and external organisational communication.
- Improved coordination with CEPIs and CECIs is needed, in particular through an effective and uniform system of written communication using new technology (e.g. intranet).
- A centralised and effective filing system is required to preserve important documents for institutional memory and to facilitate the organisation of future elections.

Independence of the NIEC

- Secure the administrative and managerial autonomy of the NIEC set out by the Electoral Code by breaking all tutelage ties – in particular financial ones – with the Ministry of the Interior.
- Determine and establish the conditions and status of the commissioners, not by decree but by law, in conformity with Article 159 of the Constitution, in order to strengthen the personal independence of the NIEC members.
- Amend the electoral law to define the limits of responsibility and substantive jurisdiction for the CEPIs to prevent them from acting as judge and defendant in electoral appeal cases.

Ethnic balance and the electoral system

- Define precise and clear criteria to guide the NIEC in exercising its power of co-optation and rectification of imbalances in the electoral registers.

- Adopt a single ballot that is more secure, less costly and easier to manage logistically.
- Amend and prepare a realistic electoral calendar by, for instance, providing for two electoral years every five years, for example, one year for the municipal and district elections, and another (three years later) for the presidential and legislative elections.
- Add more detailed practical modalities to the law governing the use of clerks during district elections to avoid abuse.
- Set out provisions in the future electoral law that guarantee greater transparency in results management, notably the publication of complete results for each polling station during the announcement of provisional results.

Management of electoral disputes

- Remove the management of district and municipal electoral cases from the jurisdiction of provincial electoral commissioners and make provision for it in local civilian courts.
- Plan, organise and implement a rational training programme for judges well before the next elections by drawing on the technical expertise of Burundian non-governmental organisations and development partners.
- Should these specialised courts not be ready for the 2015 elections, make provision for a simple and less costly alternative system of electoral mediators.
- Set out clear and simple rules of procedure for electoral litigation by facilitating appeals using request forms that are easy for candidates and the political parties to understand and complete.

Transparency in the management of elections

- Amend Article 71 of the Electoral Code by making provision for an extra copy of the ballot count minutes for the central results processing centre. A copy of these minutes should be delivered to the parties or candidates (or their representatives) who finished the electoral race in the first three positions at the polling station. Another copy should be posted up.
- Guarantee that the results from the polling stations are posted up in the voting centre immediately after the completion of the ballot count and ensure that detailed results – broken down according to polling station – are posted on the NIEC website.
- The modalities of transmission and consolidation of the results should be clearly spelt out in the new electoral law.
- Allocate adequate resources, well in advance of the next electoral meetings, for the drafting of a results management protocol to ensure transparency, particularly in relation to the speedy publication of the election results in each of the country's polling stations.

Registration and electoral operations

- Preserve and update the voters' register as it stands since it has proven its quality and credibility.
- Implement a voters' register improvement exercise as soon as possible by eliminating duplications and effecting the necessary corrections regarding voter identity (date of birth, names of parents, gender, etc.).
- In the case of biometric identification cards, waive the cost requirement for very low-income citizens to avoid jeopardising the right to vote.
- Facilitate the participation of political groups or their representatives in updating the voters' register to enhance transparency and eliminate any suspicion of fraud.
- A year before the next elections, carry out a review of the voters' register by inserting the names of voters who have reached the age of 18 but are not registered while removing the names of dead voters.
- Initiate discussions with the government and donors on the creation of a fully computerised voters' register based on information from a modern civil status register. Digital registration and the use of a bar code for each voter are options that can be pursued.

Support for civic education

- Maintain and reinforce the support to Burundi CSOs to observe elections; monitoring enhances the credibility of electoral process, as was seen in the 2010 municipal elections.
- Replicate the experience of cooperation with the media for the upcoming elections and even during the civic education campaigns, as well as amendments of the legal framework between elections.
- Allocate sufficient resources to CSOs, such as COSOME, to enable them to support and implement civic education activities on the ground, in view of their proximity to grassroots populations and expertise.
- Provide intensive support for the participation of women in the development of democracy in Burundi, well before the next elections.
- In addition to training organised for women representatives, make provision for activities with political parties to sensitise their leaders on the importance of fair play in democracy, which entails managing defeat and victory appropriately.

3

Kenya

Francis A. Aywa

A. Summary

Kenya has held regular elections since independence, but they have historically been polluted by myriad irregularities. Negative ethnicity has become a major factor of electoral politics, in part due to the combination of the 'first-past-the-post' electoral system and ethnically designed constituencies. Ethnic tensions have in turn fuelled several cycles of election-related violence.

Since the resumption of plural politics in the country in 1991, election management bodies (EMBs) have been the object of deep-seated mistrust for their real or perceived lack of political independence. Public trust in the electoral system has consequently eroded over time, and was extremely low in the aftermath of the 2007 general election. A relatively nascent institution, the Independent Electoral and Boundaries Commission (the IEBC), was in 2013 expected to help Kenya make a clean break with its past general elections history. Instead, this election divided significant sections of the country's voting population, as reflected in recent public opinion surveys.

Continuing weakness in enforcing electoral law – or a lack of political will to enforce it – has raised doubts about the IEBC's capacity to deal with law-breaking by diverse electoral role players. Enforcement of nomination procedures is also somewhat hampered by the IEBC's Nominations Disputes Committee's overlapping mandates with the Political Parties Disputes Tribunal and the courts. The IEBC also missed critical statutory election preparation deadlines, most notably in preparing the following:

- The Election (General) Regulations, 2012;
- The Election (Registration of Voters) Regulations, 2012; and
- The Election (Voter Education) Regulations, 2012.

The IEBC's handling of the nomination of special seat representatives has exposed it to unfavourable court action and further dented its image. Lastly, the IEBC's investigation and prosecution output from the 2013 general election, compared to all the allegations of malfeasance, is not apparent and the country's response to electoral crime is not sufficiently strong to send a clearly deterrent message to would-be election offenders about the cost of committing electoral offences.

Electoral transparency was one of the weakest aspects of Kenya's electoral process before 1992. This challenge continues despite the advent of, at least on paper, a revamped EMB. The IEBC has to date failed to be wholly transparent and accountable with regard to the results of the 2013 general election, in violation of the law and at great cost to its public image.

The IEBC's faulty procurement process for the biometric voter registration system and electronic voter identification devices (EVIDs), and the ensuing controversy, raised doubts on the integrity of its systems and officers and delayed voter registration by over six months. As a consequence, it continues to rely on alternative avenues for the verification of voter eligibility, such as the Green Book. This reinforces the traditional suspicion generated by a register that is perceived by electoral role players as a moving target. This is no way to build public trust in the accuracy of the register – a key confidence-building measure that is far from achieved.

The failed implementation of the IEBC's technological investments in the electoral process and the cloud that hangs over the legitimacy of the results of the 4 March 2013 general election, especially in the presidential election, are at the heart of the controversy over the quality of the 2013 elections. They require substantial improvements in accuracy and transparency to create an unimpeachably clean and transparent results tallying and transmission system.

Against the backdrop of the 2013 general election, and heated exchanges regarding the presidential elections and Supreme Court decision, one reality remains: Kenya is far from realising its aspirations for elections that provide a fair opportunity for electoral competition, free from fraud. Rather than despair, the lessons from the 2013 general election should energise all stakeholders in the electoral process to re-think the continuing shortcomings of the electoral process and its management with a view to making whatever further changes necessary to entrench electoral democracy in the country. A broad national agenda for electoral reforms can coalesce. The IEBC should consider leading the formation of an Electoral Stakeholders Forum (ESF) as a reference group for deliberations on the key measures necessary to ensure that Kenya's elections, especially the next general election, are less deficient and in conformity with international standards for credible elections. Independent commissions also need to hold the IEBC to account for its actions.

B. Political development and electoral history

Kenya gained internal self-government from Britain on 1 June 1963. It attained political independence on 12 December 1963 and became a republic on 12 December 1964. The country has, since independence, been under civilian rule, except for an attempted coup on 1 August 1982 that was swiftly put down by the army. With 11 general elections since it obtained political independence, Kenya has a long history of holding elections and using elections as a legitimating tool for governments. The current EMB, the IEBC, is nevertheless a fairly recent creation in the close to 50-year post-independence history of elections in Kenya. When it presided over the country's historic 2013 general election, the first after the promulgation of a new Constitution with enlarged freedoms and a dramatic re-organisation of governance structures, the IEBC was in its second year of existence. The EMB began its life with the appointment of the chairperson and nine commissioners, on 9 November 2011. However, it was the second time since 2007 and the fourth after the country attained political independence in 1963 that the country was re-establishing its EMB.

Early political changes and the colonial legacy

Representation in Kenya can be traced to 1905, when the Legislative Council (LEGCO) was established.[155] Members of the LEGCO were appointed by the Governor, who could dismiss them at will. Although the LEGCO represented only European interests in the beginning, a member was appointed in 1909 to represent Asian interests. A second Asian representative was appointed in 1919, and a member to represent Arab interests named in 1920. In 1925, the number of Asian representatives was increased to four.

The first elections for the LEGCO were held in 1916, following the promulgation of a Legislative Council Ordinance[156] that provided for full adult European male suffrage to elect 11 European members. In 1925, an additional four elective seats were created for Asians. In the same year, a European member was appointed to represent African interests. A second member to represent African interests, another European, was appointed in 1934. Eliud Mathu, the first African member named to represent African interests, was appointed in 1944. He was joined by Walter Odede, who was appointed a temporary member in 1946. This number was increased to four elected African representatives in 1948 and, following the Mau Mau insurgency, six in 1952.

In 1956, the Legislative Council (African Representation) Act, 1956 (No. 10) was passed, providing for the first six African elected members. In the same year, the law was amended to increase this number to eight. In the following year, the first elections in which Africans were elected were held. Following these elections, Ronald Ngala (Coast), along with Tom Mboya (Nairobi), Oginga Odinga (Nyanza Central), Lawrence Oguda (Nyanza South), Masinde Muliro (Nyanza North), Daniel arap Moi (Rift Valley), Bernard Mate (Central) and James Miumi (Southern/Ukambani) formed the African Elected Members Organisation (AEMO) to pursue African interests in the LEGCO. Since they were pushing for even more far-reaching reforms, they later issued a press

---

155   Bogonko, SN (1980) *Kenya 1945–1963: A Study of African National Movements*, Nairobi, Kenya Literature Bureau, p. 48.
156   East African Order in Council, 1919.

statement declaring Kenya's Lyttelton Constitution,[157] on which they had been elected, void, and declared that none of the African elected members of the LEGCO would take any ministerial office.[158] The 1958 Lennox-Boyd Constitution[159] would later provide for an equal number of elected representatives between the European and African communities. Each racial group had 14 elected seats. The March 1958 elections brought six more African representatives to the LEGCO.[160]

The first elections on the basis of universal suffrage were held in 1961.[161] They were made possible by the First Lancaster House Conference in London. The conference was held in 1960 to discuss Kenya's future as an independent country, after a softening of Britain's stance in regard to the Kenya Colony, under pressure from the United States, the Soviet Union and a growing bloc of non-Western states.[162] It was attended by 37 Africans, 14 Europeans, 11 Asians and three Arabs.[163] At the conference, held under the chairmanship of Secretary of State for the Colonies, Ian Macleod, the African delegation argued that Kenya needed a new Constitution. There was no agreement on the country's new Constitution, and Macleod issued an interim Constitution that, among other provisions, provided for 33 members elected on the basis of a common register of voters, with ten seats reserved for Europeans, eight for Africans and two for Arabs. The members of the LEGCO would, in turn, elect 12 special seat members.[164] All Africans over 40 years of age were allowed to vote, as was any other person over the age of 21 who was literate in any language, or with a yearly income of 75 pounds and above.

A majority of the African delegation accepted these proposals, through which the British government showed, for the first time, that it accepted majority rule, since Africans would consequently make up the majority in the LEGCO and Council of Ministers. The ban on political parties, imposed at the height of the emergency, was lifted and two political parties came into existence by the end of 1960: the Kenya African National Union (KANU) and the Kenya African Democratic Union (KADU). While KANU came to represent the interests of the two largest ethnic groups, the Agikuyu and Luo, as well as the Akamba and Abagusii, KADU came into being to protect the interests of the smaller tribes, the coastal tribes, the Kalenjin and Abaluyia.[165] In the March 1961 elections, KANU won 61% of the votes and 19 seats, while KADU won 16% of the votes and 11 seats. However, KANU leaders refused to form a government until their leader Jomo

---

157 Named after then Secretary of State for the Colonies, Oliver Lyttelton.
158 Okoth, A (2006) *A History of Africa Vol. 2: 1915–1995*, Nairobi, East African Educational Publishers, pp. 85–87.
159 Named after the Secretary of State for the Colonies at the time, Alan Lennox-Boyd.
160 Ogot, BA (1995) 'The Decisive Years 1956–63', in BA Ogot & WR Ochieng, *Decolonisation and Independence in Kenya: 1940–93*, Nairobi, East African Educational Publishers, p. 60.
161 The 1956 elections were for Europeans and Asians, whereas Africans first voted in 1957, on a 'qualified franchise'; Bogonko (1980), op. cit., pp. 173–183; Ogot (1995), op. cit., pp. 54–61.
162 Robbers, G (2007) *Encyclopedia of World Constitutions*, New York, Facts on File, Inc., p. 479.
163 Ibid.
164 Ogot (1995), op. cit., p. 61. This is the origin of the 12 nominated members, now of the National Assembly and distributed by party strength in the House.
165 Okoth (2006), op. cit., pp. 87–88.

Kenyatta was released from detention and allowed to return to politics. KADU then formed a government under Ronald Ngala. Kenyatta was eventually released in August 1961 and, after failing to persuade the two parties to unite under him, became president of KANU after James Gichuru stepped down for him. He was thereafter elected unopposed to the LEGCO on a seat vacated for him by Kariuki Njiri.

The Second Lancaster House Conference commenced in February 1962, to plot the course for Kenya's path to self-government. It was chaired by the new Secretary of State, Reginald Maudling, and attended by a KANU delegation led by Kenyatta and a KADU delegation led by Ngala. At this conference, the stickiest issue turned out to be KADU's vision of federalism and KANU's unitary approach. It resulted in a complicated framework for self-governance – the Maudling Constitution – to satisfy the latter's fears. It consisted of seven regions with entrenched local powers and a bicameral legislature at the centre. It was agreed to later thrash out further details and hold elections.

In April 1962, with the active encouragement of the British (who were keen to minimise ethnic tensions and establish a multiracial state), KANU and KADU formed a coalition government to oversee the final stages of devolution by Britain, in which Kenyatta became Minister for Constitutional Affairs and Economic Planning.[166] Immediately preceding independence, the Regional Boundaries Commission divided Kenya on the basis of either ethnic homogeneity (one tribe per district) or compatibility (more than one tribe per district or province, where they were happy to coexist).[167] Elections for the seven regional assemblies were held on 19 May 1963,[168] followed by the Senate elections on 22 May,[169] after which the elections for members of the House of Representatives were held on 25–26 May.[170]

The Third Conference was held in September/October 1963. The delegations to this conference were the two governments of Kenya and Britain. The conference finalised constitutional arrangements for Kenya's independence as a dominion, and adopted the Independence Constitution, bringing to an end more than 70 years of colonial rule.

Elections in post-independence Kenya

After independence, a number of problems confronted Kenya's politics and its elections. Though the Independence Constitution was strongly federalist, a series of political schemes and constitutional amendments resulted in the abolition of the federal system (which came to be known as *majimbo*) by the time Kenya became a republic in 1964.

---

166 Butler, LJ (2002) *Britain and the Empire: Adjusting to a Post-Imperial World*, London, IB Tauris & Co. Ltd, p. 159.
167 Fox, R (1996) 'Bleak Future for Multi-Party Elections in Kenya', *Journal of Modern African Studies* 34(4): 597.
168 KANU won 78 seats; KADU 51; Akamba Peoples' Party (APP) 8; Independents 12; Coast People's Party (CPP) 2 (total 151).
169 KANU won 19 seats; KADU 16; APP 2; Nyanza Province African Union (NPUA) 1 (total 38).
170 KANU won 66 seats; KADU 31; APP 8; NPUA 3; Independents 4 (total 112).

First, negative ethnicity (which began in the pre-independence competition for supremacy among African elites) progressively developed and ultimately became a major factor in national politics. Ethnic tensions particularly affected the structure of access to economic opportunities and redistribution of some of the land formerly owned by white settlers. Gradually, instead of elections being merely a contest for political power, they became an arena for either settling ethnic scores or a device through which political protection for ethnic groups could be assured or gained. At the resumption of multi-party politics in the early 1990s, state-sponsored ethnic clashes were part of the official response to political competition.[171] This cycle was repeated in the 1997 general election and, ultimately, the 2007 elections and the post-election violence in early 2008 in which nearly 1,300 people lost their lives. As the country tries to come to terms with the structural causes for its violent elections, it will be important to interrogate the extent to which electoral reforms also provide a structural solution to the realities of a deeply divided society.

The country's electoral system, which has all along been first-past-the-post, also gradually entrenched winner-take-all politics in which winning was a zero-sum game. Coupled with the fact that the presidency eventually became the highest position of political patronage, this further worsened inter-ethnic rivalry over the highest political office in the land. Remarkably, as various analyses and successful election petitions show, Kenya's elections have also been historically polluted by electoral vice and have been problematic in terms of both substantive electoral justice and public trust in the electoral process. It is these political problems that, over the years, constitutional, legal and administrative reforms have sought to either remedy or balance somewhat.

C. Evolution of election management reforms

Kenya's current EMB has evolved over time and is the result of fairly recent electoral reforms arising from a lengthy post-independence struggle for democratic change, culminating in the adoption and promulgation of the Constitution of 2010. Further electoral reforms received fresh impetus from the implementation of the new Constitution.

From independence to the resumption of competitive party politics

The country's first EMB at independence was the Electoral Commission, established to manage elections and demarcate constituency boundaries, established under Section 48 of the Constitution of Kenya, 1963[172] (Table 3.1). It consisted of:

- The Speaker of the Senate, as chairman;
- The Speaker of the House of Representatives, as vice-chairman;

---

171   Roberts, MJ (2009) Conflict Analysis of the 2007 Post-election Violence in Kenya (unpublished), www.ndpmetrics.com/papers/Kenya_Conflict_2007.pdf.
172   The Kenya Independence Act, 1963 (Sub. Leg.).

- A member appointed by the Governor-General,[173] acting in accordance with the advice of the Prime Minister; and

- A member representing each of the eight regions,[174] appointed by the Governor-General, acting in accordance with the advice of the President of the Regional Assembly of that Region.

The members of the commission had a term of five years and security of tenure, while the commission was not subject to the 'direction or control of any person or authority' in the exercise of its constitutional functions. Over time, however, this legal provision for functional independence was flouted with impunity.

After independence, the country underwent profound political upheaval and changes from a multi-party system in 1963 to a de facto single-party state in 1969, and then a de jure single-party state in 1982, before reverting to de jure multi-partyism in 1991.[175]

In the post-independence period of political and legal changes, the Electoral Commission's role was limited to boundary demarcation. The management of elections was unconstitutionally bestowed on the Supervisor of Elections, a relatively junior official under the office of the Attorney-General, who in turn used members of the provincial administration as election officials. District commissioners, for example, were appointed as returning officers, responsible for electoral operations at the constituency level. As all these officers were answerable to the President, who was invariably an incumbent in the successive elections in the absence of term limits on the office holder, they were patently partisan and lacked the kind of independence that would inspire public trust in the electoral process.

The Electoral Commission of Kenya (1992–2007)

With the resumption of multi-party politics in 1991, this state of affairs became untenable, owing to a deep-seated mistrust of the provincial administration from the single-party days. Establishing an autonomous body became inevitable and led to the Election Laws Amendment Act, 1991. This Act abolished the position of Supervisor of Elections and reinvested all election management powers in the Electoral Commission.

The Electoral Commission of Kenya (ECK), as it eventually came to be known, was at first not trusted to act impartially and competently, since its chairman and all its ten commissioners were appointed by the President, himself an incumbent and a candidate.[176]

---

173 At independence, Kenya's Head of State was the Queen of England, with the Governor-General as her representative, while the Prime Minister was the Head of Government. This position was done away with in the 1964 Constitution when Kenya attained full political independence from Britain.

174 Nairobi Area and Coast, Eastern, Central, Rift Valley, Nyanza, Western and North-Eastern regions. These later became provinces under the 1964 Constitution.

175 The Constitution of Kenya (Amendment) Act, No. 12 of 1991, repealed the infamous Section 2A of the Constitution that had declared Kenya a single-party state.

176 Aywa, FA & Grignon, F (2001) 'As Biased as Ever? The Electoral Commission's Performance Prior to Polling Day', in M Rutten et al., *Out for the Count: The 1997 General Election and Prospects for Democracy in Kenya*, Nairobi, Fountain Publishers Limited, pp. 102–134.

Table 3.1: Evolution of Kenya's EMB

1963	Kenya's first Electoral Commission established, with the Speaker of the Senate as chairman. Independence elections held on 19 May 1963 (regional assemblies); 22 May (Senate); and 25–26 May (House of Representatives).
1966	'The Little General Election', by-elections for 38 seats in the Senate and House of Representatives, held after the formation of the Kenya People's Union (KPU) and the requirement for members changing parties to seek a fresh mandate from the electorate.
1969	First general election held after the proscription of the KPU, in a de facto single-party political system.
1974	General election held; five seats, including that of President Jomo Kenyatta, uncontested/unopposed.
1979	General election held; President Daniel arap Moi and Vice-President Mwai Kibaki elected unopposed.
1983	First general election held under a de jure one-party system; President Moi elected unopposed.
1988	The infamous mlolongo (queue-voting) party nomination and general election held; massive electoral irregularities cited.
1991	Election Laws Amendment Act abolishes position of Supervisor of Elections and reinstates Electoral Commission's power to supervise elections.
1992	Justice (Rtd) Zacchaeus R Chesoni and ten others appointed as ECK commissioners.
29 Dec. 1992	First general election after the resumption of competitive party politics.
1997	Justice (Rtd) Chesoni and 11 others appointed as ECK commissioners.
31 Oct. 1997	President Moi appoints ten new ECK commissioners nominated by opposition political parties.
29 Dec. 1997	Second general election after the resumption of competitive party politics.
12 Nov. 2002	Samuel Kivuitu and 21 others appointed as ECK commissioners.
27 Dec. 2002	Third general election after the resumption of competitive party politics.
21 Nov. 2005	First referendum on a new Constitution supervised by ECK.
3 Dec. 2007	Samuel Kivuitu and 21 others appointed as ECK commissioners.
27–28 Dec. 2007	Fourth general election after the resumption of competitive party politics.
4 August 2010	Second referendum on a new Constitution supervised by IIEC.
9 Nov. 2011	The IEBC chairman and eight commissioners appointed by the President.
4 March 2013	The IEBC conducts the first general election under a new Constitution, the fifth after the resumption of competitive party politics.

Source: Various reports and publications on Kenyan elections

Initially chaired by Justice ZR Chesoni, a former judge who had been retired from the judiciary on bankruptcy grounds, the commission did not enjoy much public trust through the first three general elections in 1992, 1997 and 2002 (and the numerous by-elections in between) that it presided over.[177] Many of its early decisions were contested on the basis of the commission's perceived partiality to the President as the sole appointing authority: it entrenched gerrymandering in the 1997 boundary review, hardly tackled electoral vice head-on, including infractions by its officials, and was a veritable den of corruption.[178] With 22 commissioners, from 1997 onwards, it was also an unwieldy public body in which the lines between board and management were often unclear.

Despite the fact that it had dubious functional independence, the ECK gradually acquired some public trust over the years, between the 2002 and 2007 general elections. This was the result of:

- Increased transparency in regard to election results;
- The counting and announcement of results at polling stations, from 2002 onwards;
- Participation in the improvement of African election and democracy standards;
- The establishment of the political parties liaison committee as an informal mechanism for communication with key electoral stakeholders and dispute resolution;
- The eventual appointment of ten more commissioners in 1997 and 2002 by key political stakeholders rather than the President as sole appointing authority, albeit as the unlegislated part of the Inter-Parties Parliamentary Group (IPPG) reforms package in 1997;
- The outspokenness of some of its members;[179]
- Some bold proposals for electoral reforms,[180] though not always implemented; and
- Increasingly professional service delivery.

Ironically, public trust in the ECK was at its highest just before the 2007 general election.

Matters, however, came to a head in 2007, when the President single-handedly re-appointed all the commissioners (in spite of the 1997 IPPG consensus for appointment by the major political parties)[181] in the run-up to that year's general election, and the

---

177 Throup, DW & Hornsby, C (no date) *Multi-party Politics in Kenya: The Kenyatta and Moi States and the Triumph of the System in the 1992 Election*, Nairobi, East African Educational Publishers, pp. 244–246.

178 A report by the Africa Centre for Open Governance (AfriCOG) details the ECK's gross mismanagement of resources, based on recurring improprieties as reported in the Controller and Auditor-General's reports in the period between 1992 and 2007: AfriCOG (2008) *Free for All? Misuse of Funds at the Electoral Commission of Kenya*, Nairobi, AfriCOG.

179 Note should be taken of the fact that this was about the time when personalisation of successive EMBs began, with strident calls for the extension of chairman Kivuitu's term in office before the 2007 general election – apparently, many people at the time only trusted the ECK as long as Kivuitu was its chairman.

180 Such as counting of votes in polling stations from 2002 (rather than transportation to a central counting centre in the constituency).

181 This included his friend and personal lawyer, Kihara Muttu, who then became vice-chairman.

ECK ultimately bungled the presidential election, resulting in widespread violence and a governance crisis that took the intervention of the African Union (AU), through the Panel of Eminent African Personalities, to defuse.[182] It became necessary not only to disband and reconstitute the EMB, but to implement far-reaching electoral reforms.

Post-2007 reforms and the Independent Electoral and Boundaries Commission

The stage for a new EMB, following the 2008 post-election violence, was set by the Independent Review Commission of the 2007 Elections (IREC). IREC was appointed as part of the 2008 post-election settlement to inquire into all aspects of the general election held on 27 December 2007, with particular emphasis on the presidential election. In its report, IREC was withering in its findings and conclusions on the ECK, while it also criticised a diversity of other election role players, including the state.[183] It found a number of faults with the 2007 general election and recommended a number of far-reaching reforms aimed at improving Kenya's electoral practice.[184]

IREC concluded that the institutional legitimacy of the ECK and public confidence in the professional credibility of its commissioners and staff had been gravely and irreversibly impaired by the manner in which it had bungled the 2007 general election. It therefore recommended radical reform of the ECK, or the creation of a new EMB –

> with a new name, image and ethos, committed to administrative excellence in the service of electoral integrity, composed of a lean policy-making and supervisory board, selected in a transparent and inclusive process, interacting with a properly structured professional secretariat.

IREC also found Kenya's constitutional and legal framework relating to elections weak and inconsistent in ways that, in turn, weakened its effectiveness. It deplored the pollution of the electoral process by the conduct of many public participants, especially political parties and the media. It also found serious defects in the voters' register that impaired the integrity of the 2007 elections. The commission concluded that there were serious anomalies in the delimitation of constituencies that impaired the legitimacy of the electoral process. The investigation found generalised abuse of polling, characterised by widespread bribery, vote-buying, intimidation and ballot-stuffing, and determined that there had been defective data collation, transmission and tallying, and

---

182 The Panel of Eminent African Personalities had former United Nations (UN) Secretary-General Kofi Annan as chairman, and former President of Tanzania, Mr Benjamin Mkapa, and former South African First Lady, Mrs Graça Machel, as members.

183 IREC (2008) *Report of the Independent Review Commission on the General Election held in Kenya on 27 December 2007*, Nairobi, Government Press.

184 Ibid., pp. x–xi.

ultimately the electoral process failed for lack of adequate planning, staff selection/training, public relations and dispute resolution.

Fundamentally, it found that the integrity of the process and the credibility of the results were gravely impaired and irretrievably polluted. It recommended, therefore, a range of appropriate executive, legislative and political measures to enable the reconstituted or new EMB to initiate, popularise and sustain a national commitment to electoral integrity and respect for the inalienable franchise rights of Kenyan citizens – including the compilation of a new voters' register.

IREC also stated that the ECK lacked functional efficiency and independence, and was incapable of properly discharging its mandate. It therefore recommended the empowerment of the EMB to conduct the delimitation of boundaries, elections and associated activities.

Later that year, Parliament passed the Constitution of Kenya (Amendment) Act, No. 10 of 2008, dissolving the ECK and creating the Interim Independent Electoral Commission (IIEC), as the successor to the ECK for an interim period of two years, pending the conclusion of the Constitution review process, with enhanced election management powers and security of tenure. Strangely, in reconstituting the EMB, all former ECK staff were removed and re-deployed elsewhere in the public service, robbing the new body of critical institutional memory. The IIEC not only had fewer commissioners than its predecessor (nine compared to the previous 21), but they were appointed through a competitive process that was tailored to engender public trust in the successor institution.

In a departure from previous practice where the President was the sole appointing authority, the IIEC chairperson and eight commissioners were nominated from applicants following public advertisements and interviews by the Parliamentary Select Committee on the Review of the Constitution and, upon approval by the National Assembly, appointed by the President in consultation with the Prime Minister. The IIEC's functions and powers were also enhanced. It would be responsible for:

- Reform of the electoral process;
- Management of elections in order to institutionalise free and fair elections;
- Establishment of an efficient and effective secretariat;
- Promotion of free and fair elections;
- Fresh registration of voters and the creation of a new voters' register;
- Efficient conduct and supervision of elections and referenda;
- Development of a modern system for the collection, collation, transmission and tallying of electoral data;
- Facilitation of the observation, monitoring and evaluation of elections and referenda;
- Promotion of voter education and the culture of democracy;
- Settlement of minor electoral disputes during an election as may be provided for by law; and
- Performance of such other functions as may be prescribed by law.

Overall, save for a continuing inability to enforce electoral criminal law, the IIEC acquitted itself quite well, both in managing several by-elections capably and in successfully running the 2010 referendum on the Proposed Constitution of Kenya.[185]

To address past gerrymandering, the Constitution of Kenya (Amendment) Act No. 10 of 2008 conferred the politically sensitive task of boundary delimitation on the Interim Independent Boundaries Review Commission (IIBRC), comprised of a chairperson and eight members,[186] also appointed through as competitive a process as the IIEC, with security of tenure either up to the time it completed its task or when a new Constitution was adopted. The IIBRC was required to review Kenya's administrative and electoral boundaries and make recommendations to Parliament for alterations.

Unlike the IIEC, the IIBRC ended its term in relative ignominy, with internal divisions over the final boundary proposals generating wide political controversy. This also poisoned the process of adopting the report of the parliamentary committee that received the IIBRC's proposals on the new boundaries. In the end, it was agreed that the successor institution established after the conclusion of the Constitution review process would address issues left pending from the first review.

D. The Independent Electoral and Boundaries Commission

The Constitution of Kenya, 2010 (hereinafter, the Constitution), which was promulgated on 27 August 2010, established the Independent Electoral and Boundaries Commission (IEBC) as the responsible agency for conducting or supervising referenda and elections to any elective body or office established by the Constitution, and any other elections as prescribed by an Act of Parliament in Kenya. A year later, Parliament passed the Independent Electoral and Boundaries Commission Act, 2011, as the commission's enabling law. While the initial Bill had proposed five commissioners, including the chairman, the final law provided for a chairman and eight commissioners.[187] The chairperson and eight commissioners[188] were subsequently appointed in a process resembling that of the predecessor IIEC – a selection panel appointed by the President and the Prime Minister invited applicants, shortlisted and conducted interviews, then forwarded the names of the successful applicants to the National Assembly, which vetted them and submitted the approved names to the President, who then appointed them following

---

185 An Infotrak Harris poll indicated that 91% of the respondents were satisfied with the 2010 referendum results ('IIEC Sets the Ground for Free and Fair Polls as Africa Seeks Lessons', www.standardmedia.co.ke/?articleID=2000016875&pageNo=2&story_title=IIEC-sets-the-ground-for-free-and-fair-polls-as-Africa-seeks-lessons), while an Ipsos Synovate poll indicated over 90% confidence in the IIEC ('Kenya: Good Times of Confidence and Optimism Are Back', allafrica.com/stories/201008120285.html).

186 Andrew Ligale (chairman), Jedida Ntoyai, Irene Cherop Masit, Mwenda Makathimo, Joseph Kaguthi, John Nkinyangi, Murshid Abdalla, Abdulahi Sharawe and Rozah Buyu.

187 The IEBC Act, No. 9 of 2011 (hereafter 'IEBC Act'), section 5.

188 Ahmed Issack Hassan (chairman), Lillian Bokeeye Mahiri-Zaja (vice-chairman), Albert Casmus Bwire (Commissioner), Kule Galma Godana (Commissioner), Yusuf A Nzibo (Commissioner), Abdulahi Sharawe (Commissioner), Thomas Letangule (Commissioner), J Muthoni Wangai (Commissioner), Mohamed Alawi Hussun (Commissioner), OJH Oswago (Chief Electoral Officer/Commission Secretary).

consultations with the Prime Minister. Before March 2013, the IEBC managed four by-elections while preparing for the general election.

Since it is a constitutional body, the IEBC institutional framework is expected to accord with constitutional and legal requirements, as well as commonly accepted norms of public administration and corporate governance. In light of past institutional challenges in the management of elections, the legal framework sought to create a body with integrity, one that is efficient in the management of election resources, has a service orientation and a high degree of professionalism.

Behind a public image of unity, however, the IEBC's unity of purpose is under threat in diverse ways, resulting from broader board and management separation issues:

- It is still not clear what the dividing lines are between the policy and administrative domains;
- There are no institutionalised guidelines for managing this separation; and
- There is no shared understanding of the core processes of delivering an election.

Legal framework

The Constitution and various national laws contain the constitutional and legal framework for Kenya's EMB. However, in accordance with the provisions of the Constitution,[189] international conventions and treaties ratified by Kenya, as well as international standards for periodic and genuine elections, are of importance in fully understanding the state's obligations.

International law

Kenya's Constitution provides for the application of the general rules of international law (or customary international law)[190] and any treaties or conventions ratified by Kenya[191] as part of Kenyan law. The basic international legal instruments governing elections, and which are therefore binding within the meaning of the Vienna Convention on the Law of Treaties, are:

- The 1948 Universal Declaration of Human Rights;[192]
- The 1966 International Covenant on Civil and Political Rights (ICCPR);[193]
- The 1979 Convention on the Elimination of All Forms of Discrimination against Women;[194] and
- The 1952 Convention on the Political Rights of Women.[195]

---

189 Constitution of Kenya, Article 2(5) states that 'The general rules of international law shall form part of the law of Kenya'; while Article 2(6) states that 'Any treaty or convention ratified by Kenya shall form part of the law of Kenya under this Constitution.'
190 Article 2(5).
191 Article 2(6).
192 Articles 20 and 21.
193 Articles 2, 19, 21, 22 and 25.
194 Article 7.
195 Articles 1, 2, 3 and 5.

Article 25 of the ICCPR, in particular, is now widely recognised as laying down the following critical elements for periodic and genuine elections (also referred to as the global norm of participation):

i.   Periodic, meaning there must be a defined time frame within which elections are held;

ii. Genuine, in the sense that the political rights of freedom of association, freedom of assembly and freedom of speech are respected and promoted;

iii. The right to stand (or run) for elections (and the opportunity to do so) is guaranteed;

iv. Universal suffrage, meaning every citizen without discrimination has a right to participate;

v.   Voting in elections on the basis of the right to vote, which entails the rights of access to the polling station, to receive ballot materials, to mark the ballot paper in a polling booth, and to deposit the ballot paper in the ballot box;

vi. Equal suffrage, or 'one person, one vote' (each vote carrying, more or less the same weight);

vii. Secret vote, in an environment in which a voter can make her or his own choice, without undue influence or intimidation from any other person; and

viii. Free expression of the will of the voters, which implies the lack of coercion, intimidation and fraud.[196]

The 1981 African Charter on Human and Peoples' Rights (ACHPR) and the 2007 African Charter on Democracy, Elections and Governance (ACDEG) are also notable in the context of Africa.[197] ACDEG is a more recent legal instrument intended to establish regional standards on the promotion of democracy, elections and good governance in Africa. It was adopted by African heads of state and government in January 2007 at the AU Summit in Addis Ababa, Ethiopia, and entered into force on 15 February 2012. Although Kenya signed ACDEG, it has yet to ratify it (and has therefore not signified its intention to be bound by it). Nevertheless, by dint of the Kenya Constitution, other ratified international treaties and customary international law still apply.

In addition to ratified, binding treaties and decisions, there are non-binding decisions by international and regional bodies (sometimes referred to as soft law). While

---

196 NEEDS/European Commission (2007) *Compendium of International Standards for Elections*, London, NEEDS/European Commission, pp. 7–13.

197 Articles 17–26 are particularly significant since they require the strengthening of electoral institutions, guarantee access to AU observer missions, and outlaw unconstitutional changes of government (e.g. *coups d'état*).

Article 13(1) of the ACHPR states that participation in government can be either direct or through freely chosen representatives (implying elections), the Organisation of African Unity/AU Declaration on the Principles Governing Democratic Elections in Africa of July 2002 is more explicit with regard to the rights and obligations relating to elections, and is also useful for consideration of the commitment to democratic elections in the African context. In October 2005, the Global Declaration of Principles and Code of Conduct for International Electoral Observation was adopted by the UN and endorsed by the AU, Electoral Institute of Southern Africa, and the UN Secretariat. It is open for endorsement by other international organisations, through the UN's Department of Economic and Social Affairs. While binding authority may differ from instrument to instrument, many are either binding to the extent that they codify customary international law or are, at least, persuasive.

The Constitution of Kenya, 2010

The various offices, such as that of President, Governor or Member of Parliament, for which elections are the recognised mode of recruitment, are established by the Constitution. The IEBC is a constitutional commission established by Article 88. The Constitution also prescribes minimum and maximum sizes for constitutional commissions (at least three, and not more than nine members), outlines eligibility criteria for membership and confers powers and functions on the IEBC.

In regard to elections generally, the Constitution:
- Establishes the offices for which elections are the means of recruitment;
- Requires all candidates and political parties in every election to comply with the code of conduct prescribed by the IEBC;
- Lays down criteria for the fulfilment of voting rights;
- Confers jurisdiction for the settlement of election disputes; and
- Provides Parliament with the power to make enabling legislation for the conduct of elections, and for the IEBC and its functions.

The Independent Electoral and Boundaries Commission Act, 2011

The Independent Electoral and Boundaries Commission Act, 2011 (hereafter IEBC Act), was enacted to make provision for the appointment and effective operation of the IEBC. In addition to reiterating the provisions of the Constitution, the Act makes detailed provisions in regard to:
- The Chief Electoral Officer/Commission Secretary;
- The legal personality and seal of the IEBC;
- The code of conduct for candidates and political parties;
- The IEBC's financial autonomy and financial procedures;
- The procedure for the appointment of the chairperson and members of the IEBC;
- The conduct of the business and affairs of the IEBC;

- The necessary oaths and affirmations;
- The code of conduct for members and employees;
- The manner of resolving issues arising from the first review initially conducted by the IIBRC; and
- Powers to make subsidiary legislation for better performance of functions under the Act.

As the enabling statute of the EMB, it also tries to delineate the respective decision-making spheres of the commissioners, vis-à-vis the officers of the commission, and to thereby establish board/management separation of roles.

The Elections Act, 2011

The Elections Act, 2011, is Kenya's consolidated[198] electoral law. It provides for
- The conduct of elections to the office of the President, the National Assembly, the Senate, county governor and members of the county assembly;
- The conduct of referenda;
- Election dispute resolution;
- The continuous registration of voters;
- Determinations of questions concerning registration;
- Overall procedures for all elections under its remit;
- The right and procedure for recalling a Member of Parliament;
- The procedure in respect of referenda;
- The procedure regarding elections offences;
- Dispute settlement mechanisms; and
- Powers necessary for the discharge of duties conferred on the IEBC and other role players in the electoral process.

The Political Parties Act, 2011

The Political Parties Act, 2011, was enacted to provide for the registration, regulation and funding of political parties. In addition to the creation of the office of a Registrar of Political Parties (RPP), the Act provides detailed requirements for:
- Registration and regulation of political parties;
- Funding and accounts of political parties;
- Offences; and
- Powers to make subsidiary legislation for improving the functions conferred on the various public bodies with responsibilities under the Act.

---

198 It repealed the National Assembly and Presidential Elections Act (Chapter 7) and the Election Offences Act (Chapter 66) and sought to put most of the core provisions relating to elections in one legal framework.

It also established the Political Parties Liaison Committee (PPLC) as the principal platform for dialogue between the Registrar, the commission and political parties, as well as the Political Parties Disputes Tribunal (PPDT) to determine disputes between:

- Political parties;
- Members of a political party;
- A member and a political party;
- An independent candidate and a political party; and
- Coalition partners.

The PPDT mandate also includes hearing appeals arising from decisions by the RPP. Significantly, the Act requires the RPP to notify the IEBC of instances of multiple memberships to political parties.[199]

Other Kenyan laws

In addition to the foregoing laws, there are other laws that are incidental to or connected to election administration, or impinge on elections in various ways.

- The Registration of Persons Act[200] provides for the registration of persons and the issuing of identity cards. As long as the national identity card remains a mandatory photo identity for the purpose of registration as a voter and voting (for those without passports), this Act will continue to impinge on Kenyan elections.
- The Kenya Broadcasting Corporation Act[201] contains fair election coverage requirements to be implemented in consultation with the IEBC.[202]
- The Penal Code[203] covers some of the offences likely to be committed in an electoral cycle, such as violence, assault, carrying offensive weapons in public places and bribery.
- The Assumption of the Office of the President Act, No. 12 of 2012, provides a detailed procedure for how the person elected as President, and the person thereby elected as Deputy President, will assume office.
- The Publication of Electoral Opinion Polls Act, 2011, regulates the manner in which electoral opinion polls are published.
- The Public Order Act[204] is still applicable to campaign rallies as public gatherings coming under its purview. The police have residual powers under this law to disperse public gatherings on grounds of insecurity – a power that has traditionally been abused (especially in the 1992 and 1997 general elections) to interfere with the campaigns of the incumbent's opponents.

---

199 Which is outlawed by section 17 of the Act.
200 Chapter 107, Laws of Kenya.
201 Chapter 221, Laws of Kenya.
202 The Kenya Broadcasting Corporation Act (Chapter 221, Laws of Kenya), section 8.
203 Chapter 63, Laws of Kenya.
204 Chapter 56, Laws of Kenya.

Membership and staff of the IEBC

The IEBC is a body corporate with perpetual succession and a common seal and is capable, in its own name, of:

- Acquiring, holding and disposing of movable and immovable property;
- Suing and being sued; and
- Doing or performing all such acts and things as a body corporate may by law do or perform.[205]

Members and staff of the IEBC are exempted from personal liability for all acts done in good faith for the purpose of executing the powers, functions or duties of the IEBC under the law.[206]

Chairperson and commissioners

All policy decisions are the remit of the chairperson and commissioners. The Constitution and the IEBC Act envisaged the body of nine commissioners (with the chairman as first amongst equals) to operate as the board of the organisation, albeit an executive board – the latter inferred from the fact that the chairperson and commissioners are required by section 7(2) of the IEBC Act to serve full-time rather than part-time. This, however, needs to be read together with section 5(4) of the IEBC Act to the effect that the chairperson and members of the commission shall perform their functions as provided in the Constitution, and the secretariat shall perform the day-to-day administrative functions of the commission. This was an attempt to establish board and management separation, given the fact that the commissioners were expected to serve full-time. As is discussed elsewhere in this report, this intention is far from achieved and some board–management tensions do, in fact, exist in the EMB. The commissioners are appointed for a single term of six years and are not eligible for re-appointment.[207]

Secretariat and staff

The IEBC has a secretariat, established in accordance with sections 10 and 11 of the IEBC Act, that manages the day-to-day running of the commission. It has the power to hire its own professional staff subject to its approved establishment and the principle that not more than two-thirds of its staff shall be of the same gender; and that its staff shall reflect the regional and other diversity of the people of Kenya. In total, the secretariat is composed of:

- The Chief Electoral Officer;
- Two Deputy Chief Electoral Officers, one in charge of operations and the other support services;

---

205 IEBC Act, section 13.
206 Ibid., section 15.
207 Ibid., section 7.

- Eight directors (each in charge of a directorate);[208]
- 17 managers;
- 17 regional election coordinators; and
- 210 constituency election coordinators.[209]

These are the core staff usually supplemented by temporary election staff during times of increased electoral activity (typically at election time).

The IEBC's core functions are organised into nine directorates and 17 departments. Each directorate is headed by a director, while each department has a manager. In addition to the head office in Nairobi, the IEBC has the following 17 regional offices:

- Nairobi Region;
- Kakamega Region;
- Bungoma Region;
- Garissa Region;
- Thika Region;
- Nyeri Region;
- South Rift Region;
- North Rift Region;
- South West Coast Region;
- Nyanza Central Region;
- Nyanza South Region;
- Upper Eastern Region;
- Lower Eastern Region;
- North Coast Region;
- Wajir/Mandera Region;
- Central Rift Region; and
- Central Eastern Region.

The Chief Electoral Officer/Commission Secretary is the chief executive officer (CEO) of the commission, head of the secretariat, accounting officer and custodian of all the commission's records and is responsible for:

- Executing the decisions of the commission;
- Supervising and assigning duties to all employees of the commission;
- Facilitating, coordinating and ensuring execution of the commission mandate;
- Ensuring staff compliance with public ethics and values; and
- Performing other duties as may be assigned by the law and the commission.

---

208 The RPP, who used to be one of nine directors, is now independent of the commission.
209 Constituency election coordinators double up as returning officers in their respective constituencies during general elections.

The commission has two Deputy Commission Secretaries, one in charge of electoral operations and the other in charge of support services. The manager of field services, supervises the work of the regional coordinators on a day-to-day basis and in turn reports to the Deputy Commission Secretary in charge of operations.

Each regional office has four staff members:

- Coordinator;
- Warehouse officer;
- Administration officer; and
- Information and communication technology officer.

Constituency election coordinators also serve full-time and each has an office assistant. At election time, the constituency election coordinators are designated as returning officers, in charge of election operations at constituency level. For the 2013 general election, the IEBC hired county returning officers on a temporary basis.

Overall, the IEBC hired long-term staff in the professional cadres for the management of elections. Its top leadership also consists of well-trained individuals with substantial experience in the management of public affairs. However, some of the officers lacked experience in elections management prior to their appointment. They had slightly over a year to acquire this experience (chiefly from the by-elections), and the staff cadres are largely intact from the IIEC days. With this kind of leadership and management mix, the institution was expected to have fewer problems delivering than its predecessors – the IIEC and the ECK – though it would have been on a better footing if it had retained some of the good staff from the ECK. However, there are allegations of favouritism in the recruitment of staff, which are probably symptomatic of systems that are not entirely tamper-proof. The proceedings[210] and judgments of election petitions emanating from the March 2013 general election, as well as recent criminal cases against various IEBC staff may, if proven, also be evidence of lower than desirable professional standards in the staff cadres.

The disagreement between the chairman and the commission secretary, which began in the IIEC and continued to the IEBC, occasioned some divisions in the run-up to the 2013 general election. It began in the final days of the IIEC's life in August 2011 when Mr Roy Allan Otieno Odongo, the personal assistant to then IIEC CEO James Oswago, was accused of feeding a local daily newspaper with false information on the affairs of the commission and was suspended without pay.[211] In the ensuing drama, the writer of the stories in the local daily, *The Star*, Miguna Miguna (who was at the time the Prime Minister's Advisor on Coalition Affairs), was also suspended from his job. Once

---

210 For example, Daniel Nyakundi was jailed for two years after admitting that he voted twice in Makadara; see 'Kaloleni the IEBC staff face prosecution', www.the-star.co.ke/news/article-124108/kaloleni-iebc-staff-face-prosecution#sthash.RfBGQ4BP.dpuf. This is noteworthy since voting more than once requires either collusion with election officials or their negligence regarding key election procedures.

211 'Raila fires top aide over spat with IIEC', www.standardmedia.co.ke/business/article/2000040232/raila-fires-top-aide-over-spat-with-iiec.

the IEBC was constituted, it then sought to hire a new Chief Electoral Officer, leading to court action by a voter who successfully stopped the recruitment. Even though it seems to have been settled a month or so before the March 2013 general election,[212] recent events point to continuing underlying suspicions that persisted right through the general election, linked to the procurement of biometric voter registration equipment and other supplies. In response to an Ethics and Anti-Corruption Authority (EACC) raid on his house while investigating fraud, the Chief Electoral Officer reportedly demanded that all commissioners be investigated.[213]

Powers and functions of the IEBC

Article 88 of the Constitution mandates the IEBC to conduct or supervise referenda and elections to any elective body or office established by the Constitution, and any other elections as prescribed by an Act of Parliament. The functions can be grouped into three broad categories, based on a typical electoral cycle: pre-election period, election period and post-election period.

In the pre-election period, the IEBC is responsible for:
- Continuous registration of citizens as voters;
- Regularly revising the voters' roll;
- Delimiting constituencies and wards;
- Regulating the process by which political parties nominate candidates for the elections;
- Settling electoral disputes, including disputes relating to or arising from nominations, but excluding election petitions and disputes subsequent to the declaration of election results;
- Registering candidates for elections;
- Voter education;
- Facilitating the observation, monitoring and evaluation of elections;
- Regulating the amount of money that may be spent by or on behalf of a candidate or party in respect of any election;
- Developing a code of conduct for candidates and parties contesting elections; and
- Monitoring of compliance with legislation required by Article 82(1)(b) of the Constitution relating to nomination of candidates by parties.

During the election period, the IEBC is responsible for:
- Voting and other election day operations;
- Counting and verifying results;

212 'Oswago confirmed as the IEBC's CEO', *The Star*, 7 February 2013, www.the-star.co.ke/news/article-106235/oswago-confirmed-iebcs-ceo.
213 'Oswago wants EACC to investigate all the IEBC commissioners', www.ghettoradio.co.ke/oswago-wants-eacc-to-investigate-all-iebc-commissioners/.

- Announcing results; and
- Handling complaints and appeals by candidates.

In the post-election period, the IEBC is responsible for:
- Evaluating and auditing its operations;
- Organisational assessment and strengthening; and
- Promoting electoral reform.

In performing these functions, section 4 of the IEBC Act requires the IEBC to investigate and prosecute candidates, political parties or their agents for electoral offences pursuant to Article 157(12) of the Constitution and use appropriate technology and approaches in the performance of its functions. From the foregoing, we can tease out seven functions that are generic to most EMBs:
- Constituency delimitation and boundary demarcation;
- Voter registration;
- Drafting or changing electoral laws;
- Conducting and managing elections;
- Certification and proclamation of results;
- Delivering electoral justice; and
- Regulating political parties.

We analyse each of these in turn.

Constituency delimitation and boundary demarcation

Kenya is required to delimit constituencies and demarcate their boundaries because its electoral system still relies on geographical constituencies to elect a large majority of its elected officials. Kenya has, since the March 2013 general election, a bicameral Parliament consisting of a National Assembly and a Senate at the national level (Table 3.2).[214] The country has a first-past-the-post electoral system based on single-member constituencies, with gender and diversity quotas, for parliamentary and county assembly elections. In this system, 290 members of the National Assembly were elected on the basis of constituencies, while 47 women representatives were elected directly with the counties as the constituency. Another 12 members were nominated by parties according to their proportion of elected members, on the basis of party lists, to represent special interests including the youth, persons with disabilities and workers.[215]

214 In each House, there is a Speaker elected from non-members, who then becomes an ex officio member (a member by virtue of office).
215 Constitution of Kenya, 2010 (hereafter 'Constitution'), Article 97.

Table 3.2: Composition of the Parliament of Kenya[216]

National Assembly		Senate	
Men and women elected in 290 constituencies	290	Men and women elected in 47 counties	47
Elected women representatives in 47 counties	47	Nominated women representatives	16
Nominated special seat representatives	12	Nominated special seat representatives	4
Total	**349**	**Total**	**67**

Source: Constitution of Kenya

The Senate has 47 members elected by each county constituting a constituency; 16 women nominated by parliamentary political parties according to their proportion of elected members; two members, one male and one female, representing the youth; and two members, one male and one female, representing people with disabilities.[217]

Each constituency is in turn divided into wards, which are the electoral units for the county assembly elections, whose boundaries the EMB must also demarcate. The IEBC is required to review the names and boundaries of constituencies at intervals of 8–12 years,[218] and review the number, names and boundaries of wards whenever the names and boundaries of counties are reviewed.[219]

The IEBC conducted the first review of boundaries under the new Constitution from January to March 2012, in which it proposed the establishment of 290 constituencies in line with the Constitution. The IEBC also fixed the number of wards at 1,450 and delimited their boundaries. The process was viewed as generally fair but still had 134 suits filed in court against it by various people and groups. Ultimately, the High Court ruled that the IEBC's handling of the constituency and ward delimitation exercise had, by and large, been transparent and fair.[220] The country went to the general election with the constituencies resulting from this delimitation. The next delimitation exercise is due in another eight to ten years' time from when the last one was concluded.

Voter registration

The IEBC's voter registration role is provided for in Articles 82, 83 and 88 of the Constitution. The mandate to prepare a voters' register and to revise it regularly is conferred by Article 88 of the Constitution. Article 82 requires Parliament to enact legislation to provide for, among others, the continuous registration of citizens as voters. Article 83(3)

---

216 In each House, there is a Speaker elected from non-members, who then becomes an ex officio member (a member by virtue of office).
217 Constitution, Article 98.
218 Ibid., Article 89(2).
219 Elections Act, No. 24 of 2011, section 8.
220 *Republic vs Independent Electoral and Boundaries Commission & another Ex-Parte Councillor Eliot Lidubwi Kihusa & 5 others*, Miscellaneous Application 94 of 2012 [2012] eKLR.

states that administrative arrangements for the registration of voters and the conduct of elections shall be designed to facilitate, and shall not deny, an eligible citizen the right to vote or stand for election. The IEBC Act reiterates the constitutional requirements regarding the voters' register, while the Elections Act, 2011, contains detailed provisions on how voter registration is to be conducted.

After the registration process, the IEBC is expected to prepare the Principal Register of Voters (PRV). Once the PRV is compiled, the IEBC is required by law to:

- Update the PRV regularly by deleting the names of deceased voters and rectifying the particulars therein, as appropriate;
- Conduct fresh voter registration, if necessary, at intervals of not less than eight years, and not more than 12 years, immediately after the commission reviews the names and boundaries of the constituencies; and
- Revise the PRV whenever county boundaries are altered.[221]

At least 30 days before an election, the IEBC is required to publish a notice to the effect that the compilation of the PRV has been completed, and to provide every registration officer with a copy of the register relating to her or his constituency for safekeeping at the constituency office of the IEBC. A copy of the PRV is also kept at the IEBC headquarters.

When the PRV is compiled, or whenever it is altered or reviewed, the IEBC is supposed to make it available for public inspection. Members of the public are allowed to either file claims for registration or objections against registration or to make any necessary rectifications as necessary. This is the opportunity, for example, to verify claims of voter importation[222] and to take appropriate action if warranted.

Originally scheduled for August 2012, the process of registering voters for the 2013 general election began on 19 November 2012 and was concluded on 18 December 2012. The month-long exercise, initially delayed owing to failure to procure biometric voter registration (BVR) kits in time, managed to register 14.3 million voters. The IEBC implemented the BVR system in part to reinforce the integrity of the voters' register and to introduce efficiencies in the process of voter registration. The BVR process was fully automated, and capable of generating a national register, county register and constituency register more efficiently than would be the case with a manual system. It also linked the political party membership to the register – a critical element for managing the nomination of candidates.

Upon compilation of the register, the IEBC opened it for inspection and rectification on 4 January 2013 and completed this exercise on 19 January 2013. The compilation of the PRV was certified as complete on 18 February 2013 by notice in the *Kenya Gazette*,

---

221 Elections Act, No. 24 of 2011, s. 8.
222 This is the practice of bussing voters from one constituency into another to increase the number of people favourable to a particular candidate to increase her or his chances of election; such claims were rife in the 2012 registration process.

in leading daily newspapers and on the IEBC website. At this point, the indicated total number of registered voters in the BVR Register was 14,352,545, while the Special Register had 36,236 registered voters.

Table 3.3: Elements of Kenya's principal voters' register

Biometric Voters' Register (BVR)	Contains all the voter registration information for a majority of the voters (over 14 million), including biometrics.
Special Register	Contains all the voter registration information for approximately 36,000 voters, except biometrics.[225]
Diaspora Register	Contains all the voter registration information for voters registered in the Diaspora.
Green Book[226]	The primary reference at registration; used by the IEBC as the reference of last resort.

Source: IEBC interviews

As the electoral process moved towards conclusion, the IEBC's numbers were found to have either changed or had material miscalculations. On 9 March 2013, for instance, the total number of registered voters at the end of the tallying of results was indicated as 14,352,533 (a difference of 12 voters). However, if the county totals are added up, the sum of all county totals comes to 14,349,896 (a difference of 2,649 voters). On 18 July 2013 the number had changed to 14,388,781 (a difference of 36,236 voters). In the light of the requirements of the law[225] and the fact that the registration process ought to have been concluded 30 days before the general election, these changing registration figures (and the IEBC's heavy reliance on the Green Book to justify huge variances in the figures) were vigorously argued as malpractices in the Supreme Court in *Raila Odinga vs The IEBC & Others*, and continues to cast a cloud of suspicion over the quality of the PRV. In reality, even if it is accepted that the BVR register, the Special Register and the Diaspora Register are components of the voters' register, the intention of the law is that their contents should remain 'frozen' after gazetteering and should be the final reference point for the number of people who were eligible to vote.

Drafting or changing electoral laws

Neither the Constitution nor the other legislation described confers on the IEBC the power to make or propose changes to parent legislation, such as the Elections Act. It can nevertheless be inferred from the broad mandate the IEBC has in regard to elections that it can make proposals like any other electoral stakeholder.

---

223 Some due to physical disabilities (such as blindness) or other inability to capture.
224 Though its use is not contemplated after an effective voter registration process, the IEBC argued successfully in the Supreme Court that its use was necessary to avoid disenfranchising people who had been registered but whose details were omitted from the PRV due to errors in the compilation of the PRV.
225 Including Regulation 12 of the Elections (Registration of Voters) Regulations, 2012.

In regard to subsidiary legislation, the situation is different: both the Elections Act and the IEBC Act empower the IEBC to make regulations that improve the implementation of the purposes and provisions of the two Acts.[226] Given the fact that managing elections requires detailed rules, these regulations are not only an aspect of law-making by the IEBC, but also provide an opportunity for the IEBC to regulate the electoral process in a very significant way, limited only by the provisions of the parent statute. Past EMBs, especially the ECK, always made legal reform proposals, though some of these were not taken up by Parliament and legislated. It is also inconceivable that Parliament would, without valid reasons, ignore well-reasoned proposals by the IEBC for amendments to improve electoral law.

Conducting and managing elections

The Constitution and electoral laws grant the IEBC vast powers over conducting and managing elections:

- The IEBC registers voters and thereby determines who is eligible to vote. It also receives nomination papers from candidates and thereby confirms who is eligible to contest.
- All the relevant notices regarding the activities preceding the election, such as nomination of candidates, and the election date are issued by the IEBC.
- Election day activities are the responsibility of the IEBC, for which it procures all the electoral materials and ensures that there are adequate personnel (including temporary election staff) to conduct the election.
- The IEBC is ultimately responsible for the counting and announcement of results, which it then certifies through a public notice in the *Kenya Gazette*, in effect declaring the winners of the various electoral contests for which it is responsible.

There are nevertheless a number of exceptions to these general functions and powers, for which the IEBC requires the cooperation and collaboration of other state agencies. The IEBC, for instance, relies on the police service and other disciplined forces to provide election-related security – for the safety of election materials and officials, as well as the maintenance of law and order in the venues where voting and counting of votes takes place.

Certification and proclamation of results

Kenya's electoral law prescribes the formula by which votes cast in elections are translated into seats. With respect to the presidential election, for instance, the winner is the candidate who receives over 50% of all the votes cast in the election and at least 25% of

---

226 Subsequently, the IEBC did promulgate the Elections (Registration of Voters) Regulations, 2012, and the Elections (General) Regulations, 2012.

the votes cast in each of more than half of the counties.[227] All other seats are on the basis of a simple majority.[228] The EMB counts the votes and communicates the final decision regarding such seats (Figure 3.1). In keeping with Kenyan law and international legal standards, it is the responsibility of the EMB to ensure that the processes, systems and personnel involved in the counting deliver credible results devoid of fraud.

Figure 3.1: General election results processing and transmission in 2013

33,400 **Presiding Officers** supervise counting at the polling-station level, complete statutory forms, announce polling station results and relay provisional results to the IEBC headquarters.

290 **Returning Officers** aggregate and announce members of the National Assembly, county assembly members and the votes for the other seats.

47 **County Returning Officers** aggregate and announce governors, senators, county women representatives and votes for the presidential election.

IEBC headquarters announces winner of the presidential election.

Source: IEBC Interviews

Delivering electoral justice

Orozco-Henriquez et al. define electoral justice as the means and mechanisms for:

- Ensuring that each action, procedure and decision related to the electoral process is in line with the law (the Constitution, statute law, international instruments and treaties, and all other provisions); and
- Protecting or restoring the enjoyment of electoral rights, giving people who believe their electoral rights have been violated the ability to make a complaint, get a hearing and receive adjudication.[229]

The concept encapsulates a system of political (and electoral) rights, and the means to *respect, protect, promote,* and *fulfil* them. From this perspective, the EMB is both a duty bearer and an integral and important part of the means and mechanisms for ensuring that electoral processes are not marred by irregularities, and ultimately for defending electoral rights. It should not be seen to curtail the enjoyment of rights, but should instead actually expand their enjoyment. Indeed, as the primary actor and decision-maker in the electoral process, the IEBC is the first-line duty-bearer in the delivery of electoral justice. Put differently, if the EMB performs its responsibilities well and

227 Constitution, Article 138.
228 Ibid., Articles 97, 98, 181 and 193. Implied, since, though not explicitly stated, there is no provision for a special majority, as is the case with the election of the President.
229 Orozco-Henriquez, et al. (2010) *Electoral Justice: The International IDEA Handbook*, Stockholm, International IDEA, p. 1.

inspires trust in the electoral process, elections are marked by fewer disputes, which are resolved in the early stages of the dispute chain. In the long run, confidence in the process engenders trust in the final results.

It is in recognition of this broader understanding of electoral justice that the Constitution requires the IEBC to not only make fair administrative decisions, but also to settle 'electoral disputes, including disputes relating to or arising from the nominations but excluding election petitions and disputes subsequent to the declaration of election results'. Examples of such disputes include the 112 nomination cases heard by the IEBC Election Disputes Tribunal before the March 2013 general election and the complaints subsequently filed against the allocation of the list of nominees to the county assemblies following the elections. By altering the manner in which the members and staff of the IEBC are appointed and insulating the EMB from the control and influence of a section of Kenyan society, the Constitution also sought to prevent the composition of the IEBC from becoming a source of dispute, as was the case in 2007 and in the preceding elections.

The IEBC is, however, not the only actor in the electoral justice chain (Table 3.4). Other agencies, such as the police service, the Director of Public Prosecutions (DPP) and the judiciary, are also part of this chain.

Although Kenyan law has now put prosecution of electoral offences in the hands of the IEBC, the police are still required to provide election-related security, to investigate election offences and to make arrests, where necessary.

Table 3.4: Kenya's electoral justice chain

Pre-election	Election	Post-election
Political parties	IEBC	IEBC
IEBC		Judiciary
PPDT		
Judiciary		

In the case of offences committed in the context of the election process but in regard to which there may be doubts as to whether the IEBC can prosecute, such as hate speech or violence, the DPP is instrumental in sending a clear message to electoral role players that such infractions are not only frowned upon but that they will be punished in accordance with the law.

As the ultimate destination of criminal prosecutions (whether by the IEBC or the DPP) and challenges to the declaration of results, the judiciary is the final institution in the electoral justice chain. Any electoral role player who is dissatisfied with decisions made by other players in the justice chain has recourse to the courts for final decisions.

The IEBC is also mandated by law to establish the Political Parties Liaison Committee (PPLC). The PPLC has not only been a useful forum for consultation with political parties, but has also helped to defuse tensions in the process by dealing with critical challenges from a broader perspective through consensus-building. Though still in its infancy, the Political Parties Disputes Tribunal (PPDT) will also be an important part of the electoral justice machinery in the country, by resolving disputes between parties or between members or candidates and their parties.

Regulating political parties

While the Political Parties Act, 2011, envisages an independent Registrar of Political Parties (RPP), not subject to the control or direction of any person or authority, this legislation is relevant to the IEBC in two ways.

In the first instance, a substantive RPP is yet to be appointed, meaning that the previous RPP appointed under the Political Parties Act, No. 10 of 2007, is still acting as such in line with the transitional provision in section 51 of the Political Parties Act, 2011. As this previous RPP was an officer of the IIEC, designated as a director, she operated from the IEBC offices and could have been, in some ways, subject to its direction and control. She has since relocated to separate premises with initial skeleton staff, but a substantive RPP is yet to be hired.

Secondly, the fact that political parties are critical actors in the electoral process, and the inclusion of the IEBC in the PPLC means that the EMB will still have the function of maintaining dialogue with political parties and the RPP even after a substantive RPP is appointed and the new legislation is fully operationalised. Such dialogue will be critical in ensuring political parties understand their rights and responsibilities in the electoral process, are aware of major decisions in the electoral process and contribute to the IEBC's decisions on major electoral issues.

The general tenor of the law is that political parties are as subject to the law and to the IEBC's directions as any other role player. They nevertheless enjoy a special place in the scheme of things since the law requires the establishment of the PPLC as a formal forum for dialogue and consultation with political parties.[230] Nevertheless, the EMB not only has decisional independence to make decisions that are in the interest of a fair electoral process, but also has some control, by law, over the manner in which the parties conduct their nominations and manage their affairs (through the office of the RPP).

The actual relationship, though generally aligned to the structural independence established by law, has some worrying drawbacks. An analysis of the decisions taken by the EMB in which political parties have an interest shows that political parties sometimes have greater bargaining power and do get to have their way. A case in point is the manner in which parliamentary political parties made critical changes to the electoral law to allow presidential aspirants to be appointed on party lists for parliamentary seats (a fall-back position in the event of electoral defeat at the presidential elections). There was also controversy over the manner in which some political actors formally belonged

---

230 Political Parties Act, No. 11 of 2011, section 38.

to certain political parties, while their public conduct and pronouncements showed support for alternative political parties. This happened (and is expected to continue happening) in blatant disregard of the Political Parties Act, which states that:

> (4) A person who, while a member of a political party –
> (a) forms another political party;
> (b) joins in the formation of another political party;
> (c) joins another political party; or
> (d) in any way or manner, publicly advocates for the formation of another political party,
>
> shall, notwithstanding the provisions of subsection (2) or the provisions of any other law, be deemed to have resigned from the previous political party.[231]

Against this unsatisfactory backdrop in the management of political party affairs, all the RPP did was to seek the legal opinion of the Attorney-General. Three cases were filed in court – one by aggrieved party members of the Orange Democratic Movement (ODM), and two cases by aggrieved National Rainbow Coalition (NARC) and Safina MPs after their respective parties 'deemed' the members in question to have resigned from their parties and thereby lost their seats in the National Assembly. Meanwhile, the Attorney-General was apparently awaiting the courts' guidance on how this power is to be applied based on the cases in court. In the meantime, party-hopping continued right up to the end of the Tenth Parliament's term on 14 January 2013. Maybe a substantive RPP, once appointed, will deal with the matter differently – and may deem such members to have resigned from their parties, with its attendant consequences.

Political party nominations are another source of concern. They continue to be not only chaotic but also patently undemocratic, quarrelsome, and in some places even violent. Yet the IEBC has not put in place administrative mechanisms to supervise these nominations in accordance with the law and there is indeed doubt over whether, given all the imperatives of organising a successful general election, this supervisory remit of the EMB over political parties will ever be exercised at all, especially in the context of complex general elections such as the one Kenya recently held. The IEBC may have an administrative reason for not supervising the nominations, since it simply does not have enough staff to do so, but it seems that *ex post facto* supervision in the form of holding parties to account for the manner in which they followed their nomination rules and providing directives on fair nomination processes may be of some help. This is what the IEBC Election Disputes Tribunal did when it heard 120 nomination-related cases in the run-up to the last general election.[232] However, the short time set aside for the hearing

---

231 Ibid., section 17.
232 'IEBC Court Clears Kajwang, Kimunya', *Business Daily*, 28 January 2013, www.businessdailyafrica.com/ IEBC-court-clears-Kajwang-and-Kimunya/-/539546/1678138/-/e5ifboz/-/index.html.

and determination of disputes may have created a situation in which some parties felt that they did not get substantive justice.

Independence, effectiveness and regulation of the IEBC

EMB independence is critical to election administration, and is one of the most hotly debated issues in election administration. It is of crucial importance for a country's electoral process that the EMB managing the elections be *seen* to be independent of any party and of the sitting government. This is operational independence, since the funding still comes from the state. If the EMB does not have this confidence of independence, the entire electoral process and the election results might be questioned on the basis of perceived or actual lack of independence. Kenya has an EMB that is, by design and in law, intended to be free of undue influence from the executive and other electoral actors:

- Its commissioners were appointed in a competitive process that was intended to inspire public confidence in the EMB's top leadership.
- The commissioners have security of tenure.
- The EMB has the latitude to hire its own professional staff.
- The IEBC, as a constitutional commission, also has operational independence from government.

In real terms, however, there are a number of concerns. The constitutional and legal provisions do not entirely shield the appointment process from political horse-trading. This is especially so when the appointment criteria include ethnic diversity considerations that may not always be applied with perfection. In addition, some of the IEBC's decisions have raised doubts regarding its independence – chiefly the election date controversy, its waffling and prevarication over Diaspora voting arrangements until politicians waded into the fray[233] and its apparent inability to make large procurements without undue influence either from suppliers or their political proxies. Put differently, Kenya has an independent electoral commission on paper, but it is not clear if it will develop a track record of actually acting independently. If it maintains the kind of independent posture it had in the constituency and boundary delimitation process, there is a high likelihood that it will set and maintain a culture of independent decision making even when political stakes are high.

The IEBC has also tried to conduct itself as an independent manager of the electoral process. In the run-up to the March 2013 general election, it shuffled its entire regional staff in an effort to deal with the likelihood of bias as some of them were serving in regions where they were susceptible to such influences. Impartiality should nevertheless be seen as a sword that cuts both ways: the EMB is expected to treat all electoral role players the same way, whether in the context of obligations to provide services or

233 'IEBC Asked to State Position on Crucial Diaspora Vote', *Standard Digital News*, 1 December 2012, www.standardmedia.co.ke/?articleID=2000071848&story_title=iebc-asked-to-state-position-on-crucial-diaspora-vote.

addressing malpractices. So far, in spite of threats to that effect, there is no evidence to show that the IEBC has the mettle to crack down on role players who attempt to pollute the electoral process through violence, bribery and kindred election malpractices. As the BVR procurement process shows, the IEBC is also not wholly immune from the pernicious influence of corruption cartels. To fully assess the IEBC's independence, one needs to examine its relationship with key electoral role players, including the executive, the legislative and the judiciary, as well as with civil society and other non-state actors.

The IEBC and the executive

Kenyan history shows that the executive has traditionally had the propensity to control the EMB – in the era before 1991, limiting its role to boundary delimitation; after 1991, interpreting incumbency to mean reserving exclusive control over its appointment or trying to stack it with cronies.

To insulate the EMB from control and undue influence, the Constitution makes the IEBC primarily responsible for managing and conducting elections and seeks to secure its independence from the control and undue influence of other electoral actors. The law provides a process for constituting the IEBC that is both open and competitive, beginning with an independent selection panel's interviews and selections, followed by parliamentary approval and, finally, appointment by the President. Though still subject to the politics of the day, the process provides a mechanism for achieving a political consensus on the most balanced way of structuring that composition. In the transition period before the 2013 general election, this was further reinforced by the Constitution's requirement in the Transitional and Consequential Provisions (Sixth Schedule) that 'the President shall, subject to the National Accord and Reconciliation Act, appoint a person after consultation with the Prime Minister and with the approval of the National Assembly'. The commissioners have security of tenure and the commission has the constitutional and legal independence to hire its own staff, subject only to its staff establishment and budget as agreed in consultation with the Treasury. Arguably, at least on paper, the IEBC has much more structural independence than its predecessors. In real terms, the commission has conducted itself in a way that attempts to exemplify independence from the executive.

There are, however, some exceptions. The first relates to the date of the elections. The Constitution stipulates that a general election of MPs shall be held on the second Tuesday in August in every fifth year,[234] at which point the term of each House of Parliament expires.[235] It is also at this same general election that the election of a President and Deputy President,[236] Governors and Deputy Governors[237] and members of the county assemblies[238] are to be elected. However, for the first elections under the Constitution,

---

234 Article 101.
235 In accordance with Article 102.
236 Article 136(1)(a).
237 Article 180(1).
238 Article 177(1)(a).

the Transitional and Consequential Provisions provide in section 10 that the National Assembly existing immediately before 27 August 2010 'shall continue as the National Assembly for the purposes of this Constitution for its unexpired term'. Subsequently, a raucous national debate and controversy ensued regarding when the next general elections were to be held, with some contending that these elections ought to be held in August 2012, while others argued that they should be held either in December 2012 (in line with past general election practice) or March 2013 (upon the expiry of the term of the Parliament in session). The matter was eventually taken to the Supreme Court for adjudication, which referred it to the High Court. The High Court ruled that the elections would be held on 4 March 2013 or 90 days after dissolution of the Grand Coalition Government, whichever occurred sooner. The IEBC thereupon declared that it would make arrangements for a 4 March 2013 election date. At this point, the President and his side of the Grand Coalition Government proclaimed support for the 4 March 2013 date, while the Prime Minister and his supporters spoke out in favour of a December 2012 election date. The Court of Appeal upheld the 4 March 2013 date by a majority. Though public opinion is still divided on whether the IEBC exercised independent thought on the election date issue, it maintained that it was merely implementing a court decision, and that it (in fact) arrived at its decision long before the President spoke.

The second instance in which the IEBC's independence from the executive was called into question was over the BVR procurement saga. At the height of the BVR controversy, the IEBC cancelled the tendering process and it seemed evident that the country would have to fall back to the previous manual system (against huge public expectations riding on the BVR system). At this point, the executive intervened by entering into an agreement with the Canadian government, which led to the kits eventually being delivered by Safran Morpho, a French supplier sourced by a Canadian Crown corporation. Although this was seen by some commentators as executive interference in the IEBC's domain, the EMB was of the view that the intervention was necessary and, in any event, did not in any way interfere with the IEBC's discharge of its mandate. However, it is an indisputable fact that the executive would not have played a role in the acquisition of this technology had the IEBC managed the procurement process competently.

It is important to point out, though, that EMB procurement has always been problematic and accusations of corruption in the process are not new. In October 2013, Britain's Serious Fraud Office brought charges against British company Smith and Ouzman Limited, a supplier of Kenyan ballot papers, for corruptly winning tenders totalling nearly half a million pounds, contrary to the Prevention of Corruption Act. As this supplier continues to be favoured by the IEBC, public interest in the case and its outcome is understandably high.[239] Locally, James Oswago (the IEBC CEO) Wilson Kiprotich Shollei (Deputy Commission Secretary, Support Services), Edward Kenga Karisa (Finance and Procurement Director) and Willy Gachanja Kamanga (Procurement Manager) are charged in connection with the procurement of voter registration kits that were used in the 4 March 2013 general election.[240] Shortly thereafter, the IEBC Procurement Manager and four of his colleagues (Adan Katello Adano, Kennedy Guanye Ochae, Abdi Elema Ali and Gabrial Ngonyo Matunga) were charged with fraud over the purchase of solar lanterns worth KSh 200 million (USD 2.3 million). They were charged together with Benson Gethi Wangui and Joyce Makena, co-directors of Solarmak Technologies, the IEBC supplier of solar lanterns.[241] They have all since been suspended from duty.

In regard to electoral security, the IEBC relied on state security agencies throughout the election cycle, especially on Election Day. In regard to other phases of the election cycle, security agencies were critical in protecting IEBC officers in Kenya's coastal region, where the secessionist Mombasa Republican Council had warned the public against participating in voter registration and had repeatedly disrupted electoral activities, sometimes with fatalities. In respect of party nominations, the police force reportedly deployed some 66,000 police officers all over the country, with a concentration in likely trouble spots. However, there were accusations of undue involvement in the elections levelled by the ODM against the National Intelligence Service (NIS), with the support of some senior public servants.[242] Even though the IEBC wrote to the officials concerned and commenced investigations, the accusations were neither fully investigated nor proven, and had petered out by Election Day. Considering Kenya's past involvement of public servants, including those in security agencies, in elections, there is continuing concern that service delivery by security agencies is also a likely area of control by the executive.

The IEBC and security agencies

In regard to Election Day security, the IEBC consulted with the leadership of the police and had police officers seconded to it for Election Day duties, such as escorting election materials and providing security at polling centres. At a later meeting convened with

---

239   'Printing Company Faces Corruption Charges', Serious Frauds Office, www.sfo.gov.uk/press-room/ latest-press-releases/press-releases-2013/printing-company-corruption-charges.aspx; 'Ballot Paper Firm Faces Graft Charges', *Daily Nation*, mobile.nation.co.ke/News/the IEBC-Ballot-Papers-Smith-and-Ouzman/-/1950946/2047622/-/format/xhtml/-/10laitw/-/index.html.

240   'Oswago trial set for February 22–28', *The Star*, www.the-star.co.ke/news/article-143808/oswago-trial-set-february-22-28#sthash.YC4h44aA.dpuf; 'IEBC officials plead not guilty to fraud charges', *Standard Digital*, www.standardmedia.co.ke/?articleID=2000096543&story_title=iebc-officials-plead-not-guilty-to-fraud-charges.

241   'Five IEBC officials deny fraud charges', *The Star*, www.the-star.co.ke/news/article-142777/five-iebc-officials-deny-fraud-charges#sthash.D7LZYx1d.dpuf.

242   'Updated: Kimemia, Gichangi and Karangi Complicit in General Election Manipulation', cordkenya. blogspot.com/2013/02/kimemia-gichangi-and-karangi-complicit.html; 'CORD alleges plot to rig polls', *Daily Nation*, elections.nation.co.ke/news/Raila-alleges-OP-plot-to-aid-Uhuru-poll-bid/-/1631868/1696332/-/format/xhtml/-/7jisjcz/-/index.html.

the Inspector-General of Police, it was agreed that at least two armed officers would be deployed to each polling centre and that the Inspector-General would designate members of other disciplined forces, such as the Kenya Wildlife Service (KWS), the Kenya Prisons Service (KPS) and the National Youth Service (NYS) as special police officers for this purpose. The IEBC also had guidelines for the conduct of all security officers seconded to it on election duty, in respect of which the law places operational control. In the March 2013 elections, the relationship with security agencies was good:

- An election security committee was established headed by a commissioner.
- Senior police officers were seconded to work from the IEBC headquarters.
- The Inspector-General gazetted KWS, KPS, NYS and Kenya Forest Service officers as special police officers.
- The military was deployed in some limited instances (e.g. in Mombasa, following the Mombasa Republican Council attacks).
- Over 90,000 officers were trained and deployed on election duties.

According to senior IEBC officials, the NIS has no role in electoral operations at all, save to advise on specific threats. Indeed, the IEBC asserts that it only engages with the NIS in the National Security Advisory Committee.[243]

Collaboration with security agencies is also necessary for the arrest and prosecution of election offenders. Although the IEBC has recently hired an Investigations and Prosecution Manager, an Investigations Officer and a Prosecutions Officer, they are hardly enough to handle the anticipated load, given the country's election history. Collaboration with the security agencies and the DPP is, therefore, critical in the discharge of the IEBC's prosecutorial remit in respect of election offences, and has reportedly been discussed. All complaints are reportedly 'investigated, and prosecutions commenced as necessary'.[244]

However, there is a persistent problem that predates the IEBC. Regular and special police officers on election duty demand payment of election duty allowances, yet the Treasury does not provide sufficient funds, ostensibly because their participation is seen as inter-departmental collaboration. Parliament's budget committee also argues that the officers in question are doing their work and does not see the need for additional allowances. Yet the officers traditionally do not work without these allowances and at one point, close to the 2013 general election, threatened to withdraw from election duty.[245] The IEBC is of the opinion that this expense should be put in the Inspector-General of Police budget every election year.

---

243 Interview with IEBC official.
244 Interview with IEBC official.
245 Interview with IEBC official.

The IEBC and Parliament

Aside from the fact that IEBC commissioners are appointed pursuant to parliamentary vetting, the budget-making process, and parliamentary oversight in regard to the IEBC's operations, there is no other opportunity for parliamentary influence in the EMB's operations. The law shields the IEBC from being directed by Parliament.

This came sharply into focus in the debate over the manner in which the IEBC was to resolve issues arising from the first review of boundaries under the Constitution. The Fifth Schedule of the IEBC Act set out a detailed four-month procedure that was to commence with the IEBC's review of the IIBRC report and the report of the parliamentary committee on the IIBRC report and, in accordance with the Constitution and other laws, publication of a preliminary report. This would be followed by:

- Public consultations on the preliminary report for not less than 21 days;
- Submission of a revised preliminary report to the Parliamentary Committee;
- Consideration of the preliminary report by the Parliamentary Report within 14 days of its submission;
- Debate and adoption by the National Assembly, with resolutions forwarded to the IEBC; and
- Publication of a final report by the IEBC within 14 days of the expiry of the seven-day period for the National Assembly to forward its resolutions to the IEBC, 'taking into account the resolutions of the National Assembly'.

When the National Assembly forwarded its resolutions to the IEBC, the commission prepared its final report, in which it treated some of the resolutions that sought to alter its decisions in the revised preliminary report as advisory rather than directive and disregarded them. There was a hue and cry within the political class but the IEBC stood its ground. Eventually, the matter went to court, with some of the court actions filed by disaffected MPs. In the end, the High Court largely validated the IEBC's decisions, with a few alterations.[246]

Closer to the elections, the parliamentary departmental committee on justice and legal affairs summoned the IEBC over the BVR tendering process and the delays in the promulgation of election rules and regulations. After the 2013 general election, the National Assembly's Public Accounts Committee also ordered an investigation into the BVR tendering process, which continues to date. In this way, Parliament exercises a check on the manner in which the IEBC discharges its constitutional obligations. The key lesson from this second aspect of Parliament's relationship with the IEBC is that the EMB can only avoid intrusion if it conducts its affairs above board; otherwise, Parliament is entitled to inquire into its conduct and to make decisions to safeguard the public interest.

---

246 *Republic vs Independent Electoral and Boundaries Commission & another Ex-Parte Councillor Eliot Lidubwi Kihusa & 5 others* Miscellaneous Application 94 of 2012 [2012] eKLR; and *Mohamed Abdille & Others vs AG & Another* Petition 82 of 2011 [2013] eKLR.

In this regard, the IEBC's conduct in recent engagements with Parliament also raises some questions regarding its integrity.[247] After a delay of over four months, when the IEBC finally appeared before the National Assembly's departmental committee on justice and legal affairs to present the final election results in response to concerns over the delayed disbursement of the Political Parties Fund, its officials initially refused to present the results under oath. Coupled with the delay in producing the results, and the already swirling rumours about the discrepancies in the result tallies, this did not do the IEBC any favours.

The IEBC and the judiciary

The IEBC has decisional independence over electoral operations and determination of boundaries. However, as a fact of both administrative law and the requirements of the Constitution, its decisions are subject to challenge before the courts either through judicial review or election petitions. The real question of independence here is therefore not whether the IEBC is independent from the courts – for the most part the courts have not strayed into the IEBC's domain – but whether the IEBC is as much a subject of the legal process (and the courts) as other electoral role players. This can be answered in the affirmative given the EMB's track record not only with the decisions of courts relating to boundary delimitation, but also in relation a number of election petitions that have been filed against it. The IEBC generally obeys court orders and, at least in the run-up to the 2013 elections, was seen to respond publicly to the key questions of the day regarding the preparations for the elections. Its voter education campaign, though materially deficient in ways that have been critiqued elsewhere in this report, not only enabled it to enlighten voters but also to build much-needed public trust.

The courts prepared for their role by instituting the Judiciary Working Committee on Election Preparations (JWCEP), appointed by the Chief Justice in May 2012 to design and execute a programme to build the capacity of judges, magistrates and other judicial staff on electoral matters and suggest ways of working with other stakeholders. The JWCEP conducted research, capacity-building and legal reform activities to prepare relevant judicial staff for the disputes that were expected to arise from the 2013 elections, and also gave advisory guidance on how certain matters were to be handled.

A case in point was the guidance of the JWCEP on how disputes arising from party nominations were to be dealt with, which was followed by the courts soon thereafter in referring the cases that arose from the Ndhiwa and Kajiado North by-elections back to the party machinery and the PPDT. This had the effect of decongesting the electoral preparations by the IEBC.

---

247 'IEBC officials refuse to take oath', *Standard Digital*, www.standardmedia.co.ke/ktn/video/watch/2000067908/-iebc-officials-refuse-to-take-oath; 'Now Electoral and Boundaries Commission IEBC releases final presidential vote results', *Standard Digital*, 37.188.98.230/?articleID=2000088768&story_title=now-electoral-and-boundaries-commission-iebc-releases-final-presidential-vote-results&pageNo=1.

Overall, the relationship seems collaborative and cooperative. There are, however, limited exceptions, such as the decision taken by the High Court to stop the Kamukunji by-election in 2011, and also reports that the IEBC initially refused to join the National Council on the Administration of Justice (NCAJ), in spite of its supposed benefits, especially in regard to electoral law enforcement.[248]

In its first quarterly report, the JWCEP advised stakeholders that litigants should exhaust internal dispute resolution mechanisms and use other quasi-judicial tribunals before going to court. This thinking was evident in subsequent decisions of the High Court[249] in respect of the Ndhiwa, Kangema and Kajiado North by-elections in September 2012. The High Court dismissed suits filed by disaffected aspirants who rushed to court to block the electoral process on account of disputes arising from party nominations. It is now clear that the judiciary will not entertain claims (at least in the first instance) where other bodies have jurisdiction.

The judiciary – a critical role player in the delivery of electoral justice – proposed amendments to the election law that were eventually passed by Parliament, in the Statute Law (Miscellaneous Amendments) (No. 2) Act, 2012, to allow magistrates' courts to hear petitions arising from elections at the county level.[250] The Supreme Court delivered an advisory opinion to clarify its jurisdiction in respect of disputes arising from the first round of the presidential elections and the manner in which the gender quotas in representation as outlined in the Constitution will be progressively realised. In consultation with the IEBC and other role players, it subsequently drafted new election petition rules before the 2013 elections.[251]

The decision of the highest court, the Supreme Court, in three of the petitions filed after the March 2013 general election, eventually consolidated as *Raila Odinga vs The IEBC & Others* (two other petitions having been ruled inadmissible), continues to draw criticism and praise in almost equal measure.[252] In September 2013, one of the Supreme Court judges reportedly stated that elections should be won at the ballot, not in the

---

248 The NCAJ is established under Section 34 of the Judicial Service Act (No. 1 of 2011). It is a high-level policy-making, implementation and oversight coordinating body composed of state and non-state actors from the justice sector. The mandate as stipulated in the Act is to ensure a coordinated, efficient, effective and consultative approach in the administration of justice and reform of the justice system.

249 *Francis Gitau Parsimei & 2 Others vs National Alliance Party & 4 Others* Petitions 356 & 359 of 2012 [2012] eKLR.

250 The Statute Law (Miscellaneous Amendments) (No. 2) Act of 2012, section 2.

251 Supreme Court (Presidential Election Petition) Rules, 2013; Elections (Parliamentary and County Elections) Petition Rules, 2013 (Legal Notice No. 54).

252 *Raila Odinga vs the IEBC & Others*, Supreme Court of Kenya Petition No. 5 of 2013 (Consolidated with Petition No. 3 of 2013 and Petition No. 4 of 2013); 'Supreme Court Spoke Out of Both Sides of Its Mouth', *The East African*, www.theeastafrican.co.ke/OpEd/comment/Supreme-Court-spoke-out-of-both-sides-of-its-mouth/-/434750/1753630/-/b55ivbz/-/index.html; 'Verdict on Kenya's Presidential Election Petition: Five Reasons the Judgment Fails the Legal Test', *The East African*, www.theeastafrican.co.ke/OpEd/comment/Five-reasons-Kenya-Supreme-Court-failed-poll-petition-test/-/434750/1753646/-/297c6q/-/index.html.

courts[253] and that the 14 days set aside for hearing and determining presidential petitions is too short a period.[254] Overall, the courts had heard and determined 50 of the 188 election petitions arising out of the elections by 30 August 2013, while 17 had been withdrawn and 31 struck out. Ahead of the deadline of 17 October 2013, only 19% of the petitions were pending, which goes to show that the strict timelines are actually achievable.

Table 3.5: Election petitions status as on 30 August 2013

Position	Petitions filed	Judgments delivered	Petitions withdrawn	Petitions struck out	Pending judgments and formal withdrawal	Petitions pending hearing
Governor	24	7	0	2	10	5
Senator	13	1	2	4	4	2
Member of National Assembly	70	11	5	11	28	15
Women representative	9	0	1	4	1	3
County assembly representative	67	29	7	9	11	11
Speaker of county assembly	5	2	2	1	0	0
Total	**188**	**50**	**17**	**31**	**54**	**36**

Source: Judiciary

The IEBC, civil society and the media

The relationship between the IEBC and civil society is seen in the context of election observation, discussed below, and the discharge of the IEBC's voter education mandate. The latter was critical, especially given the relative complexity of holding six elections on one day. In this respect the IEBC published guidelines and regulations on voter education and accredited voter education service providers. It seems, though, that relational problems persisted late into the electoral cycle, with some IEBC staff members challenging the notion that any other agency could play the role of providing voter education. As a result, the IEBC originally intended to conduct voter education (largely funded by donors) on its own, but eventually changed its approach and sought civil society assistance in the delivery of voter education, albeit much later than would have been the case if a collaborative approach had been adopted from the start. After launching

253 'Supreme Court Debate Won't Just Go Away', *The Peoples' Court*, www.thepeoplescourt.co.ke/news/opinions/388-supreme-court-debate-won-t-just-go-away. The judge reportedly said he was misquoted.

254 Ayodo, H (2013) 'Supreme Court Judge Calls for Constitutional Amendment', www.lsk.or.ke/index.php/component/content/article/1-latest-news/308-supreme-court-judge-calls-for-constitutional-amendment.

voter education in October 2012, it was not until after the stakeholders' conference in February 2013, that it felt the pressure and handed responsibility for delivery to CSOs.

This resulted in critical delays in the implementation of voter education and may also have limited the programme's overall reach. Generally, CSOs appeared to be asking for greater engagement with the IEBC and its leadership, while the EMB's leadership seemed to view this as high maintenance (that is, too involving). CSOs wanted high-level engagement with commissioners, while the commissioners had other pressing priorities and therefore delegated the CSO engagement to the IEBC staff. CSOs interpreted this as the IEBC's indication that CSOs and their issues were a lower-order priority to the IEBC's top leadership. In its final report, the Election Observation Group decried the lack of 'effective communication and information-sharing' by the IEBC.[255] Ultimately, a compromise between these two extremes will be necessary, based on further consultations and agreement on the structure of the IEBC's relationship and collaboration with CSOs generally.

The IEBC used the media to inform the public on key stages of the electoral process. There were, however, two shortcomings in its media use:

- The first was the failure to effectively manage expectations. Many pundits questioned why the IEBC had to communicate a target for its voter registration drive, yet the previous register had been discredited. This begged the question of what the IEBC was basing its estimates on. It would probably have been wiser to just promise to register 'as many eligible voters as possible'.
- Secondly, at the height of the BVR controversy, the IEBC seemed to have totally lost its public communication strategy, giving rise to the entrenched public belief that all was not well and, ultimately, that it had been salvaged by the executive.[256] Overall, the EMB is in need of advice on how to manage expectations and project a positive image at all times, and at no time was this more evident than through the entire BVR saga and the final acquisition of the BVR kits.

The media itself was criticised for not asking the IEBC tough questions or revealing malpractices out of fear of stoking tensions similar to those related to the 2008 post-election violence, giving rise to what came to be known as the 'peace lobotomy'.[257]

255 Election Observation Group (ELOG) (2013) *The Historic Vote: Elections 2013*, Nairobi, Elections Observation Group, p. 35.

256 At one point, even the lawyer who went on to represent the IEBC in the Supreme Court presidential election petition penned an opinion piece that questioned the IEBC's integrity: Abdullahi, A (2013) 'Can electoral body pass the integrity test?', *Daily Nation*, www.nation.co.ke/oped/Opinion/Can-the-electoral-body-pass-the-integrity-test/-/440808/1682802/-/2mdtv9z/-/index.html.

257 See, for instance, Gathara, P (2013) 'The Monsters Under the House', gathara.blogspot.com/2013/03/the-monsters-under-house.html.

E. Election observation and monitoring

Kenya has a long history of election observation and monitoring, beginning with the National Elections Monitoring Unit (NEMU),[258] which observed the 1992 multi-party general election. From those early days, there has been debate on whether the country can allow election monitors or not, with the first ECK chairman declaring categorically in 1992 that Kenya had no place for election monitors. The ECK's guidelines for election observers, promulgated in 1992, also explicitly forbade monitoring and forbade observers, for instance, from talking to election officials unless they were spoken to. To date, Kenya has only had election observers participating in its elections, although in practice, much of what the ECK originally forbade is actually ignored. However, election law now recognises monitors and requires the IEBC to provide regulations for their work. Consequently, the IEBC's Guidelines and Code of Ethics for Election Observation are, for the most part, consistent with the Declaration of Global Principles for Nonpartisan Election Observation and Monitoring by Citizen Organisations, and do not place undue restrictions on observers. The result is that the lines between observation and monitoring are still blurred. In reality, however, there is some distinction between election *observation*, election *monitoring* and election *supervision*.

According to the ACE Electoral Knowledge Network,[259] the most widely accepted distinctions between election observation, monitoring and supervision refer to the role and the mandate of the different missions in terms of the level of intervention in the electoral process: observers having the smallest mandate, monitors having slightly more extended powers, while supervisors are those with the most extensive mandate (Table 3.5):

- The mandate of election observers is to gather information and make an informed judgment without interfering in the process.
- The mandate of election monitors is to observe the electoral process and to intervene if laws are being violated.
- Election supervisors certify the validity of the electoral process.

The IEBC contends that it is the supervisor, only political parties should monitor, and observers should observe.[260]

Compared to the ECK, at least in its formative years, the IEBC seemed to have a more cordial working relationship with election observers – at least until the events at the tallying centre. Kenyan CSOs were able to observe all the by-elections and the 2010 referendum conducted by the IIEC, as well as the by-elections conducted by the IEBC

---

258 NEMU was a joint initiative of the Kenyan Section of the International Commission of Jurists, the Kenyan Chapter of the International Federation of Women Lawyers and the Law Society of Kenya. It was disbanded after the elections and a new institution, the Institute for Education in Democracy formed out of its remaining structures.

259 See Ayoub, A et al. (no date) 'Observation, monitoring or supervision', ACE Project, aceproject.org/electoral-advice/election-observation/observation-monitoring-or-supervision.

260 Interview with IEBC official.

since its formation. With the exception of some of the challenges below, many observers were granted accreditation and allowed access to critical aspects of the electoral process. In 2010, a number of Kenyan CSOs[261] established the Elections Observation Group (ELOG) as a permanent national platform through which citizens can monitor general elections in Kenya and other countries in Africa. In the run-up to the general election, ELOG called for more structured dialogue and consultation with the IEBC.[262] Specifically, what the observers were demanding was a well-structured accreditation process, comprising monthly meetings with the IEBC leadership, and IEBC attendance of their events to provide clarifications.

The IEBC issued guidelines for election observers that were generally consistent with international best practice, and a Code of Conduct for Voter Educators. ELOG observed the 2013 general election and issued its report in August 2013. The EU Observer Mission and the AU Observer Mission also participated and issued reports at the conclusion of their respective missions.

Challenges highlighted in the ELOG report were that:

- ELOG did not have unfettered access to information it considered public, such as the voters' register in machine-readable format.
- They were denied a list of polling stations until much later in the day.
- Its observers found the accreditation procedures cumbersome.
- There was denial of access to observers in some stations even though an oath of secrecy was not necessary for observers.

The Africa Centre for Open Governance (AfriCOG) and Law Society of Kenya observers also reported some access and facilitation challenges. Many observers have taken issue with the fact that the tallying centre was out of bounds from the second day and that party agents were thrown out of the tallying hall at one point and were told that the area was a 'security zone'. The question was also asked why the international observers were given the voters' register earlier than domestic observers.

F. Funding of elections

Kenyan elections and the costs for the IEBC's operations are largely funded by the Exchequer. By law, administrative and other expenses of the IEBC, including salaries, allowances, gratuities and pensions of members and employees come from the

---

261 Centre for Governance and Development (CGD); Consortium for Empowerment and Development of Marginalised Communities (CEDMAC); Constitution and Reform Education Consortium (CRECO); Institute for Education in Democracy (IED); Supreme Council of Kenya Muslims (SUPKEM); Ecumenical Centre for Justice and Peace (ECJP); United Disabled Persons of Kenya (UDPK) Catholic Justice and Peace Commission (CJPC); Youth Agenda (YA); and the Federation of Women Lawyers of Kenya (FIDA).

262 See, for instance, 'Press Statement by ELOG on the IEBC's Announcement of the March 4th 2013 Elections Date', 20 March 2012; ELOG (2012) *Darubini Ya Uchaguzi*, No. 2, July/August 2012, p. 3.

Consolidated Fund[263] and remuneration is determined by the Salaries and Remuneration Commission.[264]

According to the IEBC Act, the IEBC may have the following sources of funding:

- Monies allocated by Parliament in the annual budget for purposes of the IEBC;
- Grants, gifts, donations or other endowments given to the IEBC; and
- Funds that may accrue to the IEBC in the performance of its functions under any written law (for example, through charging candidates nomination fees).[265]

Every year, before the commencement of the financial year, the Commission Secretary prepares budgetary estimates of the revenue and expenditure of the EMB for that year, which are then approved by the IEBC. The Treasury presents these estimates for consideration to the National Assembly, which approves them with or without alterations. Final budget-making authority lies in the National Assembly, which is in turn guided by the country's revenues and other fiscal constraints. In reality, the Treasury does try to moderate the estimates long before they get to the National Assembly.[266] However, in the new constitutional dispensation the Treasury is no longer the sole custodian of Kenya's financial policy; it can even be argued that it has only retained the role of a disbursing agent.

Donors have, however, continued to support critical activities and to bridge funding shortfalls in priority areas, such as voter education, technical assistance and change management. In June 2012, donors gave the IEBC USD 25.8 million as part finance towards its preparations for the general election. Donor support comes in the form of cash grants or in-kind support. Currently, this support is largely channelled through a basket fund managed by the UN Development Programme (UNDP), even though some donors still have bilateral arrangements with the IEBC for specific areas of support.[267]

Overall, the financing of elections in Kenya still raises some concerns, not in the least due to the total cost. IREC excoriated the ECK for its inefficiency. From other information sources, it is now clear that the ECK was not only inefficient but also corrupt.[268] In terms of efficiency, one of the accusations the IEBC continues to face relates to its elections budget. Before the BVR acquisition turned into a public scandal, the EMB was the subject of public discussion and controversy because of its budget. The commission was pressurised to scale down its budget, with Parliament forcing it to cut it down twice – from the initial USD 487 million it had requested to USD 370.5

---

263 IEBC Act, section 19.
264 In the transition period pending the establishment of the Salaries and Remuneration Commission, salaries and allowances were determined by the Public Service Commission in consultation with the Treasury (Interview with IEBC official).
265 IEBC Act, section 17.
266 Interview with IEBC official.
267 South Consulting (2012) *The Kenya National Dialogue and Reconciliation: Reforms and Preparedness for Elections*, p. 40.
268 AfriCOG (2008), op. cit.

million.[269] The IEBC argued that this high budget was necessary due to the acquisition of new equipment, including the BVR equipment, and that the accusations of inefficiency on its part were therefore unwarranted.[270] However, this defence will not always be available to the IEBC. It needs to evaluate its systems and streamline them in order to reduce the cost per vote to comparable African elections, such as in Ghana in 1996 (USD 0.70), Botswana in 1994 (USD 2.70) and Senegal (USD 1.20). Although the 2013 cost of USD 4.20 per registered voter (based on a reported expenditure of KSh 30.9 billion)[271] compare favourably with the 2007 cost of USD 13.74 per registered voter,[272] there is still room for improvement, given that the next general election will not involve the high establishment costs of the 2013 elections, such as the purchase of BVR and electronic voter identification equipment.

Another area of concern is the extent to which items that the national government rarely prioritises, such as voter education, would get funded if donors did not fund them. Historically, EMBs did not prioritise voter education and the push for it came from CSOs. Now that it is part of the IEBC's mandate, it is important that it be sufficiently resourced by the state. The IEBC also needs to explore ways of integrating voter education into the primary and secondary school curriculum as a way to progressively reduce voter illiteracy and sustainably manage the costs of educating voters.

G. Management of electoral disputes

The IEBC has broad powers to detect and adjudicate electoral disputes. However, the EMB is not the only actor in the electoral justice chain. Other agencies, such as the police, the DPP and the judiciary, are also part of this chain. The limits between the IEBC's jurisdiction and powers and those of the court and other agencies are nevertheless not clearly delineated. Though the EMB is also part of the justice chain, in the sense that it has the first responsibility of reaching a fair decision on the implementation of electoral law and has some adjudicative power with respect to pre-election disputes, it requires the judiciary to conclusively determine issues over which its decisions

269 Opiyo, P (2012) 'IEBC gets more money in readiness for elections', *Standard Digital News*, www.standardmedia.co.ke/?articleID=2000073872&story_title=Kenya-the IEBC-gets-more-money-in-readiness-for-elections; IEBC (2012) 'We will deliver the polls despite a lean budget – Hassan', www.iebc.or.ke/index.php/news-archive/43-july-2012/92-we-will-deliver-the-polls-despite-a-lean-budget-hassan; 'PM wants IEBC to come clean on election budget', *NTV News*, www.ntv.co.ke/news2/topheadlines/pm-wants-iebc-to-come-clean-on-election-budget/.

270 See, for instance, IEBC 'We Will Deliver the Polls Despite a Lean Budget – Hassan' www.iebc.or.ke/index.php/news-archive/43-july-2012/92-we-will-deliver-the-polls-despite-a-lean-budget-hassan in which the IEBC argues that most of its budget was 'a one-off capital investment on technology'.

271 At a modest exchange rate of KSh 85 to USD 1.

272 These were criticised by the Kriegler Commission (IREC) as 'comparable only to very special cases of post-conflict elections like Angola, Afghanistan or Cambodia. They are even higher than those observed in cases like Bosnia-Herzegovina under the Dayton Accords (USD 8).' IREC (2008) *Report of the Independent Review Commission on the 2007 General Elections*, Government Printer, Nairobi, p. 44.

have been disputed or to require the enforcement of some aspect of electoral law or procedure. This is especially so in the context of election offences and post-election disputes. Traditionally, the EMB relied on the Attorney-General to prosecute election offenders, but that power has now been conferred by law on the IEBC. The IEBC subsequently hired a prosecutor and two assistant prosecutors and will be building a cadre of prosecutors over time.

The Constitution requires the IEBC not only to make fair administrative decisions, but also to settle 'electoral disputes, including disputes relating to or arising from the nominations but excluding election petitions and disputes subsequent to the declaration of election results'. Examples of such disputes include the 112 nomination cases heard by the IEBC Election Disputes Tribunal before the March 2013 general election and the complaints subsequently filed against the allocation of the list of nominees to the county assemblies after the elections. By altering the manner in which the members and staff of the IEBC are appointed and insulating the EMB from the control and influence of a section of Kenyan society, the Constitution also sought to prevent the composition of the IEBC from becoming a source of dispute, as was the case in 2007 and the preceding general elections.

Although Kenyan law has now put prosecution of electoral offences in the hands of the IEBC, the police are still required to provide election-related security, to investigate election offences and to make arrests where necessary. As the ultimate destination of criminal prosecutions, whether by the IEBC or the DPP, and challenges to the declaration of results, the judiciary is the final institution in the electoral justice chain. Any electoral role player who is disaffected by decisions made by other players in the justice chain has recourse to the courts for final decisions.

Another aspect in which collaboration with security agencies is called for is in the arrest and prosecution of election offenders. Although the IEBC has recently hired an Investigations and Prosecution Manager, an Investigations Officer and a Prosecutions Officer, this is hardly enough to handle the anticipated load, given the country's election history. Collaboration with the security agencies and the DPP is therefore critical in the discharge of the IEBC's prosecutorial remit in respect of election offences, and has reportedly been discussed.[273] All complaints are investigated and prosecutions commenced as necessary.

The IEBC is also mandated by law to establish the Political Parties Liaison Committee (PPLC). The PPLC has not only been a useful forum for consultation with political parties, but has also helped to diffuse tensions in the process by dealing with critical challenges from a broader perspective through consensus building. Though still in its infancy, the Political Parties Disputes Tribunal (PPDT) will also be an important part of the electoral justice machinery in the country, by solving disputes between parties or between members or candidates and their parties.

---

273   Interview with IEBC official.

Amendments to the election law that were proposed by the judiciary were eventually passed by Parliament to allow magistrates' courts to hear petitions arising from elections at the county level.[274] The Supreme Court has delivered an advisory opinion to clarify its jurisdiction in respect of disputes arising from the first round of the presidential elections and the manner in which the gender quotas in the Constitution will be progressively realised. In consultation with the IEBC and other role players, it subsequently drafted new election petition rules before the 2013 general elections.[275] After the 2013 general elections, there were 188 election petitions filed against the election of various representatives. Though some are still pending, especially subsequent appeals, many of these have been heard and determined.

The most significant decision of the judiciary was the unanimous decision of the Supreme Court on three of the petitions filed in regard to the presidential elections after the March 2013 general election (two others having been ruled inadmissible).[276] Though this decision, like many of the others, was rendered within the statutory time limit, it is the most controversial, given the manner in which the process was handled, the fact that the report of the results scrutiny exercise do not seem to have been taken into account in arriving at the decision, and the reasons given by the Supreme Court for its decision. This decision is particularly criticised for the manner in which it will adversely impact on precedent for critical legal questions regarding elections, especially on the validity of the PRV, the effect of procedural impropriety on the validity of elections, and the meaning of 'votes cast'.

The judiciary has handled questions regarding the integrity of candidates in a generally unsatisfactory manner, leading to a diminution of leadership and integrity standards for elective office. The effect of the decisions in *Mumo Matemu vs Trusted Society of Human Rights Alliance & 5 Others* in the Court of Appeal, and *International Centre for Policy and Conflict & 5 Others vs the Attorney-General & 5 Others* in the High Court has been to pass the buck with regard to the legal enforcement of the integrity provisions in Chapter 6 of the Constitution. These provisions were meant to influence not only eligibility to remain in office, but also eligibility to contest office. It leaves open the question on which institution has jurisdiction to determine integrity issues if the High Court has none.

---

274 The Statute Law (Miscellaneous Amendments) (No. 2) Act of 2012, section 2.
275 Supreme Court (Presidential Election Petition) Rules, 2013; Elections (Parliamentary and County Elections) Petition Rules, 2013 (Legal Notice No. 54).
276 *Raila Odinga vs The IEBC & Others*, Supreme Court of Kenya Petition No. 5 of 2013 (consolidated with Petition No. 3 of 2013 and Petition No. 4 of 2013).

H. A critical assessment of election management in Kenya

Despite a generally good image when it was established, riding in part on the public approval ratings of its predecessor, the IIEC, the IEBC briefly ran into a number of challenges; its public approval ratings, in various public opinion surveys conducted by the Kenya National Dialogue and Reconciliation Monitoring Project and others, dipped slightly before they rose again.[277]

There were a number of institutional and operational challenges in the run-up to and following the March 2013 general election, the most significant of which were:

- Wrangles between the commissioners and management;
- Weak enforcement of the law;
- Uncertainty over the election date;
- The acquisition of the BVR kits; and
- Delays in the promulgation of election regulations.

Some of these challenges continue to date, and new ones have since arisen based on developments since the 2013 elections. All of these are important to discuss, as the IEBC was not only supposed to prepare Kenya for the general election, but also to be part of continuing efforts by the country to establish an independent and effective EMB as recommended by the Kriegler Commission and as expected by the Constitution. The rest of this section discusses each of these concerns in turn.

Weak internal governance structures

Soon after the IEBC commissioners were appointed and sworn into office in November 2011, they organised a strategic planning retreat with management to plan for the forthcoming elections and to discuss other aspects of the EMB's mandate. According to media reports,[278] towards the end of that retreat, the chairman informed his fellow commissioners at a commission meeting that the IEBC needed to appoint a Commission Secretary – in the meantime, the incumbent would be designated Acting Commission Secretary. For many watchers, this was a continuation of the controversy between the chairperson's office and the Commission Secretary's in the last days of the IIEC.[279] The IEBC proceeded to advertise for a Commission Secretary and two deputies. The matter eventually went to court and a voter obtained an injunction against the IEBC's

---

277 Although the IEBC's ratings remained comparably high and were only comparable to those of the judiciary, they are believed to have dropped after the 2013 elections; see 'Public Trust in the IEBC Plummets Over BVR Saga – Poll', *Daily Nation*, www.nation.co.ke/News/politics/Public-trust-in-the-IEBC-plummets-over-BVR-saga/-/1064/1617342/-/leuqisz/-/index.html.

278 Otieno, K (2012) 'Court blocks IEBC from replacing its CEO Oswago', *Standard Digital News*, 37.188.98.230/?articleID=2000049790&story_title=court-blocks-iebc-from-replacing-its-ceo-oswago&pageNo=2.

279 Menya, W (2011) 'Election Body Recalls CEO from Trip in Hate Probe', *Daily Nation*, www.nation.co.ke/News/politics/IIEC+suspends+Oswago+aide/-/1064/1212956/-/qhj6v4/-/index.html.

recruitment of a new Commission Secretary, pending determination of the suit.[280] The IEBC proceeded with the appointment of two deputies, pending determination of the suit regarding the Commission Secretary. While the IEBC kept a public image of unity and many of its officials stated categorically that the matter had since been buried, it is possible that it was merely a microcosm of governance issues that continue to plague the IEBC's unity of purpose in diverse ways and may, in fact, mask broader board and management separation issues.

There is a need for reflection on how to strike a balance between the executive powers of full-time commissioners, the responsibilities of the Chief Electoral Officer/Commission Secretary and the rest of the secretariat in day-to-day administration. Interviews with representatives at both levels[281] indicate that:

- It is still not clear what the dividing lines are between the policy and administrative domains.
- There are no institutionalised guidelines for how to manage this separation.
- There is no common understanding of the core processes of delivering an election.

This is fertile ground for the kind of conflicts that have sometimes flared up, as well as the managerial stasis that sometimes sets in when staff are not sure if they will be accused of crossing the policy line. The country could consider:

- Expending more effort on reinforcing board–management separation;
- Having an even smaller number of commissioners (say, three) who will focus more on policy issues; or
- Having all or some of the commissioners serve part-time.

Inadequate electoral law enforcement capacity

Given the nature of Kenya's (indeed, any) electoral process, subsequent by-elections have had claims of irregularities. Political parties have also had controversies relating to the changed allegiance of some of their elected members without suffering the consequences of by-elections as provided for in law – chiefly by publicly supporting others without writing letters of resignation to the Speaker of the National Assembly. This has largely been witnessed in the case of the ODM, the NARC and the Party of National Unity. Legally, these members should be deemed both by their parties and the RPP to have resigned in accordance with the provisions of section 17 of the Political Parties Act, 2011, but this has not been the case. Instead, the RPP has sought a legal opinion

---

280 The case was filed by a voter, Reuben Ombima, to stop the IEBC from recruiting new officials to the commission after publicly advertising the positions of chief electoral officer and two deputies. The Judge granted leave for the applicant to stop the IEBC recruitment until the matter was heard. Judge Abida Ali-Aroni also dismissed as baseless the argument by the commission that the case was not properly brought before the court.

281 Interviews with IEBC staff and officials.

on the issue from the Attorney-General, while there are a number of pending cases in the courts on the matter.

This seeming weakness in enforcing electoral law has raised doubts on the IEBC's capacity to deal with law-breaking by political parties and their members. Coming as it does when the Election Campaign Financing Bill is still pending in Parliament, it does not inspire public confidence in the IEBC's ability to rein in wayward political parties and aspirants or candidates. It is encouraging, though, that a number of people did get prosecuted successfully for electoral offences, among them IEBC officials. There is also hope that this will reduce future impunity. Enforcement of nomination procedures is also somewhat hampered by the IEBC Nominations Disputes Committee's overlapping mandates with the PPDT and the courts.

Another area in which the IEBC has experienced challenges was the promulgation of election regulations on the electoral process generally. Despite the fact that the law requires regulations to be adopted by Parliament before they become law, the IEBC had not delivered the draft regulations to the relevant Committee of Parliament six days to the original deadline. Parliament had to demand delivery in strong terms, following which the regulations were tabled by the Minister for Justice, National Cohesion and Constitutional Affairs. The Election (Amendment) Act, following a Bill by the chairman of the Constitutional Implementation Oversight Committee, saved the day by extending the time for the promulgation of the regulations. The EMB eventually submitted the election regulations, as amended and approved by Parliament, to the Government Printer for publication on 2 November 2012. While this ended the process of promulgating the Election (General) Regulations, 2012, the Election (Registration of Voters) Regulations, 2012, and the Election (Voter Education) Regulations, 2012, it is a stark reminder of the extent to which it is likely that the IEBC may not be able to discharge its obligations within the statutory deadlines. As elections are such high-pressure and time-sensitive events, this is very worrying.

The IEBC's weak capacity to enforce the law and its own regulations is in part a reflection of its vulnerability to the influence of and manipulation by political parties. Not only is this evident from the manner in which the RPP handled political parties flouting the Political Parties Act in the transition period, but also in the manner in which the IEBC has handled the nomination of special seat representatives. There was subsequently court action on the nominated members of county assemblies, in addition to the nomination of candidates for the direct elections before the general election and nominated members of the National Assembly and Senate. The IEBC has subsequently received some public condemnation for this as well, which adds to its general image problems with the rest of the electoral process.[282]

---

282 See Abdullahi, A (2013) 'Can the Electoral Body Pass Integrity Test?', *Daily Nation*, www.nation.co.ke/
    oped/Opinion/Can-the-electoral-body-pass-integrity-test/-/440808/1682802/-/2mdtv9z/-/index.html;
    Kegoro, G (2013) 'It's Sad That the IEBC Let Politicians Edge Minorities Out of Party Lists', *Daily Nation*,
    1 March 2013, elections.nation.co.ke/Blogs/-/1632026/1708404/-/118c8sn/-/index.html.

The IEBC chairman has reportedly opined that some of the commission's failures may have been due to the logistical challenges of running six elections simultaneously. He has proposed that the country considers whether it is viable and sustainable to have six elections on the same day.[283] He may well have a point, but in the absence of a well-reasoned opinion that weighs this supposed benefit against the likelihood of at least doubling Kenya's high electoral costs, it is not readily apparent that this will necessarily lead to an improvement in the IEBC's performance.

Finally, the law gives the IEBC prosecutorial powers in regard to election offenders. As indicated elsewhere in this report, the IEBC has even tried to put together a fledgling investigative and prosecution team to enable it to discharge this mandate. Its output from the 2013 elections, compared to all the allegations of malfeasance, is nevertheless not apparent. Either this is proof that the EMB was (and should henceforth be) focused on running an election rather than prosecuting malfeasance, or that the team needs to be radically revamped. Either way, the country's response to electoral malfeasance is not strong enough to send a clearly deterrent message to would-be election offenders about the cost of committing electoral crimes.

Insufficient electoral transparency and accountability

Electoral transparency was one of the weakest aspects of Kenya's electoral process before 1992. However, to its credit, the ECK had consistently taken transparency to a level where citizens trusted it – especially between 2002 and 2007. Surprisingly, this aspect seems to have weakened with the advent of a stronger EMB. For instance, while the ECK used to make public the results of many of its electoral exercises, the IIEC and the IEBC have been a bit opaque in this regard. Coupled with the kind of anxiety momentarily witnessed in the display of the results of the 2010 referendum and in the recent by-elections, this has the potential of diminishing trust in the results, with the associated consequences.

It is not enough to publicly project the results on large screens as they come in. The EMB must have all the critical information in the election results audit trail publicly available to enable its accuracy and the absence of fraud to be ascertained. There is currently some disquiet over the fact that the 2013 general election results are still not publicly available, amid claims that the IEBC cannot account for disproportionately large discrepancies (some media reports put them at close to a million votes) between the vote tallies in the presidential and other elections and that this has, among others, affected the distribution of the monies due to political parties from the Political Parties

---

283 IFES (2013) 'IEBC Chairman Reflects on Kenya's 2013 General Election and Future', www.iebc.or.ke/index.php/news-archive/286-june-2013/491-iebc-chairman-reflects-on-kenyas-2013-general-elections-and-future.

Fund.[284] This is not just an image problem for the IEBC, but could potentially reduce public confidence in both the IEBC and the Supreme Court (depending on how it handles any dispute emanating from such controversy).

Election results are such an important part of the reform of the Kenyan electoral process that analysts should not be second-guessing the EMB or deriving their accuracy from survey methodology such as the parallel vote tabulation employed by ELOG (Table 3.6). The only thing that will restore public trust is the final results in a form that will put all electoral role players at the same level in terms of the primary data, and in a form that opens up the results processing system and its products to independent verification.

Table 3.6: Comparison of parallel vote tabulation (PVT) and official results

Candidate	PVT projections	Margin of error	Range		Official IEBC result
			lower limit	Upper limit	
Kenyatta Uhuru	49.7%	2.7%	47.0%	52.4%	50.07%
Odinga Raila	43.4%	2.5%	40.9%	45.9%	43.31%
Mudavadi Musalia	4.2%	0.8%	3.4%	5.0%	3.93%
Peter Kenneth	0.6%	0.1%	0.5%	0.7%	0.59%
Dida Mohamed	0.5%	0.1%	0.4%	0.6%	0.43%
Karua Martha Wangari	0.4%	0.0%	0.3%	0.4%	0.36%
Kiyiapi James Legilisho	0.3%	0.0%	0.3%	0.4%	0.33%
Muite Paul Kibugi	0.1%	0.0%	0.1%	0.1%	0.10%
Rejected	0.9%	0.1%	0.8%	0.9%	0.88%

Source: ELOG Final statement (9 March 2013)

It is important to remember that the Kenyan EMB was designed to be both independent and accountable. Not only is it required to submit to the authority of the courts and explain itself before the relevant parliamentary committees, but it also finds itself in an environment where citizens know a lot more than they knew in the days of its precursors, and demand even more. In recent days, the EMB has had to explain not only its decisions on election requirements (such as nomination fees charged to candidates), but also the manner in which it has managed processes (such as the acquisition of the BVR kits).

284 See 'IEBC Wants Political Parties Act Amended', *The Star*, 23 May 2013, www.the-star.co.ke/news/article-121442/iebc-wants-political-parties-act-amended; Kegoro, G (2013) 'Hassan Should Stop Chasing Shadows and Release Pending Poll Vote Tallies', *Daily Nation*, www.nation.co.ke/oped/Opinion/IEBC-should-stop-chasing-shadows/-/440808/1875006/-/dar116/-/index.html; 'Independent Electoral and Boundaries Commission to Release the Elective Posts Vote Tallies', *The Standard*, 24 June 2013, www.standardmedia.co.ke/?articleID=2000086728&story_title=iebc-to-release-elective-posts-vote-tallies.

Credibility of the voters' register

To revise the much-discredited voters' register used in the 2007 general election, the IEBC resorted to BVR. However, the process of acquisition of the BVR system was marred with such opacity and controversy that it seriously damaged the EMB's image and disrupted its election planning. Intended as a technology-aided revision of the register, the process began with an international open tender for the acquisition of the BVR kits. However, as it progressed, certain interests appear to have weighed in strongly, followed by accusations of improper conduct – both by disgruntled suppliers and the EMB's leadership. Eventually, the IEBC cancelled the exercise altogether in August 2012 and announced that it would instead use the traditional manual system of registration. This immediately raised concerns over voter fraud and generated even more political controversy.

Despite public concern over what this meant for the IEBC's independence, the Cabinet finally stepped in and struck a deal with the Canadian government to procure the kits on a loan to the government of Kenya. The contract was eventually awarded by a Canadian Crown corporation to the French company Safran Morpho, which delivered the kits in three batches, with the last batch arriving on 2 November 2012. The manner in which the BVR procurement was handled and the ensuing controversy dented the IEBC's image with respect to the integrity of its systems and officers. It also delayed voter registration by over six months. As a consequence, the time originally set aside for voter registration had to be reduced to 30 day, while the IEBC proposed to Parliament that the time for inspection of the voters' register be reduced to 15 days. Parliament obliged by passing the Statute Law (Miscellaneous Amendments) Act, 2012. It does not help matters that the electronic poll books and the results transmission system eventually failed and are now the subject of EACC and parliamentary scrutiny.[285]

The IEBC argues that its use of multiple registers and the Green Book are allowed by the law; the Supreme Court agrees. The problem with this situation, though, is that it fails to allay the traditional suspicion generated by a register that is perceived by electoral role players as a moving target. Even if the reasons for the IEBC needing the Special Register and the Diaspora Register are valid, there is still a feeling that registration issues should have been settled with finality at some reasonable point before Election Day. To some electoral role players, this was not necessarily the case and they saw the Supreme Court as giving the IEBC a blank cheque.[286] Resort to the Green Book further evokes memories of the former registration system, which used optical mark readers but also had a Green Book as a fall-back position. The Green Book cannot be trusted as the primary reference when there has been a sizeable investment in technology and the public has been assured all along that technology will provide safeguards against past

---

285 'Investigations into the IEBC On-going', *The Star*, www.the-star.co.ke/news/article-117343/investigations-iebc-ongoing-eacc.

286 See, for example, 'Verdict on Kenya's Presidential Election Petition: Five Reasons the Judgment Fails the Legal Test', *The East African*, 20 April 2013, www.theeastafrican.co.ke/OpEd/comment/Five-reasons-Kenya-Supreme-Court-failed-poll-petition-test/-/434750/1753646/-/297c6q/-/index.html.

inaccuracies in the voters' register. This is no way to build confidence in the accuracy of the register, a key confidence-building measure that is far from achieved.

Credibility of the result tallying and transmission systems

The gravamen of the presidential election disputes in the last election was the results:

- The aggregate results;
- Results in specific electoral areas;
- The effect of rejected votes on the final tallies; and
- Allegations of fraud.

In certain ways, this mirrored the 2007 presidential election dispute – the only difference in 2013 being the lack of widespread violence.

According to IEBC accounts, nothing untoward happened:

- The server processing the provisional results crashed on election night;
- Engineers replaced its hard disks;
- By then the returning officers had decided to physically deliver the results to Nairobi;
- There were network issues in some areas (yet mobile telephone networks Safaricom and Airtel could not communicate on the same platform to provide the necessary redundancy);
- Some phones (e.g. in Mombasa) were not configured; and
- Information technology staff explained the difficulties using jargon, which did not help.[287]

The upshot, though, is that this was the beginning of the erosion of confidence in the results. The delayed release of the final results months after the elections (and in a form that can withstand public audit or scrutiny) still raises questions about the IEBC's transparency and accountability to the voting public, if not its overall competence as an EMB. Admittedly, some errors in the final results tallies may have been the result of fatigue, but a good results management system picks these out and provides administrative remedies before the final results are confirmed and the winners gazetted.

Ultimately, the most significant challenge from a public trust standpoint is the failed implementation of the IEBC's technological investments in the electoral process and the cloud of illegitimacy that hangs over the results of the 4 March 2013 general election – especially in the presidential elections. While the IEBC has readily owned up to technological failures, the results of the presidential election eventually were the subject of court action. In different circumstances, the Supreme Court's decision on a matter such as this would not just determine the dispute before the court, but also lay down progressive legal principles to be followed by other courts. Unfortunately, both the results

---

287   Interview with IEBC official.

and the Supreme Court's decisions are controversial. The IEBC and the Supreme Court have been roundly criticised in almost equal measure.[288] Recent opinion polls measuring public confidence in the IEBC reflect a dramatic drop in public trust – to 32% in the Ipsos Synovate poll and 44% in the Infotrak poll.[289] This has also had knock-on effects on public confidence in the Supreme Court, whose rating was down to 34% in the Ipsos Synovate poll, following the Supreme Court's decision on the presidential election petitions filed after the 4 March 2013 elections. The confidence in other courts was 18% at the time. The aftermath of the 2007 general election is enough evidence of the danger of going into another election without an unimpeachably clean and transparent results tallying and transmission system.

I. Recommendations

Given the foregoing assessment, what should be done to improve election management in Kenya? There are a number of unresolved issues from the last general election and the IEBC's role in it that suggest a continuing need for reforms. This section presents a number of points around which a post-2013 reform debate can be constructed for policy dialogue by electoral role players across the board and, above all, with the EMB:

- Establish an accurate voters' register by August 2017.
- Build a transparent, accountable results management system.
- Strengthen IEBC capacity to run efficient, effective electoral operations.
- Improve separation of board and management of the IEBC.
- Improve detection of malfeasance and enforcement of electoral laws.
- Improve accountability and transparency.
- Take tangible measures to rebuild public trust in elections.
- Deepen and strengthen regional collaboration with other EMBs.
- Make the electoral process more fair and inclusive.
- Prioritise voter education and conduct it continuously.
- Strengthen the electoral legal framework.

Establish an accurate voters' register by August 2017

Now that it has the necessary BVR solution, the IEBC should resume the continuous registration of voters and clean up all the issues that arose from the previous registration. There is now sufficient opportunity for the EMB to come up with a credible register that is certified for the 2017 elections without the shortcomings and controversies that attended the present register. It is not only a substantial trust builder, but will go a long way towards cleaning up a register that will have begun to slide into obsolescence,

---

288 See Maina, W (2013) 'Verdict on Kenya's Presidential Election Petition: Five Reasons the Judgment Fails the Legal Test', *The East African*, 30 April 2013, www.theeastafrican.co.ke/OpEd/comment/Five-reasons-Kenya-Supreme-Court-failed-poll-petition-test/-/434750/1753646/-/297c6q/-/index.html.

289 Commissioned by AfriCOG.

as all registers at some point do, and to generally learn from the operational failures that made the 2013 register a contentious matter. Above all, it will be important to comply with the requirements of section 4 of the Elections Act rather than rely on the problematic decision of the Supreme Court in regard to the validity of the voters' register.

Build a transparent, accountable results management system

While electoral fraud plagues many elections world-wide, even in advanced democracies, it can result in serious governance crises in deeply divided societies such as Kenya. A critical confidence-building measure that the IEBC can put in place before the next general election is to establish transparency requirements throughout the entire results audit trail and to make the information publicly available by using technology. This is not merely a good thing to do: the Constitution and electoral law require it. If anything, the IEBC predecessor ECK was able to ensure even better availability of results data and the new EMB was expected to improve upon it.

At the very least, a spreadsheet of the results of the presidential election (which is usually the most problematic) should be made available in a timely manner following the declaration of the winner. Polling station data should be available electronically in easily accessible formats rather than the present PDF data dumps on the EMB's website, which do not download efficiently if they do at all.

The IEBC should also institute post-election audits on a sample basis to double-check the accuracy of at least the presidential results prior to their final declaration. The marginal cost of these post-election audits is more than justified by their reinforcement of the integrity of the results. This way, either all electoral stakeholders can analyse the results and detect any malfeasance (or lack thereof) or the transparency will act as a powerful deterrent to electoral fraud.

Strengthen IEBC capacity to run efficient, effective electoral operations

There is an urgent need to focus debate on the institutional and operational failures that reduced the quality of the 2013 general election, with a view to remedying these defects before the next elections. A system-wide organisational assessment of the IEBC's institutional structures, work-flows and ability to discharge its mandate is a crucial first step, and should inform the critical capacity investments that are required to make the EMB more effective, for example:

- Board and management separation;
- Clarity on decision-making scope;
- Institutionalisation of recording critical decisions;
- Improvements in enforcement; and
- The infusion of greater transparency and accountability in its operations.

These investments should focus on the long-term goal of establishing a credible EMB that can withstand successive leadership changes, is increasingly de-personalised, and can consistently deliver credible elections through several electoral cycles beyond the next general election in August 2017.

The IEBC needs to train its staff to act impartially at all times. Employees or temporary election workers who display bias should be appropriately disciplined in accordance with the EMB's policies, and prosecuted if the infractions amount to criminal offences. All electoral law violations should be comprehensively and competently dealt with, irrespective of the social position of the offender.

Against the backdrop of the BVR saga and accusations of favouritism in staffing, the IEBC should review its procurement and hiring systems to ensure that it deals sufficiently with these integrity issues. Strengthening its internal audit function should also be a priority before the next elections. In a country where electoral expenses are competing for resources with the provision of much-needed infrastructure and basic service delivery, it is not enough to exhort people that democracy does not come cheaply.

The IEBC should conduct a comprehensive analysis of its cost per vote in the recently concluded general election and determine how to bring it down in future elections. Thereafter, it should aim to consistently bring the cost down further to a sustainable level. Possible avenues for cost-saving include:

- Local printing of ballot papers (Kenya prints its money locally);
- Streamlining procurement (and reducing pilferage and waste);
- Maximising voter education through the state broadcaster as a free public service;
- Instituting efficiency measures to avoid sequencing elections; and
- Aligning voter registration to the Integrated Population Registration System that the government intends to establish.

The IEBC should continuously review its systems and improve on them. It should particularly revisit its human resource management systems with a view to stamping out perceptions of favouritism. In order to forestall future procurement scandals, it should conduct a systems audit and improve its procurement systems. Overall, it should institutionalise election audits and evaluations in order to learn from all its electoral exercises, especially major ones like the forthcoming general election. The results of these exercises should also be documented for institutional memory and stored in a manner that facilitates easy retrieval for improved knowledge management and electoral practice.

Improve separation of board and management of the IEBC

The policy-making remit of the commissioners needs to be clearly delineated and the administrative remit of the secretariat should be outlined in the policy documents of the IEBC. Undeniably, there is no hard and fast rule about this separation and grey areas will still exist; for example, the BVR procurement was an operational issue, but seems to have consumed a great deal of the commissioners' time in managing its fallout, with continuing governance challenges for the EMB. Where overlaps exist, these should be highlighted and mechanisms of minimising organisational conflict set out. Otherwise, the country should consider the possibility of having part-time commissioners as a way of minimising board and management conflicts.

Improve detection of malfeasance and enforcement of electoral laws

Parliament, rather than the drafters of the Constitution, added the power to prosecute electoral offenders to the IEBC's mandate. By the IEBC's own admission, and from anecdotal examination of the institutional response to electoral malfeasance, the EMB has experienced challenges in enforcing electoral criminal law. It has tried to augment its capacity by establishing some inter-agency coordination with the office of the DPP, but this has not been effective.

Going forward, there are two likely paths (none necessarily better than the other) that the country could adopt:

- Either the IEBC should radically improve both its internal capacity to investigate and prosecute election offences and strengthen its inter-agency coordination with an independent DPP; or
- The law should be amended to put this prosecutorial power firmly in the hands of the DPP.

In the same vein, the IEBC should consider relinquishing jurisdiction in nomination disputes to the PPDT and the courts. In all other respects, the IEBC should ensure strict compliance with electoral law. While it should consult with all electoral role players, it should base its decisions solely on what is best for the electoral process, rather than the bargaining power of some electoral role players. It should also institute a policy of dealing decisively with critical election law breaches to send a message of zero tolerance for election offenders to the wider body of electoral role players.

Improve accountability and transparency

The IEBC should put in place a robust public communication strategy and mobilise resources for its implementation. While doing a good job is a large proportion of the expected service, communicating capably and managing public expectations is a nece--ssary adjunct to maintaining a positive image and public trust for the electoral process. The IEBC should consistently seek to improve its service delivery. Every electoral exercise is an opportunity not only to discharge its obligations, but also to learn about how to render its services better, more efficiently and more effectively. The IEBC should make customer satisfaction surveys a routine part of its service delivery through mechanisms such as an interactive website and exit surveys for appropriate events like voter registration and other areas of service provision that are amenable to such assessments.

Take tangible measures to rebuild public trust in elections

In the light of available public opinion data, there is reason to believe that unless tangible measures are instituted to rebuild broken trust, the run-up to the next general election will be marked by acrimony and calls either for the replacement of the current set of commissioners or their retention. Adverse public criticism seems to have generated an institutional siege mentality and withdrawal from public engagement in the IEBC that needs to be overcome if the institution is to make adjustments and keep improving. The EMB needs to reach out to the entire cross-section of electoral role players and constructively discuss how it can improve its effectiveness. Consideration should be given to a post-election audit that will enable the commission to gain even better insights on how to improve future performance. It should then follow through with the necessary action to ensure that it has regained public trust comparable to February 2013 levels or higher.

Deepen and strengthen regional collaboration with other EMBs

The IEBC should continue to deepen and strengthen regional and international collaboration with other EMBs and election support institutions. The objective of such collaboration and cooperation should be to consistently benchmark itself with the best regional and global standards in electoral practice, as well as to contribute to the furtherance of regional and global electoral democracy practices.

Make the electoral process more fair and inclusive

Following the Supreme Court's decisions on the gender quotas for elective offices, it is necessary to clarify how the country will progressively move towards meeting the threshold for representation by both genders. Some proposals have been mooted, including the Hon. Neto Agostinho's suggestion to reduce the number of elected leaders, but a thorough debate and some hard decisions will be necessary before August 2015 to ensure a fairer system before the 2017 general election. In the presidential system of government that Kenya now has, policy initiation resides with both the executive and the legislature. Either the Attorney-General or Parliament should initiate legislation to bring the country's election outcomes in line with its constitutional thresholds for gender and other representation.

Prioritise voter education and conduct it continuously

The country needs to move away from the current practice where voter education drives are only conducted close to general elections. To begin with, the state should take measures, including the revision of the school syllabus, to ensure all citizens with basic primary education understand Kenya's democracy and how to participate in it, including by voting. In the short to medium term, the state should adequately fund the provision of targeted voter education for diverse stakeholder groups in partnership with civil society and other civic education providers. The IEBC should provide leadership in the development of a national curriculum, set standards for voter education provision and monitor the provision of voter education.

Strengthen the electoral legal framework

The period after the promulgation of the 2010 Constitution and before the 2013 general election saw profound changes in the country's electoral laws. There are, however, still some issues that should be addressed with a view to further strengthening the legal framework. The time to negotiate changes to the constitutional and legal framework is now, rather than later. The IEBC should lead stakeholder discussions on critical constitutional and legal reforms necessary for the further improvement of Kenya's elections. Examples of possible reforms include:

- Realising the affirmative action principle on elective offices;
- Enlarging the IEBC's preparation time, which was reduced in the various electoral law amendments in the run-up to the 2013 general election;
- Passing the Election Campaign Financing Bill;
- Creating the proper institutional locus for settling nomination disputes and prosecuting electoral offences;
- Choosing between holding national and county elections on separate days and keeping them on the same day; and
- The possibility of making some further changes to the country's electoral system.

Other policy issues may also result in changes to the country's election laws.

4

Rwanda

Patrick Osodo

A. Summary

Rwanda's legal and institutional framework for elections is a product of its history, cha-racterised by decades of manipulation, violence and divisions based on ethnicity. This history, which culminated in the 1994 genocide of the Tutsi, has inspired fear and dimi-nished the incentives for free and active political expression among Rwandans. It has left in its wake a political culture of deference to authority that threatens the prospects of building a society where politicians and citizens alike can engage constructively on the basis of competing political ideas.

Over the past 18 years, Rwanda has made remarkable progress towards overcoming the burden of its history and building a society founded on the rule of law and good gov-ernance. At the heart of this progress is a resolve to 'never again' suffer another civil war or genocide. This is the primary organising basis of the country's statecraft and politics. The salient features of this resolve are captured in the country's 2003 Constitution, in a set of core commitments and principles that include pledges to fight the ideology of genocide in all its manifestations, eradicate divisionism, promote national unity and reconciliation, and protect and promote the enjoyment of fundamental human rights, including the rights to free speech, association and assembly. The Constitution also opens up the country for political pluralism through the principles of power-sharing, consensus, equality and non-discrimination.

The legal framework for the administration and management of elections derives from the Constitution and is designed to address unique domestic needs while seeking conformity with international standards and best practices. It comprises a continuously improving electoral code and a set of laws prohibiting discrimination, genocide ideology and defamation, while governing other aspects of elections such as political organising and the conduct of the media. These are buttressed by an effective national institutional infrastructure comprising a strong election management body (EMB) – the National

Electoral Commission – and a highly efficient system of national and local government administration. Ten political parties are registered and contest elections regularly under a set of governing laws. This framework remains saddled, however, with a range of fundamental legal and institutional challenges seen by observers as constraining legitimate political debate and freedom of expression. The challenges are manifested in a pre-election period and overall electoral environment often characterised by tension, suppression of critical opposition voices and media, and a general absence of plural, competitive political views.

The National Electoral Commission (NEC), which is the institution responsible for the administration of elections, is vastly improved since its establishment in 2000 and has instituted a wide range of electoral reforms. Opinion is, however, divided on its independence, capacity and ability to deliver free, fair and transparent elections.

On the one hand, the NEC has over the past years demonstrated a high level of organisational capacity in handling elections, evidenced in a number of ways:

- Its continuous self-renewal through regular revisions and updates of the laws governing its activities;
- Its respect for the overall electoral time table;
- The competence of its representatives across the country;
- The adequate numbers and distribution of polling stations and centres country-wide, giving voters easy access to, and allowing for efficient handling of, the voting exercise;
- The efficient deployment of electoral personnel and materials; and
- The efficient enforcement of electoral laws and procedures in a generally equal manner.

On the other hand, some see it as a body that is controlled by the executive and, therefore, constrained in terms of its ability to guarantee free, fair and transparent elections. This is manifested in a number of ways:

- The composition of its commissioners and officials at all levels, including polling agents, who comprise persons seen largely as affiliated or sympathetic to the ruling party;
- Cases of the NEC not investigating or sanctioning the Rwanda Patriotic Front (RPF) and local government agents who commit electoral offences;
- The NEC's sanction powers, seen as excessive and sometimes applied in favour of the ruling party;
- The domination by RPF members of the colleges for the senatorial, mayoral and other elections under the indirect ballot system;
- The NEC's locking out of election observers during certain key stages of the electoral process, such as the vote tabulation, transmission and consolidation, thus limiting transparency;

- The last-minute withdrawal of candidature by some electoral contestants, believed to arise from 'pressure from above'; and
- Charges of NEC agents influencing voters to vote for some candidates.

There are also concerns over the lack of adequate procedural safeguards to guarantee and inspire confidence in the independence of these processes, and over the lack of formal inclusive mechanisms to review and agree on key electoral reforms, particularly following the conclusion of an electoral cycle.

Two major consequences of this lack of confidence in the independence of the NEC and in its ability to deliver free, fair and transparent elections are evident – the lack of interest among political candidates and parties in petitioning unsatisfactory electoral processes and outcomes through the NEC hierarchy or the courts, and the generally low appetite among these entities for exercising their right of oversight over key electoral processes such as vote counting, tabulation, transmission and consolidation.

A particular concern relates to the NEC's delivery of civic and electoral education, a key ingredient in advancing electoral democracy – and an area identified by observers as requiring deepening. Designed perhaps to suit Rwanda's unique circumstances, the NEC's and indeed the overall national focus of civic and electoral education seems oriented more towards propagating the values of patriotism and service and getting citizens to exercise an electoral obligation, rather than advancing the greater goal and imperative of encouraging citizens to participate fully in the political life of their communities and country, and to commit to fundamental values and principles of democracy. There is no comprehensive legal framework for the participatory development and delivery of civic and electoral education in the country as yet, and the scope and content of civic education remains narrowly defined and controlled largely by the NEC, with civil society and other stakeholders participating only at the commission's discretion. As a result, a comprehensive civil society programme for civic and electoral education has not evolved.

B. History and politics of elections

The electoral landscape in Rwanda today is the product of a history characterised by manipulation, violence and divisions based on ethnicity. These characteristics culminated in the Rwandan civil war of 1990–1993 and the 1994 Genocide in which close to 1 million Tutsis and moderate Hutus were killed.

Pre-independence Rwanda (Rwanda-Urundi)

Pre-colonial Rwanda was a strong monarchy headed by a king, the *Mwami*.[290] Rwanda first became a German protectorate in 1884. Six years later, in 1890, it became part of German East Africa. In 1919, following the end of the First World War, Rwanda was administered by Belgium, under the mandate of the League of Nations. In 1946, with the end of the Second World War, it became a United Nations (UN) trust territory under Belgian administration. This period also marked the beginning of Rwanda's transition towards modern-day government. Under the trusteeship, the Belgian colonial administration was required to implement a plan for political, social and economic reforms in the colony.

The mid-1950s saw increased demands for self-rule among the Tutsi ruling elite opposed to Belgian colonial rule. It also saw an emergence of a Hutu counter-elite opposed to the monarchy and demanding greater social and economic opportunities, as well as political rights. In 1959, the Tutsi elite formed a political party, the *Union Nationale Rwandaise* (UNAR) to claim Rwanda's independence as a constitutional monarchy. In the same year, encouraged by the Belgian authorities, the Hutu counter-elite formed a rival political party, *Parti de l'émancipation du peuple Hutu* (Parmehutu). Two other political parties were founded around the same time – the Association for Social Promotion of the Masses (*Association pour la Promotion Sociale des Masses*, APROSOMA), a predominantly ethnic Hutu party, and the Rwandese Democratic Rally (*Rassemblement Démocratique Rwandais*, RADER), a more multi-ethnic party.

In November 1959, a spate of ethnically motivated violence erupted and spread across the whole country following the attack on Dominique Mbonyumutua, a popular Hutu leader and one of only ten Hutu vice-chiefs at the time.[291] Following the violence, the Belgian administration imposed a state of emergency, placed the country under military occupation and introduced a wide range of political and administrative changes, mostly favouring the Hutu. In one profound change, it replaced all the Tutsi chiefs and vice-chiefs who had been killed or displaced during the violence and others who were relieved of their duties[292] with Hutus. Most UNAR members were removed from local administration structures and replaced by APROSOMA, Parmehutu and RADER

---

290 For more reading on the history of Rwanda, see Prunier, G (1995) *The Rwanda Crisis 1859–1994: A History of a Genocide*; Mamdani, M (2002) *When Victims Become Killers: Colonialism, Nativism, and the Genocide in Rwanda*, Princeton, NJ, Princeton University Press; Anastase, S (2004) *The Rwandan Conflict: Origin, Development, Exit Strategies*; Kagame, A (1954) *Les organisations socio-familiales de l'ancien Rwanda*, Brussels; Chretien, J-P (2003) *Afrique des Grands Lacs, 2000 ans d'histoire*, Flammarion, Paris.

291 Viret, E (2010) 'Rwanda: A Chronology (1867–1994)', *Online Encyclopaedia of Mass Violence*, March 2010 edition, www.massviolence.org/fr/pdf version?id_Article=108.

292 According to Lemarchand, R (1970) *Rwanda and Burundi*, London, Pall Mall Press, p. 172, then Belgian Proconsul, Colonel Logiest, made profound changes in the composition of Rwandan administrative personnel. Of the 45 chiefs in office, 23 were dead, or had fled during the violence, as well as 158 of the 489 vice-chiefs. Logiest set up a policy to systematically replace the chiefs and the vice chiefs who were missing, had fled or had been relieved of their duties with Hutus. In the end, the administration was split 50:50 between Hutus and Tutsis.

supporters. In mid-1960, amid continuing violence, a commune-level elections were conducted for mayors and local councillors in which the Hutu parties, supported by the administration, received a massive electoral victory. Following the insurrection, Parmehutu made substantial changes to its political ideology, seeking independence under a constitutional republic where previously it had favoured a constitutional monarchy. At a party congress in May 1960, it added the suffix MDR (*Mouvement Démocratique Républicain*, or Democratic Republican Movement) to underline its break with the monarchy. UNAR and RADER protested against this racist position. In October of the same year, an interim council and government were installed based on the results of the June elections, with Grégoire Kayibanda as head. These elections had been met with protests from UNAR and RADER and were largely boycotted by supporters of the two parties. At a meeting in the UN in October 1960, *Mwami* Kigeri protested against the establishment of institutions imposed by Belgium.[293]

On 28 January 1961, a meeting of mayors and district councillors, called with the tacit support of the Belgian administration, decided to abolish the monarchy and to establish a republic. It elected Dominic Mbonyumutua as the President of the Republic and Grégoire Kayibanda as Prime Minister. It also elected a legislative assembly and appointed a government and a Supreme Court.[294] On 1 February 1961, the new legislative assembly adopted a Constitution.

These developments occurred in contravention of UN resolutions 1579, 1580 and 1605 of late 1960 and early 1961, passed to guide Rwanda's transition to independence in the final years of the Belgian trusteeship. The resolutions had laid out clear transitional steps and urged the administration, among other things, to:

- Abolish the emergency regime;
- Grant amnesty to those charged with offences linked to political violence;
- Allow an expeditious return and rehabilitation of thousands of Tutsi refugees forced into exile by the violence to enable them to participate in democratic political activities;
- Facilitate a reconciliatory conference of political parties before holding legislative elections;
- Reinstate and allow the return of the Mwami and oversee a popular referendum to ascertain people's wishes regarding him and his institution; and
- Oversee the formation of a caretaker government to conduct legitimate legislative elections leading to independence.[295]

Rwanda thus became a republic before gaining independence. At the UN, Belgium was the only state to implicitly recognise the legitimacy of what was widely regarded as a

---

293 Viret (2010), op. cit.; see also Reyntjens, F (1985) *Pouvoir et droit au Rwanda: Droit public et évolution politique, 1916–1973*, Tervuren, Musée Royal de l'Afrique Centrale, p. 285.
294 Viret (2010), op. cit.
295 Article 76, legal.un.org/repertory/art76/english/rep_supp3_vol3-art76_e.pdf.

coup d'état by governmental bodies established by irregular and unlawful means.[296] In a reverse move to show compliance with the resolutions, the Belgian administration suspended the government established on 28 January 1961 and implemented a few of the resolutions, among them those granting amnesty for political crimes. There was, however, no agreement on the establishment of a caretaker government.

On 25 September 1961 – amid a new wave of violence that saw 150 people killed, 3,000 homes burnt and more than 20,000 Tutsis displaced and forced into exile, and during which several members of the UNAR and APROSOMA parties were arrested – the UN supervised legislative assembly elections and a referendum on the monarchy. A total of 95.2% of all registered voters cast their ballots. Two ballot questions were framed on the retention of the monarchy:

> Should the monarchy in Rwanda be preserved?
> Should Kigeri V remain the King of Rwanda?

On both questions the vote was an overwhelming *No* by 80% of the voters. Both institutions were subsequently abolished. In the legislative elections, Parmehutu won the majority stake (77.6%), followed by UNAR (16.9%), APROSOMA (3.6%) and RADER (0.3%).[297]

Early in October of the same year, the new legislative assembly proclaimed the establishment of a republican regime. Grégoire Kayibanda was elected President of the Republic of Rwanda. This transition, in the midst of violence, and in contravention of the transitional arrangements laid out in the UN resolutions, caused the UN to embark on a mission to reconcile the country and to oversee the realisation of the remaining resolutions prior to granting independence to Rwanda. It subsequently established a conciliation group and a UN Commission for Rwanda-Urundi to address these resolutions, among them:

- The reconciliation of political factions;
- The return and resettlement of Tutsi refugees;
- The restoration of human rights and fundamental freedoms; and
- The maintenance of law and order.

The commission also sought to oversee the withdrawal of Belgian forces, to settle the question of the *Mwami* of Rwanda and that of economic and social support to Rwanda upon attainment of independence.[298]

In early June 1962, satisfied that these conditions had been broadly met, the UN adopted Resolution Number 1746, which would terminate the trusteeship agreement

---

296 By voting against UN resolution 1605, Belgium implicitly supported the abolition of the monarchy. Belgium also affirmed that legislative elections would be held, as well as a referendum for or against the monarchy.

297 'Elections in Rwanda', *African Elections Database*, africanelections.tripod.com/rw.html, accessed 23 October 2012.

298 Article 76, legal.un.org/repertory/art76/english/rep_supp3_vol3-art76_e.pdf, eaccessed 23 October 2012.

and pave the way for granting full independence to Rwanda.[299] On 1 July 1962, the trusteeship agreement was terminated and Rwanda emerged as an independent and sovereign state, along with Burundi. On 18 September 1962, Rwanda and Burundi were admitted as members of the UN.[300]

Rwanda's transition to independence during the period 1959–1962 was thus a difficult introduction to electoral politics. While the democratic ideals of elections and majority rule were upheld, three salient features of the transition denied it legitimacy and credibility:

- First, the elections and the referendum occurred within a highly polarised and vitriolic environment characterised by ethnic hatred, violence and manipulation, as well as massive displacement and exile of large sections of a group of the population. The electoral environment did not, therefore, offer the conditions necessary for free expression, free association or free and fair elections.
- Second, all the political parties created at the time were founded on ethnic platforms to defend and advance ethnic rather than national political, social and economic interests.
- Third, the elections – indeed the entire transition project – were led by an arbiter (Belgium) with vested political interests who steered and manipulated them to suit its interests.

These features would have a huge impact on Rwanda's electoral politics and democratic evolution in subsequent years, as will be illustrated in the subsequent sections of this chapter.

The First Republic (1962–1973)

Rwanda attained independence on 1 July 1962 as a constitutional republic with Grégoire Kayibanda as its President. However, as the new nation embarked on the path to self-government, the pattern of violence, political repression and electoral gerrymandering did not end. Disenfranchised and marginalised, the minority Tutsi community continued to mobilise politically and militarily under UNAR, mostly from Burundi and Uganda, where the majority of its members had taken refuge. From there, they continued to mount unsuccessful incursions into Rwanda: Parmehutu used these attacks as a pretext to consolidate internal unity and continue its persecution of the political opposition. Reinforced by the attacks, Parmehutu pursued and executed all leading legislators of UNAR and RADER, effectively putting an end to organised Tutsi politics in Rwanda for close to 30 years. It is estimated that between 1952 and 1967, more than 20,000 Tutsis were killed during the repression of UNAR.[301] Some 200,000 other Tut-

---

299 Ibid.
300 Ibid., p. 24.
301 Kuperman AJ (2004) *The Limits of Humanitarian Intervention: Genocide in Rwanda*, Brookings Institution Press, p. 63.

sis fled into exile, while those who remained continued to be subjected to state-sponsored violence and institutionalised discrimination. The first pronouncements by Hutu leaders of possible genocide against the Tutsis began to emerge around this time.[302]

With UNAR and RADER liquidated and their leaders killed, the focus turned to APROSOMA and its members: between 1964 and 1967, they too were gradually eased out of any political and administrative responsibility.[303] These acts of suppression and persecution gradually killed off all forms of grassroots activism in the post-independence state, leaving in its wake a docile, dependent and unquestioning population totally beholden to the mercies of an authoritarian government. This unquestioning obedience would play a tragic and central role in the unfolding of the 1994 Genocide. Between 1962 and 1965, Parmehutu dominated the political landscape, winning all presidential, parliamentary and communal elections by an overwhelming majority.[304] During the period 1965–1969, it managed to consolidate itself as the sole legal party, staying in power until 1973. In 1968, it changed its name to become the National Party of Rwanda (*Parti National du Rwanda*, NPR). With the opposition vanquished, the party's attention focused inwards, exposing considerable internal tensions previously concealed by the struggle against the Tutsis.

These tensions resulted largely from young school-leavers and graduates unable to find employment, and a critical northern Hutu political class feeling marginalised and sidelined in the affairs of government, which they saw as favouring the President's southern and central political and social elites. Keen to open up new grievances against the government, this disaffected class blamed the lack of employment of the majority Hutu on the poor implementation of the regional and ethnic quota system,[305] particu-

---

302 For example, on 23 December 1963, during a Parmehutu rally, Andre Nkeramugaba, the prefect of Gokongoro called for the assassination of the Tutsi. In response, groups of Hutus armed with spears, clubs and machetes, killed nearly 8,000 Tutsi women and children (Reyntjens (1985), op. cit., p. 465). Violence spread to the surrounding areas of Rusomo and Bugesera and up to 14,000 may have fallen victim in total (Lemarchand (1970), op. cit., pp. 224–225). In another incident, Grégoire Kayibanda, during an 11 March 1964 speech to Rwandans in exile, announced that if the troops raised by the refugees were to take the capital, this would lead to the total and sudden end of the Tutsi race (Chretien (2003), op. cit., p. 268; Semelin J (2005) *Purify and Destroy: The Political Uses of Massacre and Genocide*, Hurst Publishers, p.69.

303 Mamdani (2002), op. cit., p. 13; Prunier (1995), op. cit., pp. 57–58.

304 Parmehutu received 97.9% of the votes in the communal elections held on 18 August 1963; won an unopposed 100% mandate in the October 1965 presidential and legislative elections, and was re-elected again by the same margin in the second presidential and legislative elections held on 28 September 1969.

305 The quota system was a state policy introduced to redress historical wrongs, not just between Tutsis and Hutus, but also between Hutus of the north and those of the southern and central provinces. A law introduced in 1985 captured the spirit of this system. In the school system, the selection into schools took into account the ethnic affiliation of the child. The Hutu received over 85% of the places, the Tutsi 10–15% and the Twa 1%. In employment, allocation of posts was first on a regional basis, 60% going to the northerners and 40% to the southerners. Within each region, allocation was divided between Hutu and Tutsi/Twa, the former receiving 90% and the latter 10%. The 10% was said to reflect the relative size of the Tutsi/Twa population in the country, although the 1956 population census had put this figure at 16%. The count in the 1978 census was down to slightly less than 10%.

larly within the country's tertiary education system – then still dominated by the better-educated members of the Tutsi community.

The government responded to this agitation by establishing a new law seizing control of the education system and engineering a purge. This resulted in the removal of hundreds of Tutsis from colleges and universities and other places of employment. These developments not only re-ignited the ethnic tensions in the country, resulting in a new wave of Tutsi exiles, but also generated a new class divide, pitting the poor against the rich and the Hutu political classes of the north against those of the southern and central provinces.

The divide between the North and the South widened and on 5 July 1973, Major General Juvénal Habyarimana, a northerner, led the army in a bloodless coup, declaring himself the new President of Rwanda and launching the Second Republic.

The Second Republic (1973–1994)

The Second Republic was launched on a reconciliatory platform, allowing limited participation by Tutsis in political life and recognising their right to live as Rwandans. However, these rights remained largely in the sphere of civic and civil society life. From 1973 until the early 1990s, there was only one Tutsi minister in a 19-member Cabinet, one Tutsi ambassador, two Tutsi deputies in a 70-seat National Assembly and two Tutsis in the 16-person central committee of the country's only political party.[306] Tutsis were denied access to the organs of power, the army and the local state. Apart from one Tutsi prefect, there was almost no Tutsi representation in local government.[307] Nonetheless, no major anti-Tutsi political violence was reported from Rwanda between 1973 and 1990. Life for Tutsis was almost normal, with a number of them engaged in business and enjoying good relations with the regime as long as they stayed out of politics.

Habyarimana brought stability to Rwanda and the country enjoyed progress on the economic and social front during the period 1974–1987. By 1987, Rwanda had the lowest debt, the lowest inflation rate and the highest rate of growth of gross national product in the region. The share of agriculture in the gross national product had gone down from 80% in 1962 to 48% in 1966; secondary activities had risen from 8% to 21% and services from 12% to 31%. Mortality rate was down; hygiene and medical care were improving, while the proportion of school-going children rose from 49.5% in 1978 to 61.8% in 1986. There were no political executions after 1982 and fewer political prisoners than in most countries.[308]

However, this progress came at a political price: Habyarimana outlawed all political parties, created his own National Revolutionary Movement for Development (*Mouvement révolutionnaire national pour le développement*, MRND) and declared Rwanda a

---

306 Mamdani (2002), op. cit., pp. 138–142.
307 Ibid.
308 Mamdani (2001), op. cit., pp. 144–145.

one-party state. The country became a highly centralised developmental dictatorship under a Council for National Development instead of a real Parliament.

On 17 December 1978, the MRND organised a constitutional referendum, whose main features were a presidential republic, no presidential term limits and a single legal party. The population voted 90% in favour of all three. A week later, on 24 December 1978, presidential elections were organised and Juvénal Habyarimana was elected unopposed with 98.99% of the votes. He was re-elected unopposed again in 1983 with 99.97% of the votes.[309] In the same year, he introduced legislative elections under the framework of the National Development Council. The legislators were exclusively Hutu males.[310]

The fortunes of the Habyarimana regime began to dwindle towards the end of the 1980s. As the country grew economically, a new social elite comprising teachers, nurses and local civil servants emerged, benefiting from the state's reach into rural areas and from the proceeds of new development projects. This elite removed itself completely from the reality of the rural poor, neglecting social redistribution networks and causing sharp social polarisation in rural areas. Corruption became rampant, with most corporations turning into sites for private accumulation by politicians and businessmen.[311] Meanwhile, power continued to be concentrated in the hands of the president's northern Hutu elite, dominated by an inner core controlled by his wife and her relatives. The slump in the international price of coffee (then the bedrock of Rwanda's economy) in the period 1985–1993, and the introduction, in 1991, of the World Bank structural adjustment programmes exerted further strain on Rwanda's economy and Habyarimana's regime.[312] In June 1990, France, Rwanda's major bilateral donor, made further aid to the country conditional on democratic reforms. Other voices, from local and international civil society, from the assembly of francophone states, and from the Vatican, joined the call. The following month, Habyarimana agreed to separate the party from the state and made pronouncements about a possible transition to a multi-party system of government. He subsequently established a national commission and gave it two years to propose a new democratic charter.

309 This near-total dominance by one political party or contestant in an election has generated a popular cliché in Rwanda's latter-day electoral and developmental parlance – 'Mirongo ijana kui ijana' or '100% out of 100%'.

310 Ngabo, M (2011) 'Rwanda: Elections Are Part of Country's Culture', The New Times, allafrica.com/ stories/201103071135.html, accessed 9 October 2012.

311 A 1975 presidential decree had given civil servants permission to do private business without restriction, including owning rented houses, purchasing rented vehicles and having interest in mixed economy or commercial enterprises.

312 According to Peter Urvin, income from coffee fell from a high of USD 144 million in 1985 to a meagre USD 30 million in 1993 Uvin P (1996) Development, Aid and Conflict: Reflections from the Case of Rwanda, UN University, pp. 9–11.. The International Monetary Fund structural adjustment programme prescriptions increased the country's fiscal deficit sharply from 12% in 1991 to 19% in 1993 and caused a devaluation of the Rwandan Franc by almost 65% between 1990 and 1992. Real GDP fell by 5.7% in 1989 and further by 2% and 8% in 1990 and 1993, respectively, raising the national debt and significantly lowering the per capita income, which dropped by nearly 40% between 1985 and 1989, from USD 330 to USD 200.

As these woes were taking their toll on the country, the Rwanda Patriotic Front (RPF), a political movement of Tutsi refugees abroad, was mobilising politically and militarily for a return to the country. In October 1990, its armed wing, the Rwandan Patriotic Army (RPA), invaded Rwanda from Uganda, adding momentum to the call for democratic reforms. The following month, Habyarimana declared his support for the establishment of a multi-party system and instructed the commission to complete the draft national political charter within the year. The charter, published in December 1990, endorsed the multi-party political arrangement, provided for the right of return of refugees to Rwanda and opened up the space for political pluralism and freedom of the media. In June 1991, a draft multi-party Constitution was approved and entered into force.

By July 1991, four opposition political parties had formed and established a coalition to dismantle Habyarimana's MRND:

- Republican Democratic Movement (*Mouvement Démocratique Républicain*, MDR);
- Social Democratic Party (*Parti Social Démocratique*, PSD);
- Liberal Party (*Parti Libéral*, PL); and
- Christian Democratic Party (*Parti Démocratique Chrétien*, PDC).

The MDR was the old MDR-Parmehutu without the appellation Parmehutu, reflecting a new inclusive outlook under the leadership of Faustin Twagiramungu. All the other parties embraced this new look, shunning ethnic politics and drawing membership from both Hutu and Tutsi.[313] In a further metamorphosis, the MRND adopted a new name – the National Republican Movement for Democracy and Development (*Mouvement Républicain National pour la Démocratie et le Développement*, MRNDD) – and agreed to separate itself from the state.

The period 1991–1993 thus witnessed intense multi-party political activity and the birth of a strong political opposition in the country. The first multi-party transitional government was set up in April 1992, based on an agreement signed by the parties in March, which included peace negotiations, the settlement of the refugee problem, and the organisation of elections.

The RPA was unsuccessful in its October 1990 offensive against the Rwandan army (*Forces armées rwandaises*, FAR), which was supported heavily by the French government. Subsequently, the RPA adopted a guerrilla strategy, mounting a series of incursions into Rwanda during the period 1991–1992, aimed both at buying time and forcing the MRND to the negotiating table. The incursions caused a hardening of positions among the local Hutu political elite and a surge in anti-Tutsi sentiment. The internal opposition that had united against Habyarimana began to re-organise and coalesce around a desire to 'defend' the country. There was a resurgence of 'Hutu Power' propaganda, with

---

313   Notable for this affirmative position were the PSD and PL, which deliberately attracted members from both Hutu and Tutsi ethnic groups and those of mixed parentage.

tension rising between the extremist elements opposed to Habyarimana's reconciliation efforts and the moderate forces that were keen to continue along the path of plural, inclusive democratic reforms already started. Within each political party, a hardliner faction known as 'Power' emerged, presenting its own candidates and rooting for an all-out war.[314] These tensions resulted in widespread arrests, violence, massacres, political assassinations and displacements across the country, targeting Tutsis and moderate Hutus. The organisers and perpetrators were Hutu extremists and a growing body of militant youth from the 'Power' factions, fuelled by sections of the media. An estimated 2,000 persons are believed to have died in this climate of economic decline, violence, war and repression.[315]

The first political contact with the RPF occurred in May 1992, launching a series of negotiations that became known as the Arusha Accords (also known as the Arusha Peace Agreement). The first of these was a ceasefire agreement signed in Arusha, Tanzania, in July 1992. Continued acts of violence in opposition to the negotiations, coupled with Habyarimana's own public pronouncements against the negotiations, and an RPA offensive in March 1993, however, brought an end to the ceasefire agreement. Displeased with these developments, donor countries and the World Bank threatened the regime with an aid freeze, forcing Habyarimana to sign the last of the accords on 4 August 1993.

The Arusha Peace Agreement, comprising five protocols, touched on a range of transitional issues seeking an end to the civil war and making way for the establishment of a transitional government. These included:

- Respect for the rule of law;
- Establishment of a broad-based transitional government (*Gouvernement de transition à base élargie*, GTBE);
- Power-sharing until the general election;[316]
- Repatriation and resettlement of refugees and displaced persons; and
- Integration of the FAR and the RPA.[317]

However, the implementation of the Arusha Peace Agreement did not materialise, because of fears that it favoured the RPF. The agreement gave cabinet positions to members of all six political parties. The 21 cabinet positions created under the GTBE were divided as follows:

---

314 The MRND had *Interahamwe* ('those who work together'), the CDR had *Impuzamugambi* ('those who share the same goal'), the MDR had *Inkuba* ('thunder') and the PSD had *Abakombozi* ('the liberators') (Human Rights Watch (1999), *Leave None to Tell the Story: the Genocide in Rwanda*, p. 71).

315 CIDH (1993), p. 48, cited in Viret (2010), op. cit., p. 30.

316 According to the agreement, the general elections ending the GTBE were planned to take place no later than 22 months after the signature of the Accord.

317 Peace agreement between the Government of the Republic of Rwanda and the Rwandese Patriotic Front, signed 3–4 August 1993, peacemaker.un.org/sites/peacemaker.un.org/files/RW_930804_PeaceAgreementRwanda-RwandesePatrioticFront.pdf.

- The MRNDD, the former ruling party, was given five, including the Defence portfolio.
- The RPF also received five positions, including the portfolio for the Interior and the office of Vice-Prime Minister.
- The MDR, the major opposition party, was given four positions, including the office of Prime Minister.
- The PSD and the PL each received three portfolios.
- The PDC received one.

The agreement also granted the RPF participation in the National Assembly and allowed it to constitute 40% of the national army.

In the months following the signing of the accords, attacks and assassinations escalated. They targeted mainly civilians and politicians opposed to Habyarimana and the Hutu Power movement, and were perpetrated by militias allied to both. The UN Assistance Mission for Rwanda (UNAMIR), the UN peacekeeping force dispatched to Rwanda to supervise the implementation of the accords, and already in the country by 1 November 1993, was unable to contain these attacks or disarm those responsible for them. Meanwhile, in line with the Arusha Accords, the first contingent of the RPF entered Kigali in December 1993 and embarked on a low-key recruitment and political mobilisation drive.[318]

On 6 April 1994, a presidential aircraft carrying Habyarimana, the Burundian president Cyprien Ntaryamira and ten other passengers was shot down shortly before it was due to land in Kigali. What followed was an orgy of systematic and horrific massacres and assassinations targeting members of the Tutsi community and opponents of Hutu Power.

The violence lasted for about 100 days until mid-July when the RPA gained control of the entire country. The assassinations and massacres were organised and executed by the army and the police, the political parties and their affiliated militias or power branches, as well as the national and local administration. Initially inspired and organised by the state, the massacres eventually became a nation-wide social project performed in private and in public spaces (including stadiums and churches) by hundreds of thousands of ordinary citizens – even including judges, human rights activists, doctors, nurses, priests, friends and spouses of the victims. Short on troops and denied the official mandate to use force, the UNAMIR forces under the command of General Romeo Dallaire were completely helpless in stopping the massacres.

The number of victims remains unknown but the figure of 800,000 Tutsis and moderate Hutus has become almost official. It has been estimated that up to 75% of Tutsi civilians were massacred. Other forms of violence and crime perpetrated during this period included an estimated 250,000 acts of rape. Some 2 million civilians,

---

318   Human Rights Watch (1999) op. cit., pp. 213–214.

mainly Hutus, are believed to have fled into the Democratic Republic of Congo and Tanzania in the course of the genocide and the civil war.

On 27 May 1994, the UN Security Council recognised the systematic massacre of Tutsi civilians as genocide. In November 1994, the Security Council adopted Resolution 955 to establish a tribunal to try those with the greatest responsibility for the Rwandan genocide. In the same month, the International Criminal Tribunal for Rwanda was created with the mandate to investigate and prosecute persons within and outside of Rwanda for crimes committed between January 1994 and December 1994 within Rwanda. In February the following year, a decision was taken to base the tribunal in Arusha, Tanzania.[319]

The political situation between 1962 and 1973, and leading into 1994 when the Rwandan Genocide occurred, can thus be summarised as follows:

- 1962–1965: restricted democratic practice;
- 1965–1973: one-party state (MDR-Parmehutu);
- 1973–1975: military regime;
- 1975–1978: de facto one-party state (MRND);
- 1978–1991: one-party state (MRND); and
- 1991–1994: multi-party transition.

The Third Republic (1994 to date)

The post-Genocide period can be divided into the transitional period (1994–2003) and the post-transition period (2003 to date). After the RPA established control over the country and halted the Genocide in July 1994, a new transitional government was quickly established, guided by the spirit of the Arusha Accords and the June 1991 Constitution. Faustin Twagiramungu was appointed as Prime Minister, with Pasteur Bizimungu as President and General Paul Kagame as Vice-President and Minister of Defence – this was a new post established outside of the Arusha framework to ensure control of the government by the RPF.

The new government immediately embarked on the extraordinary task of reconciling and building a new nation. Its immediate priorities were:

- Managing the emergency situation, which included repatriating and resettling refugees;
- Rehabilitating and reconstructing the national infrastructure and economy destroyed during the Genocide; and
- Ensuring national security and transitional justice.

The government prohibited any official recognition of ethnicity as it sought ways to prosecute the over 100,000 people who had been incarcerated in the Rwandan prisons and

---

319   Strauss S (2006) *The Order of Genocide: Race, Power, and War in Rwanda*, Cornell University Press, pp. 40–52.

communal jails for complicity in the Genocide and related crimes. Politically, it entailed the crafting of a new political ideology built around national unity.

Eight political parties formed the first transitional government:

- RPF;
- MDR;
- PSD;
- PL;
- PDC;
- *Union Démocratique du Peuple Rwandais* (UDPR);
- *Parti Démocratique islamique* (PDI); and
- *Parti Socialiste Rwandais* (PSR).

The MRNDD and the CDR, the two parties that orchestrated the Genocide, were banned from taking part in the government of national unity. Shortly after the new government took office, a 70-member Transitional National Assembly comprising representatives from all the parties was formed. Political party activities were limited to the national level. In 1999, the transitional government organised its first post-Genocide local elections under the supervision of the Ministry of Local Government. In April 2000, Paul Kagame succeeded Pasteur Bizimungu as President of the Transitional National Government.

The National Electoral Commission (NEC) was established in 2000. In 2002, it prepared and supervised the first election of leaders at the district level. Both the 1999 and 2001 elections were a great test case, coming towards the end of the transitional government. On 26 May 2003, the NEC organised a national referendum to adopt a new Constitution.[320] The Constitution, whose main features were a presidential republic, a bicameral Parliament and a ban on divisionism and genocide ideology, was passed by a 93.42% vote. In August 2003, Rwanda held its first democratic presidential elections, marking another watershed in the country's electoral history.

In October 2003, the first multi-party parliamentary elections were held. RPF leader Paul Kagame won the presidential election, garnering 95% of all the votes cast. His party, the RPF, won the parliamentary elections with 74% of the votes, obtaining 40 out of the 53 seats under the direct vote system. The PSD won seven seats and the PL six. The turnout for the elections was 96.6%.

These elections were followed by the August 2008 second parliamentary elections, which were again won by the RPF and its coalition members, taking 42 out of the 53 directly elected seats, with the PSD and the PL winning seven and four seats, respectively.

In August 2010 the second presidential election since the adoption of the Constitution

---

320 Constitution of the Republic of Rwanda (*Official Gazette*, Special Issue, 4 June 2003, p. 119) as amended on 2 December 2003 (*Official Gazette*, Special Issue, 2 December 2003, p. 11) and further amended on 8 December 2005.

was held. Again RPF's Paul Kagame won with an overwhelming majority of 93%. The RPF and its coalition partners also won the senatorial elections held in November 2011 and the local elections held in February 2012 by an overwhelming majority. The third parliamentary elections were planned for September 2013.

Despite a range of shortcomings, all these elections have been rated broadly as technically well organised, peaceful and well attended.[321] What is striking about them, however, is that they have followed the same pattern of near-total voter turnout and total domination of one political party over the others that characterised elections in the pre-Genocide republics. While there is consensus that the post-Genocide regime has presided over a period of unprecedented social and economic revival and progress, many observers have drawn parallels between it and the past regimes in regard to electoral democracy, pointing to similar electoral gerrymandering. In their comprehensive report on the 2003 Rwanda presidential and parliamentary elections, the Norwegian Resource Bank for Democracy and Human Rights (NORDEM) attributes this phenomenon to pressure on the population to vote for the ruling party candidates, and to repression, harassment, intimidation and co-optation of opposition candidates, manifested in a number of ways:

- Arrests of opposition candidates and their supporters;
- Forced cancellation of pre-planned campaign meetings;
- Dissolution and denial of registration and meeting permits for opposition parties;
- Systematic presence of ruling party agents and armed security personnel in polling stations; and
- Smear campaigns against opposition parliamentary candidates.

The report goes further to say that the RPF used its financial, administrative and coercive apparatus to prepare people to vote for its candidates.[322]

Similar accounts of pressure, repression and co-optation have been reported by other election observer missions in Rwanda in subsequent years. The European Parliament observer report of the 2008 parliamentary elections raises concerns of pressure on voters to participate in the elections and the systematic presence of RPF agents and armed security personnel at polling stations.[323]

The Commonwealth Elections Observer Mission in its report of the 2010 Rwanda presidential election notes that the electoral environment was heavily influenced by

---

321 All observer missions accredited to observe elections in Rwanda are in agreement regarding the peaceful and procedural conduct of elections; see, for example, Samset, I & Dalby, O (2003) *Rwanda: Presidential and Parliamentary Elections 2003*, NORDEM Report 12/2003; Schroder, J (2008) *European Parliament Delegation to Observe the Parliamentary Elections in Rwanda (12–18 September 2008)*, p. 3; Commonwealth Secretariat (2010) *Report of the Commonwealth Observer Group, Rwanda Presidential Elections, 9 August 2010*, pp. 11, 30–31; African Union (2010) report on the 2010 presidential elections, pp. 10–13.
322 Samset & Dalby (2003), op. cit.
323 Schroder (2008), op. cit., p. 4.

political developments in the period leading up to the elections.[324] According to the report, the period preceding and following the 2010 elections was characterised by controversy, insecurity and tension across different parts of the country. Evident fractures within President Paul Kagame's RPF party saw a number of its top leaders, now exiled, come out openly to criticise his style of leadership, accusing him of being 'an absolute ruler'.[325] In what was seen widely as an assassination attempt, one of these top leaders (a former close ally of the President) was attacked and almost killed inside his residence in South Africa.[326] The government of Rwanda denied any involvement.

The final weeks of the presidential campaigns saw a journalist and a top leader of an opposition political party brutally murdered in controversial circumstances. There were several grenade attacks targeting the city of Kigali, which killed and injured a number of citizens and which the government blamed on dissident elements opposed to President Kagame's rule. A number of newspapers and broadcasting stations were closed in the lead-up to the 2010 presidential election on charges of inciting public disorder.[327] Leading opposition political parties and their supporters were intimidated, arrested and prevented from either registering their political parties or carrying out effective campaign operations.[328] In the wake of these incidents, security was intensified countrywide, reinforcing a climate of fear that was not conducive to freedom of expression or free and fair elections.

Many observers reporting on elections and the human rights situation in Rwanda are united in their concern over an electoral environment often characterised by the following:

324 Commonwealth Secretariat (2010), op. cit., p. 13.
325 Kayumba, N, Karegeya, P, Rudasigwa, T & Gahima G (2010) Rwanda briefing, pp. 19–23.
326 General Kayumba Nyamwasa, Rwanda's former military chief and a close ally of President Paul Kagame, was shot in his car at his home in suburban Johannesburg on 19 June 2010 while returning with his wife from shopping. The assassins allegedly tried to finish the job after Nyamwasa was hospitalised.
327 In April 2010, the Media High Council suspended two independent newspapers, Umuvugisi and Umuseso, for six months, effectively preventing them from covering the presidential election campaigns. Charges against them included slander, abuse and defamation targeting the President and segments of the political class, the police and the army. Umuvugisi continued to publish an online version, which was also subsequently blocked in Rwanda.
328 The main opposition parties affected were the Green Democratic Party, the Forces Démocratiques Unifiées (FDU-Inkingi) and the Social Party Imberakuri (PS-Imberakuri). The Green Party made several attempts to register, but was unable to do so, because it failed to get the necessary documents signed by the relevant authorities. Its attempts to hold a party conference where the documents would be signed failed after unruly mobs chanting RPF slogans disrupted it. Lack of police clearance and denial of permission to meet by local authorities were the other reasons. It also failed to get the documents signed by the State Notary due to a lack of cooperation by the Minister of Justice and the Ministry of Local Government. FDU-Inkingi failed to get registration when its president, Ms Victoria Ingabire, was arrested and charged with a raft of crimes when she returned to the country to contest the presidency of Rwanda in the 2010 elections, after 16 years in exile. She was convicted two years later on charges of denying the Genocide and conspiring and planning to cause state insecurity. PS-Imberakuri failed to field a presidential candidate due to serious internal conflicts believed to have been fuelled by the RPF. Its leader, Mr Barnard Ntaganda, was ousted and arrested in April 2010 on charges of propagating genocide ideology, promoting ethnic division, attempted murder, terrorism and organising illegal meetings.

- A lack of critical opposition voices in the run-up to major national elections;
- Tensions, arrests and intimidation of opposition party leaders, their agents and the media;
- A continued inability of opposition political parties to register for and contest elections freely and fairly;
- A lack of media independence;
- Restrictions on the freedoms of expression and association; and
- The lack of adequate safeguards and transparency of the vote-counting and consolidation processes.

A major point of criticism in this regard relates to the way in which the Rwanda government has enforced the laws against genocide ideology, divisionism and defamation, seen by many observers as discouraging competitive political debate and resulting in the persecution and unlawful detention of those opposed to President Kagame's government.[329] Globally, President Kagame has come under heavy criticism from opposition figures and human rights groups for suppressing dissenting political voices and smothering opposition politics. Recent assassinations and assassination attempts involving persons opposed to President Kagame's rule and style of leadership have only served to entrench these criticisms.[330]

C. Legal framework for elections in post-genocide Rwanda

Rwanda's political and electoral history has had a profound impact on the legal and institutional framework it has subsequently adopted to guide its electoral affairs. Reflecting its tragic history, Rwanda's electoral system is designed to ensure inclusive government through power-sharing and representation of various socio-economic groups and genders. At the heart of this system is the resolve to ensure that Rwanda never again goes through another experience of civil war or genocide.

Constitutional framework

In its preamble, the new Constitution adopted in 2003 underlines Rwanda's commitment to fight the ideology of genocide in all its manifestations, eradicate 'ethnic,

---

329 See the Human Rights Watch (2011) World Report, Rwanda country chapter; Schroder (2008), op. cit.; Commonwealth Secretariat (2010), op. cit.; African Union Observer Mission (2010) Report of the African Union Observer Mission to the Rwanda Presidential Elections of 9 August 2010; US Bureau of Democracy, Human Rights & Labour (2011) *Country Report on Human Rights Practices for 2010, Rwanda*, www.state.gov/j/drl/rls/hrrpt/2010/af/154364.htm; US Bureau of Democracy, Human Rights & Labour (2012) *Country Report on Human Rights Practices for 2011, Rwanda*, p. 22, www.state.gov/j/drl/rls/hrrpt/2011/af/186231.htm.

330 Following the failed first and second attempts in June 2010, a third attempt was made on the life of General Kayumba Nyamwasa in March 2014. In January 2014, a former Rwandan spymaster and a close friend of General Kayumba Nyamwasa, General Patrick Karegeya, was assassinated in a hotel in Johannesburg. Both Nyamwasa and Karegeya are co-founders and members of the Rwanda National Congress, a Diaspora-based political party fiercely opposed to President Paul Kagame.

regional and any other form of division', and promote national unity and reconciliation. It affirms Rwanda's resolve to build a nation governed by the rule of law, based on respect for human rights, political pluralism, equitable power sharing, tolerance and resolution of issues through dialogue. The Constitution grants the freedoms of press and information, association and the right to peaceful assembly.[331] These key principles and provisions constitute the bedrock of Rwanda's legal and institutional framework, which includes the framework for the management of national elections.

The principle of *power-sharing* is at the heart of Rwanda's statecraft and electoral politics. The Constitution limits the ruling party to a maximum of 50% of Cabinet seats. The remainder is divided proportionately among other parties represented in the Chamber of Deputies, although members may also be appointed from outside Parliament.[332] The Constitution provides that the Speaker of the Chamber of Deputies and the President of the Senate must be chosen from parties other than that of the President of the Republic.[333] Resolutions and disagreements must be addressed through *consensus*.[334] Other than women, youth and persons with disabilities, all 53 seats of Parliament are filled at a national level through election by universal suffrage.

The Constitution guarantees equality for all Rwandans, and between women and men. It grants a minimum of 30% of all posts in decision-making organs to women. In order to ensure adherence to this provision, the Constitution has ring-fenced this quota in key elective positions at the national and local level. Thus, out of the 80 seats in the lower chamber of Parliament, 24 are reserved for women, who hold their own elections to determine their representatives. Similarly, 30% or at least eight of the 26 seats in the Senate are reserved for women. Seats are also reserved for other vulnerable groups like the youth, persons with disabilities and historically marginalised groups. These provisions give these groups a double advantage during elections as they enable them to compete under direct suffrage, as well as through their own indirect elections. This explains Rwanda's current high number of women in Parliament (lower chamber), which at 56.4% is the highest in any parliamentary democracy.[335]

The Constitution provides for a '*multi-party system of government*' and establishes the right of political organisations to operate freely.[336] It also grants Rwandans the freedom to join political organisations of their choice[337] and the right to participate in the govern-

---

331 Articles 34, 35 and 36.
332 Article 116.
333 Article 58.
334 Article 9.
335 Based on the 2008 parliamentary elections, women occupy 45 of the 80 seats in Rwanda's lower chamber. This is 56.3% of the total seats, giving Rwanda the highest number of women in any parliamentary democracy in the world according to the Inter-Parliamentary Union based on the information provided by national parliaments by 1 February 2013, www.ipu.org/wmn-e/classif.htm. Of the 26 seats in the Senate, women occupy ten or 38.5% of the total.
336 Article 52.
337 Article 53.

ance of the country, directly or through freely chosen representatives.[338] Independent candidates may run for parliamentary and presidential elections.[339]

The *commitment to fight genocide ideology and division and to uphold national unity* is the most overriding principle and constitutes perhaps the primary organising basis of Rwandan politics. There exist two different laws, one punishing the crime of genocide ideology and the other punishing the crime of discrimination and sectarianism.[340] Genocide ideology is also addressed in the Penal Code.[341] Further, the Constitution provides that a Member of Parliament, once elected, serves the interests of all Rwandans, not any particular area or constituency.[342] It also prohibits political organising based on ethnicity, region, religion, sex or any other basis that may give rise to discrimination.

Electoral laws

The major recurring elections on a national level are:
- The election of the President of the Republic, held every seven years;
- The election of the Parliament of Rwanda; and
- The local and grassroots leaders' elections, held every five years.

The President is elected through direct and secret popular vote. Where there is equality of votes for the first two candidates, a second round for only the two candidates is organised within a month. Parliamentary elections are both direct and indirect, as are local and grassroots elections. A number of domestic laws have been promulgated to guide electoral practice in the country.

The Electoral Code

The Electoral Code[343] was enacted in 2010. It is the most comprehensive piece of legislation on elections. It is a revised version of the code first enacted to govern the 2003 elections and contains 210 articles covering general as well as specific electoral provisions and regulations spanning all phases of the electoral process. These include provisions and regulations on the following:
- Voter registration and eligibility;
- Electoral campaigns;
- Nomination of candidates;

338 Article 45.
339 Article 77.
340 Law No. 18/2008 of 23 July 2008 punishes the crime of genocide ideology. Article 2 of this law provides a definition of genocide ideology, while Article 3 offers examples of what the crime constitutes. However, there is no particular law currently criminalising division in Rwanda. The only law that appears to be a reference point for division is Law No. 47/2001 of 18 December 2001 on Prevention, Suppression and Punishment of the Crimes of Discrimination and Sectarianism. Article 1 of this law defines discrimination and sectarianism.
341 Law No. 01/2012/OL of 2 May 2012 Organic Law instituting the Penal Code, Articles 114–118.
342 Article 64.
343 Organic Law No. 03/2010 of 18 June 2010, repealing Organic Law No. 17/2003 of 7 July 2003 governing presidential and legislative elections (hereafter referred to as the Electoral Code).

- Polling operations;
- Vote counting, consolidation and results announcement;
- Petitions and resolution of electoral disputes;
- Provisions specific to the presidential election, the parliamentary elections (including both the Lower Chamber of Deputies and the Senate) and local elections; and
- The role of the National Electoral Commission in regard to the administration and management of the electoral process.

A 2013 revision has introduced new changes to the Electoral Code.[344]

Laws regulating elections for special interest groups

There are different laws governing the election of youth, women, persons with disabilities and historically marginalised communities. The laws provide minimum qualifications for election to representative bodies at different levels and the attributions of different elective offices, among other things.[345]

Law establishing the National Electoral Commission

The law establishing the National Electoral Commission[346] (NEC) details the mandate, composition, functions, funding and other relevant information relating to the organisation and functioning of the electoral commission. A 2013 review has introduced further changes to this law.[347]

Law governing political organisations and politicians

This law, passed in 2003,[348] offers guidance on the following:
- The formation, organisation and functioning of political organisations and their consultative forum;
- Their rights, obligations and conduct;
- Their funding mechanisms;

---

344 Law No. 37/2013 of 16 June 2013 modifying and complementing Law No. 27/2010 of 19 June 2010 relating to elections as modified and complemented to date.
345 The Constitution in Articles 9, 76 and 82 sets out the framework for the election of special interest groups, namely women, youth, persons with disabilities, historically marginalised groups and representatives of public and private universities. Articles 109–123 of the Electoral Code provide details and the modalities and eligibility requirements for electing such persons. Accordingly, in the Chamber of Deputies, a minimum of 24 seats are reserved for women, two for youth, and one for a representative of persons with disabilities. In the Senate, eight seats are reserved for women and two for representatives from public and private universities. Of the eight presidential appointees to the Senate, there is provision for one representative of historically marginalised communities.
346 Law No. 31/2005 of 24 December 2005 relating to the organisation and functioning of the National Electoral Commission.
347 Law No. 38/2013 of 16 June 2013 modifying and complementing Law No. 31/2005 of 24 December relating to the organisation and functioning of the National Electoral Commission as amended to date.
348 Organic Law No. 16/2003 of 27 June 2003.

- The management of their assets;
- Coalitions between parties; and
- The relationships between political parties and the media.

A 2007 review introduced new changes to this law.[349]

Laws regulating the media

The media law[350] is crucial in terms of regulating access to public media by political candidates during elections. The media law also establishes the Media High Council, which issues guidelines for election coverage by the media. A new media law has recently been passed, along with a new law governing the operations of the Media High Council.[351]

Law governing the judiciary

The law on the judiciary[352] guides the organisation, functioning and powers of the judiciary in relation to dealing with electoral offences. It complements the electoral code.

Laws on discrimination, sectarianism and genocide ideology

Although not explicitly linked to the electoral process, the laws against discrimination, sectarianism and genocide ideology[353] are indispensable when analysing the political landscape of Rwanda.

Regulations and instructions issued by the NEC

The NEC is empowered to issue instructions relating to elections at the beginning of every poll. NEC instructions are crucial in terms of complementing existing legal gaps unfilled by other electoral legislation. The instructions are reviewed during each election.

Government structure

The executive

The executive power in Rwanda is vested in the President and the Cabinet. The President is the head of state and government, and is elected by universal suffrage through a direct and secret ballot for a seven-year term, which is renewable only once. The

---

349 Organic Law No. 19/2007 of 4 May 2007 modifying and completing Organic Law No. 16/2003 of 27 June 2003 governing political organisations and politicians.

350 Law No. 22/2009 of 12 August 2009.

351 Law No. 02/2013 of 8 February 2013 regulating the media, replacing Law No. 22/2009 of 12 August 2009; Law No. 3/2013 determining the organisation, responsibilities and functioning of the Media High Council, replacing Law No. 30/2009 of 16 September 2009.

352 Organic Law No. 07/2004 of 25 April 2004 on the Organisation, Functioning and Competence of the Judiciary.

353 Law No. 47/2001 of 18 December 2001 on Prevention, Suppression and Punishment of the Crime of Discrimination and Sectarianism and Law No. 33bis/2003, Repressing the Crime of Genocide, Crimes Against Humanity and War Crimes.

President appoints the Cabinet from the political parties based on the distribution of their seats in the Chamber of Deputies, although s/he is also allowed by the Constitution to appoint other competent people who do not belong to any political party. The Rwandan presidency is, therefore, clearly a strong institution, with the current President also serving as the head of the ruling party, the RPF.

Parliament

The power to make laws is vested in a two-chamber Parliament that consists of a Chamber of Deputies and a Senate.

The Chamber of Deputies is composed of 80 members, 53 of whom are elected by direct ballot or universal suffrage for a five-year term through a system of proportional representation. Under this system, each political party must receive a minimum of 5% of the total popular vote to secure a seat in Parliament. The seats are allocated to the parties, coalitions and independent candidates by dividing the votes received by an electoral quotient, arrived at by dividing the total number of valid votes of each list that has obtained at least 5% of the votes cast by the number of seats to be contested. Of the remaining 27 seats, 24 are women who are elected indirectly by their representative organisations in the provinces; two are youth representatives elected indirectly by the National Youth Council; the remaining seat is a representative of the Federation of the Association of Persons with Disability, also elected indirectly.

The Senate is composed of 26 members, at least 30% of whom must be women. The members are appointed or elected for an eight-year term:

- Sector committees and district councils elect 12 members through secret ballot.
- Eight are nominated by the President and include a representative of the historically marginalised communities in Rwanda, such as the Twa.
- Four are nominated by the National Consultative Forum of Political Organisations (NCFP).
- The remaining two represent institutions of higher learning, one public and the other private.
- Former presidents may request to join the Senate.

The Senate has a strong mandate. In addition to amending and approving Bills, it can amend the Constitution and a range of laws linked to the management of elections:

- Organic laws;
- Laws on fundamental freedoms, rights and duties;
- Criminal laws; and
- Laws relating to the jurisdiction of courts and procedures in criminal cases, referenda, and international agreements and treaties.

Senators elect the Supreme Court's president, vice-president and judges, as well as the prosecutor-general and his or her deputy. The Constitution gives senators the power to summon political organisations that grossly violate the provisions relating to political organising and recommend them to the High Court for sanction.[354]

Local administration

Compared to many African countries, Rwanda is a small, very well-organised country. With one dominant political party and a unitary government, it is relatively easy to rule efficiently. The Constitution divides the country into provinces, districts, cities, municipalities, towns, sectors, cells and villages through which government policies, instructions and services flow.

Provinces

The five provinces (including the city of Kigali) act as intermediaries between the national government and constituent districts. The 'Rwanda Decentralisation Strategic Framework'[355] assigns to provinces the responsibility of coordinating governance issues, monitoring and evaluation in their jurisdictions. Each province is headed by a governor, appointed by the President and approved by the Senate.

Districts

There are 30 districts responsible for coordinating public service delivery and economic development in 416 sectors, 9,165 cells and 14,840 villages. Districts are governed by a district council that consists of one elected representative (councillor) from each sector, as well as representatives of youth and women. The youth and women's groups each make up at least one third of council members. The district council is headed by a team comprising a council chairperson, a vice-chairperson and a secretary, all elected through a collegiate system. The council operates independently from the district executive committee, which is headed by the mayor and two vice-mayors – one in charge of economic affairs, and the other, social affairs.

Sectors

Sectors are governed by a development committee comprising one elected representative from each cell and led by a sector coordinator. Districts and sectors also have executive secretaries – civil servants appointed through a prime-ministerial decree.

Cells and villages

Cells and villages are the smallest political units and provide a link between the people and the sectors. All resident adults above 18 years of age are members of their local cell assembly or council. From them, a ten-member cell executive committee is elected. The last elections for these local leaders were held in February 2011.

---

354 Article 55.
355 Republic of Rwanda (2007) *Rwanda Decentralisation Strategic Framework: Towards a Sector-Wide Approach for Decentralisation Implementation.*

Influence of the RPF on Rwandan politics

This decentralised administrative and leadership structure is perceived as heavily controlled by the RPF. So, too, are the various structures constituted within it to manage local elections. Leaders emerging from these structures are mostly members of the RPF or people sympathetic to it. While this may be understandable given the dominance of the ruling party across the country, opposition political parties, civil society representatives and other observers of electoral processes in Rwanda are concerned over this dominance and accuse the RPF of a range of electoral malfeasances that make it almost impossible to deliver free and fair electoral results in the country. A leader of an opposition political party interviewed for this report opined that during the 2011 senatorial elections, her party declined to present candidates for the elections because the electoral colleges[356] were dominated by RPF members and could not, therefore, be trusted to vote for opposition candidates.[357]

Similar views were expressed by other respondents, including a number of representatives from diplomatic missions in Kigali. According to a political officer and election observer from the US Embassy, more than 90% of the district electoral college for the 2011 senatorial elections was drawn from members of the RPF.[358] The officer observed further that days before the elections, a number of contestants were instructed by the RPF to remove their names from the elections list and they did so 48 hours before the polls opened.

In its 2011 Annual Human Rights Report on Rwanda, the US Department of State observes that several successful candidates (including non-RPF candidates) were asked by the RPF to run for office and given assurances that they would win.[359] The report adds further that some voting members indicated receiving a text message from the provincial RPF headquarters on the morning of the election instructing them to vote for particular RPF and non-RPF candidates.

These examples illustrate the immense powers and influence that the RPF holds over the electoral process and politics in Rwanda. Pre-eminent in the rebuilding of the Rwandan state following the civil war and the Genocide, the RPF, referred to fondly as 'the family', retains a monumental hold on Rwanda's political and social life, even on business. It wields a robust, hugely complex and deeply rooted administrative, financial and political machinery that has been compared, in terms of organisation, financial muscle and political weight to parties such as the Chinese Central Committee, South Africa's African National Congress and Ethiopia's ruling party, the Ethiopian People's Democratic Revolutionary Front. In a recent publication, the RPF was ranked as one of

---

356 The electoral college is a group of electors who are selected to elect candidates for political positions such as mayors and senators; for example, the electoral college of the district executive committee that elects senators and mayors comprises members of the district council and council members from all sectors constituting the district.
357 Interview, 21 September 2012.
358 Interview, 27 September 2012.
359 US Bureau of Democracy, Human Rights & Labour (2012), op. cit., p. 22.

the richest political parties in the world.[360] Its political manoeuvring has resulted in a systematic co-optation and smothering of the opposition, which has rendered the latter completely irrelevant on the country's political landscape. The only visible opposition is that operating from the Diaspora. Its 'regime change' agenda has, however, failed to resonate with the local and international public.

Legislation on political organisations

Political organisations are free to operate in Rwanda within a multi-party framework. Citizens are free to join political parties of their choice. Nonetheless, as noted by the Secretary-General of the PSD, 'Political parties were reluctantly agreed to by Rwandans during the 2003 Constitution because of their bad legacy.'[361] This view, believed to have been advanced by the legal and constitutional commission established in 2000 to draft the initial text of the Constitution has, however, been disputed by some observers.[362] Nevertheless, safeguards were included. The Constitution prohibits political organising on the basis of 'race, ethnicity, tribe, clan, region, sex, religion or any other division which may give rise to discrimination'.[363] It requires political parties to 'constantly reflect the unity of the people of Rwanda and gender equality and complementarity, whether in the recruitment of members, putting in place organs of leadership, or in their operations and activities'. The Constitution further requires all registered political parties to join the NCFP as the space for exchanging ideas on ways to improve governance, promote national unity, as well as resolve conflicts arising within and between political organisations.[364] The Constitution even anticipates violations of these provisions and empowers the Senate to summon and seek High Court sanctions against political parties that violate them.[365]

These constitutional provisions constitute the basis of the law governing political organisations and politicians.[366] The law offers general and specific principles and guidelines with regard to organising for political purposes. It underlines the constitutional freedoms to form and join a political party, but also the imperative to do so in a way that unites, does not discriminate and preserves Rwanda's territorial integrity and security. To operate, political parties must register with the Ministry of Local Government. For a political party to be registered, it must secure at least 120 persons from the whole country, including at least five persons living in each province or in City of Kigali

---

360 Wallis, W (2012) 'Rwanda: The RPF Builds A Formidable Business Group', *The Rwandan*, 26 September 2012, www.therwandan.com/blog/rwanda-rpf-builds-a-formidable-business-group.

361 Interview with the Hon. Damascene Ntawukuriryayo, Secretary-General of the PSD and Speaker of the Senate.

362 Remarks by Eugene Ntaganda, who reviewed this report and, was an expert for the 2000 commission. According to Ntaganda, this may have been a view pushed by the RPF apparatus to legitimise its appeal to the population (comments made on draft report submitted 7 October 2013).

363 Article 54.

364 Article 56.

365 Article 55.

366 Organic Law No. 16/2003 of 27 June 2003 governing political organisations and politicians.

as signatories to its statutes.[367] An amendment of the law on political parties passed in 2007 now allows parties to organise at all levels of government.[368]

Currently, Rwanda has ten legally registered political parties, which are all members of the NCFP:

- Rwandan Patriotic Front (RPF Inkotanyi) or *Front Patriotique Rwandais* (FPR);
- Democratic Union of the Rwandan People (*Union Démocratique du Peuple Rwandais*, UDPR);
- Liberal Party (*Parti libéral*, PL);
- Ideal Democratic Party (*Parti démocratique idéal*, PDI);
- Social Democratic Party (*Parti social démocrate*, PSD);
- Party for Progress and Concord (*Parti du Progrès et de la Concorde*, PPC);
- Christian Democratic Party (*Parti Démocratique Chrétien*, PDC);
- Rwandan Socialist Party (*Parti Socialiste Rwandais*, PSR);
- Solidarity and Progress Party (*Parti de la solidarité et du progrès*, PSP); and
- Social Party Imberakuri (*Parti Social Imberakuri*, PS-Imberakuri).

Considered against the background of the Genocide, a focus on re-uniting the Rwandan people is justified. However, the law on political parties may conflict with the provisions endorsing political pluralism in Rwanda's Constitution. On the subject of power-sharing, there are concerns over the absence of solid legal safeguards to ensure that the current ruling party – the RPF – does not exceed the 50% quota. The Constitution is silent on the formula for calculating this quota where the ruling party is in coalition with opposition groups. It is not clear whether coalition members of the ruling party are considered as opposition parties sharing the remaining 50% quota. Further, it is silent on the number of non-party members who can be offered Cabinet seats vis-à-vis active political parties with seats in Parliament.[369] This could create room for manipulation of the principle of power-sharing in favour of the ruling party.[370]

There is also a strong view that the NCFP is dominated by allies of the ruling RPF, undermining plurality of political views and generating political parties that are complementary rather than in opposition to the ruling party.[371] Currently, six out of the nine opposition parties are in coalition with the ruling party.[372] Yet, they are considered as

---

367 Ibid., Article 9.
368 Organic Law No. 19/2007 of 4 May 2007 modifying and completing Organic Law No. 16/2003 of 27 June 2003 governing political organisations and politicians.
369 Article 116 of the constitution states 'members of Cabinet are selected from political organisations on the basis of their seats in the Chamber of Deputies without excluding the possibility of appointing to Cabinet other competent people who do not belong to any political organisations.'
370 More than half of the current Rwandan Cabinet of 29 ministers, including the Prime Minister, are known RPF members. In the 53-member Chamber of Deputies representation is as follows: 35 (66%) RPF, seven PSD, four PL, two PDI, one each for the other five parties. PS-Imberakuri is not represented, having fielded no candidates for the parliamentary elections.
371 Interview with Marcel Museminali, managing editor, *The Business Daily*, 28 September 2012.
372 'Elections in Rwanda', *African Elections Database*, africanelections.tripod.com/rw.html#2003_Presidential_Election, accessed 23 October 2012.

independent political parties. This is unfair, according to the Secretary-General of the PSD, who also feels that under such an arrangement of shared power, parties other than the RPF have difficulties showcasing and mobilising political support and membership on the basis of their political agenda and contribution to national development.[373]

Further, the requirement to operate in a way that 'constantly reflects the unity of the people of Rwanda'[374] makes it easy for opposition political parties to be constrained or banned for not acting in accordance with the law. This was the case with the Christian Democratic Party and the Islamic Democratic Party, which had to change their names to Centrist Democratic Party and Ideal Democratic Party, respectively, to be in line with the provision prohibiting political parties from having religious, ethnic, or other labels seen as discriminatory.[375] Others such as the Green Party, PS-Imberakuri and United Democratic Forces (FDU-Inkingi) have also faced registration impediments due to technicalities linked to this and other related laws.

Other challenges are found in the regulations barring candidates from campaigning on party platforms. The electoral code prohibits the use of party emblems and manifestos by candidates contesting senatorial and local elections, as well as elections for special interest groups.[376] These, together with a host of other restrictions in the sections on campaign regulations[377] are seen as severely constraining the freedom of speech guaranteed in Article 33 of the Constitution.

The commitment to fight genocide ideology and divisionism is, however, the one principle that has drawn the greatest concern among political organisations, civil society and human rights groups, legal professionals and international development partners. The group of laws that governs these commitments is at the heart of the debate around electoral democracy in Rwanda. While it is widely agreed that genuine instances of hate speech or conduct still occur in Rwanda, and that this group of laws is well intentioned and understandable in its proper context,[378] there are widespread and legitimate concerns that as currently framed, these laws are not specific enough with respect to the principles of legality, intentionality and support for freedom of expression, in line with

---

373 Interview with the Hon. Damascene Ntawukuriryayo, Secretary-General of the PSD and Speaker of the Senate, 20 September 2012.
374 Article 56.
375 *African Elections Database*, africanelections.tripod.com/rw.html#2003_Presidential_Election.
376 Articles 30 and 152.
377 Articles, 29, 30, 149, 150, 152, 153.
378 A number of reports generated within Rwanda point towards the continued existence of genocide ideology within the country. Examples include: Rwanda Senate (2006) Genocide ideology and strategies for its eradication, pp. 18–19; Rwanda National Assembly (2007) 'Rapport d'analyse sur le problème d'idéologie du génocide évoquée au sein des établissements scolaires, (unofficial French translation).

international law.[379] They do not, therefore, offer sufficient legal basis or guidance to fairly prosecute hate speech or conduct. In a 2008 governance assessment undertaken jointly with the government of Rwanda, development partners working in the country identified four specific concerns with regard to this group of laws:

- It is doubtful that the laws were drafted clearly enough to allow a person to know whether their conduct would amount to a breach of the law violating the principle of legality.
- The laws do not include the requirement of intentionality (that the offender intended to cause harm).
- The penalties do not allow for sufficient judicial discretion to ensure that sentencing is proportionate to the circumstances of each case.
- The law may not strike the appropriate balance between prohibiting hate speech and supporting the freedom of expression.[380]

Citing a range of examples in which these laws have lent themselves to misinterpretation and have in fact been used to criminalise expression and suppress legitimate political debate and opposition in Rwanda, the development partners and a number of other observers have called for an urgent revision of these laws to align them with international standards so that genuine incidents of hate conduct can be differentiated from legitimate freedom of expression.[381]

In the lead-up to the 2010 presidential election, three prominent leaders of opposition parties were charged and later convicted under these laws in what was seen by many observers as an attempt by the state to clamp down on the opposition and critics of government. Victoire Ingabire, the leader of the exiled opposition party FDU-Inkingi, was arrested in April 2010. She was sentenced two years later to eight years imprisonment on charges of genocide denial and conspiracy, and planning to cause state insecurity. Bernard Ntaganda, leader of the PS-Imberakuri, was twice summoned

---

379 Article 19 of the International Covenant on Civil and Political Rights, to which Rwanda is a signatory, guarantees the right to freedom of opinion and expression. Freedom of expression may be restricted to preserve the rights or reputations of others, national security, public order, public health or public morals. Such restrictions must, however, be defined by law and must be necessary, meeting the requirement of proportionality, for example. Importantly, they must not take away the right itself. Article 20 prohibits propaganda for war and any advocacy of national, racial or religious hatred that constitutes incitement to hostility, discrimination or violence. Any such prohibition must also comply with the same requirements prescribed for Article 19.

380 Joint Governance Assessment: Rwanda, Draft Final, 23 July 2008, pp. 34, 79.

381 A good discussion of this is found in Amnesty International (2010) *Safer to Stay Silent: The Chilling Effect of Rwanda's Laws on Genocide Ideology and Sectarianism*, pp. 13–16. According to this report, some 608 and 749 cases related to genocide ideology were brought up and charged in 2008 and 2009, respectively. Various other groups and reports have drawn attention to the vagueness and ambiguity of these laws and sought their repeal: US Bureau of Democracy, Human Rights & Labour (2011), op. cit., pp. 16–17; US Bureau of Democracy, Human Rights & Labour (2012), op. cit.; Commonwealth Secretariat (2010), op. cit., pp. 11–16; Article 19 (2009) *Comment on the Law Relating to the Punishment of the Crime of Genocide Ideology of Rwanda*, London, www.article19.org/pdfs/analysis/rwanda-comment-on-the-law-relating-to-the-punishment-of-the-crime-of-genocid.pdf.

to the Rwandan Senate on similar accusations.[382] On 24 June 2010, he was arrested and charged with endangering national security, divisionism and attempting to organise illegal demonstrations. On 11 February 2011, he was sentenced to four years in prison on these charges. Deogratias Mushayidi, leader of the Pact for Peoples' Defence (*Pacte de Défense du Peuple*, PPD), was arrested in Burundi on 3 March 2010 and extradited two days later to Rwanda. He was charged on 17 September 2010 with promoting genocide ideology, revisionism, divisionism, threatening state security, using false documents and collaborating with a terrorist group. He was sentenced to life imprisonment. On 24 February 2012 the Rwandan Supreme Court upheld his conviction and sentence.

Two journalists, Agnès Uwimana and Saïdati Mukabibi, who worked for the Kinyarwanda-language newspaper *Umurabyo* in Rwanda, were arrested in July 2010 on charges of publishing defamatory articles against the person of the President, endangering national security and inciting divisionism and denying the Genocide. They were sentenced to 17 and seven years, respectively, by the High Court. Their sentences were later commuted to four and three years, respectively.[383]

The government has acknowledged its challenges in defining these laws, indicating since April 2010 its intention to review and update them.[384] In November 2012, Rwanda's Minister for Justice presented to Parliament an amended version of the 2008 genocide ideology law. The revised version contains improvements, in particular a narrower definition of the offence and a reduction in prison sentences. It suggests that only conduct should be punished, if it is manifested in public, unlike in the existing version, which punishes ideas and thoughts as well.[385] Observers, however, say the revisions still do not go far enough in defining genocide ideology and removing vague language that could still be used to criminalise free speech.[386] In recent high-profile cases linked to elections, where divisionism and genocide ideology were identified as charges, the accused persons were able to successfully contest aspects of these laws. Their victories were, however, always clawed back through other related charges and legislation.[387] According to the media freedom organisation Article 19, other laws continue to pose challenges

---

382   On 14 December 2009 and on 15 January 2010.

383   'Rwanda journalists jailed for genocide denial launch supreme court appeal', *The Guardian*, 20 January 2012, www.guardian.co.uk/world/2012/jan/29/rwanda-journalists-genocide-denial-appeal.

384   'Government Announces Review of Contentious Genocide law', *Rwanda News Agency*, 5 April 2010, rwandinfo.com/eng/rwanda-kagame-is-now-willing-to-review-the-contentious-genocide-law.

385   'Govt. seeks to amend genocide ideology law', *Rwanda New Times*, 3 November 2013, www.newtimes.co.rw/index.php?i=15165&a=60288.

386   Human Rights Watch (2013) *World Report 2014: Rwanda*, www.hrw.org/world-report/2013/country-chapters/rwanda; see also Article 19 (2013) 'Rwanda: Media Law Does Not Go Far Enough', 18 March 2013, www.Article19.org/resources.php/resource/3665/en/rwanda:-media-law-does-not-go-far-enough.

387   For example, Victoire Ingabire was convicted on two counts of genocide denial and conspiracy and planning to cause state insecurity, but acquitted on four other charges, which included promoting genocide ideology, inciting ethnic divisionism and supporting armed groups. Deogratius Mushayidi was cleared of charges of promoting genocide ideology, revisionism and divisionism and terrorism. In the case of Uwimana and Mukabibi, the Supreme Court found no clear evidence of creation of divisionism and denial of genocide, but upheld the charges of disrupting national security and defamation.

to free speech and free political expression.[388] Defamation and slander remain criminal offences under the Penal Code,[389] while the revised media law[390] does not go far enough in guaranteeing media independence from government.

D. The National Electoral Commission

Mandate, functions and institutional framework

Although the National Electoral Commission (NEC) was formally established in 2000, the idea of an independent electoral commission had been conceived as early as 1993 as part of the Arusha Peace Agreement.[391] In 1999, the first post-genocide local elections were held. They were managed by a small department within the Ministry of Local Government. A 2000 law established the NEC for the first time. [392] Over the years, the NEC has evolved in response to demands for a more independent commission that is able to organise freer and fairer elections.[393] The current version of the commission's legal framework is Law No. 31/2005 of 24 December 2005 establishing the National Electoral Commission,[394] which was updated in June 2013.[395]

The 2003 Constitution reaffirmed the commitment to have an independent electoral commission,[396] stating in Article 180:

> The National Electoral Commission is an independent commission responsible for the preparation and organisation of local, legislative and presidential elections and referenda or such other elections the responsibility for the organisation of which the law may vest in the Commission.

---

388 Article 19 (2013) 'Rwanda: Media Law Does Not Go Far Enough', op. cit.
389 'Rwanda: Draft Penal Code, a Legal Analysis', *Article 19*, 29 November 2011, www.Article19.org/ resources.php/resource/2881/en/rwanda:-draft-penal-code; see also 'New Penal Code Comes into Force', *The New Times*, 3 July 2012, www.newtimes.co.rw/news/index.php?i=15042&a=55485.
390 Law No. 02/2013 of 8 February 2013 regulating the media replacing Law No. 22/2009 of 12 August 2009.
391 See Article 24(c) of the Protocol of Agreement on Power-Sharing Within the Framework of a Broad-based Transitional Government between the Government of Rwanda and Rwanda Patriotic Front signed on 30 October 1992, https: //peaceaccords.nd.edu/site_media/media/accords/Rwanda_Peace_Accord.pdf.
392 See Law No. 39/2000 of 28 November 2000 setting up the NEC, *Official Gazette*, Special Issue, 29 November 2000.
393 Interview with Charles Munyaneza, Executive Secretary of NEC, 10 September 2012; Law No. 38/2013 of 16 June 2013 modifying and complementing Law No. 31/2005 of 24 December 2005 relating to the organisation and functioning of the NEC, as modified and complemented to date, Article 1,8.
394 Law No. 31/2005 of 24 December 2005 relating to the organisation and functioning of the NEC, *Official Gazette*, Special issue, 3 January 2006 (hereafter 2005 NEC Law).
395 Through Law No. 38/2013 of 16 June 2013 modifying and complementing Law No. 31/2005 of 24 December 2005 relating to the organisation and functioning of the NEC as modified and complemented to date.
396 See Article 180 of the Rwandan Constitution as amended to date.

Apart from mandating the President of the Republic to sign presidential orders appointing the commissioners or terminating their service, and requiring the commission to submit annual reports to Parliament, the Constitution leaves all other matters concerning the organisation and functioning of the NEC to be determined by law.[397] Under the 2005 NEC Law and the Electoral Code,[398] the commission has full responsibility for all matters linked to the conduct of elections. While the law did not specifically mandate the NEC to propose electoral reforms, this mandate is now affirmed in its 2013 review.[399]

Organisational structure and functioning

The NEC is a national body with decentralised structures that enable it to implement its mandate as stipulated by law. It is composed of three organs:

- Council of Commissioners;
- Bureau of the Commissioners; and
- Executive Secretariat.[400]

Council of Commissioners

The Council of Commissioners is the supreme organ in charge of ensuring the functioning of the NEC. It is made up of seven commissioners, including the president and the vice-president of the NEC. The Council of Commissioners is appointed through an order prepared by the Cabinet and signed by the President of Rwanda.[401] It is not clear how the commissioners are identified and selected. There is a lacuna in this regard in the Constitution, the Electoral Code and the 2005 NEC Law. Interviews with a number of sources, however, point towards an informal consultative process that involves the Ministry of Local Government, the NCFP, the Office of the President, and the National Security Service.[402] From this consultation, an inclusive list of names is drawn up and presented to the Cabinet for vetting.[403] The Cabinet then presents a list of seven nominees, including the president and the vice-president, to the Senate for further scrutiny

---

397 According to Article 113 of the Constitution, the President signs the presidential orders deliberated in the Council of Ministers concerning the appointment and removal of NEC commissioners.

398 Law No. 27/2010 of 19 June 2010 relating to elections.

399 Article 12 (sub-articles 3 and 18) of the NEC Law empowers the NEC commissioners to take decisions on electoral matters and to advise the government on ways in which the commission may perform better. This could be interpreted to include a role in proposing new electoral laws. The June 2013 review of the NEC law (Law No. 38/2013) affirms this mandate in Article 1 (sub-article 8).

400 Article 6 of Law No. 31/2005 establishing the NEC.

401 Article 113, 6 (i) of the Constitution of Rwanda.

402 Interviews with the Hon. Appoliniare Mushinzimana, Senator and Member of the Rwandan Senate Appointments Committee, interview, 15 September 2012; the Hon. Zephanir Kalimba, Senator, telephone interview, 15 June 2013; Mr Gisagara, legal advisor of the NEC, telephone interview, 19 June 2013.

403 The political affiliation of the commissioners represents a key aspect and benchmark of the independence of any given EMB. The NEC's official website makes reference to its members being drawn from 'different' political parties and from civil society, see 'Structure', National Electoral Commission, www.nec.gov.rw/details/?tx_ttnews[tt_news]=6&cHash=0f5ec824d1c539eab95af356101f5 ca1, accessed 23 March 2013.

and approval.[404] Two of the seven commissioners must be lawyers and, in line with Constitution, at least 30% of members must be women. Once approved, the names of the nominees are sent back to the Cabinet. A presidential order is then prepared and signed by the President appointing them.[405]

The Council of Commissioners is not a full-time organ. Once appointed, members continue with their ordinary duties. During elections, commissioners convene meetings whenever necessary. However, during non-electoral periods, the commissioners meet once every three months, or when necessary. During the election period, the commissioners are required to suspend their other duties one month before the elections in order to monitor activities until the announcement of the final results.[406] They resume their normal non-commission duties at the end of that period.

Commissioners are not paid a salary but receive a fee during the election period and a sitting allowance determined by a presidential order during meetings outside of the election period. The commissioners serve a term of three years, renewable once.[407] A June 2013 review[408] of this law has now changed this to five years, renewable once. The quorum for the Council of Commissioners is at least two-thirds of its members.[409] Meetings are summoned and chaired by the president, and by the vice-president in the absence of the former. In case both are absent, the commissioners elect from among themselves a temporary chairperson. Decisions of the Council of Commissioners are taken by consensus, or by a simple majority vote of two-thirds of the commissioners present. The commission can create its own internal regulations.[410]

In order for a person to be a commissioner, he or she has to be:

- A Rwandan;
- A holder of at least a bachelor's degree from a university or a state-recognised higher learning institution; and
- A person of integrity.

On assumption of office, the commissioners take an oath administered by the president of the Supreme Court. They can be removed from office by a presidential order.[411] A member of the commission ceases to be a commissioner due to one of the following reasons, in addition to that of completing his or her term of office:[412]

- Resignation from duty and notification in writing to the President of the Republic;

---

404 Article 8 of the 2005 NEC Law.
405 Articles 88 and 113(5i) of the 2003 Constitution of Rwanda.
406 Article 10 of the 2005 NEC Law.
407 Ibid., Article 7.
408 Law No. 38/ 2013 of 16 June 2013 modifying and complementing Law No. 31/2005 of 24 December 2005 relating to the organisation and functioning of the NEC as modified and complemented to date.
409 Article 23 of the 2005 NEC Law.
410 Ibid., Article 30.
411 Ibid., Article 8.
412 Ibid., Article 31.

- Failure to discharge his/her duties for various reasons;[413]
- Upon request by the President of the Republic;
- Upon request by at least a half of the members of the Senate;
- Upon death.

Bureau of Commissioners

The Bureau of Commissioners is composed of the president, the vice-president and the executive secretary of the NEC. It is responsible for preparing:
- Urgent actions to be forwarded to the Council of Commissioners;
- Points to be discussed in the Council of Commissioners; and
- Forwarding to the Council of Commissioners the programme for electoral activities.

The president is responsible for:
- Representing the NEC before other institutions;
- Convening and directing the meetings of the Council of Commissioners;
- Convening and directing the meetings of the Bureau;
- Coordinating the activities of the NEC; and
- Performing other duties related to his/her responsibilities as may be assigned by the Council of Commissioners.

The vice-president is responsible for:
- Assisting the president of the NEC, replacing him/her in case of his/her absence, and
- Performing other duties related to his/her responsibilities as may be assigned by the Council of Commissioners.

Bureau members serve for a term of office similar to the commissioners and are replaced in the same way.

Executive Secretariat

The Executive Secretariat is the technical office of the NEC, responsible for its day-to-day functioning. It is headed by the executive secretary, who is supported by directors in charge of finance, electoral operations, civic education and information and communication technology. It has supporting staff in accordance with the NEC organisational structure, who are deployed at national headquarters and at decentralised levels in the provinces, City of Kigali and at district headquarters. The national secretariat also

---

413 Including those articulated in Articles 32 and 33 of the 2005 NEC Law. These include abuse of office through behaviour seen as hindering the smooth running of the elections or standing for/holding other elective positions while still occupying the position of a commissioner.

maintains a pool of experienced coordinators and volunteers,[414] who manage elections at polling centres at cell and sector levels. The Executive Secretariat is specifically in charge of:

- Preparing the action plan of the NEC and its budget;
- Executing the decisions of the Council of Commissioners;
- Preparing draft instructions governing the electoral process;
- Preparing draft civic education on elections;
- Preparing the electoral list; and
- Performing other duties assigned by the Council of Commissioners.

During election periods, the NEC is mandated to establish branch offices at provincial, City of Kigali and district levels.[415] The number of personnel is determined by the particularity of each level and the election. The mandate of the branches is to prepare electoral activities at their levels in accordance with the instructions of the NEC.

The executive secretary is appointed by an order of the Prime Minister on permanent service terms following approval by the Cabinet. Like the commissioners, s/he is sourced through a consultative process that involves the line ministry, the NCFP, and the office of the President. The executive secretary's qualifications are the same as those of the commissioners. Other staff members of the secretariat are recruited and managed in accordance with the general statute on public servants and the approved NEC structure. To emphasise its independence, the Office of the Secretariat of the NEC is located in a separate building from the various institutions that oversee its operations and interact with it.

Functions and powers

In 2005, the law regulating the NEC was amended to address shortcomings observed by the NEC itself, the various missions accredited to Rwanda to observe elections, and other stakeholders such as Parliament and the political parties.[416] The NEC is mandated to discharge the following duties:

- Prepare, conduct and supervise elections;
- Establish electoral constituencies;
- Establish commission branches in the provinces, City of Kigali, and in the districts;
- Appoint members of the Electoral College, give them instructions, receive their reports and supervise them during elections;
- Prepare and teach civic education on elections;
- Monitor, announce and publish in writing election results;

---

414 The NEC currently manages up to 65,000 volunteers during universal suffrage elections, interview with the executive secretary of the NEC.
415 Article 26 of the 2005 NEC Law.
416 Interview with Charles Munyaneza, executive secretary of the NEC, 10 September 2012.

- Put in place strategies to ensure elections are free, fair and transparent;
- Accredit national and international election observers;
- Monitor whether candidates are enjoying equal access to public media during elections; and
- Participate in the elaboration of draft laws governing elections, which the NEC has to organise and conduct.

The Electoral Code gives the NEC the mandate to ensure respect for laws and regulations governing the electoral process.[417] The NEC secretariat is charged with preparing the electoral roll and drafting the instructions governing the electoral process.[418] The NEC is required to submit its Plan of Action, activity report and the decisions of its Council of Commissioners to the President, copying the President of the Senate, the Speaker of the Chamber of Deputies, the Prime Minister, the President of the Supreme Court and the minister in charge of Local Government.[419] The Council of Commissioners has the following functions:[420]

- Determining electoral policy;
- Approving the NEC action plan;
- Taking decisions on electoral matters;
- Analysing and approving:
  - NEC reports;
  - Electoral instructions;
  - Electoral education materials;
  - Electoral equipment and materials;
  - The electoral time table and the final electoral list of candidacies; and
  - The draft budget for the NEC so that it may be forwarded to competent authorities;
- Approving representatives of the NEC in its branches at province, City of Kigali and district levels during elections;
- Monitoring electoral campaigns and the electoral process;
- Announcing election results;
- Coordinating NEC activities; and
- Advising the government on how the NEC may perform better.

Voter registration
The Electoral Code charges the NEC with the responsibility of preparing and maintaining the voters' register and managing the entire registration process.[421] Accordingly, the NEC is mandated to:

---

417 Electoral Code, Article 5; see Law No. 27/2010 of 19 June 2010 relating to elections, *Official Gazette*, Special Issue, 19 June 2010.
418 Ibid., Article 19.
419 Ibid., Article 28.
420 Article 12 of the 2005 NEC Law.
421 Articles 7–23.

- Draft electoral instructions specifying the time for beginning and closing the voters' register and the content of that register;
- Define the modalities for registration in the voters' register;
- Monitor and regulate registration in the voters' register;
- Update the voters' register at least once per year. Where an election is held within two months of the previous one, the register used in the previous election is maintained;
- Determine eligibility for and monitor registration in the voters' register;
- Receive and keep the voters' register; and
- Issue and replace a voter's card to registered voters

A voters' register is established in each village and in every embassy of the Republic of Rwanda. Bona fide Rwandan citizens (with Rwandan identity cards or passports or other document issued by a competent authority) of at least 18 years of age and not prohibited by the electoral law are allowed to register as voters. The Electoral Code identifies eight categories of persons considered ineligible to register as voters.[422] They are:
- Persons deprived of the right to vote by a competent authority and who have not been rehabilitated or granted amnesty by the law;
- Persons convicted of murder and manslaughter;
- Persons definitively convicted of the crime of genocide against the Tutsis or crimes against humanity;
- Persons who plead guilty to the crime of genocide and crimes against humanity in the first degree;
- Persons convicted of the crime of defilement;
- Persons convicted of the crime of rape;
- Prisoners; and
- Refugees.

Registration is carried out by NEC-designated officials, whose mandate includes ensuring registration is done in accordance with the law, as well as maintaining the security of the registration materials. Upon completion, a provisionally approved register is displayed in public to enable registered voters to verify their details. This is done over a period of 30 days before polling day.

A list of persons removed from the voters' roll for reasons of ineligibility is published before the release of the final register. Upon the final closure of the registration process, electoral coordinators at the provincial and City of Kigali level transmit a written statement on the registration process to the president of the NEC. The voters' register is kept in the archives of the NEC, where it is available for consultation on request. Persons interested in lodging a complaint related to registration may do so in writing

---

422 Article 11 of the Electoral Code.

to the branch of the NEC where the complaint arose before the publication of the final voters' register. The branch of the NEC that receives the complaint must issue a decision within 48 hours, which may be appealed within 24 hours to the next level of the NEC if not satisfactory. All final decisions made by the NEC regarding registration and correction of the voters' register may be appealed in court.

Any registered voter who wishes to transfer from the register of the village or the embassy where he or she was originally registered to another does so by presenting a written document issued by a competent NEC staff member from the original place of registration showing that he or she has been removed from the original voters' register. He or she is then issued with a new voter's card.

Approval of party candidates

The Council of Commissioners is mandated to monitor, analyse and approve political candidates in line with stipulated provisions in the Constitution, the Electoral Code and the code of conduct for politicians and political organisations.[423] The law governing politicians and political organisations obliges politicians and political organisations to:[424]

- Avoid any speech, writing or action that may discriminate or divide;
- Educate the members of a political organisation or a politician to participate in political competition peacefully and with mutual respect and in tranquillity;
- Respect their opponents and avoid disparaging or defaming them;
- Tell the truth during political competition;
- Inform Rwandans of the fundamental principles and the political programme of the political organisation, with a view to building the nation;
- Avoid spoiling ballot papers, cheating in the polls and disturbing the elections or the counting of votes;
- Avoid unsound legal disputes or disparaging any election that was held in accordance with the law; and
- Use established legal procedures and abide by the final decision made by the authorised institution where election results are being challenged.

Before publication of the final list of candidates, a candidate who is disqualified by the NEC is informed in writing of the documents that are missing in his/her dossier and is granted time to complete it. This is done within five days after publication of the provisional list of candidates and before publication of the final list. The NEC approves and announces the final list of candidates at least seven days before commencement of election campaigns.[425]

---

423 Article 12 of the 2005 NEC Law.
424 Article 38 of the law governing politicians and political organisations.
425 Article 63 of the Electoral Code, amended and modified by Article 18 of Law No. 37/2013.

Constituencies

The role of the NEC in establishing electoral boundaries is set out in the 2005 NEC Law and the 2013 update.[426] Electoral constituencies in Rwanda vary according to the various elective positions.[427]

For the presidency, the electoral boundary comprises the entire country and eligible Rwandans living in the Diaspora.[428]

For members of the Chamber of Deputies in direct elections, it is also the entire country, with the same provision for Rwandans living in the Diaspora.[429]

For women MPs, the 24 deputies are elected directly by an electoral college that consists of members of executive committees of the National Women's Council at the national, provincial, district, sector, cell and village levels, as well as members of councils of districts and sectors within the respective electoral constituencies. A Presidential Order determines the electoral constituencies and the number of women deputies to be elected within each constituency in accordance with the administrative entities of the country.[430]

Senators are elected through a combination of direct and indirect methods:

- Twelve senators are elected directly through secret ballot by an electoral college comprising members of sector committees and district councils who form an electoral constituency;
- Eight are nominated by the President and include a representative of the historically marginalised communities in Rwanda such as the Twa;
- Four are nominated by the NCFP; and
- Two represent institutions of higher learning, one public and the other private, elected by the academic and research staff of these institutions.[431]

The elections of local administrative leaders at district and City of Kigali levels are by direct or indirect suffrage through secret ballot. The local administrative organs for which elections are held are councils, the bureaux of councils and the executive committees. The district council members comprise one representative (councillor) elected from each sector, and representatives of the youth and women who make up one-third of the council members. The district council is headed by a bureau comprising a chairperson, a vice-chairperson and a secretary, all elected directly by an electoral college.

The female members of the council (30% of all council members) are elected through indirect and secret ballot, as well as by members of the council bureau of sectors constituting the district, members of the executive committee of the National Women's

---

426 Article 5(2) of the 2005 NEC Law and Article 1(2) of Law No. 38/2013 of 16 June 2013.
427 Set out in the Electoral Code, Articles 87, 104, 109–111, 116, 136, 159–161.
428 Article 87.
429 Article 104.
430 Article 109.
431 Article 116.

Council at the district and sector level, and cell-level coordinators of the national council of women.

Working alongside the council is the district executive committee, headed by the mayor and two vice-mayors. Members of the district executive committee are elected by indirect and secret ballot, through an electoral college comprising members of the district and the sector councils constituting the district. Similarly, each sector is governed by a development committee comprising one elected representative from each cell and led by a sector coordinator. The cells and villages are the smallest political units providing the link between the people and the sectors. All resident adults (above the age of 18 years) are members of their local cell assembly or council. They elect a ten-member cell executive committee, which in turn elects two women and one youth to represent the village in the cell council.

Electoral calendar

The Bureau of Commissioners is charged with preparing and forwarding to the Council of Commissioners the programme for electoral activities.[432] The Council of Commissioners have the mandate to analyse and approve the electoral time table.[433] The time table outlines the range of activities related to the planning and conduct of elections, along with the dates and duration for undertaking them during an election year. Key activities include the following:

- Preparation and mobilisation of the electoral budget;
- Preparation and conduct of civic education;
- Preparation of electoral instructions;
- Upgrading the voters' register;
- Recruitment and deployment of electoral staff;
- Procurement of electoral materials;
- Invitation and accreditation of electoral observers;
- Determination and publication of the list of candidates;
- Announcement of the dates for and the conduct of election campaigns, and
- The actual elections.[434]

The polling date and the period for the election campaigns is determined by a Presidential Order.[435] According to the June 2013 update of the law, the period for election campaigns is now at least 20 days, revised from 18 in the 2010 version of the Electoral Code.

---

432   Article 14 of the 2005 NEC Law.
433   Ibid., Article 12.
434   For an example of the range of activities undertaken by the NEC during an election year, see Mbanda, K (2013) *Electoral Calendar for Legislative Elections, 2013*, NEC, Kigali, www.nec.gov.rw/uploads/media/ Electoral_Calendar_for_legislative_elections_2013_01.pdf.
435   Article 19 of the Electoral Code.

Appointing members of the Electoral College

An Electoral College is a group of people who have the right to vote.[436] The Electoral College system is used in the election of senators, women deputies and representatives of the youth and persons with disabilities at the district level. The 2005 NEC Law empowers the Council of Commissioners to appoint members of the Electoral College, give them instructions, receive their reports and supervise them during elections.[437] In all cases where an Electoral College is used, elections take place when a quorum of two-thirds is present. If the quorum is not attained, elections are postponed for a period not exceeding five days. If the quorum is not attained in the second instance, then those present proceed with the elections.

Civic and voter education

The NEC has a mandate to prepare and teach civic education, and to draft relevant voter education materials.[438] The NEC's civic and electoral education programme aims to teach citizens the importance of voting and encourage them to vote responsibly. The NEC targets the general population directly and through their representative groups, such as political parties, women, youth councils and trade unions.

Other institutions are also involved in delivering civic and electoral education. The law on political organisations mandates politicians and political organisations to educate citizens on politics based on democracy and elections.[439] Other constitutional institutions such as the National Unity and Reconciliation Commission (NURC) and the National Human Rights Commission also offer civic and political education to Rwandans. The *Itorero ry'Igihugu* (a form of national informal education) and *Ingando* (national solidarity camps) initiatives are two specific civic education programmes run nationally under the NURC. The two initiatives aim to inculcate the values of integrity, patriotism, service and national unity and reconciliation as key ingredients of national development. *Itorero ry'Igihugu* targets the general population and special groups such as returning exiles, while *Ingando* targets school-going and school-leaving youth.

Management of electoral campaigns

The Electoral Code determines how electoral campaigns are carried out in Rwanda,[440] based on provisions contained in the Constitution and other relevant laws. Citizens have the right to campaign freely.[441] An amendment of the law on political parties passed in 2007 now allows parties to organise and campaign at all levels of government.

---

436 As defined in Article 2(9) of Law No. 37/2013 of 16 June 2013 modifying and complementing Law No. 27/2010 of 19 June 2010 relating to elections.
437 Article 5(3).
438 Articles 5(4) and 19(4) of the 2005 NEC Law.
439 Article 2 of the Electoral Code.
440 Ibid., Articles 28–30, 64–69 and 147–153.
441 Ibid., Articles 19 and 28.

Regulating access to the media: The NEC and the Media High Council

Articles 67 and 68 of the Electoral Code regulate the relationship between the NEC and the Media High Council (MHC). The MHC is required to ensure equal access to public media for all independent candidates, political organisations and coalitions in competition. The NEC is mandated to receive copies of all communication regarding requests for use of public media by political parties and candidates. A candidate who wishes to campaign using state media sends a written request to the directors of such media outlet at least three days before the commencement of the event, indicating the date and the time of the event. This time has now been changed to five days under the June 2013 update of the Electoral Code. The directors of the media outlet must reply in writing within 24 hours (changed to 48 hours in the updated law) before the commencement of the event.

Law No. 30/2009[442] sets out the mission, organisation and functioning of the MHC and provides the legal framework for the role of, and access to, the media during elections. The MHC is mandated to:[443]

- Monitor whether political organisations and coalitions of political organisations enjoy equal access to public media during electoral campaigns;

- Establish regulations governing programme content and coverage of electoral campaigns by public and private media; and

- Ensure that the public media organs give equal coverage to various election-related news.

The MHC issues instructions regarding the implementation modalities for these provisions.

The relationship between the NEC and the MHC is, however, set to change in light of recent policy and legislative changes with regard to media regulation and operations in Rwanda. On 30 March 2012, the Cabinet adopted a media policy document outlining major reforms in the sector. The key reforms relevant to the MHC's relationship with the NEC included the following:

- The MHC would no longer be responsible for media regulation, but rather for media development and the promotion of media freedom.

- Print journalists would self-regulate under a mechanism to be determined.

- The government-run Rwanda Bureau for Information and Broadcasting (ORINFOR) would transform into the Rwanda Broadcasting Agency (RBA), to be regulated by its own board made up of civil society and private-sector individuals.

---

442 Law No. 30/2009 of 16 September 2009 determining the mission, organisation and functioning of the Media High Council.
443 Ibid., Article 6 (12–14).

- The Rwanda Utility Regulatory Authority (RURA) would have regulatory authority over electronic media (under the supervision of the RBA's board of directors) for the allocation and use of the electromagnetic spectrum.

- Content regulation would be devolved to a self-regulatory mechanism.

The Cabinet ordered that these reforms be enacted through new legislation and changes to existing media laws. On 30 June 2012, the Office of the Government Spokesperson replaced the Ministry of Information. On 1 July 2012, the Cabinet approved new draft legislation on access to information and on the RBA, as well as amendments to the media law, the MHC law, and the law governing RURA.

On 11 March 2013, Parliament adopted Law No. 02/2013 regulating the media, Law No. 03/2013 outlining the responsibilities, functioning and organisation of the Media High Council, and Law No. 04/2013 on access to information.

The role of the MHC under the new law is identified as helping to develop the capacity of Rwanda's media to make it more vibrant and professional. The role of media regulation is transferred to a media practitioners' self-regulatory body and to the national utilities regulator RURA. The day-to-day functioning of the media and the conduct of journalists is to be managed by a self-regulatory body, while the regulation of audio, audio-visual media and the internet is to be carried out by RURA.

The roles related to media monitoring during elections, which were previously performed by the MHC, have now been transferred to the NEC.

Sources: Law No. 37/2013 of 16 June 2013 modifying and complementing Law No. 27/2010 of 19 June 2010 relating to elections as modified and complemented to date; Law No. 03/2013 of 8 February 2013 outlining the responsibilities, functioning and organisation of the Media High Council, replacing Law No. 30 of 16 September 2009; Law No. 02/2013 of 11 March 2013 regulating the media, replacing Law No. 22/2009 of 12 August 2009; Law No. 38/2013 of 16 June 2013 modifying and complementing Law No. 31/2005 of 24 December 2005 relating to the organisation and functioning of the National Electoral Commission as modified and complemented to date.

All candidates have the right to equal access to state media.[444] A candidate who wishes to campaign using state media must request it through a written notice, against acknowledgment of receipt, addressed to the NEC at least five days before the commencement of such a campaign. The candidate must indicate the date and time s/he intends to conduct the campaign, and if it is on state radio or television. The NEC, in turn, must reply within 48 hours of such notice after consultation with the management of the media outlet on which the candidate wishes to conduct his/her campaign. However, candidates are barred from campaigning on the basis of their political parties.[445]

444 Ibid., Articles 68 and 69 (updated through Articles 20 and 21 of Law No. 37/2013 of 16 June 2013).
445 Article 125 of the Electoral Code.

Candidates are further barred from campaigning on the basis of race, ethnicity, region, religion and in other discriminatory or divisive ways; from abusing, defaming or slandering other candidates;[446] and from using national insignia and party emblems, photos and write-ups.[447] The Code also prohibits any form of corruption to influence voters and the use of state property during campaigns. Candidates who contravene these provisions are to be removed from the list of candidates,[448] but have the right of appeal to a higher instance of the NEC or a competent court.[449]

Recently, the June 2013 update of the Electoral Code has allowed candidates to use posters and other means during campaigns,[450] stating that:

> A candidate may, for his/her election campaign, use posters, banners, distribution of letters and circulars, public rallies and public debates, radio, television, print media, and any other means which is not contrary to the law.

The modalities for use are, however, to be determined by the NEC instructions.

Voting and vote counting, consolidation and announcement

The responsibilities of the NEC for vote counting are established by the Electoral Code. Responding to previous criticisms of the voting process, the June 2013 amendment now provides for voters to tick or cross with a pen against the candidate of their choice in elections where the ballot paper is used.[451] Previously, only the use of an inked thumbprint was allowed.

In line with the provisions barring certain individuals from registering as voters,[452] the code temporarily disqualifies the following categories of individuals from voting:[453]

- Persons in preventive detention in accordance with the provisions of the Criminal Procedure Code;
- Persons in detention in the execution of a sentence;
- A person with, or who shows signs of, mental illness; or
- Any other person who disrupts public order at a polling site.

Counting begins immediately after voting ends, without the requirement of an hour's interval between the closing of polls as was previously the case.[454] The counting must be public and before all present.

---

446 Ibid., Article 30.
447 Ibid., Article 152.
448 Ibid., Article 153.
449 Ibid., Article 165.
450 Law No. 37/2013 of 16 June 2013, Articles 9 and 20.
451 Article 15 of the Electoral Code.
452 Ibid., Article 11.
453 Ibid., Article 49, modified and amended by Article 16 of Law No. 37/2013 of 16 June 2013.
454 Ibid., Article 58.

The Electoral Code sets out an elaborate process for vote counting, declaration, consolidation, transmission and announcement of results.[455] This involves:

- Public counting and announcing of all valid votes cast at the polling station, noting the invalid votes and all votes against the voters' register,[456]
- Signing of NEC-provided tally sheets by voting room assessors, polling agents and representatives of candidates present at the polling station;
- Public declaration of election results immediately upon completion of vote counting;
- Consolidation of all results after voting by members of the polling room committee;
- Preparation of a statement of conduct of elections by the coordinator of the polling room and other polling room members;
- Signing of the statement by the polling room committee, candidates or their representatives or representatives of lists of candidates;
- The coordinator of the polling room places in the ballot box of the polling room the statement on the conduct of elections, sealed in an envelope and stamped by him/her before the public, together with the valid and invalid ballot papers, and hands them over to the chairperson of the polling station, and
- The chairperson of the polling station, after collecting all the electoral results from each polling room, sends them to the district level through the sector electoral coordinator.

Representatives of candidates are entitled to follow up the entire vote counting process and to request that their observations and contestations be recorded in the statement. There is a three-tier process for vote consolidation from polling centre to district, and on to the national level, for which the NEC is responsible.[457] Accordingly, the election coordinator at each level of consolidation of election results merges the results at the preceding level and communicates them to the public.

Powers of the NEC to sanction misconduct
The Electoral Code charges the NEC with the responsibility of monitoring and ensuring respect for laws and regulations governing electoral activities[458] gives specific powers of sanction to the EMB. For example, the NEC is empowered to remove from the

---

455 Ibid., Article 59.
456 A valid vote and an invalid vote are defined in Article 60 of the Electoral Code. Accordingly, a ballot paper is considered null and void if it bears signs other than those specified, does not clearly indicate the elected list or candidate, is returned in the ballot box without indicating any choice of candidate, has additions, or if it is not in compliance with the Electoral Code or NEC instructions. Such a ballot shall not be considered as a vote cast and shall not be considered in the calculation of the percentage of votes obtained by a candidate.
457 Electoral Code, Article 61.
458 Ibid., Article 5.

candidates' list anyone who violates campaign laws.[459] Such violations may include campaigning on the basis of a political organisation, using national or an organisation's symbols or write-ups during such campaigns,[460] or posting campaign materials in unauthorised places.[461] They may also include candidates acting in contravention of the code of conduct for politicians and political organisations.[462]

The procedure for sanction entails:

- An oral warning;
- A written warning where a candidate persists; and
- A nullification of candidature in writing within 12 hours of being officially informed of the violation, if the violation persists.

The same procedure is followed with candidates belonging to a political organisation or a coalition of political organisations. In such cases, the NEC summons the party or coalition concerned and advises it to remove the candidate in question. If the party or coalition fails to do so, the NEC delists the candidate by a notice to the political organisation or coalition concerned, the Senate, the NCFP and the Supreme Court. A candidate thus delisted can appeal the decision to a competent jurisdiction within 24 hours.

Article 55 of the Constitution gives power to senators to summon and recommend to the High Court for sanction political organisations that grossly violate the provisions relating to political organising. Such powers have been exercised before, for example, in the case of Bernard Ntaganda, leader of the Ideal Social Party, in 2010. A person who is removed from the list of candidates may appeal against the decision through the NEC hierarchy. If dissatisfied with the NEC decision, the person may appeal to a competent court of law.

Accreditation of election observers

The Electoral Code mandates the NEC to give accreditation to domestic and foreign election observers upon request.[463] The observers are required to abide by electoral laws and instructions issued by the NEC. The law allows observers unhindered access to all electoral activities for which they are accredited, including being present in the polling rooms. Responding to recent criticisms levelled against the NEC, the June 2013 review of the Electoral Code now codifies a range of additional rights for election observers.[464] Accordingly, electoral observers and representatives of candidates are allowed the following rights:

---

459 Ibid., Articles 69 and 153.
460 Ibid., Articles 125 and 152.
461 Ibid., Article 151.
462 Articles 35–41 of the law governing political organisations and politicians constitute the code of conduct for politicians and political organisations. Article 38 in particular, provides the code of conduct during the election period.
463 Electoral Code, Article 205.
464 2013 update of the Electoral Code, Article 30.

- To be informed about the electoral calendar;
- To be informed about how elections are organised and conducted;
- To be informed about where all electoral operations are done;
- To have access to all documents related to elections;
- To have free access to where all electoral operations are conducted, except the polling booth after the commencement of polling operations; and
- To be informed about election results within the period provided by law.

The updated Electoral Code also sets out the obligations of observers:[465]
- To avoid any activity that may disrupt the smooth electoral process;
- To be impartial in electoral activities;
- To comply with laws in force in general and laws related to elections in particular;
- To respect national culture;
- To avoid giving instructions to electoral officers;
- To operate in the area to which they have been accredited;
- To respect electoral officers at all levels;
- Not to publish elections results before the competent organ does so; and
- To produce a report based on evidence or facts observed during the elections and submit it to NEC within 60 days of the closure of polling.

Power to propose laws and regulations

The NEC's powers to prepare electoral regulations are set out in the law establishing it.[466] The instructions are meant to complement the electoral laws in guiding the electoral process. The power to draft the instructions is vested in the NEC's Executive Secretariat. Once drafted, the instructions are analysed and approved by the Council of Commissioners.[467] The powers to propose electoral laws remained dormant for some time until June 2013. These powers are now codified in an update of the 2005 NEC Law, which now empowers the NEC to participate in the elaboration of draft laws governing elections the commission organises and conducts.[468] These are analysed and approved by the Council of Commissioners before they are submitted to Parliament for review and enactment.

Independence and integrity

Article 180 of the Constitution establishes the NEC as an independent commission responsible for the preparation and organisation of local, legislative and presidential elections and national referenda and other elections determined by law. The law requires

---

465 Ibid., Article 31.
466 2005 NEC Law, Article 19(3).
467 Ibid., Article 12(6).
468 Article 1(8) of Law No. 38/2013 of 16 June 2013 modifying and complementing Law No. 31/2005 of 24 December 2005 relating to the organisation and functioning of the NEC.

that the NEC and its commissioners are independent and conduct their activities with the highest integrity. A requirement for appointment as a commissioner is that the person be a man or woman of very high integrity.[469] The oath of assumption of office requires the commissioners to be:

- Be loyal to their office;
- Serve selflessly without discrimination or favour; and
- Promote fundamental freedoms and rights.

Commissioners are barred from standing for any elective post during their tenure.[470]

The 2005 NEC Law grants temporary immunity against detention to members of the NEC at national or branch level during the elections period.[471] However, if accused of behaviour that may hinder the smooth running of the elections, such as revealing secrets, vote rigging, damaging electoral documents and materials, and other related offences, a commissioner is liable to prosecution in accordance with the electoral laws and the Criminal Procedure Code of Rwanda.

The NEC and the national Parliament

The NEC is a creation of the Constitution and, as such, is subject to parliamentary control. It is mandated to propose draft electoral laws through the ministries of justice or local government, and instructions for approval by Parliament. The NEC is required to submit its Plan of Action, activity report, as well as decisions of its Council of Commissioners to the President of the Republic, with copies to the President of the Senate, the Speaker of the Chamber of Deputies, the Prime Minister, the President of the Supreme Court and the minister in charge of local government.[472] The NEC may also recommend to Parliament further sanctions against politicians or political organisations that violate the provisions of the Electoral Code.

E. Funding of elections

The NEC budget

The budget of the NEC comprises a recurrent budget and a special budget for elections.[473] Both budgets are included in the national budget. The Council of Commissioners approves the annual budget before it goes to the Ministry of Finance and to Parliament for final approval. The 2005 NEC Law allows it to solicit additional funding from development partners.[474]

---

469 2005 NEC Law, Article 11.
470 Ibid., Article 32.
471 Ibid., Article 33.
472 Ibid., Article 28.
473 Ibid., Article 29.
474 Ibid.

The NEC has made tremendous efforts in seeking to end its dependence on donor funding. It plans to achieve 100% funding from domestic sources by 2013 and to phase out donor funding of national elections altogether. Indeed, the NEC has lived up to this plan.

In the 2008 parliamentary elections (15–18 September 2008), the NEC spent RWF 7.7 billion, of which the government contributed 63% (RWF 4.8 billion);[475] the remaining 37% came from development partners and was managed under a joint basket fund.[476] In 2010, up to 83% of the RWF 8.5 billion (USD 10 million) budget required for the presidential election came from the national budget.[477] This amount stood at 89% in 2012.[478] The budget for the September 2013 parliamentary elections was estimated at about RWF 5 billion (USD 8 million),[479] with 96% of this money coming from the national budget.[480] The remaining 4% was raised by NEC Printing Services and UNDP support. The Commonwealth Expert Team report notes that between 2008 and 2013, Rwanda managed to reduce its expenditure per voter by nearly 50%, from USD 2.9 to USD 1.4.[481] On average, about 40% of this budget goes into recurrent expenditure, while the rest is spent on the actual conduct of the elections.[482]

Among the strategies employed by the NEC to reduce costs and donor dependency include the use of volunteers, currently estimated at around 65,000 countrywide, and the re-use of materials procured from previous elections such as ballot boxes, stamp pads and printing papers. More recently, the NEC has procured its own state-of-the-art printer to print ballot papers, voters' registers, as well as civic education and other materials used during elections. The printer is hired out to other government institutions during non-election periods to generate income for the NEC. Some key respondents expressed reservations, however, about an in-house printer, citing fears of possible fraud through overprinting of ballot papers and ballot stuffing in the absence of adequate independent oversight.

---

475 The Commonwealth (2013) *Report of the Commonwealth Expert Team, Rwanda Legislative Election (Chamber of Deputies), 16–18 September 2013*, thecommonwealth.org/sites/default/files/project/documents/Rwanda_Elections_2013_Commonwealth_Expert_Team_Report.pdf.

476 Ibid.

477 Commonwealth Secretariat (2010) *Report of the Commonwealth Observer Group, Rwanda Presidential Election, 9 August 2010*, p. 9, aceproject.org/ero-en/regions/africa/RW/rwanda-observation-report-presidential-elections-1.

478 'NEC should be aid free – Karangwa', *The New Times*, 10 March 2012, www.newtimes.co.rw/news/index.php?i=14927&a=51187.

479 'Rwanda Parliamentary Elections to Cost US$ 8 Million', *The Independent*, 29 March 2013, allafrica.com/stories/201304011094.html.

480 The Commonwealth (2013), op. cit.

481 Ibid., p. 7.

482 For example, the NEC 2008 budget was RWF 5,793,799,622, allocated as follows: RWF 3,608,235,105 (62.3%) to preparing and conducting the 2008 election of MPs and the Chamber of Deputies; RWF 1,044,921,316 (18%) to building the institutional capacity of the NEC; RWF 42,715,000 (0.7%) to promotion of relations and collaboration with other organs.

Auditing

By law, the commission is obliged to submit, by March of each year, an annual activities report, an action plan and a budget to the President of the Republic – with copies to the Parliament, the Supreme Court, all Cabinet members and the Ministry of Local Government.[483] The reports are prepared by the relevant departments and offices of the NEC and pre-approved by the Council of Commissioners. Upon approval, the NEC's budget is presented to the Ministry of Finance. The NEC's internal auditor prepares quarterly and annual audit reports, which are submitted to the Council of Commissioners for review. In addition, the NEC is subject to an audit by the Auditor-General at his/her discretion, and upon request by Parliament and the executive.[484] Every year, the Auditor-General must submit a complete report on the state financial statements for the previous year to each chamber of Parliament, prior to the commencement of the session devoted to the examination of the budget of the following year.[485]

Financing of political parties

Rwandan political parties have three main sources of financing:
- Limited state support channelled through the NCFP to all registered parties in equal measure;
- Independent contributions from membership; and
- Income from party assets.

According to the law regulating political parties, any political party that obtains at least 5% of the valid votes is eligible for an equal share of financing from the government. The NCFP has a capacity-building grant available to parties every year. The grant, issued upon application, comes from the national budget and depends on the available budget for the year. Parties are required to submit yearly financial statements and inventories of assets to the Ministry of Local Government, the Ombudsman and the NCFP. Donations from public or quasi-public enterprises, foreigners and trading companies are not allowed. Any donation exceeding RWF 1 million has to be declared within 30 days. Except in the case of the RPF, membership contributions are paltry and irregular, and the small parties depend almost entirely on the funding made available by government through the NCFP.

The small parties have practically no assets. The RPF, on the other hand, draws on an extensive base of financing that includes:
- A fixed percentage of members' income;
- Special contributions during election times;
- Ongoing fundraising activities involving public pledges;

---

483   Article 180 of the Constitution; Article 4 of the 2005 NEC Law.
484   Article 183 of the Constitution; Law No. 05/98 of June 1998 establishing the Office of the Auditor-General of State Finances.
485   Article 184 of the Constitution.

- Sales of party paraphernalia; and
- Contributions from the Diaspora.

It also has a robust business and asset base built over many years. This formidable base affords the RPF an overwhelming financial and political advantage over its competitors, and a capacity to access, mobilise and recruit members in ways that the opposition political parties can never hope to match.

Representatives of various political parties interviewed for this study opined that the government should provide an operational budget to political parties since they are not allowed to receive funding from foreign sources. In their view, political parties in coalition with the ruling party should equally benefit from such funds. A concern was raised about the late reimbursement of funds to political parties that obtain the 5% vote threshold. The key concern, however, was in relation to the challenges faced by opposition political parties' in mobilising funding from the public. While a 2007 amendment of the law on political organisations now allows these entities to organise at all levels of government, parties other than the RPF continue to be frustrated by local authorities in their efforts to mobilise and recruit membership based on issues important to them. A member of the opposition observed, 'If a priest can be jailed for merely expressing a different opinion on a government programme, how about a politician or anyone else on a matter in which the government has a strong interest?'[486] According to PSD and PS-Imberakuri, because of the history of Rwanda, a negative perception has been formed about opposition political parties, diminishing their value and making it difficult for them to recruit members and mobilise resources for their activities.[487]

F. Management of electoral disputes

Electoral disputes can be taken to the Supreme Court, or directly to the NEC, depending on the type of election to which the complaint pertains.

Supreme Court

The Supreme Court is the highest appellate court in the country. Its jurisdiction includes receiving and hearing petitions related to referenda and presidential and legislative elections.[488]

The Electoral Code lays out the mandate of the Supreme Court in regard to resolving disputes related to a presidential candidature.[489] Any petition regarding presidential or

---

486 This was in specific reference to a priest who was jailed for 18 months for criticising the government's *Nyakatsi* and family-planning programmes. The *Nyakatsi* programme was a national campaign to phase out grass-thatched houses (known as *nyakatsi* in Kinyarwanda) across the whole country and re-roof them with iron sheets.
487 Interviews with the leaders of both parties, 20–21 September 2013.
488 Article 145 of the Constitution.
489 Article 85 of the Electoral Code.

parliamentary candidature must be lodged with the Supreme Court within 48 hours of the publication of the list of candidates. Upon receipt of the petition, the President of the Supreme Court must, within 24 hours, inform the president of the NEC and the Ministry of Local Government.[490]

Any petition related to presidential or legislative election results are to be lodged, in writing, with the President of the Supreme Court within 48 hours of the provisional outcome being announced by the NEC, with a copy to the President of the NEC.[491] In both cases, the petition must indicate the identity of the complainant and the nature of the complaint.[492] When the petition is declared admissible, the President of the Supreme Court must inform the president of the NEC within 24 hours after the receipt of the petition.[493] The Supreme Court must, in turn, issue a ruling on the petition within five days of the filing.[494] Within this time, the Supreme Court examines the petition and notifies the parties concerned of the date when the hearing of evidence will take place in the court registry. It also informs them of the period granted to them to make their submissions. If a cancellation of the results is not warranted, the Supreme Court declares the final results within another five days.[495] However, if the flaws petitioned against have altered in a determining way the result of the elections, the Supreme Court nullifies the election and declares a fresh poll within 90 days of the first election.

NEC

The NEC is mandated to resolve electoral disputes at levels other than presidential and parliamentary elections within its hierarchy. Disputes may be related to the organisation of elections or contested electoral results.[496]

Disputes at the cell, village and sector level are to be lodged with the electoral supervisors at the concerned level immediately after the end of the elections. They are settled publicly in front of the population. Decisions taken at these levels may be appealed at higher levels of the NEC, depending on their hierarchy.

At the district or City of Kigali levels, electoral results may be contested in the first instance at the branch of the NEC where the elections occurred. Any person with a petition may submit it in writing to the branch within 48 hours from when it occurred, indicating the irregularities in the electoral process and providing substantive evidence of it. If the petitioner is not satisfied with the decision of the NEC officials at this level, s/he may appeal to the next level of the NEC in the province or the City of Kigali, and to the national level if necessary. The level of the NEC that receives the appeal is required to decide it within 48 hours of receipt.

---

490 Ibid., Article 75.
491 Ibid., Articles 71–73.
492 Ibid., Article 73.
493 Article 22 of Law No. 37/2013, updating Law No. 27/2010.
494 Articles 77, 85 of the Electoral Code.
495 Ibid., Article 78.
496 Articles 164–169 of the Electoral Code.

A person who files a petition at the highest level of the NEC and is not satisfied with decisions taken, is entitled to file his or her case in a competent court within a period not exceeding 24 hours. The court in turn is obliged to render a decision on the petition within a period not exceeding 48 hours and before the day of the announcement of the final results. In the case of a petition related to the organisation of elections, the competent court must determine it and render a judgment before the day of the elections.

Types of complaints

Complaints on infringement of electoral laws and provisions during elections have been lodged with the NEC at national and local levels. The main infringements include:

- Intimidation and beating up of opposition party members, agents and supporters by local authorities and supporters of the RPF;
- Local authorities impeding opposition party campaigns and preventing citizens from attending their rallies;
- Confiscation and destruction of campaign materials belonging to opposition candidates;
- Warnings to supporters of opposition candidates that they risk being excluded from government programmes such as 'one cow per family'; and
- Arrests of opposition party activists on charges of illegal campaigning (illegal political speeches, illegal distribution of leaflets and wearing of party T-shirts).[497]

The NEC has addressed some of these complaints; however, there is a general concern that it has been reluctant or slow in responding to others, thus creating disincentives for opposition candidates and their representatives to lodge complaints on electoral misconduct.[498] As a result, the appetite for court petitions has died down. Apart from the high-profile petitions lodged by opposition party leaders against their state sentences and imprisonment, there were no instances of electoral process disputes that were formally lodged with the High Court, a lower instance court, or the Supreme Court, by a politician or a political party or a coalition against a decision made by the NEC.

Respondents gave a number of reasons for opposition politicians, political parties and activists being disinclined to formally appeal the rulings of the NEC either through

---

497 US Bureau of Democracy, Human Rights & Labour (2012) *Country Report on Human Rights Practices for 2011, Rwanda*, p. 22, www.state.gov/documents/organisation/186443.pdf; Schroder (2008), op. cit., p. 17.
498 Some of the examples given included the NEC's lack of action on allegations of influence peddling and fraud committed by the RPF during the 2011 senatorial elections and reports of intimidation of agents of opposition political parties during the 2010 presidential elections reported by the Commonwealth Observers (Commonwealth Secretariat (2010), op. cit., p. 17). Accordingly, PSD had recruited over 170 party agents to observe the polling in the district. After the agents had been trained and registered, a number of them reported being intimidated by RPF representatives and local authorities. In the end, the party had only 50 party agents to field in the area. The PSD representatives also reported the destruction of their campaign posters by supporters of the RPF to the NEC district coordinator, but no action was taken by the NEC.

its hierarchy or in the courts. These reasons included a fear of reprisal from the NEC or the state, and a belief, based on precedence, that neither institution would grant them a fair hearing. A number of respondents from civil society and opposition political parties associated the NEC and the Supreme Court with the executive and the RPF, and thus doubted their commitment to render fair and independent rulings on electoral matters. They observed that in all recent petitions brought by members of the opposition political parties to the Supreme Court, the judges had ruled in favour of the state, largely upholding the initial sentences.[499]

The lack of formal complaints has also been explained by the existence of informal forums for dispute settlement, such as the NCFP and the Office of the Ombudsman.[500] These institutions offer mediation services in internal as well as inter-party disputes. The NCFP may also address cases of political misconduct and, if necessary, bring them to the attention of other relevant authorities such as the Ministry of Local Government, the Office of the Ombudsman and the Senate Commission on Political Affairs for further action. Political party and civil society leaders, however, observed that these mechanisms were largely informal and did not offer any guarantees of action.[501]

Other concerns with potential to generate electoral disputes relate to the time limits allowed for submission and resolution of petitions in contested local, legislative and presidential elections. For local elections, the four days (less in village, cell and sector elections) provided to lodge and resolve a disputed election result is seen by respondents as insufficient. For legislative and presidential elections, the period of five days given between lodging and resolving a disputed electoral result by the Supreme Court was seen by respondents as too short to enable a proper judicial determination in elections of this magnitude.

G. A critical assessment of election management in Rwanda

Over the past 18 years, Rwanda has made remarkable progress in breaking away from its past and moving towards a path of greater electoral democracy. It has promulgated a

---

499 The main recent petitions are those of Victoire Ingabire, Bernard Ntaganda and Deogratius Mushayidi. On 7 March 2012, Victoire Ingabire launched an appeal in the Supreme Court challenging the constitutionality of Rwanda's genocide ideology and divisionism laws, charging that they are vague and used by the state to restrict freedom of expression. The Supreme Court dismissed the petition on 18 October 2012 on grounds of lack of merit. On 17 December 2012, she appealed her 30 October 2012 eight-year conviction on charges of genocide denial and conspiracy and planning to cause state insecurity. Her appeal was dogged by postponements, and confessions of duress and framed testimonies by prosecution witnesses. In December 2013, Rwanda's Supreme Court upheld her conviction and increased her jail term from eight to 15 years. Similarly, the appeal of Deogratius Mushayidi's life sentence handed down in September 2010 was dismissed by the Supreme Court in February 2012 after several hearings on the ground of lack of adequate mitigating evidence. Also dismissed was Bernard Ntaganda's appeal of his four-year sentence handed down in February 2011 on charges of organising illegal meetings, inciting ethnic divisions and threatening state security. The appeal was dismissed in April 2012 on grounds of lack of merit.
500 Commonwealth Secretariat (2010), op. cit., p. 17.
501 Ibid.

wide range of relevant electoral laws and established the requisite institutions to implement them. However, the commitments and the principles underlined in the Constitution are also the bane of Rwanda's electoral system. While progressive, the system remains saddled with fundamental legal and institutional challenges that still stand in the way of Rwanda's move away from its burdening past towards a path of greater democracy and freer, fairer and more transparent elections.

Key among these are the challenges posed by the set of laws relating to divisionism, sectarianism, genocide ideology and defamation applied by Rwandan authorities to prosecute and deter speech and other conducts deemed as constituting hate or likely to divide or cause conflict among Rwandans.

Another major concern relates to the delivery of civic and electoral education. The NEC's strategy for civic and electoral education is generally oriented more towards getting citizens to exercise an electoral obligation and propagating notions of patriotism and service, rather than advancing the greater ideal of encouraging citizens to participate fully in the political life of their communities and country, and to commit to fundamental values and principles of democracy.

Institutional framework

Rwanda's NEC has strong powers in the management of the electoral process, which would put it in the category of 'strong central referee commissions', according to a comparative study of EMBs in West Africa.[502] While it lacks the power to register political parties, distribute and monitor government-allocated funds to them and adopt the electoral calendar without the prior approval of the executive,[503] it enjoys a wide range of other powers. It has the power to manage all the affairs in the preparation and conduct of elections, and to ensure respect for laws and regulations governing the electoral process. These include determining electoral boundaries, establishing the electoral list, approving the final list of candidates, overseeing electoral campaigns and the voting process, announcing the results of all elections, and invalidating and correcting them before their announcement and publication. The NEC is also mandated to sanction and disqualify individuals infringing on electoral laws and instructions, and to propose new ones to Parliament.

Political parties and other stakeholders see these powers as excessive. Of particular concern are the powers to approve and sanction candidates. While there is consensus that Rwandan elections are generally conducted peacefully and within the law, there is

---

502 Hounkpe, M & Fall, IM (2011) *Electoral Commissions in West Africa: A Comparative Study*, 2nd edn, ECOWAS & Friedrich-Ebert-Stiftung, pp. 40–41, aceproject.org/ero-en/misc/electoral-commission-in-west-africa-a-comparative; see also Hounkpe, M, Fall, IM, Jnadu, AL & Kambale, P (2011) *Election Management Bodies in West Africa: A Comparative Study of the Contribution of Electoral Commissions to the Strengthening of Democracy*, AfriMAP & Open Society Initiative for West Africa, www.afrimap.org/english/images/report/AfriMAP_WestAfrica_EMB_Full_EN.pdf.

503 The polling day and the period of elections are determined by a presidential order, according to Article 64 of the Electoral Code.

deep concern over the NEC's perceived excessiveness and selective application of sanctions. A number of instances where such excesses and selective sanctions were applied have been identified in the various election observer reports. They include instances where candidates were barred from contesting, delisted or pressurised to withdraw their candidacy on unclear grounds, or where the NEC failed to investigate or act on reported breaches of electoral law by politicians or their agents. These have already been identified in this report. Other concerns such as the NEC not consulting enough during the review and reform of electoral laws and instructions and not granting sufficient opportunity to ventilate other important electoral concerns have also been noted elsewhere in this report.

Management of elections

Since 2000, the NEC has organised and conducted the following elections:

- First local elections of 2001;
- First constitutional referendum and first presidential and parliamentary elections of 2003;
- Second local elections of 2006;
- Second parliamentary elections of 2008, held to elect members of the lower chamber of Parliament;
- Second presidential election of 2010;
- Second local leaders elections and second senatorial elections of 2011; and
- Parliamentary elections of 2013.

In addition, the NEC was involved in organising special elections, such as those of community mediators and Gacaca[504] judges.

Voter registration and the right to run as a candidate

The voters' register is now electronic and is updated annually before any election. It is possible to check one's status online or using a mobile telephone; the register now also includes the voter's photograph. According to the European Union (EU) Observer Mission, the voters' register has become more inclusive.[505] Cases of missing names on the register have reduced considerably. The NEC has also increased the number of polling stations and polling rooms to reduce the long queues during voting. Each polling room handles no more than 500 voters.

Further, the rights to register as a voter or run as an independent candidate have been broadened. Citizens convicted of genocide crimes from category three (crimes such as theft or destruction of property) and those who have committed minor offences

---

504 A system of community justice established in 2001 to try people involved in the Genocide.
505 European Union Election Observation Mission (2008) *Final Report: Republic of Rwanda Legislative Elections to the Chamber of Deputies 15–18 September 2008*, p. 12, eeas.europa.eu/eueom/pdf/missions/ eueom_rwanda_final_report_en.pdf.

may now vote.[506] However, a number of important restrictions still exist regarding the right to vote or run as a candidate, including the denial of these rights to prisoners, persons in temporary confinement such as those in pre-trial detention or in hospitals, and persons with dual nationality.

Relationship with political parties

The NEC enjoys good working relations with the NCFP.[507] This relationship is, nevertheless, informal and is without any structured mechanisms for engagement and feedback or any legal requirement to share reports. A number of political party representatives interviewed for this study were concerned that the NEC was not engaging them sufficiently as key stakeholders in the electoral process. In particular, they were concerned about the lack of adequate consultation in the drafting of electoral laws and instructions, terming the NEC's powers in this regard as excessive.[508] They were concerned that there was no formal mechanism for consultation and dialogue at the level of the NEC, the NCFP and civil society to resolve important electoral process matters such as those identified by the elections observers, and that the NEC did not involve them enough in the process of reviewing and reforming electoral laws and instructions. They observed that often the NEC prepared draft laws and instructions too late into the election calendar, thus allowing little or no time to debate them before they go to Parliament for review and approval.

In its report on the 2010 presidential election, the Rwandan Civil Society Election Observation Mission (CSEOM) recommended that a formal mechanism be established to bring together the NEC, political groups, civil society and other important stakeholders to debate key electoral concerns.[509] This recommendation has not been acted upon to date, despite numerous promises by the NEC.[510]

Civic and voter education

There is a need to broaden and deepen civic and political education among Rwandans, especially among young Rwandans, and to create room for other players both in determining the content of civic and voter education, and in planning and delivering it. 'I would like to see my children free to think,' remarked the Secretary-General of the PSD and President of the Senate.[511] He observed further:

---

506 Article 11 of the Electoral Code.
507 Mr Kabagema Anicet, the executive secretary of the NCFP, interview, 19 September 2012.
508 The Hon. Damascene Ntawukuriryayo, interview, op. cit.; Mme Christine Mukabunani, interview, op. cit.; Senator Apollinaire Mushinzimana, interview, 15 September 2012.
509 CSEOM (2010) *Final Report: Presidential Election 2010*, p. 33, www.rcsprwanda.org/IMG/pdf/Report_on_Presidential_Elections_9_August_2010.pdf.
510 Eugene Rwibasira, former chairperson of the Rwanda Civil Society Platform and spokesperson of the CSEOM, interview, 24 September 2012.
511 The Hon. Damascene Ntawukuriryayo, interview, op. cit.

Political parties remain too weak, waking up only at elections, and our media is too immature; yet the challenges facing Rwanda today require more open debate on many facets of our national development. There is need for more forums for debate in schools and universities and for universities to engage in more research and discussion of important social issues.[512]

According to the LDGL, the government of Rwanda should introduce civic and political education in the school curriculum at all levels and promote the culture of debate.[513] In their report on the 2010 presidential election, the Rwanda CSEOM notes:

Although voter education programmes took place across the country, citizens in rural areas in particular would benefit from more concerted efforts to ensure they are aware of the mechanics and meaning of elections.[514]

The Commonwealth Observer Group, in their report on the same election, note the lack of familiarity among a large number of voters with the proper voting procedures[515] and underline the importance of increased civic and voter education, targeting especially the elderly and the youth.[516]

There was a concern that the NEC's focus seemed geared more towards getting citizens to exercise an electoral obligation rather than empowering them to exercise an important constitutional and democratic right.[517] While perhaps designed to suit Rwanda's unique circumstances, the NEC's and indeed the national approach to delivering civic and voter education ought to move beyond voter information and education and responsible citizenship to embrace civic education in its complete sense, encompassing such aspects as the meaning of democracy, citizenship and rights, democratic principles and procedures, and democratic institutions and laws, among other things. The aim should be to encourage citizens to participate fully in the political life of their communities and country, committed to the fundamental values and principles of democracy. In this regard, the annual national dialogue and the civil-society-led national dialogue forums are good examples of efforts to engage the public in wider conversations around important national issues. The success of such forums holds enormous potential for

---

512 Ibid.
513 LDGL (2013) *Rapport de la LDGL sur la observation des élections Présidentielles du 9 Aout 2010 au Rwanda*, p. 73, www.ldgl.org/wp-content/uploads/2014/03/Rapport-LDGL-sur-les-%C3%A9lections-parlementaires-sept-2013-au-Rda.pdf.
514 CSEOM (2010), op. cit., p. 19.
515 Ibid., p. 23.
516 Ibid., p. 32.
517 Article 48 of the Electoral Code makes it obligatory to vote in Rwanda. In the draft electoral law currently with Parliament, this will no longer be the case.

opening up the society to discussions on other issues such as elections, democracy and the rule of law.

There is a need to broaden the planning and delivery of civic and voter education to involve other actors, such as civil society and political parties. Currently, content development, planning, and delivery of civic and voter education remains the preserve of the NEC. The NEC Law is silent on the role of other potential providers such as civil society and political parties. Currently, the NEC engages with these entities only at its discretion. In countries like Kenya, a more liberal legal provision allows for multiple actors to participate in preparing and delivering civic and voter education, including developing education materials.[518]

Other challenges identified as hindering effective delivery of civic and voter education include the late publication of electoral laws and instructions, denying both the electorate and candidates sufficient time to familiarise themselves with them. For example, the Electoral Code came into force 38 days before the commencement of the presidential election campaigns, which began on 20 July 2010. This period was 'too short for the citizens to know the contents of the law'.[519] Similarly, the law governing the organisation and functioning of the National Women's Council[520] and the law on the organisation and functioning of the National Council for People with Disabilities[521] were published in the *Official Gazette* on 11 February 2011, two days before the elections. While the NEC blamed these delays on Parliament's slow pace in reviewing the draft laws, the latter blamed the NEC for submitting the draft laws to Parliament late.

Management of electoral campaigns

The NEC has been accused of bias in favour of the ruling party, thus creating disincentives for opposition candidates and their representatives to approach it for redress. Among the accusations levelled against the NEC include non-action on allegations of influence peddling by the RPF and on reports of intimidation of agents of opposition political parties by RPF agents and local authorities. The NEC has also been accused of being excessive in the application of its sanction powers, in particular the power to bar candidates from contesting elections or to remove them from the list of candidates. Respondents felt that such powers should be vested in competent courts so that due process can be followed. This is also the view of other commentators on Rwanda's electoral laws.[522]

---

518 Section 40 of the Kenya Elections Act, 2011, p. 34 states: 'The Commission shall, in performing its duties under Article 88(4)(g) of the Constitution, establish mechanisms for the provision of continuous voter education and cause to be prepared a voter education curriculum.'

519 CSEOM (2010), op. cit., p. 7.

520 Law No. 02/2011 of 10 February 2011.

521 Law No. 03/2011 of 10 February 2011.

522 For example, Lutz, G (2009) *Notes on Rwanda's New Electoral Code.* Report on behalf of the Rwandan National Electoral Commission & Swiss Agency for Development and Cooperation, p. 8.

Other concerns include the short duration allowed for political campaigns and the conduct of public servants during campaign periods. The period of 18 days (now increased to 20 in the June 2013 review of the Electoral Code) allowed for campaigns is seen by political parties and other observers as too short to enable citizens to sufficiently know the candidates. During the senatorial elections, candidates are allowed as little as ten minutes to campaign and two minutes to present their manifestos before the Electoral College, as was the case during the 2011 senatorial elections.[523]

Further, the Electoral Code remains silent on the conduct of public servants during campaigns. Many state officials have been known to actively participate in the preparation and conduct of political campaigns, dressed up in the colours of their political parties.[524] This is attributed to the lack of clarity over what constitutes illegal campaigning, especially as a guide for local authorities in their handling of political campaigns. This lack of clarity has been a major cause of the unequal application of campaign regulations by political parties and the harassment meted out to opposition party politicians and their agents by local authorities. Some clarity has now been introduced, through changes to the Electoral Code,[525] but this still does not go far enough, particularly in regard to the conduct of public servants during elections.

Voting, vote counting, consolidation and announcement

Over the past years, there has been a significant improvement in the NEC's management of voting, vote counting, consolidation and results announcement. The consolidation documents are displayed where the elections have taken place. The president of the NEC carries out the consolidation of election results at the national level on the basis of the consolidated electoral documents at the district level. The Electoral Code provides for provisional results of the presidential election to be announced by the NEC within five days of the polls closing, and the final results within seven days after the declaration of provisional results.[526] In theory, the voting and vote counting, consolidation and transmission processes remove any possibility of electoral fraud. The consolidation process is in principle accessible to observers and candidate representatives. The law, therefore, provides a sound basis for good practice.

In practice, however, there have been instances of irregularities and lack of transparency in these processes. In their report of the 2008 legislative elections, the EU observer group outlined a range of countrywide gross disorders in relation to the tabulation and consolidation of election results.[527] These included:

523 CSEOM (2011) *Report of Senatorial Elections Took Place on 26–27 September 2011*, p. 18, www.rcsprwanda.org/IMG/pdf/Senatorial_election_final_english_version.pdf.
524 Civil Society Elections Observer Mission Report, Rwanda 2010 presidential elections, p. 18.
525 Articles 9, 10 and 20 of Law No. 37/2013 of 16 June 2013 modifying Articles 29, 30 and 67 of Law No. 27/2010 of 19 June 2010.
526 Article 70 of the Electoral Code.
527 European Union Election Observation Mission (2008), op. cit.

- Shifting the location for the organisation of indirect elections for the seats reserved for women representatives from the province to the district;
- Including sectors as additional consolidation points contrary to NEC procedures;
- Failure to follow consolidation procedures in relation to securing and sealing ballot boxes;
- Transmission of election results from the polling centres to the sectors and to the district level by telephone, without the physical transfer of the tallying forms and materials as required by NEC instructions (thus not being fully observable by election observers);
- In Kigali, polling centre results being delivered directly to the NEC office, by-passing the district; and
- Observers being barred from entering some district consolidation offices and being informed the following day upon re-visiting the centres that they could only get the results from the NEC headquarters.[528]

The CSEOM raised similar concerns in its report on the same elections, noting that the processes could be improved and made more transparent. In their report on the 2010 presidential election, they further observed that:

> Electoral procedures regarding the transmission of results and physical location of district level consolidation were lacking in detail, and this was reflected in practice. Practice was inconsistent around the country, as was information provided to observers …. In summary, consolidation of results was a problematic element of this electoral process.[529]

The Commonwealth Observer mission in its report on the 2010 presidential election also notes a range of counting, transmission and consolidation irregularities:
- Ballot boxes not being sealed properly or certified empty before commence-ment of voting;
- Haphazard application of ink on voters' fingers;
- Lapses in the counting procedure, such as the start of the count not being announced formally or reconciliation of votes not being done in accordance with the stipulated law and NEC instructions;
- Delays in transmission of ballot boxes; and
- Tabulation and consolidation processes shrouded in secrecy in many districts.[530]

---

528 Ibid., pp. 20, 39–41.
529 CSEOM (2010), op. cit., pp. 15, 28–30.
530 Commonwealth Secretariat (2010), op. cit., pp. 25–28.

These challenges continue to weigh down Rwanda's electoral process as observed by the CSEOM in the September 2013 parliamentary elections.[531]

There are also legal challenges affecting the voting and vote counting and consolidation processes. These include the obligation to vote, the start time of voting, the use of thumbprints to cast a vote, and the display and publication of results at the polling and consolidation stations.

Overall, there have been no problems with the actual voting and the process has been praised as well organised and peaceful by many observers, with the voters' register generally in order, enabling all eligible voters to exercise their right to vote. The idea of voting as an obligation[532] has been problematic, with the NEC sometimes employing tactics that were deemed inappropriate in an effort to implement the law.[533] The 6am start time for voting has also been considered inappropriate as it is still dark at this time and most rural polling stations do not have electricity. Further, the current practice of voting using a thumbprint has been criticised, with observers concerned that it could be used to trace a ballot to a voter.

The Electoral Code provides for an obligatory public display of election results at polling-station level and at later stages of the consolidation process. The manner of this display is, however, not prescribed in law and is left to the discretion of the NEC. In most cases, there has been no public display or posting of electoral results at the polling stations or at the district consolidation centres. In its report on the 2010 presidential election, the CSEOM noted that transparency of polling station counting would be enhanced through a legal or procedural requirement to immediately post results outside each polling centre.[534]

Some of these challenges have, however, been recognised by the NEC and are addressed in the June 2013 revision of the electoral law:

- Voting will be a civic duty rather than a legal obligation;[535]
- Polling will start at 7am and end at 3pm for direct elections;[536]
- The time for a candidate to review his or her dossier in case of disqualification before announcement of the final list has been increased to five days from two;[537]
- More rights for electoral observers have been granted;[538] and

531 'Rwanda: Civil Society Cite a Number of Irregularities in Parliamentary Elections', *La Tribune Franco-Rwandaise*, 23 September 2013, www.france-rwanda.info/article-rwanda-civil-society-cite-a-number-of-irregularities-in-parliamentary-elections-120200085.htm l, accessed 4 November 2013.

532 Article 46 of the Electoral Code.

533 A case in point was NEC officials' use of loudspeakers in the early hours of the morning (approximately 2–3am) in Eastern Province (Rwamagana District) to call people to come to vote, reported by the Commonwealth team (Commonwealth Secretariat (2010), op. cit., p. 23).

534 CSEOM (2010), op. cit., p. 28.

535 Article 3, modifying Article 8 of Law No. 27/2010.

536 Article 14.

537 Article 18.

538 Articles 30 and 31.

- Casting of votes using a thumbprint or pen where ballot papers are used, unlike before when the thumbprint was the only option.[539]

Election observation

The NEC has over the years established good working relations with election observers, giving them accreditation and permitting them access to observe elections at different levels.

Since 2000, Rwandan civil society has deployed domestic observers to monitor key national elections. Notably, the *Programme d'Observatoire des Elections au Rwanda* (POER), a coalition of some 150 local CSOs, was established in 2000, monitoring the March 2001 local elections at district level, the March 2002 local elections at sector-level, the December 2002 elections of judges for the *Gacaca* courts, and the May 2003 referendum on the new Constitution.

POER delivered generally favourable observation reports until 2003, when a split occurred in the organisation between those who wanted the report watered down and those who sought to include more critical remarks in the report on the 2003 referendum. Afraid to be denied accreditation if it formed its own organisation, the critical group remained within the organisation. During the 2003 presidential election, it decided to write its own report but was denied accreditation by the NEC. On the day of the election, POER managed to get accreditation, but suffered a range of frustrations, including being denied access to both the voting and vote consolidation processes and the electoral results. Faced with a wide range of leadership and funding challenges, POER disintegrated and died in the years that followed.

In 2008, it was replaced by the Rwandan Civil Society Election Observation Mission (CSEOM), which was established under the Rwanda Civil Society Platform (RCSP). The RCSP is the national apex organisation of some 15 umbrella organisations representing a majority of the non-governmental and community-based organisations operating in Rwanda. The CSEOM, bringing together some 500 long-term and short-term observers drawn from member organisations, has observed every national and grassroots-level election since 2008. Since its establishment, the CSEOM has enjoyed increased capacity, resources and goodwill from development partners and has generated reasonably objective reports of the conduct of elections in the country. This performance has, however, tended to vacillate, depending on who heads the RCSP and in turn the CSEOM.[540]

Another civil society group that has been involved in the monitoring of elections is the *Ligue Des Droits de personnes des Grands Lacs* (LDGL), a regional non-governmental organisation (NGO) working on democracy and human rights issues. Steered by

---

539 Article 15.
540 This researcher observed the operations of the CSEOM during the tenures of the immediate former chairperson of the RCSP and the CSEOM and the incumbent.

leaders and staff from the three Great Lakes countries,[541] LDGL has been monitoring Rwandan elections since 2003.

In practice, election observers have faced numerous challenges in following the various stages of the electoral process, as shown in their various reports. This aspect of the NEC's work presents perhaps one of the main transparency tests for Rwanda's electoral process. In the run-up to the 2008 parliamentary elections, for example, the LDGL was prevented from deploying its full election observer mission, fiercely attacked by the president of the NEC even before its report came out, and implicitly threatened with denial of registration as an NGO in Rwanda. The NEC president accused the LDGL of altering an earlier version of its observation report to make it more critical.[542]

In its report of the 2008 parliamentary elections, the EU Election Observation Mission recounts being deliberately excluded, obstructed, and in some cases even misdirected during the district level consolidation processes. The report notes that the mission was only able to receive preliminary results on the same day as consolidation in two out of the 30 electoral districts and that the results were relayed directly to the NEC National Centre in Kigali by telephone, and without being announced or published at the districts.[543] The CSEOM made the same observations in its report on the same elections, stating that it only observed the consolidation of results at sector level in 50% of the sectors. In some cases, observers were actually prevented from observing, while in others they were not informed of the location of the sector-level consolidation, making it impossible for them to confirm the accuracy of consolidated results at any stage beyond the polling centre. The CSEOM observed further that at the district level, observers often had to negotiate to be allowed to attend, were at times directed to the wrong location, and that the transmission of results from sector to district level was inconsistent and in some cases took place by telephone.[544]

Similar accounts are given of the 2010 presidential election, with the Commonwealth Elections Observer Mission reporting lack of transparency in the tabulation process in a number of districts:

> Prior to the day of the election, observers had met with district officials in order to gain an understanding of the plans for the tabulation, among other things. However, on the evening after the close of polls and the subsequent days, the district offices were in many cases not active and the process was not apparently ongoing despite earlier assurances that it would be. Observers sought to gain clarification from relevant officials but in some cases it was not possible to ascertain quite where, how or when the tabulation was to be completed. As a

---

541 Burundi, DRC and Rwanda.
542 Samset & Dalby (2003), op. cit., pp. 33–34.
543 European Union Election Observation Mission (2008), op. cit., pp. 40–41.
544 CSEOM (2008) Final Report: Rwandan Parliamentary Elections 2008, pp. 14–15, www.rcsprwanda.org/ IMG/pdf/CSEOM_final_report-englishfinal_2008.pdf.

consequence, this part of the process lacked the requisite transparency in some districts.[545]

The CSEOM also reports being denied access to observe the voting procedures and the district-level consolidation process for the same election.[546] One respondent, citing 'reverse rigging'[547] observed:

> There is no value added in supporting elections. We were able to monitor everything, except when it came to consolidation of the votes at the district level. They slammed the door on our faces at this point.[548]

The Electoral Code also provides for candidates or representatives of candidates to follow the entire process of vote counting and to sign on the tally sheets and have their observations recorded in the statement of the conduct of elections. These provisions are, however, not obligatory and the failure to follow the process or sign on the tally sheets and on the statement of conduct of elections does not invalidate the election results. Elections observation reports show that apart from the candidates and agents of the ruling RPF, the other candidates or their representatives have not followed the counting and consolidation processes as keenly as they should, or signed or registered their complaints in the designated forms. Likewise, ordinary citizens have not shown a keenness to follow the vote counting and consolidation processes once they cast their ballots. For the candidates and their agents, the reasons are linked mainly to the lack of resources needed to deploy personnel in all the polling and consolidation points across the country, although some of them attributed it to despondency among opposition candidates and agents arising from their diminished faith in the fairness of the electoral process and the limited prospects of them winning against the ruling party. According to respondents, the electoral law appears deficient in not making it a requirement for the agents or representatives of political candidates to sign on the tally sheets or establish their right to receive copies of the signed results forms from the polling stations, and in not requiring the NEC to immediately post the results of the elections outside the polling stations. They proposed increased political education and changes to the Electoral Code, both to build demand for oversight and to ensure that these are made legal requirements of the electoral process.[549]

---

545 Commonwealth Secretariat (2010), op. cit., p. 25.
546 CSEOM (2010), op. cit., p. 30.
547 Reverse rigging refers to the illegal practice where votes are adjusted backwards during the consolidation process at the district level to avoid a situation where one party secures more than 95% of the total votes, thus prompting a constitutional crisis in regard to the formation of government.
548 View of a respondent from the Dutch embassy, interview, 27 September 2013.
549 Interviews conducted in September and October 2012.

Independence

While the Constitution establishes the NEC as an independent EMB, a number of observers question its independence. In the words of one respondent, the 'NEC is only as effective as the mandate from above. There is not much it can do .... [It] conducts a very efficient electoral process, but does not deliver a free and fair result.'[550] A member of the opposition referring to the 2011 mayoral elections remarked: 'Some knew the results, had even relocated and were already celebrating their elections.'[551]

Other reasons cited for the low confidence in the ability of the NEC to deliver free, fair and transparent elections include those discussed earlier, among them:

- The last-minute withdrawal of candidature by some electoral contestants, even with their names and photographs already printed on the ballot papers, believed to arise from 'pressure from above';
- Concerns about NEC agents influencing voters to vote for specific candidates;
- Cases of the NEC not investigating or not imposing sanctions on the RPF or RPF agents who commit electoral offences such as deploying government resources or wearing party colours during their campaigns, previously forbidden by the law; and
- The NEC locking out election observers during certain stages of the electoral process.

According to the Commonwealth Observer Group report on the Rwanda presidential election in 2010, serious concerns were raised about the implicit political affiliation of members of the NEC, given the importance attached to its independence. The report recommended thus:

> It would be helpful for this to be clarified to ensure transparency of and confidence in the electoral process. There are various models for the composition of an electoral management body, and they can comprise independent, non-political figures or be broadly representative of political contestants depending upon what is felt to be most suitable in any given context. Whichever model is preferred, it is important for the process to be clear and transparent.[552]

Commissioners were implicitly drawn from different political parties.[553] In reality, however, the composition of the NEC commissioners was criticised, with many observers concerned that it comprised people affiliated to or biased towards the RPF. Respondents felt that in the context of Rwanda, where the political and administrative setup

---

550   US Embassy staff, interview, 27 September 2012.
551   Member of PS-Imberakuri, interview, 21 September 2012.
552   Commonwealth Secretariat (2010), op. cit., p. 11.
553   Interviews with Charles Munyaneza, Apollinaire Mushinzimana, Damascene Ntawukuriryayo, all op. cit.

is dominated by one strong political party, the commissioners and members of the NEC at decentralised levels should be balanced between different political parties and civil society. This would avoid any perception that the commission is an extension of the RPF, hence eroding its independence in the eyes of political stakeholders. The CSEOM in its report of the 2010 presidential election observed:

> It would be helpful to be clearer about the background and/or affiliation of members as it is vital that the body responsible for managing the electoral process be inclusive and representative. Ideally, such a body either needs to be completely independent of any political affiliation or comprise a good representative balance.[554]

Other commentators have recommended that, at a minimum, the president of the NEC should be someone not affiliated to any political party.[555]

Relationship with the media

The NEC and the Media High Council (MHC) enjoy good working relations in facilitating and monitoring access to the media by political parties.[556] A monitoring report of the coverage of the 2010 presidential election by the MHC shows substantial improvement in the media's respect for electoral law and regulations, as well as general reporting on electoral matters. Key improvements included live coverage of presidential campaigns by Rwanda Television (RTV), respect for the regulatory requirement of equal and fair coverage for all competing political parties and candidates, and improvements in the levels of professionalism in coverage.[557] However, the report also identified shortcomings, among them:

- The failure to respect the principle of equal airtime in the print and electronic media;
- The dominance of RPF and its candidates as news sources;[558]
- Limited political analysis and interpretation of events;
- Lack of interest among some segments of the media, in particular the faith-based media, in covering political campaigns; and
- A general urban bias in the coverage of political campaigns by the media.[559]

Independent election observers, on the other hand, portray the public media in different ways. While the CSEOM expressed satisfaction with the public media's coverage

---

554 CSEOM (2010), op. cit., p. 31.
555 An, M et al. (2008) *Idealism Without Illusions: Lessons from Post-Conflict Elections in Cambodia, Rwanda and Sudan*, Woodrow Wilson School of Public Policy and International Affairs, pp. 24–27.
556 Mr Eric Bazirema, Director of the MHC, interview, 22 September 2012.
557 An et al. (2008), op. cit., pp. 3–4.
558 Ibid., pp. 6–7.
559 Mr Eric Bazirema, op. cit.

of the 2010 presidential election,[560] groups like the LDGL portrayed it as biased towards the ruling RPF.[561] In the same vein, key informants were concerned over the reluctance of journalists working for the state-owned media (ORINFOR) to report the activities of opposition political parties, and about the MHC's inability to immediately sanction state-owned media outlets that violate regulations relating to equitable and fair coverage of candidates or party activities during elections. According to the 2009 media law,[562] the MHC can only inform the NEC and offer recommendations where they observe irregularity. This does not offer the needed immediate redress for candidates whose rights may have been infringed. Under the 2013 revision of both the Electoral Code and the 2005 NEC Law, the responsibility for media monitoring during elections has now been moved away from the MHC to the NEC.[563]

Overall, the media environment in Rwanda, especially its role in promoting free expression, remains constrained. According to the media organisation Article 19, the reforms adopted in 2013 through the new media law do not go far enough in guaranteeing the independence of the media from the government.[564] While providing some useful safeguards for the freedom of the press, the new law regulating the media contains many provisions that still pose threats to journalists and the independence of the media in the country, including online media. Defamation remains a criminal offence under the penal code, while definitions of a number of criminal offences are still vague, unclear and broad, making it easy for legislation to be manipulated to restrict expression and media freedom. In its report of Rwanda's September 2013 parliamentary elections, the East African Community Election Observer Mission noted that the coverage of the elections was generally lacklustre. 'Despite the existence of various media outlets, the media did not significantly engage with the electoral process.'[565]

These limitations remain troubling and put to question the role of the media in promoting a free, fair and transparent electoral process in Rwanda.

H. Electoral management and the debate on democratic reforms

An interesting point of discussion was whether Rwanda could now open up more and genuinely address the questions of political space and freedom of expression identified in this report. Opinion was divided. Some felt that Rwanda was already 'letting go' and that the question was one of how much, not whether, to let go.

---

560 CSEOM (2010), op. cit., p. 8.
561 LDGL (2013), op. cit., pp. 64–65.
562 Law No. 30/2009 of 16 September 2009.
563 Article 1(7) of Law No. 38/2013 of 16 June 2013 modifying and complementing the 2005 NEC Law.
564 Article 19 (2013) 'Rwanda: Media Law Does Not Go Far Enough', op. cit.
565 'Reservation of the EAC Mission on Rwanda Polls', *The Citizen*, 30 October 2013, www.thecitizen.co.tz/ magazine/political-reforms/Reservations-of-EAC-mission-on-Rwanda-polls/-/1843776/2053324/-/item/1/- /6ysr6nz/-/index.html, accessed 4 November 2013.

Others felt that given the country's history, it was important to move cautiously on democratic and electoral reforms. This group observed that 50 years on, the Holocaust of the Jews was still fresh, yet Rwanda was being asked to let go hardly two decades after the Genocide. They observed that there was still evidence of divisionism and genocide ideology in the country and that more time was needed to heal and unite the country. It was, therefore, both inevitable and necessary to put stability first.

The first group concurred, but felt that the current levels of openness were disproportionate given how far the country had come. While there were grounds to be cautious, they felt these must not become pretexts for closing the door on legitimate political opposition and fundamental freedoms. They observed that while it was too soon to expect Rwanda to be a liberal democracy, the question of whether it was moving fast enough towards being one, or whether it could move faster without endangering the evident gains of stability and prosperity needed to be addressed by the ruling party. They also pointed out the risks of maintaining the status quo and allowing authoritarian norms to become ossified into the political system.

In conclusion, Rwanda's NEC has been effective in handling elections since 2000. However, it remains a young institution operating in an extremely volatile and dynamic political environment, calling for the constant reform of institutions and procedures in order to fulfil the mandate of delivering free, fair and transparent elections. Key stakeholders and observers are challenging its structural and institutional framework and independence in this regard and calling for further reforms.

I. Recommendations

Legal and institutional reforms to improve the overall electoral environment

- The NEC should immediately act on its promise to establish a formal mechanism to facilitate the collaborative review and reform of electoral laws, in line with the recommendations of various election observer missions.
- The NEC should work closely with Parliament to improve the timeliness of the review, adoption and publication of electoral reforms to allow candidates, voters and other stakeholders sufficient time to familiarise themselves with the new laws and to conduct effective civic and voter education.
- Improve the Electoral Code and NEC instructions to clearly define what constitutes illegal campaigning to ensure equal application of campaign regulations.
- Review and amend the group of laws relating to divisionism, sectarianism, genocide ideology and defamation to further clarify and bring them in line with international standards on freedom of expression, so that genuine incidents of hate speech or conduct and slander can be differentiated from legitimate freedom of expression.

- Review the 5% vote threshold set for entry into Parliament, which especially disadvantages independent candidates.
- Speed up the processes of ratifying the East African Draft Protocol on Good Governance and educate the public on its content and meaning, along with those of the East African Principles for Elections Observation, Monitoring and Evaluation, and ways to make both fully operational.

Electoral dispute management and powers of sanction
- Revise the provisions on time for submission and resolution of petitions in disputed local legislative and presidential elections.
- Review NEC's sanction powers with a view to limiting them, especially the powers to de-list candidates.

Independence and transparency
- Establish a clear and transparent process for identifying and recruiting the seven commissioners of the NEC. Institute a public advertisement and recruitment process for the president of the NEC. Revise the 2005 NEC Law accordingly.
- Increase efforts to improve the transparency of the vote tabulation, transmission and consolidation processes. The revision of the electoral law to allow observers more access to these processes is welcome. The results of vote counting, tabulation and consolidation should be publicly displayed and posted outside each tallying and consolidation centre immediately upon completion of counting and consolidation.
- Legal reform should require the NEC to make available signed copies of the tally sheets and the statement on the conduct of elections from polling and consolidation centres to representatives of political candidates and the electoral observers on request.
- The NEC should increase electoral and voter education for political parties, their agents and observers to increase their appetite for and participation in overseeing the electoral process, in particular to ensure that the procedures stipulated for handling the voting, results transmission and consolidation processes are clearly understood and properly followed.
- Increase the capacity of the NEC through recruitment of more permanent staff and proper training, to remove the current system of engaging thousands of volunteers with unclear political affiliation.
- Detail electoral procedures in relation to transmission of results and the physical location of district-level consolidation to avoid the current confusion regarding how to handle these processes that lead to claims of lack of transparency.

Broaden meaning, approach to delivering civic and electoral education

- Expand the delivery of civic and electoral education by involving more providers in its design, planning and delivery. A key step towards this is changing the 2005 NEC Law to allow it to legally enlist other providers through a legal forum that brings together electoral stakeholders to agree on the scope, content and plans for country-wide delivery and management of civic and electoral education. This is also necessary to encourage providers to develop programmes for civic and electoral education and to fund-raise for such activities.

- Work closely with political parties to expand their role in offering civic and political education in line with their mandate, building on the legal opportunity that now allows them to decentralise their activities down to the lowest level of government. This is important to remove the fear of politics and elections from the population, build the profiles parties need to mobilise membership and raise funds locally, while increasing both political awareness and the appetite for greater political engagement, particularly in regard to increasing oversight of electoral processes and pursuing the redress of electoral disputes through established legal channels.

- Together with other relevant institutions, continue the efforts to promote the culture of dialogue and debate at different levels of society, building on existing successful models such as the annual national dialogue and the civil society-led national dialogue forums, which could be further improved by decentralising them to the grassroots to capture communities' voices. These efforts could be extended to schools and higher institutions of learning where the youth could be encouraged to establish forums to debate issues of national concern freely, unburdened by their history and an intransigent old guard.

5

Tanzania

Alexander B. Makulilo

A. Summary

Tanzania's federal structure, requiring separate elections for the Mainland and the islands of Zanzibar, has necessitated the creation of two election management bodies (EMBs) with different mandates. The National Electoral Commission (NEC) is responsible for Union elections, in both the Mainland and in Zanzibar, while the Zanzibar Electoral Commission (ZEC) is responsible for Zanzibar elections.

Both EMBs face significant challenges, the most critical of which is the perception that they are not independent and impartial, despite apparent legal guarantees of freedom from political interference. The system for appointment and removal of commissioners, especially for the Mainland, does not ensure their full independence from the executive; while financial and logistical dependence on the executive undermines the timeous completion of significant activities. There is a need to revise the requirements for the composition and tenure of commissioners, and also to ensure the adequate financial security of the two institutions.

In reality the legal framework for EMBs has not protected them from encroachment by the government and incumbent parties – on the Mainland, Chama Cha Mapinduzi (Party of the Revolution, CCM), and in Zanzibar, CCM in a government of national unity (GNU) with the Civic United Front (CUF).

The NEC and ZEC commissioners are appointed by the Union President and the President of Zanzibar, respectively, with very limited requirements for the qualifications stipulated in the Constitution. The only significant restriction for appointing ZEC commissioners is that the President of Zanzibar has to choose two out of seven names proposed by the official opposition. This requirement, however, ensures that the commission would always be split 5:2 whenever there is a controversial issue relating to party interests. The security of tenure of commissioners is legally precarious for the NEC, because the President can remove a commissioner for incompetence without being questioned. None has been removed to date, partly because these commissioners have been 'safe' handpicked appointees. In the case of the ZEC, the President has to receive a report from an investigative committee made up of High Court judges before removing a commissioner.

Institutionally, the EMBs are not autonomous – they are dependent on the government for physical facilities, personnel and budget. They have to request resources from the Prime Minister's Office on the Mainland (NEC) and the Second Vice-President's Office in Zanzibar (ZEC).

The NEC has a small secretariat at the national level with no office and personnel outside the headquarters in Dar es Salaam. During elections, it utilises space in regional and district government offices, and uses designated government officials as returning and assistant returning officers. The independence of these officials is highly contested. Members of opposition parties believe that the officials have vested interests in the victory of the ruling party, as their positions are dependent on the continued incumbency of the government in power. The ZEC has offices up to the district level and has more leeway in employing personnel; yet in some cases the ZEC has not been able to prevent some Zanzibar government officials and politicians from influencing the conduct of elections.

The performance of the two EMBs in managing elections, from registration to vote counting and declaration of winners, remains inadequate.

There are glaring weaknesses in how the EMBs register voters. Neither receives adequate funds to update the permanent voters' registers, which are updated twice in five years. The NEC register uses outdated technology. While the ZEC register is updated and fully digitised, registration problems are more serious in Zanzibar due to a legal provision that requires a person to have lived on the islands continuously for three years to register as a voter. Many potential voters are thus denied their constitutional right to freedom of movement and the right to vote.

The NEC approves nominated candidates to stand for election after intra-party candidate selections, but it has no role in supervising internal party processes. The paperwork required to submit candidate names to NEC officials is considerable and bureaucratic. A small error could lead to a nomination being nullified. As a result, the many contending political parties on the Mainland look for such errors to have contestants disqualified on technicalities. The process should be simplified and corrections to technical errors allowed. The nomination process has been less controversial in Zanzibar, where there are only two major contending parties, the CCM and the CUF.

The campaign process on the Mainland is increasingly characterised by corruption, use of abusive language and violence. The situation in Zanzibar has improved following the formation of the GNU. The main protagonists in the increasingly acrimonious election campaigns are the party in power – the CCM – and the most powerful opposition party, CHADEMA (*Chama cha Demokrasia na Maendeleo*, or Party for Democracy and Progress). The electoral code of conduct allows the NEC to sanction candidates and political parties, including suspending them from campaigning, but it has hardly exercised these powers.

Voting, vote counting and declaration of results have been marred by controversy, particularly where opposition parties are strong, with fears of attempted manipulation of results often expressed. In highly contested constituencies, crowds have often massed around vote tallying stations waiting for results to be announced, often leading to confrontations when the police attempted to disperse them. The NEC's use of government officials as returning officers has undermined any trust it might enjoy among opposition parties.

Foreign and domestic observers have at best given a qualified 'free and fair' verdict for the NEC and a 'poor' rating for the ZEC in the first three elections after the re-introduction of multi-party politics in 1995, 2000 and 2005. These elections led to deaths in Zanzibar in each instance. In 2010, the modality of a GNU was agreed on before the vote and no deaths occurred during the elections. Violence is now largely concentrated on the Mainland, where a contestation over the results of the 2010 elections ended in three people being killed in Arusha.

Tanzania is in the process of crafting a new Union Constitution. The NEC is likely to undergo significant changes following recommendations for transparently selected commissioners and to give the organisation more autonomy. At the same time, the CCM has been accused of trying to take advantage of its larger number of delegates (about two-thirds of the members) in the Constituent Assembly to manipulate the Constitution-drafting process to its advantage. In Zanzibar, attention to the ZEC in the constitution-making debate is limited, as debate is focused on increased power and autonomy for Zanzibar in the Union rather than internal constitutional arrangements. It is widely believed that the 1984 Constitution of Zanzibar is largely acceptable. The ZEC is seen as having improved considerably from the past, not in terms of its structure, but largely due to the GNU. Yet cracks in the GNU are beginning to emerge, and once the Union is settled, differences between the two main rival parties are likely to resurface.

B. Political history

Tanzania's Constitution has evolved through four phases:
- The Independence Constitution of 1961;
- The Republican Constitution of 1962;
- The Interim Constitution of 1965; and
- The permanent Constitution of 1977 currently in use.

These constitutions have six distinctive features in common:
- Their making did not involve public debate and discussion;
- With the exception of the independence Constitution, the rest tend to

concentrate and centralise power in the executive arm and particularly in the chief executive, namely, the President (who is head of state, head of the government, head of the public service, and commander-in-chief of all armed forces);

- They raise the ruling party to the acme of power by making it the supreme organ in the United Republic;
- They suffocate autonomous organisations such as trade unions, cooperative unions and other civil societies;
- They do not incorporate the Bill of Rights (note that the Bill of Rights first appeared in the Constitution of the United Republic in 1984); and
- The ruling party can solely make or un-make the Constitution through amendments.

The net product of these characteristics is the politics of hegemony by the ruling party and the resultant repressive political culture over the past four decades since independence. Currently, the United Republic is writing a new Constitution, expected to be completed in April 2014. In order to understand the constitutional development in Tanzania and its impact on democracy, particularly on the electoral process and management, it is imperative to highlight such developments in Tanganyika and Zanzibar both before and after the Union of 1964.

Tanganyika (Mainland Tanzania)

Tanganyika went through different political and constitutional phases of development from the colonial period to 1964, when it joined with Zanzibar to form the United Republic of Tanzania.

Tanganyika was a German colony from 1884 to 1918, and then a British one from 1919 to 1961. The British colonial system was run through indirect rule. Each African 'tribe' at the local government level would be ruled by its own chief. As there were no clear-cut ethnic lines in many areas, the British created 'tribes' and chiefs.[566] Colonial rule was not based on democracy, and elections came late to British Tanganyika. A legislative council was established in 1926 but its 20 members were all appointed by the British Governor. Only in 1956 did the Governor announce that the first elections would be held in Tanganyika in 1958, based on limited suffrage and race. Voters had to meet criteria based on education and income in order to vote for three candidates – a European, an Asian and an African (black) in a three-member constituency. This was intended to avoid an African majority as it was thought they could only win a third of the seats under the system.

The Tanganyika African National Union (TANU), the main nationalist party formed in 1954 and led by Julius Nyerere, was split on the issue of participation in the racially based elections. Though many of its leading figures called for a boycott of the elections,

---

566 Ranger, T (2010) 'The invention of tradition in Colonial Tanganyika' in R Ginker et al. (eds) *Perspectives on Africa: A Reader in Culture, History and Representation*, Wiley-Blackwell, p. 456.

Nyerere convinced the party to participate while mobilising White and Asian candidates to run on the TANU ticket. TANU won 28 out of the 30 seats; the other two being won by the African National Congress (ANC), a splinter from TANU established by those who had initially called for a boycott.[567] After the divisive issue of race, TANU had to deal with other issues that threatened its nationalist future. The first opposition came from traditional chiefs, who had formed the United Tanganyika Party (UTP) with the assistance of the British colonial government. TANU also faced negative mobilisation from the All Muslim Nationalist Union of Tanganyika (AMNUT), a political party that campaigned for independence to be delayed so as to bridge the gap in the level of education between Christians and Muslims.[568] TANU was able to win the support of moderate Muslims by promising to deal with the disparities in education after independence. As it would turn out, though, these challenges reappeared after independence and would influence the declaration of single-party rule.

Tanganyika won independence from Britain under the Westminster parliamentary model of government.[569] The party with the highest number of seats in the legislature would form the government under a Prime Minister. The electoral system was that of simple plurality in single-member constituencies. In the 1960 elections, which were held before the independence date of 9 December 1961, TANU won a landslide victory with 70 out of 71 seats.[570] The remaining seat was won by an independent candidate who was in fact a member of TANU; it meant that effectively, the country had a Parliament without an opposition. The popularity of TANU was still intact when it decided in 1962 to adopt a new Republican Constitution, creating a presidential system of government. In the elections for that position, Nyerere of TANU won 99.2% of the votes, and the other candidate, Zuberi Mtemvu of the ANC, won only 0.8%.[571]

Although TANU seemed to be hegemonic in the early 1960s, serious political contestations had begun to emerge. In 1964, the army staged a mutiny against the continued presence of British officers, the East African Muslim Welfare Society (EAMWS) agitated for more positions for Muslims in state structures, and other state workers called for more Africanisation of the civil service and better pay. New political parties were formed: the People's Convention Party, under Samson Mshalla; and the People's Democratic Party led by Kasanga Tumbo.[572] The mutiny was crushed and the army was disbanded to be replaced by a new national army. The EAMWS was banned in 1968, its Kenyan leaders expelled from the country and many trade union leaders detained.[573]

---

567   Nohlen, D et al. (1999) *Elections in Africa: A Data Handbook*, pp. 875–879.
568   Iliffe J (1979) *A Modern History of Tanganyika*, Cambridge University Press, pp. 551–552.
569   The Tanganyika (Constitution) Order in Council, 1961.
570   Nohlen et al. (1999), op. cit.
571   Ibid.
572   Consolata, R (2010) Political Party Institutionalisation in Tanzania, Dissertation, University of Dar es Salaam.
573   Mhina, A (2007) 'State-religion relationships and religious views on development policies', in A Mhina (ed.) *Religions and Development in Tanzania: A Preliminary Literature Review*, Religions and Development Programme, University of Birmingham, Working Paper 11, p. 8.

Zanzibar

Zanzibar colonial politics was dominated by deep divisions based on race, partly due to slavery and the slave trade; these were reflected by the political parties. Three political parties participated in the elections in 1957, January 1961, July 1961 and 1963, which elected unofficial members of the colonial legislative council.[574] The parties were the Afro-Shirazi Party (ASP), the Zanzibar and Pemba Peoples Party (ZPPP) and the Zanzibar Nationalist Party (ZNP). In terms of race, the ASP had its base among Africans and poorer Shirazi.[575] The ZPPP was mainly supported by the higher-income Shirazi, while the ZNP was seen as the party of the Arab elites, although its language sought to appeal to multi-ethnic Zanzibar nationalism rather than narrow Arab nationalism.[576]

There was a perception within the ASP that the colonial Commissioner of Elections was gerrymandering constituency boundaries in favour of the ZNP and ZPPP. In the 1963 elections, for example, the ASP won 54% of the vote and obtained 13 seats, while the ZNP–ZPPP coalition received 46% of the vote and won 18 seats. These results were very contentious.

Independence was granted on 10 December 1963 by the British to a ZNP–ZPPP parliamentary coalition government under the Sultan of Zanzibar. The ASP responded by staging a revolution on 12 January 1964 and establishing the Revolutionary Government of Zanzibar. ASP leader Sheikh Abeid Amani Karume suspended the 1963 Independence Constitution and proclaimed a constitutional decree that abolished all political parties except the ASP. He also abolished all elections.[577] The ASP agenda centred on redistribution of power from the previous Arab elites to Africans.

The revolution was the culmination of deeply divisive and contested electoral politics. In a first-past-the-post electoral system, it is not uncommon to have disparity between the total number of votes and the number of seats. The controversy in Zanzibar over this issue was, however, so intense that the disparity was not accepted. As a result, its elections were mostly followed by violence. After the June 1961 election, for example, rioting led to the deaths of 69 people. The political violence intensified during the revolution in 1964. It was estimated that around 5,000 people were killed, most of them Arabs – especially the poorer ones living in the rural areas of Zanzibar.[578] The ills of the past and the violence of the revolution left a lasting scar on Zanzibar, which came to haunt the re-entry of multi-party politics in 1992 as the contending political parties came to reflect the pre-revolution cleavages.

---

574 Sharrif, A (2001) 'Race and Class in the politics of Zanzibar', *African Spectrum* 36(3): 310.

575 Zanzibar people who trace their origins to the Shiraz province of Iran.

576 Mohammed, B & Makulilo, AB (2012) 'Beyond Polarity in Zanzibar? The "Silent" Referendum and the Government of National Unity', *Journal of Contemporary African Studies* 30(2): 195–218, dx.doi.org/10.10 80/02589001.2012.669565.

577 Responding to journalists' questions, Karume declared that there would be no election in Zanzibar in the next 50 years (EISA (2010) 'Zanzibar: 1963 Legislative Council Elections', www.content.eisa.org.za/old-page/zanzibar-1963-legislative-council-election).

578 Sharrif (2001), op. cit., pp. 314–315. There are no credible sources to get the exact figures of the deaths to date.

The Union

The events of 1964 on the Mainland and islands led to the establishment of a union between Tanganyika and Zanzibar. Confirmed in its authority after the suppression of the mutiny, TANU negotiated with the revolutionary government of Zanzibar for the creation of a new united republic named Tanzania.

The Interim Constitution of Tanzania of 1964 established the powers of the respective parts of the Union:

- Article 5 highlighted 11 activities where the Union President and legislature had authority in the entire United Republic;
- Article 5(b) allowed for a separate legislature and executive constituted according to the existing law in Zanzibar; and
- Article 5(d) referred to representation from Zanzibar in the Union legislature (without indicating how the candidates would be selected).[579]

The Union, therefore, gave birth to two governments: the United Republic of Tanzania government, which managed Union affairs together with all Mainland affairs, and the Revolutionary Government of Zanzibar, dealing with non-Union matters in Zanzibar.

The Union of April 1964 was closely followed by the legal establishment of a one-party state in the Mainland as well as in Zanzibar (where the revolutionary government was already a single-party entity). A commission was appointed in January 1964 to look into the matter and reported in March 1964. Proposals were presented to the National Assembly and passed as constitutional amendments in June 1965.[580] The elections in 1965 were, therefore, contested within the context of single-party politics.

It was officially argued that the reason for instituting a one-party state was to give voters a choice. TANU was so hegemonic, it was argued, that all TANU candidates would have carried the day. It was, therefore, seen as important to give voters a choice between two TANU candidates for parliamentary and council elections.[581] The introduction of one-party rule was also seen by the commission as a way of rescuing the National Assembly from decline and decay, as the institution had turned into a rubber stamp because of lack of an opposition. As a result, legislation was passed rapidly and uncritically.[582]

Under the new electoral system, voters had the choice between two parliamentary and local government council candidates from whom they could elect one for each level. There were, however, some limitations to potential candidates: they were screened by the party and only those who supported the system were allowed to participate. The same arguments for having two parliamentary candidates were not used for the

---

579   Union of Tanganyika and Zanzibar Act, 1964 (The Interim Constitution), 25 April 1964.
580   Nyerere, J (1968) *Freedom and Socialism*, Oxford University Press, p. 35.
581   Ibid.
582   Kjekshus, H (1974) 'Parliament in a One-Party State: The Bunge of Tanzania, 1965–70', *Journal of Modern African Studies* 12(1): 19.

presidential election. In presidential elections, only one candidate was allowed to stand and arguments in favour of one candidate were blurred.

The single-party parliamentary elections were keenly contested on the Mainland and a good number of incumbent members of Parliament (MPs), including cabinet ministers, usually lost their seats. In the 1965 elections, when 94 constituency seats were in contest, 29 out of 50 incumbent MPs lost their seats, including two ministers and nine junior ministers. In the 1970 elections, half of the 74 incumbents, that is 38, were not returned.[583]

The new political system was centralised and unitary – a political culture based on consensus. In 1967, this consensus was given an ideological identity in the form of the socialist Arusha Declaration. Single-party rule was legitimised as socialist democratic centralism or 'participatory democracy'. However, this new political system was seen by some as authoritarian; for example, the Preventive Detention Act of 1962 was used to quell dissent, while the Trade Union Ordinance stifled workers' rights.[584]

During the period of single-party rule, the National Assemblies had many MPs who were not elected directly by the population. Since it was not a parliamentary system with an opposition where most of the seats would have been determined by direct votes, the government decided to introduce non-constituency seats that would not be openly contested. In the 1965 National Assembly, there were, for example, 94 such seats, exactly the same number as for constituency MPs. Fifteen MPs chosen by the National Assembly acted as an electoral college, representing special interests such as trade unions, cooperatives and women. Another 32 MPs came from Zanzibar as members of the Revolutionary Council; 20 other members were nominated from Zanzibar. The state decided that 17 Regional Commissioners would enter the National Assembly by virtue of their office. Ten members were nominated by the President. All MPs from Zanzibar were appointed because at that time, there were no elections in Zanzibar except for the Union President. The first legislative and Zanzibar presidential elections came with the 1979 Zanzibar Constitution, which allowed for such elections to be held in 1980.[585]

By the time of the 1985 general election, when President Ali Hassan Mwinyi took over from Nyerere, the number of constituencies had been increased from 106 to 119; but the National Assembly had 274 members – meaning there were 155 members who were not directly elected. During that time, 15 special seats were introduced for women. Most of those elected by the National Assembly sitting as an electoral college came from what were called party-affiliated organs, that is, for women, youth, workers, cooperatives and parents. In the last National Assembly under single-party rule in 1990, the number of constituencies increased to 130 but the number of MPs in the National Assembly

---

583 Nohlen et al. (1999), op. cit.
584 Mwesiga, B (1994) 'The Rise and Fall of One Party State' in J Widner (ed.) *Economic Change and Political Liberalisation in Sub-Saharan Africa*, Johns Hopkins Press.
585 Lodge, T, Kadima, D & Pottie, D (2002) 'Tanzania' in *Compendium of Elections in Southern Africa*, Electoral Institute for Sustainable Democracy in Africa (EISA), p. 354.

was 284, the difference being 154.[586] It became clear that the directly elected MPs were a minority in the National Assembly, further lowering the democratic value of the general election. The logic of the ruling party, which had become supreme in 1975, was to allow for various groups in the society to be represented in the National Assembly. The practice was corporatist in the sense that anyone wishing to participate in decision-making in the society had to be screened by party organs. This situation fuelled the clamour for multi-party politics and democracy in Tanzania.

The situation in Zanzibar was quite different. Despite the fact that Tanzania was declared a single-party political system in 1965, there were effectively two sister parties, TANU on the Mainland, and ASP in Zanzibar. For a long time, Zanzibar did not have elections because it was under a revolutionary government. However, as part of the Union, some elections were imposed on Zanzibar. The first was the union presidential election in 1965, which in reality was just a plebiscite whose results were known beforehand. A joint party committee came together to appoint a presidential candidate.[587] The people of Zanzibar at the time were not voting for MPs to the Union National Assembly. The MPs were simply picked by the Zanzibar Revolutionary Council (ZRC).

TANU and ASP decided in the 1970s to end the anomaly of having two political parties in a single-party state. They established a joint party commission consisting of 20 members to draw up a new party constitution, which led to the formation in 1977 of Chama Cha Mapinduzi (CCM). The same 20-person commission was charged with the task of drawing up a new draft Constitution for the United Republic of Tanzania. This was enacted by a Constituent Assembly exclusively made up of MPs in 1977, and it is still in force. The Union Constitution of 1977 created a uniform system for the whole of Tanzania and provided for a de jure one-party state until 1992, when it was amended to allow for multi-party politics. In 1979, a new Zanzibar Constitution was also adopted, allowing the first Zanzibar elections since 1964 to be held in 1980. The people of Zanzibar could now vote for one presidential candidate and for representatives to the newly created House of Representatives for Zanzibar, as well as for MPs to the Union Parliament. The ZEC was established to manage these elections. The electoral politics and management of Zanzibar in 1979 seemed to imply the creation of a homogeneous system with the Mainland. However, in 1984, a new Constitution for Zanzibar was promulgated, which created a separate electoral system for Zanzibar.[588]

Multi-party politics returned to Tanzania in 1992, following various sources of pressures on the regime in power. There was pressure from Western donor countries, which threatened to cut off development aid unless there was progress towards democratisation. There was also the collapse of socialism in Eastern Europe, poor economic

---

586   Numbers were compiled from Nohlen et al. (1999), op. cit., pp. 881–885.
587   Ibid., p. 39.
588   Makulilo, A (2011) 'The Zanzibar Electoral Commission and its Feckless Independence', *Journal of Third World Studies* 28(1): 268.

performance at home and the ever-growing agitation of Tanzanian civil and political groups.[589] It also followed recommendations of the presidential commission, chaired by Chief Justice Francis Nyalali, on whether Tanzania should be a single-party or multi-party system.[590] In 1992, the Political Parties Act No. 5 was enacted to allow for a multi-party political system in Tanzania.

Currently, there are 21 political parties of which six are active. These are:

- CCM;
- CUF;
- CHADEMA;
- Tanzania Labour Party (TLP);
- National Convention for Construction and Reform–Mageuzi (NCCR-Mageuzi); and
- United Democratic Party (UDP).

The first general election for Union government following the return of multi-party politics was held in October 1995. There were a number of Union by-elections run under the auspices of multi-party politics held in 1993 and 1994, all won by the CCM.[591]

Since 1992, there have been four general elections: in 1995, 2000, 2005 and 2010. Results from these elections indicate that the number of CCM parliamentary seats rose from 186 in 1995 to 202 in 2000, and 206 in the 2005 general election before dropping to 186 in 2010. It should also be noted that throughout these elections, there were unopposed candidates[592] running on CCM tickets. The number of unopposed candidates was 25 in the 2000 elections and eight in the 2005 polls. This number rose to 17 in the 2010 elections. Figure 5.1 summarises parliamentary election results of the different political parties.

In presidential elections, the CCM's support is still high and has increased over the years. In the 1995 elections, the party mobilised 61.8% of the vote; in 2000 the figure increased to 71.7% and in 2005 to 80.28%. However, in 2010, the CCM's support dropped to 62.84%. It is interesting to note that Augustino Lyatonga Mrema, who obtained 27.8% of the vote through the NCCR-Mageuzi in the 1995 elections, received only 7.8% of the vote when he ran for the TLP in the 2000 elections, which dropped to 0.75% in the 2005 elections. Even Prof. Ibrahim Haruna Lipumba of the CUF, who mobilised up to 16.3% of the vote in the 2000 elections, received only 11.68% in the 2005 elections and 8.28% in the 2010 elections. Figure 5.2 provides a summary of the political parties and their performance in presidential elections.

---

589   Mhina, A (1999) 'Le pluralisme politique, une "transition démocratique" contrôlée', in Baroin, C et al., *La Tanzanie Contemporaine*, Karthala, Paris, pp. 233–234.

590   United Republic of Tanzania (URT) (1999) *The Presidential Commission on Single-Party or Multi-Party System in Tanzania*, Dar es Salaam University Press.

591   The first was held in 1993 at Kwahani in Zanzibar, followed by Ileje and Kigoma on the Mainland in 1994; see Tanzania Affairs, www.tzaffairs.org.

592   Unopposed candidate means that no votes are cast and the candidates are declared to have won the election.

Figure 5.1: Parliamentary election results by political party (1995–2010)

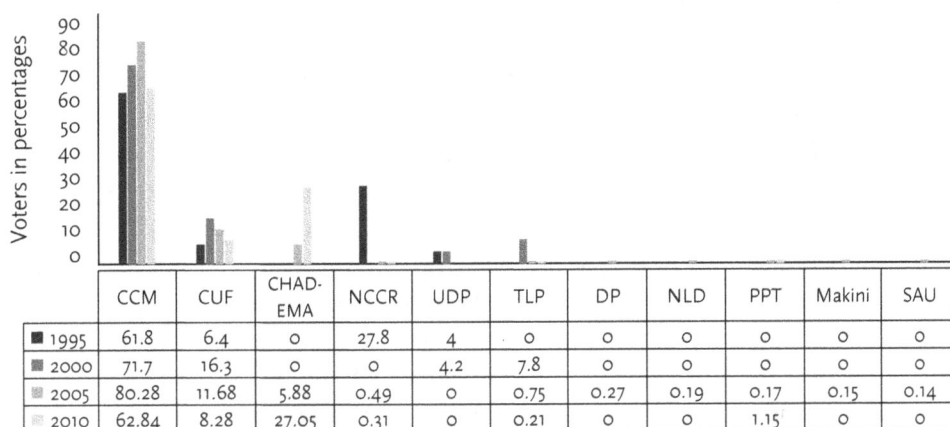

	CCM	CUF	CHAD-EMA	NCCR	UDP	TLP	DP	NLD	PPT	Makini	SAU
■ 1995	61.8	6.4	0	27.8	4	0	0	0	0	0	0
■ 2000	71.7	16.3	0	0	4.2	7.8	0	0	0	0	0
■ 2005	80.28	11.68	5.88	0.49	0	0.75	0.27	0.19	0.17	0.15	0.14
■ 2010	62.84	8.28	27.05	0.31	0	0.21	0	0	1.15	0	0

Source: Adapted from the NEC, Tanzania (1996, 2001, 2006 and 2011).

Figure 5.2: Presidential election results by political party (1995–2010)

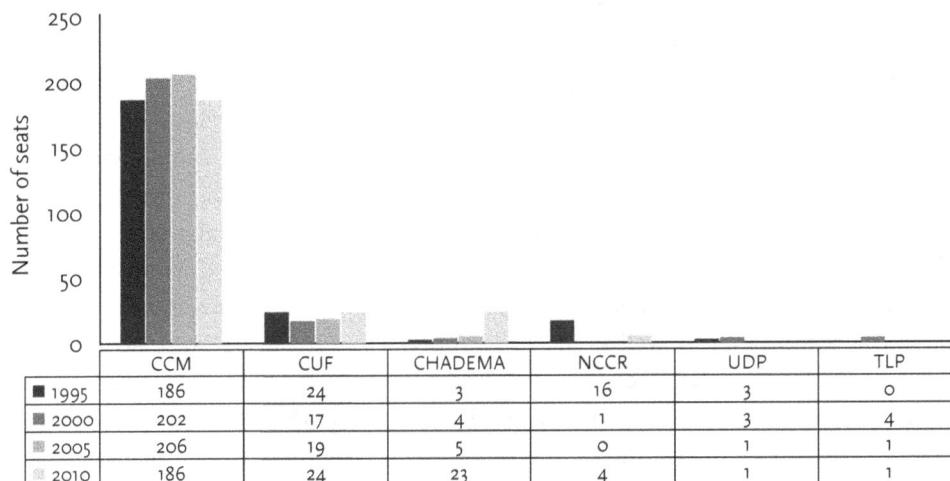

	CCM	CUF	CHADEMA	NCCR	UDP	TLP
■ 1995	186	24	3	16	3	0
■ 2000	202	17	4	1	3	4
■ 2005	206	19	5	0	1	1
■ 2010	186	24	23	4	1	1

Source: Adapted from the NEC, Tanzania (1996, 2001, 2006, and 2011).

Zanzibar elections since the return of multi-party politics

In Zanzibar, the return of multi-party politics rekindled, albeit with some modifications, the pre-independence politics.[593] There were only two major contending political parties in Zanzibar: the CCM, the incumbent party, which is dominant on Unguja Island, and the CUF, which is dominant in Pemba. These two parties became violently opposed to each other – the CCM seeing itself as the custodian of the Zanzibar revolution, while

---

593   Bakari & Makulilo (2012), op. cit., p. 197.

the CUF positioned itself as the champion against the ills of the past and the present that were linked to that revolution. Consequently, the CUF has been accused of being linked to Arab interests.

A closer analysis of the political situation produces a more nuanced understanding of the position of the parties. Suffice it to say, though, that they fought bitter battles until taking the decision to work together in a GNU.

In all general elections in Zanzibar before 2010, the results were contested and the CUF did not recognise the elected President. Violence usually ensued and resulted in deaths, the largest number being recorded in 2001 when 31 people were killed in Pemba and many CUF supporters fled to Kenya and Somalia as refugees. Efforts were made to reconcile the two parties. The first attempt was made in 1999 by the Commonwealth in the aftermath of the 1995 elections. That attempt, referred to as *Muafaka I* ('Accord I'), failed. The second attempt was brokered locally by the two political parties at the national level. It was known as *Muafaka II*. The key issues in reference to *Muafaka II* were the recognition of Aman Abeid Karume as Zanzibar's President by the CUF, and in turn, the CUF received pledges that the ZEC would be reformed and the Constitution reviewed to make it compatible with multi-party democracy. This was partially fulfilled, and notably called for the participation of political parties in the constituting ZEC, with each party providing two commissioners. The ZEC was reorganised in 2003 to allow for the inclusion of four commissioners, two from the CCM and two from the CUF. The President at that time faltered in implementing other agreements.[594]

A third *Muafaka* followed the 2005 elections, proposing a GNU, but failed because of last-minute disagreements between the two parties. Unexpectedly, however, the two top leaders of the CCM and the CUF in Zanzibar held secret talks that produced *Maridhiano* ('Compromise'), which gave birth to the GNU in 2010.[595] Two issues were part and parcel of the *Maridhiano*, namely the inclusion of the CUF in government through a free and fair election, as well as the issue of peace in Zanzibar. Notwithstanding, in one incident, the CUF demanded the immediate disbandment of the ZEC and the NEC before the 2010 general election on the grounds that the EMBs were neither independent nor impartial. Similarly, the CUF expressed concerns over election-rigging by the ZEC in favour of the ruling party.[596] Even after conceding defeat after the announcement of presidential election results, the CUF candidate, Seif Shariff Hamad, expressed his mistrust of ZEC officials.[597]

The GNU has facilitated the sharing of power between the CCM and the CUF. The

---

594 'Tanzania: Main electoral trends (1961–2005)', EISA, www.content.eisa.org.za/old-page/tanzania-main-electoral-trends-1961-2005.
595 Bakari & Makulilo (2012), op. cit., p. 196.
596 The CUF through its letters CUF/HQ/ZEC/037/010/056 dated 18 October 2010 and CUF/HQ/KR/MU/030/59 of 30 October 2010 to the ZEC and other key stakeholders.
597 Tanzania Election Monitoring Committee (TEMCO) (2011) *The 2010 Zanzibar Elections: Report of the Tanzania Election Monitoring Committee*, http://www.temco.udsm.ac.tz/images/2010Reports/TEMCO_2010_General_Elections_Report.pdf.

winner occupies the Presidency and appoints the Second Vice-President, who is the head of government in the House of Representatives. The CUF obtained the position of the First Vice-President of Zanzibar and a number of cabinet ministries. Members of the smaller opposition parties in Zanzibar, which do not have a single MP or member of the House of Representatives, have protested against this CCM–CUF hegemony. While the constitutional amendments do not mention the CCM or the CUF as the sole participants in a GNU, in the current situation, only these two parties qualify to participate in government.[598]

C. Election management bodies

Election management in Tanzania is under the mandate of two bodies, namely the National Electoral Commission (NEC) for Union elections and the Zanzibar Electoral Commission (ZEC) for Zanzibar elections. The two bodies manage elections through a number of functions such as registration of voters, demarcation of electoral boundaries, nomination of candidates, voter education, voting and vote counting, and declaration of results.

The National Electoral Commission

The Independence Constitution created the first Electoral Commission of Tanganyika, under the chairmanship of the Speaker of the National Assembly, assisted by three to five appointed commissioners.[599] The Electoral Commission had two phases during the single-party era. The first worked from 1965 to 1990 and the second was established in 1990 and worked until 1992 when multi-party politics was restored. The EMB established by the Independence Constitution became the Electoral Commission of Tanzania (ECT), and in the 1977 Union Constitution came to be referred to as the Electoral Commission of the United Republic of Tanzania, albeit with unchanged powers. From 1965 to 1990, the ECT had five commissioners under the chairmanship of the Speaker of the National Assembly. The legal and administrative framework of Tanzania's elections was set out in the following documents:

- The Interim Constitution of 1965;
- The Constitution of the United Republic of Tanzania, 1977 (hereafter 'the Constitution');
- The National Assembly (Elections) Act, 1964, and its Amendment Act of 1965; and
- The Report of the Election Rules Committee.

---

598 Interviews with Zanzibar offices' party leaders of CHADEMA, the NCCR and TADEA, Zanzibar, September 2012.
599 Parliament of Tanzania 'History', www.parliament.go.tz/index.php/home/pages/5; Tanganyika Independence Constitution 25(1), 9 December 1961.

The Clerk of the National Assembly was the head of the secretariat, known as the Directorate of Elections, while senior government officials in the regions and the districts were appointed as returning officers.[600]

From 1990, amendments to the 1985 Elections Act No. 1 replaced the Speaker of the National Assembly as head of the ECT with a judge of the High Court or Court of Appeal. The number of commissioners rose from five to seven. The Clerk of the National Assembly, however, remained Director of Elections. All members of the ECT were appointed by the President at his discretion. One change introduced in 1990 was to give the ECT some authority to deal with election complaints. Election petitions were handled by a panel consisting of the commission chairman, who was from Tanzania Mainland. He was assisted by a judge of the Zanzibar High Court and another member of the commission appointed by the chairman.[601] The 1990 amendments were an attempt to make the commission more effective in dealing with more demanding electoral contestations, but it lasted only a short while because of the return to multi-party politics in 1992.

In 1993, the ECT was replaced by the NEC. The constitutional and legal framework for the NEC today is found in Article 74 of the Constitution, as elaborated by the Elections Act No. 1 of 1985. Both instruments have been amended several times to allow for a patchwork of reforms in electoral laws and regulations. The Constitution was last amended on this mandate in 2005. Article 66 of the Constitution was amended to allocate women special seats constituting 30% of the total in the National Assembly. Moreover, it provided for the appointment of up to ten MPs (five of whom must be women) by the President. The Elections Act was amended in 1992, 2000, 2005 and 2010. At the same time, the 1979 Local Government Elections Act was amended in 1994 to give the NEC the mandate to manage local government (councillor) elections on the Mainland. Since then, the law has been amended before every general election. The logic of the amendments was to allow for reforms agreed to by the government, such as the counting of votes at the polling stations (1995) or the introduction of the permanent national voters' register (2004). However, changes to legislation repeatedly recommended by the NEC over the years, such as an independent act for the NEC or legislation to allow an independent budget, have been ignored.[602] The Electoral Laws (Miscellaneous Amendments) Act No. 7 of 2010 was enacted to empower the NEC to make and publish in the *Government Gazette* – after consultation with political parties – the Electoral Code of Conduct in order to promote free and fair elections.[603]

600 Chaligha, A (2010) 'Management of Elections in Tanzania' in REDET, *Democracy and Political Competition in East Africa*, Dar es Salaam, E & D Vision Publishing, p. 399.
601 Ibid., p. 400.
602 See, for example, NEC (2006) *The Report of the National Electoral Commission on the 2005 Presidential, Parliamentary and Councillors Elections*, United Republic of Tanzania (URT).
603 NEC (2010) *Electoral Code of Conduct for the Presidential, Parliamentary and Councillors' Elections*, www.tz.undp.org/ESP/docs/Legal_Documents/2010_NEC_Electoral_Code_of_Conduct.PDF.

The Zanzibar Election Commission

The Zanzibar Constitution of 1979 created an Electoral Commission of Zanzibar (ECZ) along similar lines as the ECT established under the 1977 Union Constitution. The Speaker of the House of Representatives became the Chairperson of the ECZ and the Secretary of the House of Representatives became the Director of the ECZ. The President of Zanzibar appointed five other members to the commission. The ECZ ran closely monitored party elections, but the controls and screening of candidates was more stringent than on the Mainland because of fears of the old Arab regime working against the Zanzibar revolution. A new Constitution for Zanzibar was promulgated in 1984, together with the Zanzibar Election Act 11 of 1984. These became the legal instruments for the ECZ. The name and structure remained the same until in 1993, just as was the case for the Union, when the ZEC was formed at the return of multi-party politics in 1992.

Today, the legal and institutional framework of the ZEC is based on the following:

- Constitution of Zanzibar of 1984 (Articles 119 and 120);
- Political Parties Act No. 5 of 1992;
- Zanzibar Election Act No. 11 of 1984 as amended by Act No. 4 of 1990;
- Act No. 8 of 1992;
- Act No. 5 of 1995;
- Act No. 3 of 2000; and
- Elections (Amendment) Act No. 12 of 2002.

The major reform in the composition of the ZEC was, however, implemented in 2001, following the signing of *Muafaka II*, which required the President of Zanzibar to consult with the leader of the opposition in the House of Representatives in appointing two members from the opposition parties to serve as ZEC commissioners.

Constitutionally, the ZEC's mandate is restricted to the management of Zanzibar's elections. However, the NEC delegated to the ZEC the management of Union elections in Zanzibar in the multi-party elections of 1995 and 2000. That assignment was withdrawn after the 2000 elections, which were seen as the most chaotic in Zanzibar since the return of multi-party politics in 1992 and affecting the Union polls in the Isles.

Structure, composition and staffing

NEC commissioners

There are seven NEC commissioners, all appointed by the President of Tanzania for a renewable term of five years.[604] Commissioners serve on a part-time basis. The chair-

---

604 Article 74 of the Constitution and Section 4(1) of the National Elections Act, Chapter 343. The current members are Rtd Judge Damian Z Lubuva (chairman), Rtd Judge Himid Mahamoud Himid (vice-chairman), Prof. Amon E Chaligha (member), Mchanga H Mjaka (member), Rtd Judge John J Mkwawa (member) and Rtd Judge Mary HCS Longway (member).

man and vice-chairman have to be judges of the High Court or Court of Appeal of Tanzania. It is also a constitutional requirement that when the chairman comes from Tanzania Mainland, the vice-chairman must be from Zanzibar and vice versa.[605] One member of the commission is appointed from among members of the Tanganyika Law Society (the law association for Mainland Tanzania). The other four members can be appointed by the President from among Tanzanians 'possessing adequate experience in the conduct and supervision of parliamentary elections'. However, there are no other restrictions on the President's discretion in appointing members of the NEC.

The President has unfettered powers to remove a commissioner. The Constitution states that the President can remove a commissioner from his/her position for reasons of incompetence, ill health, or losing the qualification of being a commissioner.[606] The President would have to state a reason for removal, but effectively, his/her decision cannot be questioned. So far, the President has not dismissed any commissioner. NEC commissioners have been appointed from among judges, former Inspectors-General of Police, lawyers and academics. Usually, there has been one woman, but no other considerations have overtly been made. In the ongoing constitution-making process, there is a call for the involvement of other groups like civil society organisations (CSOs) and political parties, but apart from gender balance, it is unlikely that other considerations, such as religion, will be pursued, as the principle of a secular state is strong in Tanzania.

ZEC commissioners

The ZEC has seven commissioners. The chairman is appointed by the President of Zanzibar as s/he sees fit, but the person has to have the qualifications and status equivalent to a High Court judge in any Commonwealth country. Two commissioners are appointed by the President on the recommendation of the Second Vice-President, who is the head of government in the House of Representatives. Two other commissioners are appointed by the President on the recommendations of the leader of the opposition in the House of Representatives. Another member is appointed from among the judges of the High Court, and the last member is appointed by the President as s/he sees fit. The President thus appoints three members, including the chairman, with the only limitations being based on qualifications, and two other members on the recommendation of the head of government in the House of Representatives, who belongs to his party and is also appointed by the President. Only the two commissioners put forth by the opposition are appointed with the President's hands tied. All commissioners, including the chairperson, work part-time.

New members of the ZEC were appointed in May 2013 after the previous commissioners' term expired.[607] All appointees are men, a fact that led the Tanzania Media

---

605 Constitution of the United Republic of Tanzania, 1977 (hereafter 'Constitution'), Article 74(1&2).
606 Ibid., Article 74(5).
607 The current members are Jecha Salim Jecha (chairman), Omar R Mapuri, Salmin Senga, Haji Ramadhani Haji, Nassor Khamis Mohammed, Ayoub Bakari and Judge Abdulkarim Ameir Issa.

Women's Association (TAMWA) to comment that the current ZEC was worse on gender representation than the previous commissions, which had had at least one woman commissioner.[608]

The qualifications of some commissioners, including chairpersons, have often been questioned.[609] Constitutional loopholes allow the appointment of unqualified members, including chairpersons. For example, the Constitution specifies that the chairperson shall be appointed by the President as s/he deems fit.[610] It states that the chairperson shall be a person who is qualified to be a judge of a High Court or Court of Appeal in any Commonwealth country or a person who is respected in society.[611] Under this provision, the President appears to be at liberty to appoint anybody whom s/he deems fit, since being qualified to be a judge is not a binding requirement. A good example was in 1995 when the chairperson was only a district magistrate. It has been pointed out that only the vice-chairpersons (who are appointed by the commissioners themselves) have been meeting the criteria of being lawyers, which implies that the chairmen have been appointed on the basis of their loyalty to the ruling party.[612]

Commissioners are appointed for a period of five years and can be removed for reasons of illness or failure to perform their tasks properly. The President, in such circumstances, is required to form a special committee of at least two High Court judges or those of the Court of Appeal to investigate and make recommendations to him. No commissioner has been removed to date.

The NEC secretariat

The NEC consists of the chairman and commissioners, as well as a small national secretariat headed by the Director of Elections, who is appointed by the President, on recommendation from the commission.[613] The secretariat has the following ancillary units:

- Administration and personnel;
- Accounting and auditing; and
- Legal.

Below the units, there are four sections:

- Information technology;
- Research and statistics;
- Election management; and
- Voter education.[614]

---

608 MI Ali, TAMWA Coordinator, Zanzibar, press release, 'Gender Equality Needed in Zanzibar Decision-Making Bodies', 5 May 2013; see also 'Zanzibar Government Criticised for Disregarding Gender Parity', *Daily News*, 6 May 2013.

609 TEMCO (2011), op. cit., p. 56.

610 Constitution, Article 119(1)(a).

611 Ibid., Article 119(2)(a).

612 Zanzibar Legal Society, interview, Zanzibar, September 2012.

613 Chaligha (2010), op. cit., p. 401.

614 NEC (2006), op. cit.

At the field level, the structure of the NEC operates only during elections. At the regional level, a Regional Election Coordinator is appointed during elections.[615] A returning officer is appointed for every constituency and is assisted by a number of assistant returning officers. Since the 2000 amendments to the Elections Act,[616] the executive directors of local councils have been appointed as returning officers by virtue of their position, and ward executive secretaries have been the assistant returning officers. In practice, therefore, elections are managed at the local level by administration officials. The law does not, however, prevent the NEC from appointing another person if there are issues with the council executive.

The ZEC secretariat

The President also appoints the Director of the ZEC from two names proposed by the commissioners. The Director heads the permanent secretariat of the ZEC; unlike the NEC, the ZEC has offices down to the district level. There is also a registration officer for every constituency assisted by assistant registration officers. During elections, the ZEC has a freer hand than the NEC in choosing its returning officers and assistant returning officers, although civil servants are not proscribed from holding these positions.

Powers and functions of the EMBs

The Constitution and the Election Act of 1985 give the NEC the following seven responsibilities:

- Supervise and coordinate the registration of voters in the election of the President and MPs of the United Republic of Tanzania;
- Supervise and coordinate the conduct of the presidential and parliamentary elections;
- Review the boundaries and demarcate the United Republic into various constituencies;
- Coordinate the registration of voters for the election of councillors in Mainland Tanzania;
- Declare MPs and councillors for women special seats; and
- Perform any other function in accordance with the law enacted by Parliament.[617]

The powers of the ZEC are described in the Constitution of Zanzibar 1984,[618] its functions are laid out in the Election Act of 1984,[619] namely:

- The overall supervision of the general conduct of all presidential, members of the House of Representatives and local authorities leaders elections in Zanzibar; and
- The promotion and coordination of voter education.

615 Section 8(1) of the Election Act of 1985 as amended in June 2010.
616 Ibid., Section 7(1).
617 Constitution, Article 74(6).
618 Constitution of Zanzibar 1984, Articles 119 and 120.
619 Chapter 1.

The ZEC is also responsible for the determination of constituencies.[620]

Demarcation of boundaries

The NEC is empowered by the Constitution to review boundaries and to demarcate Tanzania into different parliamentary constituencies.[621] It gives the NEC the authority to demarcate constituencies after obtaining the consent of the President.[622] The President, therefore, retains the power to decide on the creation of new constituencies.

The Constitution further sets out the criteria for creating new constituencies, including population, geography and communication.[623] Furthermore, the NEC, after learning from Zambia, Malawi, Mozambique, South Africa and Botswana, and having consulted various stakeholders – including leaders of political parties – added the following criteria:

- Population quota;
- The economic status of the constituency;
- The size of the constituency;
- Administrative boundaries;
- A constituency not to cut across two districts or councils;
- A ward not to lie in two constituencies;
- Existing pattern of human settlement;
- The Union environment;
- The physical capacity of the Parliament building; and
- The number of special seats for women.

Hence, in 2010 the United Republic of Tanzania was divided into 239 constituencies instead of 232, as was the case in 2005.[624]

The ZEC is empowered by the Constitution of Zanzibar to review boundaries and to divide Zanzibar into different constituencies.[625] The limit on the number of constituencies is voted for by the House of Representatives, the lowest being 40 and the highest 55.[626]

Registration of voters

The Constitution empowers the NEC to establish a permanent national voters' register.[627] To enable the commission to carry out this mandate, the Elections Act[628] and the Local Authorities (Elections) Act[629] are amended from time to time.

---

620 Constitution of Zanzibar, Article 120.
621 Constitution of the United Republic of Tanzania, Article 74(6)(c).
622 Ibid., Article 75(1).
623 Ibid., Article 75(3).
624 The commission published all the constituencies in the *Government Gazette* No. 271 of 30 July 2010.
625 Constitution of Zanzibar, Article 120(1).
626 Ibid., Article 120(2).
627 Constitution of the United Republic of Tanzania, Article 5(3).
628 Act No. 1 of 1985.
629 Act No. 4 of 1979.

The Constitution of Zanzibar states that every Zanzibari who has attained the age of 18 years is entitled to vote in elections.[630] According to this provision, a Zanzibari:[631]
- Must be a person who resided in Zanzibar prior to 12 January 1964; or
- Was born in Zanzibar, and has at least one Zanzibari parent; or
- Must be a Tanzanian citizen after 26 April 1964 and should not have lost such citizenship; or
- Has acquired citizenship by naturalisation.

After 2005, stringent measures were taken by law requiring a potential voter to carry an identity card.[632]

Voter education

The Election Act gives the NEC the responsibility of providing voter education throughout the country, and to coordinate and supervise persons who provide such education.[633] The ZEC is similarly mandated to provide voter education.[634] It performs this function with the assistance of other stakeholders, such as CSOs and political parties. There is, however, no central voter education curriculum as yet.

Nomination of candidates

The Constitution provides that a person shall only be entitled to be elected to hold the office of President of the United Republic if s/he:
- Is a citizen of the United Republic by birth in accordance with the citizenship law;
- has attained the age of 40 years;
- is a member of, and a candidate nominated by, a political party;
- is qualified to be an MP or a Member of the House of Representatives;
- has not been convicted by any court of any offence relating to evasion to pay any tax due to the government within a period of five years before the general election.[635]

A person is qualified for election or appointment as an MP if s/he:
- is a citizen of the United Republic;
- is at least 21 years old;
- can read and write in Kiswahili or English; and
- is a member and a candidate proposed by a political party.[636]

---

630 Constitution of Zanzibar, Article 7(1).
631 Legislative Act No. 5 of 1985, Section 3(1)–(4). These conditions are repeated in Section 12(1) of the Zanzibar Election Act No. 11 of 1984 (hereafter the Zanzibar Election Act).
632 Section 12(1) of the Zanzibar Election Act. Identity cards are issued under Legislative Act No. 7 of 2005.
633 Section 4(c) of the Election Act No. 1 of 1985.
634 Under the Zanzibar Election Act and the Referendum Act, 2010.
635 Article 39(1) of the Constitution.
636 Ibid., Article 67(1).

The nomination process is cumbersome and bureaucratic because there are many conditions in the electoral law.[637]

In Zanzibar, legal provisions for nomination to contest the Zanzibar presidency,[638] procedures for nomination of members for election to the House of Representatives,[639] and of candidates for councillorship[640] are stipulated in the Zanzibar Election Act.

Management of elections

The Constitution and the National Elections Act mandate the NEC to manage elections for the United Republic of Tanzania.[641] Such powers extend to three types of elections, namely presidential, parliamentary and local government. The NEC manages the use of funds during elections.[642] It performs this function with the assistance of the Office of the Registrar of Political Parties (RPP).

The ZEC is the sole manager of elections in Zanzibar and Election management in Zanzibar is governed by a framework of laws,[643] which have been the subject of intense debate since the return of multi-party politics.

Declaration of results

Parliamentary and councillor election results are declared at the local level.[644] However, in presidential elections, the NEC is empowered to officially declare the election result after adding returns received from the 239 returning officers.[645]

The ZEC is the only institution mandated to declare election results in Zanzibar.[646] It is an offence for any other institution or person to perform this role.

Independence of the EMBs

Independence of the NEC

The independence and autonomy of the NEC is enshrined in the Constitution.[647] The NEC is an independent department and has no obligation to follow any order or directives from any person or government department, or opinion from any political party. Moreover, 'No court is allowed to inquire into the election of a presidential candidate who

---

637   Articles 38, 38(a) and 39 of the Election Act.
638   Zanzibar Election Act, Chapter 3.
639   Ibid., Chapter 4.
640   Ibid., Chapter 5, sections 56–58.
641   Chapter 343 of the Constitution.
642   Election Expenses Act No. 6 of 2010.
643   Constitution of Zanzibar; Zanzibar Election Act; Political Parties Act No. 5 of 1992.
644   National Elections Act, Chapter 343; Local Authorities (Elections) Act, Chapter 292.
645   National Elections Act, Chapter 343, sections 35(e), 35(f)(8) and 81(b).
646   Constitution of Zanzibar; Zanzibar Election Act.
647   Article 74(11) and (12) of the Constitution of the United Republic of Tanzania.

is declared by the electoral commission (NEC) to have been duly elected'[648] and neither is any court allowed to inquire into any matter done by the NEC in discharging its duties.[649]

In its report on the 1995 general election, the Tanzania Elections Monitoring Committee (TEMCO), a civil society coalition, posed the question: 'Is the NEC independent?' It responded by arguing that 'ideally, Article 74(7) and 74(11) of the Union Constitution purports to accord independent status to [the] NEC at least at national level ... Practically, however, the NEC does not pass the basic tests of an independent institution.'[650] TEMCO advanced four reasons for its position:

- First, the appointment of NEC commissioners is made by the President, who is also the chairman of the party in power.
- Second, appointees to the NEC have no security of tenure since the President can revoke their appointment at his or her discretion.
- Third, neither the Constitution nor the Elections Act secures funds for use by the NEC.
- Fourth, the NEC does not have its own staff at the regional and constituency levels. It relies on staff in local government administrations, who in most cases are CCM cadres.

TEMCO concluded:

> And how could the National Electoral Commission delink itself from [the] CCM given its composition, manner of its appointment, reliance on CCM government discretionary funding, and even more compromising, reliance on borrowed government personnel, most of whom were believed to be (or to have been in the immediate past) CCM members?[651]

The report of the Commonwealth Observer Group stresses the importance of having an independent and impartial electoral commission.[652] It states:

> According to Article 74 of the Constitution, the Electoral Commission of the United Republic shall be appointed by the President. Further, the Director of Elections is also appointed by the President on the recommendation of the commission. There is no requirement for such an appointment to be supported by a decision of Parliament

648 Ibid., Article 41(7).
649 Ibid., Article 74(12).
650 TEMCO (1997) *The 1995 General Election in Tanzania: Report of the Tanzania Elections Monitoring Committee*, Dar es Salaam University Press, p. 137.
651 Ibid., p. 193.
652 Commonwealth Secretariat (2010) *Report of the Commonwealth Observer Group: Tanzania General Elections 31 October 2010*, aceproject.org/ero-en/regions/africa/TZ/tanzania-final-report-general-elections-commonwealth.

and no requirement for the President to seek input from Parliament with regard to potential appointees. Such a provision does not reflect good practice because it does not adequately provide for consultation and political confidence in a vital body that needs to be impartial and inclusive. Further, the ability to continuously renew a commissioners' mandate can impact on the independence of the EMB. This concern is compounded by the fact that on the mainland, election officials are drawn from among government administrators. Further, the Regional Election Coordinator appointed by [the] NEC is marginalised and lacks authority vis-à-vis the returning officers.

While the NEC sees these provisions as a way of protecting it from litigation (which might paralyse an election process), opposition parties, CSOs and some academics see it as curtailing the rights of voters and candidates.[653]

The immunity clause for the NEC in the Constitution was put to the test in a 1996 appeal brought by the Attorney-General and two others against Amani Walid Kabourou of CHADEMA, who had successfully challenged the parliamentary victory of CCM candidate Azim Suleman Premji. The Court of Appeal of Tanzania held that the

CCM was given more air time on Radio Tanzania Dar es Salaam than were given other political parties, and its broadcasts generally were biased in favour of the CCM candidate, such that it must have influenced the by-election results in favour of the CCM candidate.[654]

This meant that the NEC, which was responsible for managing that election, was biased.

While the NEC can claim that the Constitution legally protects its independence and autonomy, its powers belong to the appointing and controlling authority. All members of the NEC and its Director of Elections are appointed by the President. The only limitations to such appointing powers are the requisite qualifications of the chairman and the vice-chairman, and the requirement that there must be a candidate from the Tanganyika Law Society. Otherwise, in terms of actual individuals to be appointed, the President has no limitation, as there is no competition among the candidates to be selected.

The matter went to court in 1993 through a case filed by Mabere Nyaucho Marando and Edwin Mtei of CHADEMA, arguing that the President had no right to monopolise the exercise of creating the NEC. The High Court ruled that 'the mere fact that members of the commission are appointed by the President, who is leader of a political party, does not *ipso-facto* imply that the commission cannot act independently'.[655]

653 Makulilo, A (2009) 'Independent Electoral Commission in Tanzania: A False Debate', *Representation* 45: 435–453.
654 *Attorney-General vs Aman Walid Kabourou* [1996] T.L.R 156.
655 High Court of Tanzania, Dar es Salaam, Civil Case No. 168 of 1993.

Some scholars agreed with the ruling, and Chaligha argued that the impartiality of the NEC depends on the credibility of individual commissioners.[656] Mwaikusa likewise argued that the President has many appointees: s/he appoints the Chief Justice, judges of the Court of Appeal and High Court of Tanzania and there have never been any registered claim on the decisions of the Court of Appeal and the High Court to have favoured the government.[657]

This view has been seriously challenged by Alexander Makulilo,[658] who argues that it is 'too simplistic as it purports to equate the NEC and the court in terms of their independence'. Instead of considering the basic tests of independence, the argument is centred on 'the appointing authority as the common factor of independence to all presidential appointments'. The distinction of independence between the court and the NEC seems to be misplaced, since the court enjoys a relatively higher degree of independence:

- First, the President appoints judges of the Court of Appeal after consultation with the Chief Justice,[659] and judges of the High Court after consultation with the Judicial Service Commission.[660]

- Second, the tenure of judges is secured and protected by the Constitution. Judges are not responsible to the President after their appointment. They cannot be removed from office at the pleasure of the President. Their removal requires investigation by an independent commission of judges from Commonwealth countries.[661] Moreover, the opinion of the commission is binding on the President.

- Third, the remuneration of the judges of the Court of Appeal and of the High Court is drawn from the Consolidated Fund of the Government of the United Republic of Tanzania.[662] It should be noted that the NEC does not enjoy these advantages, while judges do.

- Fourth, in terms of mandate, the NEC's is specific to elections, which determine who is to form the government, whereas the judiciary, as one of the three branches of government, deals with a wider mandate of administration of justice on all matters ranging from civil to criminal.

656 Chaligha A (1997) 'Management of the elections: The role of the National Electoral Commission' in SS Mushi and RS Mukandala, *Multiparty Democracy in Transition. Tanzania's 1995 General Elections*, Dar es Salaam, Mkuki na Nyota Publ., p. 33.
657 Jwani MT (2001) 'Sheria na Kanuni za Uchaguzi: Haja ya Uhuru, Haki na Usawa' in RS Mukandala et al (eds) *Ushindani wa Kisiasa Nchini*, Dar es Salaam University Press, pp. 53–64, p. 61.
658 Makulilo, A (2009) 'Independent Electoral Commission in Tanzania', op. cit., pp. 443–444.
659 Article 118(3) of the Constitution.
660 Ibid., Article 109(1).
661 Ibid., Article 110a(2).
662 Ibid., Article 142(5).

Thus, equating the NEC and judges is a serious error. The NEC relies heavily on the government to carry out its duties; it is dependent on the government for offices, vehicles and personnel. This does not sit well with opposition political parties, which want an independent and autonomous EMB with its own offices, funds and personnel.

Even more contested is the practice of appointing government officials as regional elections coordinators and local government officials as returning officers and assistant returning officers. Apparently, in an attempt to ensure their impartiality, the NEC makes the co-opted officers sign an agreement that makes them liable to prosecution in case of professional misconduct.[663] There is, however, no evidence of any returning officer being penalised for partisanship or incompetence. There has been some evidence of pressure from the executive on the appointment of returning officers and regional elections coordinators where the government had sought to influence appointment or dismissal.[664]

Independence of the ZEC

The provisions in the Zanzibar Constitution, which give powers to the ZEC, are similar to those in the Union Constitution that grant powers to the NEC. The Zanzibar Constitution states that the ZEC is an independent department and that it has no obligation to follow any order or directives from any person or government department or opinion from any political party.[665] The ZEC has legal immunity from government departments, political parties and the courts.[666]

The Director of the ZEC believes that these constitutional and legal provisions grant the commission independence and autonomy, which he estimates to be around 75%.[667] The impartiality and independence of the ZEC has, however, been a matter of contention since the return of multi-party politics in 1992. The CUF, the main opposition party in Zanzibar, has consistently called for the disbanding of the ZEC. Its position apparently did not change even after two members of the party joined the ZEC in 2003. On the eve of the 2010 elections, when the GNU was imminent, the Secretary General of the CUF was still calling for the disbanding of the ZEC and the NEC.[668]

In an attempt to determine the independence and impartiality of the ZEC, TEMCO used three criteria:

- Procedures for nominating commissioners;
- Security of tenure for commissioners; and
- An independent budget decided directly by the House of Representatives.

---

663 A Chaligha, interview with Chaube Varanya, 20 November 2008, http://successfulsocieties.princeton. edu/sites/successfulsocieties/files/interviews/transcripts/3473/amon_chaligha.pdf.
664 NEC (1997) *The Report of the National Electoral Commission on the 1995 Presidential and Parliamentary Elections*, URT.
665 Constitution of Zanzibar, Article 119(9&12).
666 Ibid., Article 119(12&13).
667 Salim Ali Kassim, Director of Elections, ZEC, interview, 2012.
668 *The Guardian*, Dar es Salaam, 1 October 2010.

According to TEMCO, the ZEC does not pass the test.[669]

Makulilo is also of the view that the ZEC does not pass the minimum test of an independent and impartial body. Using the 2005 elections and the ZEC report as a reference, he has argued that the use of employees of the state invites the influence of regional and district commissioners, who wield considerable arbitrary powers in Zanzibar and who have been known to interfere with some of the decisions of the ZEC.[670] For example, the CUF presidential candidate in the 2010 elections was prevented from campaigning in Zanzibar North Region on the orders of the regional commissioner. The same candidate and his party were prevented from campaigning in Donge constituency in the same region. A seasoned Cabinet minister had declared that the 'people' of Donge did not want to hear campaigning in their area.[671] It is evident, therefore, that although the ZEC has a freer hand in choosing its returning officers and assistant returning officers, these officials operate in a political system in which some administrators ignore the ZEC and the law with impunity.

The legal and constitutional contestation against the ZEC by the main opposition party was reduced when the Constitution of Zanzibar was amended to allow for the GNU, and the presence of two CUF nominees in the commission. In the context of the current debates over the new Constitution for the Union and for Zanzibar, the smaller political parties in Zanzibar oppose entrenching the composition of the GNU as established since 2010, thus making permanent an interim situation, which is almost of equal strength between the CCM and the CUF, into a permanent constitutional position. They argue that there is a need to have wider party participation within the ZEC to avoid the hegemony of the two main parties. Alternatively, they propose that the ZEC be a non-partisan organisation made up of commissioners who are technocrats.[672]

D. Funding of elections

According to the Elections Act, the cost of elections should be paid out of the Consolidated Fund[673] – as is the case with funds for the judiciary.[674] In practice, however, this does not happen for elections.[675] The question of funding for the NEC and the elections in Tanzania has raised many complaints from the NEC itself, opposition political parties and academics. The NEC has been consistent, through periodic reports, in requesting

669 TEMCO (2011), op. cit., p. 52.
670 Makulilo (2011) 'The Zanzibar Electoral Commission', op. cit., pp. 275–277.
671 TEMCO (2011), op. cit., p. 72.
672 Interviews with Zanzibar offices' party leaders of CHADEMA, the NCCR and TADEA, Zanzibar, September 2012.
673 Election Act, section 122.
674 Article 142(5) of the Constitution.
675 NEC (1997), op. cit., p. 62.

fiscal autonomy from the government, but these requests have not been granted. The NEC receives funding on an ad hoc basis when there are elections or by-elections.

The NEC budget

The NEC budget comes from two sources: the government and the external donor community. Both sources are sometimes unreliable because funds can be inadequate or can be delayed. The NEC does not have a budget directly voted for by the legislature, instead its funds are voted for as part of the budget of the Prime Minister's Office. Each time the NEC organises elections or a by-election, it has to request requisite financial and other resources from the Prime Minister's Office. The availability of funds is, therefore, dependent on the state of funds in the Prime Minister's Office as well as the Treasury.

Most donor contributions pass through a basket fund that pools resources to create an election project. Such a single project provided funds for both the NEC and the ZEC, as well other organisations engaged in voter education and local election monitoring covering both the Mainland and Zanzibar. These include CSOs and academic institutions, as well as the media.

The experience from the 1995 general election illustrates the funding problems the NEC faces. In February 1995, the NEC had estimates of Tsh 25.3 billion (approximately USD 14 million). By March 1995, the Treasury had paid only Tsh 1.15 billion (less than USD 1 million) when there were extensive preparations for the elections that needed to be completed. Finally, the total cost for the election came to Tsh 38.6 billion (approximately USD 20 million). The funds were paid in phases, without taking into consideration the elections time table. Some of the funds were paid after the election, which meant that for a considerable time, the NEC was indebted to many service providers.[676]

In the 1995 elections, donors had promised to give Tsh 8.6 billion (approximately USD 4 million). In the final analysis, the amount was paid, but they were paying only at the speed the government was paying, which was little by little. Consequently, some of the funds were also paid after the elections. The NEC was emphatic that inadequate and untimely funding was a source of many problems facing electoral management during those elections.[677]

Donor funding was significant in the 1995 and 2000 elections, which gave donors some say in the manner in which the polls were managed. In the 1995 elections, for example, donors pressurised the NEC to allow the counting of votes at polling stations. This was adopted and since then, it has reduced tensions surrounding the transfer of ballot boxes. A commission report indicated that a senior government official from the Prime Minister's office tried to attend a NEC meeting where that decision was made; the NEC prevented him from doing so.[678]

676 Ibid., p. 31.
677 Ibid., p. 32.
678 Ibid., p. 62.

It would also appear that the improved funding by the government for subsequent elections was partially an attempt to reduce donor influence in the conduct of elections in Tanzania. In the 2005 elections, the government funded 95% of the elections budget, while donor funding accounted for only 5%. The total amount of funds for that election came to Tsh 62.53 billion (approximately USD 33 million), of which the government gave Tsh 58.7 billion (USD 30 million) and donors Tsh 3.53 billion (USD 3.05 million). It needs to be pointed out, however, that donors provided some funds before the elections by funding the permanent national voters' register. In the course of producing the register, the government provided Tsh 30 billion (USD 16 million), while the basket fund (UNDP, Denmark, the Netherlands, UK, Norway, Canada, Finland, Germany, Sweden, Ireland and Switzerland) gave USD 9.53 million. Italy gave EUR 160,000 and Japan donated Tsh 400 million (USD 218,000).[679]

In the 2010 elections, the government of Tanzania released to the NEC all funds budgeted for conducting the elections. The approved budget amounted to Tsh 60.5 billion (approximately USD 32 million). The amount is lower in dollar terms than the sum for the 2005 elections, but it needs to be noted that the elections in 2005 took much longer because they were postponed for six weeks following the death of a vice-presidential candidate for CHADEMA. This delay called for more funds for NEC activities, including the production of new ballots for the presidential election. In the 2010 elections, the NEC also received funds from the UNDP under the Election Support Programme (ESP). These funds purchased election materials and paid for voter education and capacity-building for NEC officials (Table 5.1).[680]

Despite improved funding from the government, NEC reports have consistently urged for a change to the law to grant it its own budget voted directly by the National Assembly and allocated through the Treasury. It has also asked for annual budget allocations so as to allow for the continuous updating of the national voters' register, as well as the management of by-elections when the need arises. These requests have not been granted.

Table 5.1: Funds for the general elections in 2005 and 2010 in Tanzania

Year	Government	Donor basket
2005	Tsh 58.7 billion (USD 30 million)	Tsh 3.53 billion (USD 3.05 million)
2010	Tsh 60.5 billion	Tsh 19 billion

Source: NEC 2006 and 2011

---

679 NEC (1997), op. cit., pp. 14–15.
680 TEMCO (2011), op. cit., p. 88.

Funding of elections in Zanzibar

As is the case for the Mainland, the ZEC does not have its own budget directly approved by the House of Representatives in Zanzibar. Its budget has to be requested from the Office of the Second Vice-President, just as the NEC requests funds from the Prime Ministers' Office. The Second Vice-President reviews the ZEC requests and makes decisions in consultation with the Ministry of Finance.

The Director of the ZEC believes that the problem with funding is not linked to the relationship with the Second Vice-President, but rather to the constraints emerging from the limited size of the Zanzibar economy and government revenues. According to him, the experience of the 2010 elections indicated that the Office of the Second Vice-President did not unnecessarily block the ZEC from receiving its budgeted funds. The funds are generally adequate taking into account the limited resources Zanzibar has and the many priorities of the government. Other observers mention the government exerting pressure on the ZEC by withholding funds until certain decisions are made. Funds were, for example, withheld during voter registration until the ZEC acceded to instructions to accept only Zanzibar identity cards.[681] The smaller political parties and CSOs believe that the ZEC needs to have its own budget, controlled by an independent board, to allow for effective and timely implementation of its activities. They point out, for example, that since 2010, the voters' register has not been updated, thus denying the youth who have attained voting age and who are eager to register as voters the right to do so.[682]

Another source of funding for the ZEC is donor contributions, which are obtained through the same basket fund from which the NEC also gets its election grants. The contributors were the same (UNDP, Denmark, the Netherlands, UK, Norway, Canada, Finland, Germany, Sweden, Ireland and Switzerland) and operated under the ESP. There are some delays in the disbursement of funds from the ESP owing to the high standards of control set to ensure financial accountability; the limited accounting capacity within the ZEC prevented speedy disbursement of funds from the ESP.[683] In previous elections, donor funds had political conditions following the acrimonious politics that attended the return of multi-partyism in 1992 in Zanzibar. Such conditions had included votes being counted at the polling stations, as well as pressure for a permanent national voters' register. In the 2010 elections, no political conditions were linked to donor funds in Zanzibar, most likely because of the imminent formation of the GNU.[684]

---

681   Makulilo (2011) 'The Zanzibar Electoral Commission', op. cit., p. 276.
682   Interviews with local representatives of political parties and CSOs, Zanzibar, September 2012.
683   TEMCO (2011), op. cit., p. 51.
684   Ibid.

Table 5.2: Funds for the general elections in 2005 and 2010 in Zanzibar

Year	Government	Donor basket	NEC
2005	Tsh 1 billion	Tsh 1.3 billion	Nil
2010	Tsh 2.95 billion	Tsh 59.6 million	Tsh 125.9 million

Source: ZEC 2006 and 2011

E. Management of electoral disputes

Presidential elections

A particularly controversial provision of election law in Tanzania is that presidential election results declared by the NEC cannot be challenged in the courts. Once a presidential candidate is declared a winner by the NEC, no court of law can question that decision.[685] This position is highly contested and there is a conviction among opposition parties and many analysts that it needs to be changed, while placing a time limit on such litigation and court decisions.[686] There is already considerable pressure to remove this immunity in the new Constitution, which is currently being debated.

Similarly, in Zanzibar no court can inquire into the election of a presidential candidate who has been declared by the commission to have been duly elected.[687] The provision contradicts the role of the judiciary,[688] which makes the judiciary the final authority in adjudication of disputes. The High Court has had to invoke 'inherent jurisdiction' in order to circumvent the Constitution[689] and settle disputes related to pre-election functions, the conduct of legislative elections, and their results.[690] Generally, for election disputes, courts should be allowed to hear and decide on disputes arising from presidential electoral results. The current constitutional draft allows the court to decide on the validity of presidential results.

Parliamentary elections

Electoral disputes for parliamentary elections arise from the nomination stage. A candidate in a constituency (or ward, for councillors) can lodge an objection against the nomination of any of the councillor or parliamentary candidates. The objection is lodged with the returning officer in the case of a parliamentary candidate, and assistant returning officer if it is a councillor candidate. These officers then decide these cases. Aggrieved candidates can appeal to higher authorities – to the returning officer for councillor

---

685 Chapter 2 of the Constitution, Article 41(7).
686 John Tendwa, RPP, interview, Dar es Salaam, September 2012.
687 Article 34(7) of the Zanzibar Constitution.
688 Ibid., Article 93(1).
689 Ibid., Article 119(13).
690 Makulilo (2011) 'The Zanzibar Electoral Commission', op. cit., p. 275.

candidates, and to the NEC national office for parliamentary candidates.[691] Returning officers and assistant returning officers have been accused by opposition parties of rejecting the nomination of candidates without valid reasons.[692]

In the 2010 elections, for example, the NEC upheld the appeals of two CHADE-MA parliamentary candidates who had been disqualified by returning officers following objections to their nominations. The two had competed against two former Cabinet ministers, who, after the nullification of the other candidates' nominations, were declared as having been elected unopposed. The experience of these appeals points to the impunity of returning officers, which the NEC ought to have penalised but did not. In the first case, involving a candidate in Nyamagana, Mwanza Region, the returning officer refused to issue the candidate with the appeal form. The candidate had to fly to Dar es Salaam to obtain the form from NEC headquarters in order to meet the 24-hour appeal deadline. In the second case, which involved the parliamentary candidate for Mtama, Lindi Region, the NEC had ruled in favour of his appeal against disqualification, but the returning officer kept the letter from him for two weeks, making the candidate lose valuable campaign time. Overall, the NEC received 56 appeals in relation to parliamentary elections and 124 in relation to council elections. Of these, the NEC allowed four appeals, all involving reinstating opposition party candidates who had been disqualified.[693]

The system of lodging complaints in the High Court once the elections are over has a number of hurdles. The aggrieved party (candidate, voter or Attorney-General) has to lodge the petition within 14 days of the elections.[694] A person seeking redress needs to pay a deposit of Tsh 5 million (approximately USD 3,200) for every accused respondent.[695] The three possible respondents targeted for litigation could be the winning candidate or his/her party, the NEC and the Attorney-General. For any other respondent mentioned, a similar deposit is required. One may request the court to reduce the deposit by arguing that one has limited means.[696] The law states that the petitioner has to formally consult the judge on the amount s/he is able to pay. However, the election law states that the petitioner shall request the court to consider the amount to be paid as deposit.[697] As a result, a number of cases were later thrown out of court on the technicality that the petitioner had paid the amount without consulting the court. It is a bizarre twist that

---

691 Election Act, Article 40.
692 TEMCO (2001) *The 2001 General Election in Tanzania: Report of the Tanzania Elections Monitoring Committee*, Dar es Salaam.
693 TEMCO (2011), op. cit., pp. 66–67.
694 Election Act, Article 111(3).
695 Ibid., Article 111(2).
696 The clause to give the judge the choice to reduce the amount to be paid was put into law after the Ndyanabo case, in which the lawyer successfully petitioned the Court of Appeal in 2002, which ruled that the law requiring every election results petitioner to pay Tsh 5 million was unconstitutional because it denied some citizens access to justice.
697 Election Act, Article 111(3).

one has to request the court to make a decision even when one did not request a reduction of the amount to be paid.

After the parliamentary elections in 2010, only two results were overturned by the High Court for the elections in Arusha Urban and Sumbawanga, but on appeal, the deposed MPs – for CHADEMA and the CCM – won back their seats. In the case of Arusha constituency, for example, CHADEMA candidate Godbless Lema initially lost in court to three voters who challenged his election on the grounds that he had campaigned in such a way as to exploit religion, sex and residence differences to undermine the opposing candidate, Dr Batilda Buriani. The Appeal Court overturned the High Court decision on the grounds that the respondents in the appeal case did not have *locus standi* to challenge the election. In other words, the voters had no right to bring the election petition when their rights as voters had not been violated in any way.[698] The appeal did not comment on the accusations against Lema.

Parliamentary elections in Zanzibar

Electoral disputes in Zanzibar have mainly been generalised and have hardly involved individual cases. The CUF rejected the results of the elections in 1995, 2000 and 2005.[699] Attempts to resolve major electoral disputes took the form of reconciliation talks – *Muafaka I, Muafaka II* and ultimately *Maridhiano*. There were, therefore, no individual candidates going to court to challenge the declared results. Though the ruling CCM has remained in power in Zanzibar since the return of multi-partyism in 1992, this state of affairs is anything but 'stable'. Notwithstanding the fact that elections have been neither free nor fair, the margin of victory between the CCM and the major opposition party, the CUF, has in most cases changed only slightly. Since 1992, Zanzibar has conducted four general elections, that is, in 1995, 2000, 2005 and 2010. The CCM won all these elections. In 1995, the CCM obtained 50.2% of the total valid votes against 49.8% for the CUF. In 2000, the CCM won 67.04% of the vote and the CUF 32.96%. The 2000 elections were described by TEMCO as 'aborted', while international observers called them 'a sham' owing to open rigging, manipulation, and violence. In 2005, the CCM won 53.2% of the vote and the CUF 46.1%. In contrast, in 2010, the CCM obtained 50.1% and the CUF 49.1%.

In the 2010 elections, individual electoral disputes were expected within the context of the prospective GNU. The ZEC established sub-committees to deal with these disputes. The results of their deliberations have not been made available. At the same time, election clerks had been instructed not to issue complaints forms to people who needed them. Many of the clerks were allegedly recruited on the basis of their party affiliation and their closeness to ZEC officials.[700]

It seems that candidates in Zanzibar are not used to contesting election results

698 Court of Appeal of Tanzania, Civil Appeal No. 47 of 2012.
699 TEMCO (2011), op. cit.
700 Interview with Zanzibar Legal Society officials, Zanzibar, September 2012.

through the courts. Many observers found it curious that in Zanzibar, where people are politically sensitive and there are many political complaints, there was not a single post-election court case. The partial explanation for this is that in the past, closely contested constituencies were few; generally parties had strong areas where they dominated. Another reason is that many parties did not have adequate funds for the legal costs involved in court cases, even though there are no cash guarantee deposits required for Zanzibar election petitions.[701] In addition, lack of trust in the judicial system is said to discourage parties and candidates from pursuing legal action.

F. EMB relations with other actors

The NEC's relationship with the ZEC
The Union election mandate is not problematic on Mainland Tanzania but it is so for Union elections in Zanzibar. The Constitution requires the NEC to consult with the ZEC from time to time.[702] This implies that there is no hierarchy in the relationship between the NEC and the ZEC. The relationship is informal and there are no joint committees. That would not have been a problem if the NEC was able to adequately fulfil its Union elections mandate in Zanzibar. There was a time when it was not the case, as the NEC was forced to delegate the running of Union elections to the ZEC. When the 2000 election in Zanzibar was aborted, results in 16 Union constituencies out of 50 were nullified. The NEC did not issue a statement to condemn what happened, although Union elections were adversely affected. The NEC took over the mandate of running Union polls in Zanzibar during the 2005 elections and has been doing so ever since, using the ZEC register and its own for those not registered by the ZEC.

Relations with the Registrar of Political Parties
The Political Parties Act – legislation which came with the constitutional amendments that allowed multi-party politics in 1992 – states that 'There shall be a RPP in the office of the Prime Minister or in such other office as the President may determine who shall be appointed by the President.'[703] The office of the RPP in Tanzania is separate from the NEC and the two have different mandates.

This different mandate was reflected in 2010 when CHADEMA complained that the rallies of the CCM presidential candidate were systematically going beyond the prescribed 6pm deadline. The RPP announced an extension of the daily campaign time to 7pm. The chairman of the NEC renounced the Registrar's intervention, stating that

701 TEMCO (2011), op. cit.
702 Article 74(13) of the Constitution.
703 Section 4(1) of the Political Parties Act No. 5 of 1992.

it fell outside his mandate and reiterated that the time limit was 6pm. The Registrar publicly admitted the error.[704]

The two offices are likely to remain separate because there are no apparent advantages of joining them. However, the independence of the office of the RPP vis-à-vis the incumbent party has often been questioned by opposition political parties.

Relations with political parties

The relationship between the NEC and political parties, especially opposition parties, has not always been easy. Since its inception, the NEC has sought to engage political parties through meetings to discuss electoral laws and make recommendations that have not been taken up by the government or implemented. Proposals for changes to the electoral system have been ignored. A few proposals such as the counting of votes at polling stations and more balanced reporting by the public media were taken up.[705] When two opposition parties refused to sign the Code of Conduct that was created as a voluntary pact in 2005, it was quickly enacted into a law and thus became binding in the 2010 elections. CHADEMA refused to sign the declaration to accept the Code of Conduct in protest.[706]

Both the NEC and the ZEC involve members of political parties in seven out of their eight committees, namely:

- Electoral Authorities and Electoral Process;
- Voter Education and NGOs (non-governmental organisations);
- Supplies and Logistics;
- Information and Public Relations;
- Government and Political Parties;
- International Organisations and Observers; and
- Code of Conduct for Elections.[707]

However, the eighth committee on the management of elections is the most important because it makes most of the critical decisions on the running of elections. No political party members are part of this committee and parties consequently have no effect on the most important decisions.

---

704 TEMCO (2011), op. cit.
705 NEC (1997), op. cit., p. 65.
706 NEC (2010) *Electoral Code of Conduct*, op. cit., p. 31.
707 NEC (2006), op. cit., p. 24; Salim Ali Kassim, op. cit.

Relations with the judiciary

The Constitution stipulates that in election matters, all complaints, except those pertaining to a presidential election, shall first be heard by the High Court in respect of parliamentary elections:[708]

> (1) Every proceeding for the purposes of determining the question of whether – (a) the election or appointment of any person to be MP was valid or not; or (b) an MP has ceased to be an MP and his seat in the National Assembly is vacant, or not, shall, subject to the provisions of sub-article (2) of this Article, first be instituted and heard in the High Court of the United Republic.

The jurisdiction of the High Court in hearing election petitions is not only statutory but constitutionally stipulated. The Constitution provides further that a petitioner dissatisfied with the decision reached by the High Court can go to the Court of Appeal, which has the final say in all matters including election petitions, except presidential elections, which cannot be contested in any court of law.[709]

In the case of the election of a councillor, the Local Authorities (Elections) Act[710] provides as follows:

> The election of a candidate as a member shall not be questioned except in an election petition ... The election of a candidate as a member shall be declared void on any of the following grounds which are proved to the satisfaction of the court.

Relations with Parliament

The Union Parliament and the House of Representatives of Zanzibar are the sole organs responsible for law-making. The NEC and the ZEC are creatures of the Constitutions of the Union and Zanzibar, respectively. The law-making bodies in the respective countries enact laws under which the EMBs operate. The NEC and the ZEC simply implement laws as enacted by the Houses. Indeed, it is a one-way relationship, except that in the course of implementing the laws enacted by the legislative bodies, the NEC and the ZEC exercise delegated powers by creating operational rules and regulations in the administration of elections.

---

708 Article 83(1) of the Constitution.
709 Article 83(4) of the Constitution.
710 Local Authorities (Elections) Act, section 107(1&2) (Chapter 292 R.E. 2010).

Relations with the media, civil society and election monitors

The NEC describes its relationship with the media as being very good[711] – it has organised several meetings with the media and other stakeholders during general elections
and has tried to be transparent with them. This is, however, largely an exercise in public
relations. It is the responsibility of the NEC to ensure that the media, especially public
media, are fair to all candidates and political parties during the elections.

There are problems with the public media, which have the tendency to favour the
incumbent party. The pressure on the media can be illustrated by an incident in which
the CCM presidential candidate collapsed on the podium during the inauguration of
party campaigns in front of TV cameras on 21 August 2010. Not only did the TV stations decline to show the footage, but there was a total blackout on the news in both
public and private media, including the newspapers on the following day.[712] One can
only imagine the type of pressure that was exerted on the media to produce such an
outcome.

Likewise, when the competition heated up, the government newspaper, *Daily News*,
published two controversial editorials. The first was on 24 September 2010, which stated that the CHADEMA presidential candidate would not be the fifth president of Tanzania. The second was on 31 October 2010, the voting day, which stated blatantly: 'Vote for
CCM, Vote for Unity'.[713] The NEC did not comment on the two editorials even though it
was its responsibility to ensure that the public media was not biased.

The media situation was better in Zanzibar during the 2010 elections. The voter
education information disseminated by the electronic media in Zanzibar was produced
by the Tanzania Broadcasting Corporation and validated by the ZEC.[714]

The relationship between the NEC and CSOs has often been cordial. The NEC holds
meetings with NGOs during election preparations. However, it has not prevented those
organisations from reporting anomalies during elections. The NEC is responsible for
coordinating voter education in the whole country and CSOs wishing to engage in voter
education have to obtain permission from the NEC. The impact of that relationship on
voter education is limited.

The same applies to election monitoring bodies. TEMCO, the largest and most systematic domestic election monitoring body, was established in April 1994 by 22 member organisations (most of them CSOs), including the University of Dar es Salaam. In
the 1995 elections, TEMCO deployed 136 monitors in 180 constituencies from 6 August
to 31 October 1995.[715] It has observed all elections since that time. In the 2010 elections, it had 152 member organisations and was funded by the UNDP. It had long-term
observers in most constituencies on the Mainland and Zanzibar, as well as about 7,000

---

711   NEC (2006), op. cit.
712   TEMCO (2011), *Tanzania 2010 Elections* op. cit., p. 152.
713   Ibid.
714   TEMCO (2011), op. cit., p. 81.
715   Makulilo, AB (2011) '"Watching the Watcher": An Evaluation of Local Election Observers in Tanzania',
      Journal of Modern African Studies 49: 244, dx.doi.org/10.1017/S0022278X11000036.

short-term observers.[716] It has operated without many barriers from the NEC, except bureaucracy. All of its observers have to be vetted and issued with identification cards by the NEC and the ZEC, which can be cumbersome.

The same applies to international observers, who usually arrive in the country a few weeks before the voting day. This leaves them at the disadvantage of not knowing what has been happening prior to the elections. Many reports end up being favourable to the results. In the 2010 elections, for example, foreign observers congratulated the people of Tanzania for holding credible, peaceful, free and fair elections. The African Union team also congratulated Tanzanians on their political maturity, as well as the NEC, the ZEC and the security agencies. The East African Community mission commended the elections as conducted and believed that they had been free and fair. The European Union (EU) team commended the peaceful and generally orderly election day, although key stages of the electoral process lacked transparency.[717]

Security issues

Violence in Tanzanian politics used to be a serious problem during the Zanzibar elections. All elections before 2010 had cases of violence, as discussed earlier. In Zanzibar, the relationship between the CUF and the police was very hostile. Electoral violence has now become a serious problem on the Mainland and is undermining the credibility of the NEC, which has not been able to deal with it. It has been indicated that the CCM and CHADEMA have fuelled violence by operating with party security systems that are becoming increasingly lethal.[718]

The performance of the police has been uneven – some regional police commanders and officers commanding districts have done a good job of neutralising volatile situations, while others have made tense situations worse. The police have often, however, been the cause of violence. Opposition party members believe that most police commanders see their role as protecting the incumbent party. They believe that change will come only when the present high echelon of the police retires.[719] The police have also attacked members of the media, confiscating their cameras and computers.[720]

Security presents a major challenge for by-elections and the general election in 2015. The question is not only the training of police about political and human rights, which has already been carried out. The problem lies with political party leaders who fear losing power (in the case of the CCM) and their desire to capture political power (in the case of CHADEMA). CCM politicians pile pressure on the police to take action against their strongest political opponents, while CHADEMA uses youth to mobilise for confrontations. Both are a recipe for violence.

716 TEMCO (2011) *Tanzania 2010 Elections* op. cit., p. 1.
717 'Tanzania: 2010 Elections Observer Missions and Reports', EISA, www.content.eisa.org.za/old-page/tanzania-2010-election-observer-missions-and-reports.
718 J Mtatiro, CUF Deputy Secretary-General, interview, August 2012; Deus Kibamba, interview, August 2012.
719 Faustine Sungura, Secretary of NCCR-Mageuzi, interview, Dar es Salaam, August 2012.
720 Deus Kibamba, interview, August 2012.

G. A critical assessment of election management in Tanzania

Voter registration

The NEC is responsible for keeping a voters' register for presidential, parliamentary and local council elections. Until 2004, voter registration was carried out during the six months before each election, and the process was contentious, with allegations of phantom voters in the form of false voting stations and ballot boxes. There were, therefore, calls for a permanent voters' register.[721] In 2004, a permanent national voters' register was introduced after amendments to the law.[722] The amendments replaced the old system of periodic registration during each election by empowering NEC to establish the national voters' register and to operationalise it.

Actual registration in the permanent national voters' register started in October 2004 and was generally well received. Voter turnout has been high. In 2005, the projection was to register 16,570,230 voters; this is the estimated number of people above the age of 18, based on the 2002 national household survey. In the end, 15,942,824 people were registered – 96% of those targeted.[723] The voters' register was upgraded in different country zones in the period 2007–2008. The total number of those registered increased to 18,014,667. Out of these, 2,074,065 were new voters.[724]

The significant weakness of the NEC's management of the voters' register is the failure to allow an easy transfer of registration from one constituency to another or even from one ward to another. Before the national voters' register, the transfer process was simple: voters just needed to take a letter from the returning officer of the previous constituency where they had registered, to the returning officer of the new constituency where they intended to vote and they were allocated a new polling station, as well as eligibility to vote in all three elections. At present, voter registration transfers are cumbersome, especially close to elections; even if one succeeds, one is not allowed to vote in all three elections (presidential, parliamentary and local government). The justification in preventing people from voting in the three elections on the Mainland, which is governed as a unitary system, is difficult to establish. This restriction is contrary to Tanzanians' constitutional right to freedom of movement and of settling anywhere in the country. It results in a denial of citizens' rights to vote for an MP or a councillor anywhere on the Mainland.

Another problem related to registration is the lack of funds to update the voters' register. At present, it can only be updated twice every five years. The process of updating, which is done from one zone to another, allows only two weeks for people to appear and register. This time is inadequate as people have to allocate time for registration within

---

721 TEMCO (1997), op. cit.; TEMCO (2000).
722 Section 12(1) of the Elections Act No. 1 of 1985 and section 15B(1) of the Local Authorities (Elections) Act No. 4 of 1979.
723 NEC (2006), op. cit.
724 TEMCO (2011), *Tanzania 2010 Elections* op. cit., p. 23.

their schedules. Youth are more affected when there are by-elections, because these occur between general elections and new registration is done only before the general elections; youth who have turned 18 since the general elections are therefore excluded from voting in by-elections.

Failure to transfer registered voters to new polling stations was one of the numerous factors that contributed to low voter turnout in the 2010 elections, with the national average standing at 42.8%. This compared very poorly to 84.4% and 72.28% for the 2000 and 2005 elections, respectively.[725] A study by Research and Education for Democracy in Tanzania (REDET) identified many reasons given by respondents for the low turnout. These included dissatisfaction with political parties, the NEC and the political system, as well as the buying of voting cards to prevent some supporters of the opposition from voting. However, a good number of Tanzanians could not vote because they were away from the places where they had registered to vote.[726] The most talked-about case was that of university students who had registered at their campuses, but were on long vacation in different parts of the country during the elections. This constitutes disenfranchisement of Tanzanian citizens, who were exercising their constitutional right of freedom of movement.

Voter registration in Zanzibar

Voting rights in Zanzibar are exclusive and highly controversial. Indeed, since the return of the multi-party system in 1992, it is alleged that mechanisms have been designed by the ruling party and its government to ensure that members and followers of the CUF are systematically disenfranchised.[727] The critical question is 'Who is eligible to vote in Zanzibar?' The spirit of the law is that for one to vote, one must have attained the age of maturity and must be a citizen. These were the conditions applied during the single-party elections and they were inclusive enough to allow all potential voters to vote.[728]

However, restrictions on registration were imposed after 1995, when a requirement of five years residence on the islands was imposed for one to be eligible to vote.[729] After the 2000 general election, the Zanzibar Election Act was amended to change the criterion of residence.[730] A resident, according to this provision, is a person who resides permanently in a constituency, and has lived there for a period of not less than 36 months consecutively prior to the registration day. Students, security officers, government employees and people who serve in international organisations are exempted. After 2005, stringent measures were taken by law to require a potential voter to carry a Zanzibar identity card.[731] To get the Zanzibar identity card, however, one must pro-

---

725   TEMCO (2011), *Tanzania 2010 Elections* op. cit., p. 40.
726   REDET & ZLSC (2012) *Report on the Low Voter Registration for the Zanzibar 2010 Elections.*
727   TEMCO (2011), op. cit.
728   Bakari & Makulilo (2012), op. cit.
729   TEMCO (2011), op. cit.
730   By Act No. 12 of 2002, Section 12(2) & (3) (ii) (a–e) of the Zanzibar Election Act.
731   Through amendments to Section 12(1) of the Zanzibar Election Act.

duce a birth certificate (which costs Tsh 2,500) and an introduction letter from the street/village executive officer (*Sheha*).[732] Voter registration is thus highly contested and politicised by the two major political parties, the CCM and the CUF. The CCM and its government dominate the process of defining who is an eligible voter, mainly to their advantage.[733]

The requirement for a prospective voter to hold a Zanzibar identity card has posed two critical problems on franchise. One is that the process of securing the identity card is relatively expensive. TEMCO estimates the total cost in the region of Tsh 32,000 (about USD 22) and time-consuming. In a way, potential voters have to buy their right to vote.[734] Second, the *Shehas* who initially have to issue a letter of introduction as a gateway towards registration are often CCM cadres. For example, at the *Shehia* (village) of Machui in Unguja South region, the *Sheha* was at the same time the CCM branch publicity secretary.[735] Indeed, *Shehas* occupy a strategic position to deny potential voters registration. It must be emphasised that in Zanzibar, party identification is quite known by individuals and even by households, making it easy for the *Shehas* to play the politics of exclusion, mainly to the detriment of CUF members.[736]

TEMCO observed that a requirement for prospective voters to have the Zanzibar identity card was a hindrance to, and prevented a significant number of potential voters from, registering.[737] The overwhelming powers of the *Shehas* interfered with the voter registration process, since they determined the eligibility of potential voters by deciding who could receive the identity card. The CUF director for elections, Juma Said Sanane, for example, remarked that about 200,000 CUF supporters in Unguja and Pemba were denied a Zanzibar identity card by the *Shehas*.[738]

The permanent voters' register was updated before the 2010 elections, and in Zanzibar the ZEC organised this in two stages between July 2009 and May 2010, with a voter education campaign through radio, TV and the press to encourage eligible voters to register. The register is fully digitised and more advanced than the NEC's. However, only 407,658[739] people registered as voters, a 20% reduction from the 507,225 registered in 2005. The Commonwealth Observer Group attributes the low voter registration for Zanzibar to three major reasons:

- The overly stringent requirement in order to qualify register: 'In order to qualify to register to vote a person must have permanent residency for a period of 36 months in a given constituency, thereby excluding Zanzibaris who may have been residing abroad during that period.'[740]

---

732 Legislative Act No. 7 of 2005.
733 Bakari & Makulilo (2012), op. cit.
734 TEMCO (2011), op. cit., p. 4.
735 TEMCO (2011), op. cit., p. 4.
736 Bakari & Makulilo (2012), op. cit.
737 TEMCO (2011), op. cit., p. 3–4.
738 TEMCO (2011), op. cit., p. 4.
739 A further 44,406 voters were registered to vote in the Union Elections but not in the Zanzibar elections.
740 Commonwealth Secretariat (2010), op. cit., p. 15.

- The condition that voters produce an identity card, 'which required a formal application procedure and payment of costs equivalent to some USD 20'[741] that many people were not ready to spend.
- The discretionary authority of the *Shehas*, 'whose powers in this regard, though circumscribed by the constitutional amendments governing the 2010 elections, remain controversial'.[742]

In some instances, *Shehas* facilitated under-age voter registration in favour of the CCM. In Donge Vijibweni in Unguja North B, TEMCO witnessed

> a large number of under-age youth appearing for registration. They were brought in groups by a person who, upon request by the TEMCO observer, refused to identify himself. Even when the observer tried to inquire about the issue with the registration officials, they were uncooperative and said they were not allowed to answer any question.[743]

What this implies is that the *Shehas* cleared them for the Zanzibar identity cards and ultimately allowed them to qualify for registration as voters. The problem of under-age voters was pervasive throughout the registration process. TEMCO contends that:

> the allegation of registering under-age voters surfaced at several registration centres. Some of the people who came for registration appeared too young to be 18 years old. Indeed, registration of the under-age was one of the common objections raised by the CUF party agents.[744]

A study commissioned on the question of low voter registration for the 2010 elections in Zanzibar and conducted by REDET and the Zanzibar Legal Services Centre (ZLSC) shows that 154,350 people with Zanzibar identity cards – the prerequisite for registration – were not on the ZEC voters' register of 2010.[745] The difference was considerable in the islands, which have a small population. The ZEC director argued, in response, that the qualification for obtaining a Zanzibar identity card was easier in 2005 than in 2010 when the system was tightened. In addition, restrictions on registration of people in Zanzibar who are on the move is important for planning purposes, such as ensuring that there is the right number of ballots in a polling station.[746] Neither planning

---

741   Ibid.
742   Ibid.
743   TEMCO (2011), op. cit., p. 2.
744   TEMCO (2011), op. cit., p. 5.
745   REDET & ZLSC (2012), op. cit., p. iv.
746   Salim Ali Kassim, op. cit.

exigencies nor the narrow interests of the two main political parties, the CCM and the CUF, can justify the denial of constitutional rights to ordinary citizens. At present, it is possible for one to be born in Zanzibar and remain there all one's life and still fail to qualify to be a voter, just because one has not remained in the constituency one was going to vote in for three consecutive years.

In 2009, CHADEMA and the NCCR filed a case in the High Court of Zanzibar against the ZEC and the Attorney-General. The two institutions were accused of deliberately denying the people of Zanzibar their rights to vote by introducing a minimum residency criterion. The case was dismissed on the grounds that it was not presented to the court by a competent lawyer. The two parties could not take it to the Court of Appeal (Union) because the written ruling has not been issued to date.[747]

All other stakeholders, apart from the party in power, have criticised the registration process in Zanzibar. The registration time of two weeks in every zone is seen as limited because it goes according to zones and many voters are left unregistered. There is also an over-reliance on the lowest government administrator at the village level, the *Sheha*, who is given wide discretion to determine who is and who is not to be registered. These administrators are consulted to establish whether someone has lived in the area of registration for three years and whether that person qualifies to have a Zanzibar identity card. *Shehas* have systematically favoured CCM cadres and have disowned members of other political parties, leading to many complaints and, at times, violence.

The REDET and ZLSC study dismissed the excuse of apathy as the reason for low registration, as well as the submission by the ZEC that for the 2005 elections many people registered as Zanzibar voters with the intent of selling their vote. The major reasons given by the study are linked to purposeful restrictions on eligible citizens, either directly by the *Sheha* or technically by imposing a fee. Needless to say, many of those who were not registered were rural area residents.[748]

The ZEC should be made more independent and autonomous to ensure that it acts impartially. The *Shehas* should not work directly in connection with elections in Zanzibar, since many of them are CCM cadres.

Nomination of candidates

Nomination of candidates starts at the party level. Competition is intense in the larger parties and vicious in the ruling party because of the general belief that once one wins the CCM nomination, one is likely to be elected.[749] Nomination issues only come to the NEC once the parties formally submit the names of their candidates on the day of nomination – not less than 60 days and not more than 90 days before an election is held.[750]

---

747 CHADEMA (Zanzibar) and NCCR-Mageuzi (Zanzibar), interviews, Zanzibar, September 2012.
748 REDET & ZLSC (2012), op. cit., p. 41.
749 TEMCO (2011), op. cit.
750 Section 46(1) of the National Elections Act, Chapter 343 R.E. 2010.

After the nomination day, the NEC has to deal with objections placed on candidates so as to disqualify them should the need arise. Such objections are raised either by rival candidates or by their political parties.

Challenges against candidates' nomination forms are common on the Mainland because of the desire to eliminate strong opposition on a technicality, so as to reduce competition or even eliminate it and win unopposed.[751] Candidates and parties make huge efforts to avoid errors in their nomination forms because they would not be able to correct them after the nomination day. With so many candidates returning their forms on the nomination day, there are, at times, illegal manoeuvres to prevent some candidates from presenting their papers before the deadline. For example, in the 2010 elections, one candidate had his briefcase containing his nomination forms stolen on the nomination day and he could not fill in new forms in time.[752]

The NEC's problems in performing its functions lie with its credibility and the trust it enjoys among key stakeholders. The EMB is sometimes unable to make decisions owing to legal limitations. It is because of this that the NEC has consistently demanded to have its own Act of Parliament as its foundation.[753]

Nominations in Zanzibar

Nomination of candidates has been less controversial in Zanzibar than on the Mainland because only two political parties are dominant. The Union legal provisions discussed earlier are equally applicable in Zanzibar for Union parliamentary seat candidates. Only the CCM and the CUF have elaborate participatory systems for nominating candidates. They have a minimum of two contestants in every constituency and so no candidate is nominated unopposed. For the other small parties, candidates are usually hand-picked by party authorities or are self-appointed.[754]

The approval of nominations by the ZEC consists of receiving and accepting forms from candidates. In the 2010 elections, the ZEC received only five objections to nominations: one from Unguja, and four from Chake Chake, Pemba. One objection, of a CCM candidate against an NCCR-Mageuzi opponent from Chake Chake, relating to an inadequate number of nomination signatures where two supporters had signed twice under different names, was affirmed by the ZEC.[755]

Demarcation of constituencies

The demarcation of constituencies is always contested. Although the Constitution gives the NEC the power to demarcate constituencies, in practice the decision to establish new constituencies is often political. While in some countries population is the only criterion for determining constituencies for the legislature, in Tanzania other factors come

---

751   TEMCO (2011), op. cit.
752   TEMCO (2011), *Tanzania 2010 Elections* op. cit., p. 64.
753   NEC (2001, 2006), op. cit.
754   TEMCO (2011), op. cit., pp. 34–38.
755   TEMCO (2011), op. cit., p. 44.

into play. Some of these are geography and communication. Politicians from various regions have been mounting pressure to create new constituencies. Decisions to create new constituencies are, however, made at the central government level by the Prime Minister in consultation with the President.

In exercising its own powers, the NEC has been conservative in recommending the establishment of new constituencies. In the 2005 elections, for example, the NEC stated that it did not find reason to conduct any extensive review of the boundaries of the constituencies and added only one new constituency, following the establishment of a new town council at Kibaha.[756]

The situation was different in the 2010 elections. Constituencies were increased from 232 to 239. The seven new constituencies were not originally the NEC's idea but resulted from a tendency of President Jakaya Kikwete to expand different establishments as part of his populist politics. While his predecessor, Benjamin Mkapa, created only one new region, Kikwete created four regions and 19 districts.[757]

It is recommended that a body be legally mandated to demarcate constituency boundaries. The present practice is perceived as being biased in favour of the party in government.

Constituency demarcation in Zanzibar

Demarcation of election constituencies in 2005 resulted from the implementation of the requirements of the Zanzibar Constitution, the Zanzibar Election Act and the Declaration of the House of Representatives of January 2004. According to the declaration, the House of Representatives ordered the ZEC to:

- Probe the numbers, boundaries and names of the election constituencies;
- Take into consideration the requirements of section 120(2&3) of the Zanzibar Constitution while conducting the probe; and
- Officially publish a notice specifying the alteration of numbers, boundaries and names of those constituencies before the end of 30 April 2004.

The ZEC announced its report on the constituencies' boundaries for the general election of 2005 on 15 February 2005 (Table 5.3).

756 NEC (2006), op. cit.
757 *Daily News*, Dar es Salaam, 9 March 2012.

Table 5.3: Demarcation of boundaries in Zanzibar in 2005

District	Population	No. of constituencies before	No. of constituencies after
North A	84,147	5	5
North B	52,492	3	3
Central	62,391	3	3
South	31,853	2	2
West	184,204	4	9
Urban	205,870	12	10
Wete	102,060	6	5
Micheweni	83,266	5	4
Chake Chake	82,998	5	4
Mkoani	92,473	5	5
Zanzibar	981,7754	50	50

Source: ZEC 2006

Voter education

The NEC is empowered to conduct and coordinate voter education in the whole country.[758] CSOs and other organisations wishing to engage in voter education have to obtain permission from the NEC. This task, however, occurs only during elections and the NEC mostly acts as a clearinghouse of voter education, rather than a permanent coordinator. As a result, issues of civic education have lagged behind. It has been observed that the NEC has not been provided with meaningful financial assistance to engage in voter education.[759] The result is that most of the voter education has been conducted by CSOs, political parties, churches and other faith-based organisations through donor funds managed by the UNDP. There is no standard voter education curriculum that is issued, except that any organisation or individual wishing to provide such education must present the materials to the NEC for approval. The UNDP commissioned a resource book to be used in the 2005 and subsequent elections.[760] Even then, voter education efforts were sporadic and the majority were held in urban areas.[761]

The challenge in Tanzania is to link voter education to civic education in general, especially considering the trend of low voter turnout. Voter and civic education need to be long-term because during elections, it is difficult to compete with partisan positions provided to potential voters by the political parties. It is recommended that a standard curriculum be developed to enhance the provision of voter education. There should be an adequate budget to fund country-wide voter education.

758 National Election Act, 1985, Section 4(c).
759 TEMCO (2011), op. cit.
760 Mallya, E, Ndumbaro, L & Kanyinga, K (2004) *Raia Makini*, UNDP, Dar es Salaam.
761 Masterson, G (2002) 'Tanzania and Zanzibar' in *Compendium of Elections in Southern Africa 1989–2009: 20 Years of Multi-Party Democracy*, EISA, Johannesburg, pp. 536–537.

Voter education in Zanzibar

The ZEC is responsible for promoting and coordinating voter education in Zanzibar.[762] There is also no voter education curriculum. CSOs and other entities wishing to offer voter education have to get permission from ZEC, but these organisations do not have adequate funds to carry out this kind of education. A law should be enacted to ensure civic education is provided continuously. CSOs should be given adequate resources to assist in providing voter education.

Management of campaigns

Overall, the NEC's legal power is not sufficient in relation to management of campaigns, violence, election expenses, and enforcing the Code of Conduct. There is no proper coordination among the institutions that are involved in the management of elections such as the police and RPP.

Campaigns are an important part of general elections and for more than two months, the country is dominated by campaign activity. The legal period for campaigns starts immediately after the nomination of candidates and runs up to the eve of Election Day.[763] Since the first multi-party elections in 1995 and through to 2010, the NEC has sought to manage the process to address the major problems linked to this activity. The election regulations require political parties and candidates to provide the NEC with a proposed schedule of campaign meetings to enable the commission to prepare a coordinated programme for campaigns that would then be binding on all parties.

The increasing chaos and violence linked to election campaigns led the NEC to convene a conference of all political parties to come up with a Code of Conduct for the 2005 elections. The Code of Conduct became a voluntary document in 2005 after two political parties, CHADEMA and the NCCR-Mageuzi, refused to sign it because they believed the CCM would not have respected it and the NEC would not be able to sanction the party in power.[764] By 2010, the Code of Conduct for presidential, parliamentary and councillor elections had become compulsory because the National Assembly had passed it through amendments to Section 124A of the 1985 Election Act in August 2010. Many legislative proposals over the years had been ignored by the National Assembly but this one was taken up without delay. It was clear that the state had an interest in it and CHADEMA and the NCCR-Mageuzi were bound by the code, notwithstanding their reservations.

The code is legally binding on candidates, political parties, the government and the NEC. The task of enforcing the code is given to committees at national, constituency and ward level under the chairmanship of NEC officials. The secretary is also an NEC official, with only one participant coming from political parties. The law is silent on how

---

762 Zanzibar Election Act, section 1(5).
763 The Elections (Presidential and Parliamentary Elections) Regulations, Government Notice No. 279, Article 39, 13 August 2010.
764 Faustine Sungura, Secretary of NCCR-Mageuzi, interview, Dar es Salaam, August 2012.

the parties' representative is to be selected. The committees seek to ensure that the regulations and the Code of Conduct are respected by all political parties and candidates.[765]

The Code of Conduct for political parties specifies up to 35 items, among them the requirement to respect electoral laws and ensure party members and supporters adhere to it. Parties are also expected to respect the NEC and its decisions, to avoid chaos, as well as to avoid campaigning on the basis of insults, race, ethnicity, gender and religious segregation.[766]

In implementing the Code of Conduct, the NEC faces three important challenges:

- The first is addressing the question of a level playing field for all political parties. The NEC, under the National Elections Act, sets the campaign time limits and draws up time tables to ensure that political parties do not clash at sites.
- The second issue concerns campaign violence, which usually is the consequence of verbal attacks between party leaders and supporters.
- The third problem is the use of bribes and other forms of inducement to woo potential voters, which is illegal. This problem has persisted and is growing at an alarming rate in spite of the enactment of the Election Expenses Act, 2010, intended to curb electoral corruption and the excessive use of money in elections.

Over the years, opposition parties have complained that there is no level playing field when it comes to election campaigns and that the ruling party has not been penalised for violating regulations, such as ignoring the campaign time limit of 6pm, and undermining the NEC's authority. There have been incidents in which the police have taken down opposition leaders from the podium at 6pm without extending similar sanctions to CCM leaders. For example, in the 2010 elections, following CHADEMA's complaint that the CCM presidential candidate's campaign rallies were consistently going beyond the 6pm time limit, the RPP tried to extend the campaign time to 7pm. The NEC chairman pointed out that the matter was not the prerogative of the RPP and that the time limit for political campaigns would remain 6pm. There was, however, no warning to the CCM or its candidate.[767]

The problem of violence has over the years involved supporters of the CCM and the strongest opposition party of the time – the NCCR-Mageuzi in 1995, the CUF in 2000 and 2005, and CHADEMA in 2010. While the police dealt with actual issues of criminal violence, the NEC could have taken more decisive steps to reinforce the work of the police force. The Code of Conduct allows NEC-dominated committees to penalise offenders. Council candidates can be fined Tsh 50,000 (USD 32) if their supporters engage in violence, and parliamentary candidates can be fined Tsh 200,000 (USD 128) for a similar offence. More importantly, the NEC can prevent a candidate or

---

765   NEC (2010) *Electoral Code of Conduct*, op. cit.
766   Ibid., Chapter 2.
767   TEMCO (2011), op. cit., p. 109.

party from campaigning.[768] It is important for the NEC to take such a stance because there are increasing incidents of the Code of Conduct being violated during elections. The prevalence of violations such as violence, bribery and insulting language during campaigns gives the impression that the NEC is largely ineffective in enforcing the Code of Conduct.[769]

Campaign management in Zanzibar

The election campaign period in Zanzibar has also been characterised by irregularities and violence. In the 2000 elections, for example, three issues were of major concern:

- The role of the police;
- The problem of getting space for conducting rallies, which mostly affected the CUF; and
- The use of threatening language in campaign rallies by CCM and CUF leaders.

There was tension between the police and CUF supporters, who believed the law enforcement officers were biased and employed excessive force against them. In one incident, CUF supporters beat up three police officers and confiscated a gun. In another, policemen shot and wounded five CUF supporters.[770]

The conduct of the campaigns for the 2010 elections improved because of the context of the *Maridhiano* compromise leading to the GNU. For the first time, the election in Zanzibar was not a winner-take-all contest. The GNU agreement before the elections made sure that the two competing parties would be in office.

The campaign rules and regulations used in the 2010 elections in Zanzibar were laid down by relevant Union and Zanzibar laws. Union election campaigns in Zanzibar were guided by the Elections Regulations, 2010, the Code of Electoral Conduct, 2010 and the Elections Expenses Act, 2010.[771] Zanzibar elections applied the laws, regulations and Code of Conduct for political parties.

The Code of Conduct for political parties in Zanzibar disallowed 14 practices, which included:

- Disrupting the rallies of opposing parties;
- Using language that was insulting, slanderous or demeaning to other candidates or parties;
- Campaigning in mosques, churches or other religious buildings;
- Soliciting votes on the basis of tribe, religion, denomination or race; and
- Transporting people to campaign rallies.[772]

---

768 Ibid., p. 24.
769 TEMCO (2011), op. cit., pp. 122–130.
770 TEMCO (2001), op. cit., pp. 117–118.
771 The Election Expenses Act, 2010, Government Notice No. 246.
772 TEMCO (2011), op. cit., p. 63.

During the campaigns, there were instances of the use of abusive language, some use of religious discrimination and in one case, two people were seriously injured following an incident of stone throwing. These were, however, minor compared to the 1995, 2000 and 2005 elections, which were a security nightmare.[773]

Other stakeholders attest to the improved environment and attribute it to police maturity and the formation of the GNU. However, there were cases in the 2010 elections where the police were engaged in skirmishes with voters.[774] In a recent by-election in Bububu, violence between the police and CUF supporters re-emerged, marking the return of tensions between the GNU partners. Six suspected CUF supporters were arrested and charged with rioting.[775]

Voting, vote counting and declaration of results

There was a marked improvement in the management of the voting day in the 2010 elections compared to 2005 and previous polls. In the 2005 elections, for example, names in voter lists were not alphabetically arranged. In centres with multiple polling stations, voters could not find the correct polling station easily. The problem was significant in Dar es Salaam. In the 2010 elections, the lists were alphabetical and voters were guided by an election clerk to the correct polling booth. There were, however, isolated cases where some voters were allocated polling stations far from where they had registered. In some cases, the distances were long enough to discourage people from voting. As it would become apparent later, the calm on voting day was partly due to low voter turnout.[776]

The NEC's performance in vote counting and the declaration of election results has not been exemplary. It was observed and documented that where opposition parties were strong and likely to win, vote counting and tallying took a long time, and declaration of the winner was significantly delayed.[777] The NEC attributed the delays in declaring results to the failure on the part of returning officers and assistant returning officers to adequately master the new vote tallying procedure, the Results Management System (RMS). Kibamba, Tendwa and Mtatiro have attributed these delays to politics and not technicalities, especially when it occurred mostly in areas where the opposition was strong.[778] That tendency has encouraged some opposition parties to take a confrontational stance from the beginning by urging followers to stay around polling and tallying stations after casting their ballots to 'protect their votes', implying that delays signified

---

773 According to the Director of the ZEC (Salim Ali Kassim, interview, op. cit.), there were no election-related deaths in the run-up to the 2010 elections. In 1995, more than 20 people died after the elections, while the aftermath of the 2000 elections had the highest number of casualties. There were also deaths in the 2005 election in Pemba.

774 Interviews with Zanzibar offices' party leaders of CHADEMA and TADEA, Zanzibar, September 2012.

775 *The Citizen*, Dar es Salaam, 18 September 2012.

776 TEMCO (2011), op. cit.

777 Ibid., pp. 192–193.

778 Deus Kibamba, interview, August 2012; John Tendwa, interview, Dar es Salaam, September 2012; J Mtatiro, CUF Deputy Secretary-General, interview, August 2012.

attempts to change results through vote rigging. Violent confrontations were recorded as the police tried to remove such supporters in Segerea and Ubungo constituencies in Dar es Salaam, Nyamagana constituency in Mwanza, and Arusha Urban constituency.[779]

The EU, which was the largest external observer group, stated in its report that the NEC was deficient in such fundamental areas as effective communication within the different levels of the commission. Public information, which could have enhanced transparency, for example, in the registration of voters and in the transmission of results, was lacking. Information was not effectively conveyed to stakeholders and the general public, thus creating unnecessary mistrust.[780]

The largest internal observer group, TEMCO, in its final statement declared the performance of the NEC in the 2005 and 2010 general elections to be free and fair. Makulilo has questioned this assessment, arguing that there were no qualitative changes from the 1995 and 2000 Union elections, which had been characterised as free but not fair.

Legal reforms are recommended to ensure that election observers and party agents get an opportunity to monitor the tallying of presidential aggregated results.

Voting, vote counting and declaration of results in Zanzibar

The processes of voting, vote counting and declaration of results have always generated tension in Zanzibar because outcomes are generally very close. The conduct of the ZEC has often been called into question by the CUF for lacking impartiality. In the 1995 elections, the ZEC was very ambivalent in proclaiming electoral results. There were initial unofficial reports that gave the CUF victory, in response to which the CCM wrote a letter of protest calling for the nullification of the results. The ZEC was silent for four days before declaring the CCM the winner.[781] Inevitably, the CUF did not accept defeat, and violence resulting in deaths followed.

The experience of the 2000 elections has been discussed earlier: the ZEC decided to go ahead with elections in spite of the chaos and disorganisation that characterised them. Many polling stations opened late and there were not enough ballot boxes. The ZEC interrupted the counting process and later nullified results in 16 constituencies where reruns were held in the week that followed.[782] The ZEC declared votes between the CCM and the CUF that did not fit the trend of other elections: in 1995, it was 50.8% for the CCM to 49.8% for the CUF; in 2000 it was 67.04% to 32.96%; and in 2005 it was 53.2% to 46.1%.[783] The 2000 elections stood out as being very different because of a boycott by the opposition in the re-run of the polls.

779 TEMCO (2011), op. cit., p. 192.
780 EU Election Observation Mission (2010) *Final Report: General Elections, October 2010.* eeas.europa.eu /delegations/tanzania/documents/page_content/tanzania_final_report_final_en.pdf.
781 Makulilo (2011) 'The Zanzibar Electoral Commission', op. cit.
782 'Zanzibar: The October 2000 Elections', EISA, www.content.eisa.org.za/old-page/zanzibar-october-2000-elections.
783 Makulilo (2011) 'The Zanzibar Electoral Commission', op. cit., p. 269.

The Director of the ZEC believed that the declaration of elections results in 2010 was exemplary because it was done within 24 hours after voting ended. There is no strict legal limit to the time allowed for declaring results, but in previous elections the EMB took several days before it announced outcomes, usually amid raised political temperatures. There was still some tension outside the central tallying station in 2010 when the ZEC declared the CCM candidate winner. Finally though, and reluctantly, the CUF presidential candidate accepted the victory of the CCM candidate. CUF supporters joined CCM followers to celebrate the GNU.[784] The reaction, therefore, can be attributed to *Maridhiano*, which created an atmosphere where the ZEC could operate smoothly since, for the first time, it was not a winner-take-all election.

H. Constitutional review and reform of EMBs

During the ongoing process of crafting a new Constitution, both the NEC and the ZEC have to be reformed and fundamentally restructured. Some opposition political parties have called for reforms to the EMBs even before a new Constitution because they argue that the Constitution might not be ready before the 2015 elections. They would not abide elections held under the current EMBs for fear that they could compromise and again use government or local government officials as returning officers and assistant returning officers. This has been categorically stated in presentations by CHADEMA and the CUF to the Constitutional Review Commission (CRC).[785]

Reform of the NEC

Demands for reforms first focused on the NEC, and were initially voiced by CUF, followed by other political parties.[786] The chairman of the CRC has argued that one could not change the election law before Tanzanians have established the nature of the electoral system they want to have in the new Constitution. He believes that the process of getting a new Constitution will be completed by April 2014 and that there will be more than a year to make the requisite changes to the law.[787] Whether the draft Constitution will receive majority support at the referendum remains to be seen. Regardless of the outcome, the NEC is likely to undergo radical changes before the next elections. The views presented to the CRC show an overwhelming desire for substantial changes.

It is instructive that the recommendations presented recently by the chairman of the NEC to the CRC call for significant changes to the structure of the EMB. The NEC proposed that 'independent' needs to appear in the name of the EMB. It recommended that candidacy for the position of commissioner needs to be open and transparent, and that the commissioners need to be selected by an independent technical body. The

---

784 TEMCO (2011), op. cit., p. 102.
785 *Jamhuri Media*, Dar es Salaam, 29 January 2013.
786 J Mtatiro, CUF Deputy Secretary-General, interview, August 2012; J Mnyika, IPP media, interview, 14 December 2012.
787 Warioba, S, *Raia Mwema*, 2 January 2013.

recommended candidates then need to be confirmed by Parliament and appointed by the President. It is proposed that the commissioners be sworn into office by the Chief Justice. Other propositions from the NEC include the supremacy of the courts on election matters, the institutional independence of the EMB, and the possibility of an MP changing parties without losing his/her seat.[788]

The NEC recommendations are progressive but they also indicate that the commission is aware that as it stands today, it is neither independent nor autonomous. These proposals would be acceptable to many; unfortunately they have not been reflected in the first draft of the Constitution, which is quite weak in the area of EMBs. The draft Constitution provides for commissioners to be appointed by the President on the recommendation of an appointing committee made up of the Chief Justice, judges and Speakers of the proposed legislatures. The proposed appointing committee would not be independent since the Speakers would have been elected by the party or coalition with the majority in each legislature.[789] In addition, there is the question of how to get Speakers to appoint commissioners before the elections. These proposals have not respected popular views expressed by the people, who do not support appointment of commissioners by government officials.

Alternative views have come from some political parties proposing that commissioners be appointed from political parties. CHADEMA, for example, proposed a commission of 25 members – 18 of whom would come from political parties.[790] The idea of a partisan EMB is not popular even among opposition parties, such as the CUF. Many call for a new process for selecting and confirming members of the EMB. There might be differences about the final appointing authority, with some proposing the National Assembly and others the President, but the critical factor is the transparency in the selection and confirmation process.

One important proposition in the ongoing Constitution debate is that all actions of the new EMBs could be questioned in a court of law, including the declaration of the winner in the presidential election. This is included in Article 78 of the draft Constitution, which proposes that the aggrieved candidate lodges an appeal within seven days and the court gives judgment within 14 days.[791]

Reform of the ZEC

The calls for reforms of the ZEC in Zanzibar have been muted because of the GNU. The most vocal voices had been within the CUF, but the party is now in the coalition government. The participation of the two political parties in the ZEC has been seen as beneficial for them and there is reluctance to reopen the debate. The Director of the ZEC stated that it would not be prudent for the elections management body to propose

788 Lubuva, D, *Habari Leo*, Dar es Salaam, 19 January 2013.
789 URT (2013) *Rasimu ya Katiba ya Muungano wa Tanzania* [Draft Constitution of the United Republic of Tanzania], Articles 181 & 182.
790 *Jamhuri media*, 29 January 2013.
791 URT (2013), op. cit., p. 42.

changes. Experience has shown that when the ZEC proposed changes, they were rejected even if the same proposals were being adopted when proposed by political parties.

The smaller parties and CSOs propose a completely new EMB with a diversity of independent-minded and academically qualified commissioners coming from CSOs, academic institutions and other non-governmental sources. They propose that the EMB needs to have its own office, equipment and budget.

In the constitutional review process, participants from Zanzibar have not analysed the organs of the Zanzibar government. They are interested in increasing the power and autonomy of Zanzibar within the Union. They argue that they have their own Constitution, which is popular in Zanzibar, especially following the ten amendments that gave greater autonomy to Zanzibar in 2010, and which some observers see as usurping the sovereignty of the Union Constitution. While the structure of the ZEC is still contested by the opposition in Zanzibar, the honeymoon for the GNU and a preoccupation with the demand for greater autonomy for Zanzibar in the ongoing constitution-making process have temporarily reduced the intensity of the pressure to restructure the ZEC.

I. Conclusions

Free and fair elections are critical to Tanzania's quest for democracy and citizens' participation in public affairs. The integrity of EMBs is more critical today than it has been before for a number of reasons.

- First, a very clear trend that became evident in the 2010 elections, and is becoming more apparent in by-elections held since then, shows that the majority of Tanzanians are staying away from the polls. Part of the reason is that they do not trust the electoral system, including the EMBs. The possible danger is that they might believe that the solution to participation in public affairs is outside the system.
- Secondly, while the CCM could in the past claim to be truly hegemonic in terms of having a sweeping majority, that claim cannot be sustained today. It is fast losing support and the opposition is getting stronger. Any serious political fallout after contested election results could be very destructive to the society.
- Thirdly, the call for a new Constitution started as a quest to reform the NEC and the ZEC. Attempts to retain the EMBs in their current form are likely to undermine the whole constitution-making process.

The challenge of delivering free and fair elections cannot be addressed by EMBs alone. There is the question of reforming the political system, especially by dealing with the domination of regimes that purport to support democratic practice when they actually harbour authoritarian tendencies. There is also the issue of political culture. The tendency in African elections is for both ruling and opposition political parties not to accept electoral defeat. However, in a situation where the ruling party wants to remain in power at any cost and the opposition wants to capture power at all costs, the existence of an independent and autonomous EMB can avert chaos.

This study examined the independence of the NEC and the ZEC and the possibility of having autonomous EMBs in the ongoing constitutional reform process. The independence of the NEC has been questioned consistently by opposition political parties and independent analysts since the first multi-party by-elections after 1992 and the first multi-party elections in 1995. Those who argue that the NEC and the ZEC are independent point to constitutional provisions, which apparently guarantee their autonomy. The reality, however, is that those legal provisions have been used to protect the NEC and the ZEC from being questioned for malpractices and faults in the management of elections.

Meanwhile, the incumbent political parties have been reluctant to change the structure and character of both the NEC and the ZEC. Despite requests for specific laws that would enhance the EMBs' budget autonomy and freedom to employ staff, these legal reforms have not been undertaken.

At the same time, the appointment of commissioners gives the Union and Zanzibar presidents a great deal of leeway. While constitutions point to the qualifications of commissioners – especially the chairpersons, who are expected to be senior judges – the appointment process is not transparent. This situation has fuelled perceptions among members of the opposition, as well as other political parties, that the President could appoint commissioners who would favour the ruling party.

The performance of the NEC and the ZEC in the management of elections has been mixed, from a qualified free and fair rating to poor, according to observers' reports. Union elections managed by the NEC have exposed problems with elections in the region of Dar es Salaam in 1995 and chaos in Zanzibar in 2000. As for the ZEC, observers' reports show its performance as being very poor except in the 2010 elections.

One of the practices most contested by opposition parties is the use of civil servants as returning officers and assistant returning officers. These are seen as interested people whose continued appointments depend on the incumbent party's continued stay in power.[792]

J. Recommendations

This study makes the following specific policy recommendations.

Independence of the NEC and the ZEC

- With the ongoing process of writing a new Constitution in Tanzania, the independence of the NEC and the ZEC from the state needs to be recognised and enforced.

---

792 J Mtatiro, CUF Deputy Secretary-General, interview, August 2012; Faustine Sungura, Secretary of NCCR-Mageuzi, interview, Dar es Salaam, August 2012.

- The process of appointing NEC and ZEC commissioners – even where it is based on compromise – needs to be open and transparent. Candidates need to be interviewed and screened by an independent technical team, and a gender-balanced list presented to the National Assembly for confirmation before appointment by the President.
- Members of the NEC and the ZEC need to have security of tenure enshrined in the Constitution. They should be removed only on grounds of gross misconduct after being investigated by a committee of High Court judges.
- The NEC and the ZEC need to have their own organisational law, physical infrastructure and secretariat represented right up to the district level. Most opposition political parties have no confidence in government officials running elections at the constituency and sub-constituency level. Government officials should not be involved in managing elections.

Funding of elections
- The NEC needs to have its own funds voted directly by the legislature and paid from the Consolidated Fund in the Treasury. Similarly, the ZEC needs to have its own organisational law and its own funds voted directly each year by the legislature and paid from the Consolidated Fund in the Zanzibar Treasury.
- The two EMBs need to improve their relations with donors, particularly those involved in elections support, to facilitate the financing of activities related to elections, including the provision of voter and civic education.
- Donors, on the other hand, should make sure that they honour their financial pledges to the EMBs adequately and on time. This would allow the EMBs to prepare for the management of elections.
- Likewise, donors should adequately fund CSOs so that they can provide civic and voter education to the majority of citizens.

Demarcation of constituency boundaries
- There should be an independent body, composed of seasoned professionals and civil society representatives, in charge of boundaries demarcation on the Mainland as well as in Zanzibar.

Voters' register and voter registration
- The technology of the permanent national voters' register needs to be updated and digitised to modern standards.
- The national voters' register has to allow citizens to register continuously and to vote anywhere in the country within the limits set by best practices in the EAC and the Southern African Development Community.
- The three-year residence requirement for registration of Zanzibar voters is contrary to the Bill of Rights in the Zanzibar Constitution and should be abolished.

Nomination of candidates

- The process for nominating election candidates needs to be simplified so as to verify the identity of the candidate.
- It needs to be less bureaucratic in order to avoid nullification of nominations for small technical errors.
- Emphasis needs to be placed on the identity and curriculum vitae of candidates. This will reduce attempts by candidates and parties to disqualify competitors.

Electoral violence

- The NEC and the ZEC need to mete out penalties as outlined in the Code of Conduct for political parties, which include suspending a candidate or a political party from campaigning.
- While the Zanzibar election campaigns were less violent in 2010, there was apparent impunity in a politician preventing the CUF from campaigning in his area. The ZEC should not be silent in the face of political impunity.

Voting, vote counting and declaration of results

- The process of vote counting and relay of results is still contested because the NEC gives a lot of leeway to returning officers and assistant returning officers, while the ZEC is not seen as being transparent enough.
- The NEC needs to institute strict appointment standards for personnel and to closely supervise them to avoid their manipulation.
- To avoid heightened political tensions in Zanzibar, transparency in vote counting, tallying and announcement of results needs to be well entrenched. Transparency should be promoted, particularly during the final tallying of presidential election results.

Voter education

- The NEC needs to deal not only with voter education but also with civic education in light of the recent decline in voter turnout. The NEC can use CSOs to conduct this activity during the period between elections.
- The NEC needs to develop a standard voter education curriculum.
- Voter education by the ZEC is limited to short periods before elections. The ZEC needs to engage academics and CSOs to develop voter and civic education.
- The ZEC needs to develop a civic education curriculum.
- The ZEC can use CSOs to coordinate this activity in the period between elections.
- CSOs should actively engage in providing civic and voter education. They should make sure that they reach the majority of citizens in both rural and urban areas.

- CSOs should also be accountable to the people and the financiers who fund their activities.

Electoral disputes

- All NEC and ZEC electoral decisions should be open to challenge in courts of law, including the declaration of the winner in the presidential elections.
- Litigation needs to be conducted promptly and judgment delivered within a specified short period so as to avoid a governance vacuum. The limits of seven days for litigation and 14 days for judgment seem reasonable.

Relationship with other actors

- The NEC and the ZEC need to build good relations with the legislature in order to ensure that legal reforms to the electoral system are implemented.
- The EMBs need to work closely with political parties in order to improve transparency in election administration and hence boost its credibility.
- The NEC and the Office of the RPP should be merged to harmonise their activities and to be cost effective.
- The government should embrace comprehensive reforms that would separate the ruling party from the state. This would ensure fair political competition and independent and impartial EMBs.
- Similarly, the ruling party should be limited from using the state machinery to its own advantage.

6

Uganda

Margaret Sekaggya

A. Summary

The Electoral Commission of Uganda has been perceived negatively and does not enjoy great trust among stakeholders, including opposition parties and civil society organisations. Its composition, the manner of its appointment and how it has executed its mandate in conducting elections in the recent past have all contributed to this trust deficit. Recent elections have been conducted in an environment where media freedom is limited; freedom of assembly, association and expression are constrained; and political parties are weak.

The Electoral Commission (EC) has had challenges in the following areas:

- Updating the national voters' register, resulting in disenfranchisement of some voters;
- Demarcation of constituencies when new districts are formed;
- Oversight of political parties and candidates;
- Ensuring equal access to public media;
- Conducting elections;
- Voter education;
- Delays in publishing results, particularly of parliamentary elections;
- Delays in hearing and determining complaints, especially at the district level; and
- Inadequate remuneration for its staff.

The EC's strategic plan for 2013–2017[793] attempts to address some of these concerns, and is based on five pillars, namely:

- An institutionally strengthened election management body;
- Free, fair and transparent elections;

---

793 EC (2013) *The Strategic Plan 2013–2017 of the Electoral Commission, Uganda*, EC of Uganda, Kampala, www.ec.or.ug/docs/EC%20Strategic%20Plan%202013-2017.pdf (hereafter *'Strategic Plan'*).

- A credible, accurate and accessible national voters' register;
- Effective and comprehensive voter education; and
- A more service-oriented election management body (EMB).

The strategic plan is, however, inadequate for addressing all the issues surrounding the electoral process – such as the EC's own independence, strict implementation of all electoral laws, and review and amendment of existing laws that have an impact on the elections, among other things. The EC is one of the many key players in the electoral process.

This study makes the following recommendations:

- Law reform by Parliament should provide for a more credible, participatory and transparent process for the appointment and removal of the members of the EC, and increased media access to electoral processes.
- The EC should improve the execution of its mandate, particularly in civic education, updating the national voters' register, adjudication of complaints and the conduct of elections.

B. Political history of elections

Before independence, elections in Uganda were not greatly valued, as the colonial government handled the affairs of the country.[794] Prior to gaining independence from Britain in 1962, the only elections in Uganda were for the Legislative Council (LEGCO). It was small and composed only of Europeans. Its legislative powers were limited, since all important and major decisions came from Her Majesty's Government in the United Kingdom. The LEGCO was created by the British colonial government in 1920 through an order-in-council and held its first meeting on Wednesday, 23 March 1921. It was made up of the colonial governor as president, four officials and two nominated non-officials, all of European descent; in later years, a few Indians were added.

Although there was a provision for five elected members from Buganda, elections did not take place, because the Buganda Government and Lukiiko had advised people in Buganda to boycott the elections. There was no representative from Karamoja. There were six nominated Europeans and six nominated Asians. The government side had 32 members while the representative side had 30 members, including the five vacancies for Buganda. The government effectively had a majority of seven (32 minus 25). The LEGCO also had, at the time, five nominated women members.

After independence, the political, social and economic dynamics of the country began to take shape as citizens developed an interest in Uganda's democracy.

---

794 Ogwang, C (2000) 'A Brief History of the Electoral Commission in Uganda' in *The Electoral Commission Today*, 10th Anniversary Edn, EC of Uganda, p. 5.

Transition to independence

In 1961, the colonial government organised elections contested by two political parties, the Democratic Party (DP) and the Uganda People's Congress (UPC), leading to the formation of the first ever internal self-government headed by Chief Minister Benedict Kiwanuka. The 1961 elections were characterised by violence instigated by the Buganda Government in an effort to prevent the Baganda from registering to vote.

In 1962, the colonial government organised another election in which the DP won the majority of seats in Parliament. The DP's victory led to the first alliance of political parties in Uganda, composed of a merger between the UPC and Kabaka Yekka (KY) to become the UPC-KY. This new majority took over government, headed by the first Prime Minister, Milton Obote, and Major General Sir Edward Frederick Mutesa II (Kabaka of Buganda) as the first President.

Following the 1962 elections, Uganda gained independence from Britain on 9 October 1962. The LEGCO was replaced by the National Assembly, also called the Uganda Parliament.

Constitutional change (1962–1986)

The 1962 Constitution was abrogated by Prime Minister Milton Obote in 1966, who imposed an interim Constitution on the legislature through military force. The regime, among other things, removed the constitutional recognition for kingdoms in Uganda.

The 1962 Constitution was replaced with the 1967 Constitution, which though widely debated, extended Obote's rule for five years without elections and established a republic, with a strong presidency that had powers to appoint officers who should normally have been elected into office. Elections that had been scheduled for 1967 were abandoned and the tenure of Members of Parliament (MPs) was automatically extended for another five years. In 1969, political parties were banned in an effort to consolidate Obote's rule and Parliament turned the country into a one-party state.

In 1971, Idi Amin overthrew Obote's government. The country sank further into dictatorship as the Constitution and political activity were suspended. Amin ruled through military decrees passed by the military council. Elections were suspended and replaced by military appointments until Amin's removal from power in April 1979.

Thereafter, Uganda was governed by the Uganda National Liberation Front (UNLF), which was composed of a group of exiles who had taken over power with the assistance of the government of Tanzania. The National Consultative Council, the legislative structure of the UNLF, elected Prof. Yusuf Lule and then Godfrey Binaisa as President in quick succession.

In 1980, elections were organised by the Military Commission, an organ of the UNLF, in conjunction with the EC. The electoral process was marred by gerrymandering, ballot box stuffing, coercion, violence, fraud, discrimination and harassment of non-UPC candidates.[795] During these elections, each political party had its own ballot box, which intimidated supporters of parties other than the UPC. Furthermore, the counting of votes was carried out at the district headquarters and not at the polling stations. The electoral process was largely described as irregular and was characterised by violence, harassment and intimidation of non-UPC members. Afterwards, it was alleged that the DP had won the elections, but an announcement was made prohibiting the EC or any person other than the chairman of the Military Commission from announcing the results. Eventually, when the results were announced declaring that the UPC's Milton Obote had won the presidency, they were rejected by the parties that had participated. The alleged fraudulent elections prompted Yoweri Museveni and others to resort to an armed struggle to restore democracy.[796]

The period between 1980 and 1986 was politically unstable, with a civil war raging. There were no elections. Obote was overthrown as President in July 1985 by General Tito Okello, who was in turn deposed in January 1986 by Museveni of the National Resistance Movement.

The National Resistance Council

In 1986, the National Resistance Movement (NRM) came to power after overthrowing the military regime of General Tito Okello. This group formed the National Resistance Army government and, using the National Resistance Council (NRC), which served as Parliament, enacted Statute No. 5 in 1988 to establish the Uganda Constitution Commission. The commission began the process of writing and developing a new Constitution for Uganda. Justice Benjamin Odoki was its chairman.

The first elections under the NRM were held in 1989, specifically to fill the positions in the NRC from the village to the national level, including the legislature. The 1989 elections were held under an umbrella movement without political parties. Candidates stood on individual merit. The elections were criticised for their lack of direct participation, which was limited to the village level. Direct participation did not extend to the national level, where elections were conducted through electoral colleges and were removed from the people. Although these elections were praised as an improvement on the 1980 polls because the process was more transparent with votes counted at the polling stations and gerrymandering eliminated, they were also characterised by lack of voter education, bribery and partiality.

795 Sekaggya, M (2010) *Uganda: The Management of Elections*, Open Society Initiative for Eastern Africa, p. 12; Mbazira, C (2009) *Reform Overdue: Making the Case for Electoral Restructuring in Uganda*, HURIPEC Working Paper No. 26, p. 10.

796 Museveni, YK (1997) [reprinted 2007] *Sowing the Mustard Seed*, Moran Publishers, pp. 121–126.

The restoration of multi-party politics

In 1993, the Commission for the Constituent Assembly (CCA) was established and mandated to organise and conduct Constituent Assembly elections.[797] Elections to the Constituent Assembly were direct, with provision also made for special groups, such as women, to participate through electoral colleges. The elections were characterised by inadequate voter education, as well as allegations of fraud and bribery, among other irregularities. Elected members of the Constituent Assembly would later be tasked to debate, pass and adopt a new Constitution.

The 1995 Constitution restored presidential and parliamentary elections in Uganda. Nonetheless, Uganda has yet to experience a change in occupancy of the presidency through the ballot box.

The 1996 and 2001 elections were held under the 'movement system', in which individual political parties were not permitted. Elections were held for posts at different levels within the structures of the NRM. The 1996 elections were the first since the military takeover in 1986 and the major issue of contention for observers was the lack of political party participation. Nevertheless, the elections were, by and large, deemed free and fair and there were no major complaints of irregularities and voter intimidation or harassment. In the referendum held in 2000, Ugandans voted for the retention of the NRM. The 2001 elections, however, faced many allegations of malpractice and were challenged in the Supreme Court, which confirmed anomalies like multiple voting, evidence of pre-ticked ballot papers and harassment of voters.[798]

The 2006 and 2011 elections were held under the multi-party political dispensation, following amendments to the Constitution. This followed a recommendation from the Constitutional Review Commission and a referendum in July 2005, which showed overwhelming support by Ugandans for a multi-party political system. Therefore, in 2005, Parliament approved a constitutional amendment to return the country to a multi-party political system – but also scrapped presidential term limits. The NRM, which had transformed into a party, won both elections, with 214 of the 309 seats in the Eighth Parliament, which served between 2006 and 2011.

The 2006 elections were particularly marred by harassment and arrest of the opposition presidential candidate on charges of rape and treason. The NRM won that election with a lower margin than before[799] and the Supreme Court acknowledged widespread electoral malpractices and vote rigging; however, according to the court, this did not substantially affect the result of the elections.[800]

The 2011 general elections for the President and 375 MPs were the second multi-party polls held since 1980. They were less violent than previous elections and deemed by observers to be, by and large, free and fair, though not perfect. Some of the issues

---

797 Constituent Assembly Statute No. 6 of 1993.
798 *Col. Dr Besigye Kizza vs Museveni Yoweri Kaguta, Electoral Commission* (Election Petition No. 1 of 2001).
799 President Yoweri Kaguta Museveni won the election with 59.26% of the vote, which was 10% less than his 2006 election win.
800 *Rtd Col. Dr Kizza Besigye vs Electoral Commission, Yoweri Kaguta Museveni* (Election Petition No. 1 of 2006).

of concern related to the negative perception of the independence of the EC, commercialisation of elections, disenfranchisement of voters because of errors in the national voters' register, intimidation and harassment of voters and other administrative glitches.[801] Nevertheless, these polls stood out as some of the best organised in the country when compared to the rest. Parliament passed the necessary laws to help standardise regulation of the electoral administration and management, media coverage and political parties.

The 1995 Constitution provides for measures to ensure the representation of particular groups in Parliament, including women and persons with disabilities. According to these provisions, there is a woman representative for every district in Parliament. However, women representatives for non-reserved constituencies are very few. Persons with disabilities were elected through an electoral college constituted by members of the National Union of Disabled Persons in Uganda (NUDIPU).[802]

Although there were 38 registered political parties, only seven presented presidential candidates for the 2011 general election; one candidate ran as an independent. The presidential election results are presented in Table 6.1.

Table 6.1: Summary of the 2011 presidential election results

Candidate	Party	Votes	Percentage
Abed Bwanika	People's Development Party (PDP)	51,708	0.65%
Besigye Kizza Kifefe	Forum for Democratic Change (FDC)	2,064,963	26.01%
Beti Olive Kamya Namisango	Uganda Federal Alliance (UFA)	52,782	0.66%
Bidandi-Ssali Jaberi	People's Progressive Party (PPP)	34,688	0.44%
Mao Norbert	Democratic Party (DP)	147,917	1.86%
Olara Otunnu	Uganda People's Congress (UPC)	125,059	1.58%
Samuel Lubega Mukaaku	Independent	32,726	0.41%
Yoweri Kaguta Museveni	National Resistance Movement (NRM)	5,428,369	63.38%
Total valid votes cast		**7,938,212**	
Total ballot papers counted		**8,272,760**	**59.29% of registered voters**

Source: EC

801 Uganda Human Rights Commission (UHRC) (2011) *Report on the 2011 Uganda Elections.*
802 Section 8 of the Parliamentary Elections Act and Regulations 10 and 11 of the Parliamentary Elections (Special Interests Groups) Regulations, 2001.

The electoral context

The legal framework, political environment and institutional capacities before, during and after polling day have an impact on how rights are enjoyed during elections.[803]

Media

The media play an important role in elections. However, media freedom was scaled down by law and access to media remains a major challenge.[804] The EC has no control over media organisations to ensure that there is an equitable distribution of airtime to all political parties.[805]

During the 2011 elections, the Forum for Democratic Change (FDC) opposition candidate Kizza Besigye was denied access to several radio stations, including Nakaseke FM, Bunyoro Broadcasting Services, King's Broadcasting Services, Radio Kitara, Spice FM, Hoima FM, Liberty Broadcasting Services, Voice of Teso, among others.[806] The Uganda Broadcasting Corporation (UBC) gave him considerably less coverage than it gave the President.[807] Some radio stations denied Besigye access even after he had paid for services.[808]

Freedom of the media is largely constrained. Media organisations have been closed for certain periods or threatened with closure when they report issues that are considered sensitive by the government.[809] A number of individual journalists were threatened with criminal prosecution for offences related to their work.[810]

The merger of the Broadcasting Council and the Communications Commission under the Uganda Communications Act, 2013, also had an effect on media operations. The new law came into force on 18 January 2013. Originally, the Broadcasting Council granted licences, whereas the Communications Commission performed duties of a regulatory nature.[811] The Communications Commission has threatened media institutions that give vent to divergent views or those considered contrary to the government

---

803 United Nations (2013) *Report of the Special Rapporteur on the Rights to Freedom of Peaceful Assembly and of Association*, A/68/299, p. 4, www.ohchr.org/Documents/Issues/FAssociation/A_68_299_en.pdf, accessed 13 November 2013.

804 Sekaggya (2010) *Uganda*, op. cit., pp. 37–39.

805 Ibid., p. 39.

806 African Centre for Media Excellence (2011) *The Views Expressed Must Represent Those of Management: Radio Ownership and its Impact on Political Speech in Uganda.*

807 European Union Election Observation Mission (2011) *Uganda Final Report: General Elections 18 February 2011*, p. 28. eeas.europa.eu/eueom/pdf/missions/eueom_uganda2011_final_report_en.pdf, accessed 10 October 2013.

808 African Centre for Media Excellence (2011), op. cit.

809 African Centre for Media Excellence (2011), op. cit.; also see AfriMAP (2010) *Public Broadcasting in Africa Series: Uganda*, OSIEA, p. 29; also see Human Rights Watch (HRW) (2010) *A Media Minefield: Increased Threats to Freedom of Expression in Uganda.*

810 African Centre for Media Excellence (2011), op. cit.; HRW (2010) *A Media Minefield*, op. cit.

811 For background, see AfriMAP (2010) *Public Broadcasting in Africa Series: Uganda*, OSIEA.

position.[812] More recently, media that reported an alleged plot by the President to groom his son, Muhoozi Kainerugaba, to take over from him were closed for a while.[813]

In addition, the Interception of Communications Law, coupled with the requirement that all mobile telephone numbers be registered in the absence of a data protection law, will likely make journalists cautious of who they speak to by telephone because of fears about who might be listening in.[814]

Freedom of assembly and freedom of association

Freedoms of assembly and of association are pertinent to the democratic process, both during the election period and between elections.[815] The Constitution provides that every person has the right to freedom of assembly and freedom of association, including the freedom to form and join political organisations.[816] It also guarantees every person the right to participate in the affairs of government, individually or through his or her representatives in accordance with the law, as well as to participate in peaceful activities to influence the policies of government through civic organisations.[817] The National Objectives and Directive Principles of State Policy established at the beginning of the Constitution provide that 'the state shall be based on democratic principles which empower and encourage the active participation of all citizens at all levels in their own governance'.[818]

However, there are legislative restrictions on freedom of assembly and freedom of association. For example, Statutory Instrument No. 53 of the Police Act, which came into effect in September 2007, places restrictions on meetings of more than 25 people. The African Peer Review Mechanism Country Review Report for Uganda recommended the repeal of this provision.[819]

The Public Order Management Act, 2013, seeks to regulate the rights of citizens to hold demonstrations and assemble. It gives the Inspector-General of Police powers to regulate the conduct of all public meetings. This law has undergone various changes.

---

812 Freedom House (2013) 'Uganda: Freedom of the Press', www.freedomhouse.org/report/freedom-press/2013/uganda, accessed 14 October 2013.

813 Wesonga, N 'UCC threatens to withdraw licences over Tinyefuza', *Daily Monitor*, 15 May 2013 www.monitor.co.ug/News/National/UCC-threatens-to-withdraw-radio-licences-over-Tinyefuza/-/688334/1853030/-/rgroh7z/-/index.html; also see Biryabarema, E 'Uganda threatens to punish media over succession reports', 16 May 2013, *Reuters*, www.bdlive.co.za/africa/africannews/2013/05/16/uganda-threatens-to-punish-media-over-succession-reports all websites, accessed 14 October 2013.

814 Regulation of Interception of Communications Act 18 of 2010 and the Uganda Communications Act 1 of 2013.

815 United Nations (2013) *Report of the Special Rapporteur*, op. cit.

816 Article 29 of the Constitution of the Republic of Uganda, 1995 (hereafter 'the Constitution'), provides that 'Every person shall have the right to freedom to assemble and to demonstrate together with others peacefully and unarmed and to petition'.

817 Article 38 of the Constitution.

818 Principle II(i).

819 African Peer Review Mechanism (APRM) (2009) *Republic of Uganda*, APRM Country Review Report No. 7, paragraphs 276 and 284, www.africa-platform.org/sites/default/files/resources/Uganda%20Country%20Report.pdf.

Human rights and civil society organisations (CSOs) argued that the Bill, when it was first published, had the potential to stifle public debate on government policies and practices in violation of the Constitution by seeking to restrict the content of matters or issues that can be discussed at public meetings.[820] However, the law that was eventually passed is not as restrictive. Nevertheless, it has had an impact on how citizens can demonstrate and assemble, as it provides guidance and regulates their activities.

The NGO Registration (Amendment) Act, 2006, which revised the NGO Registration Act of 1989, places a significant legislative hindrance on the exercise of the freedoms of assembly and association for CSOs by allowing the government to exert considerable control over their operations. It does so through requiring that non-governmental organisations (NGOs) be registered. The NGO Board has the authority to monitor NGO operations and develop policy guidelines for community-based organisations. In addition to the existing obligation for NGOs to register with the national board, the Registration (Amendment) Act further requires them to obtain a periodic permit in order to operate. The law also expands the ministry's power to regulate the dissolution of NGOs. Giving the government such expansive powers over NGOs' right to assemble significantly undermines their space to consistently carry out operations. This could have serious implications on democratic processes as their activities may be unnecessarily restricted by the government.[821]

Political parties

Ugandan political parties are fledgling and fragile. From 1962 to 1967, Uganda had several political parties. However, this changed in 1967 under Obote's one-party system up to the time when he was deposed by Idi Amin. During Amin's reign, from 1971 to 1979, Uganda was under military rule. Political parties re-emerged after Amin was overthrown – between 1980 and 1985. However, political party activities were suspended for over two decades after 1986 when the country was placed under the 'movement' system. The movement system of government, which was widely criticised, was perceived as a one-party state. It was only in 2005 that the ban on political parties was lifted on the recommendation of the Constitutional Review Commission and the July 2005 referendum in which Ugandans expressed overwhelming support for a return to multi-party politics. Currently, there are 39 registered political parties but some of them risk being de-registered for failure to comply with requirements for the declaration of sources of

820 Human Rights Centre Uganda (2011) *Annual Report 2010–2011*, www.hrcug.org/index.php?option=com_docman&task=doc_download&gid=25&Itemid=175; also see Uganda Human Rights Commission (2011) *Annual Report to the Parliament of Uganda*.

821 HRW (2012) *Curtailing Criticism and Obstruction of Civil Society in Uganda*, www.hrw.org/sites/default/files/reports/uganda0812ForUpload.pdf; also see 'NGO Law Monitor: Uganda', International Centre for Not-For-Profit Law, www.icnl.org/research/monitor/uganda.html, accessed 13 October 2013.

funds and other assets.[822] The parties face many challenges, including the availability of resources to mobilise and to conduct campaigns effectively.[823]

The National Resistance Movement (NRM) dominates the political landscape, but other parties of some significance include the Forum for Democratic Change (FDC), Conservative Party (CP), Democratic Party (DP), Justice Forum (JEEMA), Peoples Progressive Party (PPP) and the Ugandan People's Congress (UPC). Some opposition parties have formed a coalition known as the Inter-Party Cooperation (IPC).

The political parties are governed by the Political Parties and Organisations Act, which was enacted in 2005 but underwent several amendments in 2008 in preparation for the 2011 elections. In order to address the issues relating to financing, lawmakers passed the Political Parties and Organisations (Amendment) Bill in a record seven minutes during the last sitting day of Parliament in 2009.[824] The action opened the way for political parties to be funded by government, most likely with money sourced from tax revenues. The main beneficiary in the amended law was the NRM, which has the highest numbers in Parliament, because it introduced a new clause that the funding from government would be based on the numerical strength of the party. However, in reality, no party received funding in 2011, as money was not made available for this purpose and there was no follow-up from any of the political parties and other stakeholders to lobby the Ministry of Finance for funding. The opposition parties rejected the kind of funding the law would impose and the issue was put on hold and remains outstanding. The law was further criticised for not adequately providing a comprehensive framework for party financing that covers private contributions and financial spending.[825]

Notably, the parties operate in a highly commercialised environment with a consumerist approach characterised by voter bribery. The voters actually demand gifts or money in exchange for their vote and the candidates comply. Political candidates who are unable to buy gifts or give money to voters are generally at a disadvantage.

C. Legal framework for the Electoral Commission

History of EMBs

There have not been many EMBs since independence. The 1962 Constitution created an Electoral Commission consisting of a chairman and no less than two other members appointed by the President, who acted in accordance with the advice of the Prime Minister.[826] The 1962 Constitution further required that the members be appointed in consultation with the leader of the opposition and that they hold office for a term of four

---

822 Patrick Byakagaba, Head Political Parties Desk, EC, interview, EC offices in Kampala, 3 October 2013.
823 Semogerere, PK (2011) *Reality Check: Political Party Financing in Uganda: A Critical Analysis in Reference to Other Countries*, Konrad-Adenauer-Stiftung.
824 Gyezaho, E 'How Key Election Law Was Passed in Seven Minutes', *Daily Monitor*, 12 March 2010.
825 Semogerere (2011), *Reality Check*, op. cit.
826 Article 45(1).

years.[827] This Constitution was abrogated by Obote, who introduced an interim Constitution in 1966 and then the 1967 Constitution, which extended his government in office for five years without elections.

In the 1980 elections, the first since independence, the Electoral Commission headed by KMS Kikira with Vincent Sekkono as secretary managed the contest. The Electoral Commission at the time was largely influenced by the Military Commission, which more or less took over the elections and departed from the usual tenets of a free and fair election, such as the secrecy of the ballot.

The 1995 Constitution established the Interim Electoral Commission (IEC). Appointments to the IEC were made by the President, with the approval of Parliament. It was funded by the government and development partners, mainly the United Nations Development Programme (UNDP) and was chaired by Steven B Akabway.[828] The purpose of the IEC was to organise and conduct the general election of 1996 – the first direct presidential and parliamentary elections in Uganda.[829]

In May 1997, Parliament enacted the Electoral Commission Act (1997) to establish a permanent EMB to replace the IEC in line with Article 60 of the Constitution. The first permanent EC was chaired by Hajji Aziz K. Kasujja.[830] It was this EMB that organised the 2001 elections.

The 2006 and 2011 elections were held under the chairmanship of Dr Badru Kiggundu, with a few changes in membership.[831] The commissioners were appointed by the President and approved by Parliament. Given that they serve for a seven-year term that began in November 2009, the commissioners are likely to be in charge of the 2016 general election. The members of the EC have diverse backgrounds and qualifications but have largely been perceived as NRM cadres by the opposition parties, among other stakeholders.[832]

---

827 Article 45(3)(a).
828 The other members were Mrs Flora Nkurukenda (deputy chairperson), Mr Charles Owor, Mrs Margaret Sekaggya, Mr Philip Idro, Ms Syda Bumba and Mr Aziz K Kasujja.
829 Statute 3 of 1996 and Parliament (Interim) Provisional Statute No. 4 of 1996.
830 The other members were Flora Nkurukenda (deputy chairperson), Mr Ted Wamusi, Ms Mary Maitum, Mr Robert Kitariko, Ms Nassanga H Miiro and Mr Charles D Owiny. In August 2000, Sister Margaret Magoba was appointed to the EC to replace Ms Mary Maitum, who had been appointed judge of the High Court. Mr Andrew Muwonge served as Secretary.
831 The current commission is composed of Dr Badru M Kiggundu, Mr Joseph Biribonwa (deputy chairperson), Dr Jenny Okello, Mr Tom Buruku, Mr Steven Ongaria, Dr Tomasi Sisye Kiryapawo and Ms Justine Mugabi Ahabwe. (The contract of Dr Kiryapawo expired in February 2011.)
832 Fisher, J (2013) 'The Limits – and Limiters – of External Influence: Donors, the Ugandan Electoral Commission and the 2011 Elections', *Journal of Eastern African Studies*, dx.doi.org/10.1080/17531055.2013.809206; Murison, J (2013) 'Judicial Politics: Election Petitions and Electoral Fraud in Uganda', *Journal of Eastern African Studies* 7(3): 492–508, dx.doi.org/10.1080/17531 055.2013.811026; De Torrenté, N (2013) 'Understanding the 2011 Ugandan Elections: The Contribution of Public Opinion Surveys', *Journal of Eastern African Studies* 7(3): 530–548, dx.doi.org/10.1080/1 7531055.2013.810839; 'Are Electoral Commissioners cadres of the NRM Party?', *The Independent*, 9 March 2010, www.independent.co.ug/cover-story/2579-are-electoral-commissioners-cadres-of-the-nrm-party/, accessed 31 October 2013; also see 'Uganda: Museveni and Parliament Re-appoint Controversial Electoral Commission', Wikileaks, 25 August 2009, www.cablegatesearch.net/cable.php?id=09KAMPALA979, accessed 31 October 2013.

Institutional framework

The EC consists of a chairperson, a deputy chairperson and five other members appointed by the President with the approval of Parliament.

The EC is mandated under Article 61 of the Constitution to:

- Ensure that regular, free and fair elections are held;
- Organise, conduct and supervise elections and referenda in accordance with the Constitution;
- Demarcate constituencies in accordance with the provisions of the Constitution;
- Ascertain, publish and declare in writing under its seal the results of the elections and referenda;
- Compile, maintain, revise and update the voters' register;
- Hear and determine election complaints arising before and during polling;
- Formulate and implement civic educational programmes relating to elections; and
- Perform such other functions as may be prescribed by Parliament by law.

The EC members make policy decisions, which are implemented by the secretariat, headed by the secretary to the commission. The secretary is in charge of the management of funds as well as the day-to-day operations of the commission – with the assistance of the directors for operations, technical support services, and finance and administration, among others. Members of the commission work full time.[833] The EC secretariat does not have legislative authority, but can make proposals for electoral reform to Parliament through the Ministry of Justice and Constitutional Affairs. The EC has offices at the regional and district levels.

Appointment, removal and remuneration of commissioners

Both the Constitution and the EC Act stipulate that the President shall appoint the seven members of the commission with the approval of Parliament.[834] The Constitution requires that commission members must be of 'high moral character, proven integrity and ... [must] possess considerable experience and demonstrated competence in the conduct of public affairs'.[835] Where an appointment is being renewed, the renewal should be done at least three months before the expiry of the first term.[836] Each commissioner's term lasts seven years and is only renewable once. Parliament determines the commissioners' remuneration.[837]

The nomination processes for all constitutional bodies and the judiciary follow the same procedure: appointment by the President on approval by Parliament. Within Parliament, the Appointments Committee, headed by the Speaker, is responsible for vetting

---

833 Section 5 of the Electoral Commission Act, 1997 (hereafter 'EC Act').
834 Article 60(1) of the Constitution.
835 Ibid., Article 60(2).
836 Ibid., Article 60(4).
837 Ibid., Article 60.

presidential nominations for constitutional bodies such as the EC. The independence of the person appointed is thus, in theory, dependent on the personal integrity and professionalism of the individual, and her or his ability to resist pressure from all sides.

Commissioners can only be removed from office by the President for inability to perform the functions of his or her office arising out of physical or mental incapacity, misbehaviour or misconduct, or incompetence.[838]

The members of the EC, who work full-time, are remunerated on the same basis as members of all other constitutional bodies under the Salaries and Allowances (Specified Officers) Act, including the Uganda Human Rights Commission (UHRC) and the Equal Opportunities Commission.[839] Remuneration for the EC is charged to the Consolidated Fund.[840] Nevertheless, there have been concerns about the inadequate remuneration paid to the EC. Currently, the commissioners are not as well remunerated as the Inspector-General of Government, the Executive Director of the Kampala Capital City Authority, the Auditor-General, and the Governor of the Bank of Uganda, whose salaries are negotiated and are not regulated under the Specified Officers Act.[841] In order to address this disparity, the EC intends to harmonise the salary and benefits of its staff with those of other statutory bodies.[842]

Secretariat

The EC secretariat is headed by the secretary, who is appointed by the members of the commission in consultation with the Public Service Commission. The secretary is assisted by the directors of Finance and Administration, Operation, and Technical Support Services.

The Directorate of Operations has four departments:
- Voter Data Management;
- Field Operations;
- Election Management; and
- Voter Education and Training.

The directorate of Finance and Administration consists of three departments:
- Finance;
- Human Resources; and
- Administration.

---

838 Ibid., Article 60(8).
839 Salaries and Allowances (Specified Officers) Act, Chapter 291.
840 Article 66(3) of the Constitution.
841 Nagaaga, W 'There is Urgent Need to Harmonise Salary Structures in Government', *Daily Monitor*, 3 April 2013.
842 *Strategic Plan*, op. cit., p. 11.

The directorate of Technical Support Services has two departments:
- Information Technology; and
- Planning and Research.

The Legal Department, Public Relations Unit, and Internal Audit and Procurement Unit report directly to the secretary of the commission. At the district level, electoral offices are headed by district registrars. All of these are permanent staff.

Staff members at lower levels are hired on a temporary basis to execute specific election activities like registration of voters, display of voters' registers, and polling. They include:
- Sub-county/town/municipality division supervisors;
- Parish/ward supervisors;
- Registration officials;
- Display officials; and
- Polling officials.

The EC has noted that given the large numbers of staff, the periodic nature of their tasks and the expenses required, it is not prudent to appoint all staff on a permanent basis.[843] In 2010/2011, the EC had a total of 776 regular staff. Of these, 102 were Uganda Police Officers who had been assigned to work with the EC.[844] The EC used a total of 8,561 temporary officials – 1,327 at the sub-county and 7,234 at the parish level – to conduct the 2010/2011 general election.[845]

Mandate of the EC

Preparing, managing and updating the voters' register
The EC Act provides that the commission shall compile, maintain and update on a continuous basis a voters' register, which shall include the names of all persons entitled to vote in a national or local election.[846] Furthermore, the commission is required to maintain as part of the voters' register, a voters' roll for each constituency and for each polling station.[847]

Demarcation of electoral constituencies
Under the Constitution, Uganda is divided into a number of constituencies as prescribed by Parliament by resolution, which are demarcated by the EC and published in the

---

843 Information from Leonard Mulekwah, Director of Operations, EC, interview, 3 October 2013.
844 EC (2011) *Report on the 2010/2011 General Elections*, p. 22, www.ec.or.ug/docs/General%20election%20 Report%202010-2011.pdf.
845 Ibid.
846 Section 18(1) of the EC Act.
847 Sections 18(2&3) of the EC Act.

Gazette.[848] The EC has a duty to demarcate constituencies and to organise the election of MPs for them.[849] The EC has to ensure that each county, as approved by Parliament, has at least one MP, and that no constituency falls within more than one county.[850] The EC is required to review the demarcation of constituencies within 12 months after the publication of the results of a census of the population of Uganda, and may as a result re-demarcate the constituencies. The electoral districts are dependent on the number of administrative districts.[851]

Oversight of parties and candidates

Register and oversee political parties

The Political Parties and Organisations Act requires the EC to register all political parties and organisations.[852] The EC has the obligation to maintain a register of political parties and organisations,[853] as well as maintain oversight over them. Parties are required to submit to the EC a written declaration of their assets and liabilities. Failure to make such a declaration within 21 hours after notice from the EC may cause the commission to apply to the High Court for an order to de-register the political party or organisation.[854] Political parties and organisations are also required to provide information to the EC regarding their records and audits.[855]

Nomination of candidates

The EC oversees the nomination of all candidates, whether independent or belonging to a party. The EC receives the nomination papers of all candidates – presidential, MP, or local council – on appointed dates, which are published in the *Gazette.*[856] A candidate's nomination can be rejected on account of failure to meet the statutory requirements of age and number of supporters, among other things. When a candidate fulfils all requirements, s/he is duly nominated to run for elections.

Supporting the National Consultative Forum and Code of Conduct

The Political Parties and Organisations Act provides both for a Code of Conduct and for the establishment of a National Consultative Forum (NCF), in which political parties

---

848 Article 63 of the Constitution.
849 Ibid., Article 63(1).
850 Ibid., Article 63(2).
851 EC Act, Article 20.
852 Section 4 of the Political Parties and Organisations Act.
853 Section 6(2) of the Political Parties and Organisations Act 2005 (as amended).
854 Ibid., section 9(6).
855 Ibid., sections 15 and 12.
856 Presidential Elections Act, 2005 (as amended); Parliamentary Elections Act 2005 (as amended); Local Governments Act, Chapter 243 (as amended); Political Parties and Organisations Act, 2005 (as amended).

and the EC discuss and try to avoid points of conflict and tension.[857] The NCF is composed of:

- One representative from every registered political party or organisation;
- The chairperson of the EC (or his or her representative);
- The Attorney-General (or his or her representative); and
- The secretary of the EC, who is also the secretary to the NCF.[858]

This means that the EC is a member of the NCF and plays an important role in the administration of the forum. Like any other member, the EC has a duty to ensure that all political parties and organisations comply with the Code of Conduct.[859]

The chairperson for the NCF, who must be selected from the party with the most representatives in Parliament,[860] is currently Dr Ruhakana Rugunda of the NRM. The vice-chairperson is Mr Amanya Mushega. The NCF liaises with the EC on matters pertaining to political parties and organisations, and ensures that political parties and organisations comply with the Code of Conduct. It also communicates the complaints and grievances of political parties and organisations to the EC, and makes recommendations to the minister on any matters under the Act.[861]

The NCF has held several meetings where it has developed an action plan, as well as reviewed and approved a Code of Conduct, which has been submitted to the Ministry of Justice and Constitutional Affairs for presentation to Parliament for enactment.[862] The MPs will need to carry out the necessary consultations before the code is passed. The NCF has also considered and agreed on several electoral reforms and has made recommendations to Parliament and the executive. Some of the recommendations relate to the provision of civic and voter education to enhance citizen participation, compliance with the law, to secure a level playing field, to maintain a credible voters' register and to ensure a competent, efficient and credible EMB, among others.[863]

Overseeing party financing

The EC oversees party financing. Political parties and organisations are required to submit written declarations stating their sources of funds, assets and liabilities.[864] Furthermore, parties and organisations are required to submit information relating to records of donations, contributions or pledges of contributions, statements of accounts

---

857 Sections 19 and 20 of the Political Parties and Organisations Act 2005 (as amended).
858 Ibid., Section 20(2).
859 Ibid., section 20(4)(b).
860 Ibid., section 20(a).
861 Ibid., section 20(4).
862 Hon. Dr Ruhakana Rugunda, chairperson of the NCF, interview at the Ministry of Health, 30 September 2013.
863 Ibid. Also see proposals for electoral reforms by the NCF on file with the author.
864 Section 9 of the Political Party and Organisations Act 2005 (as amended).

showing sources of funding, property and how it was acquired, and a copy of their audited accounts, among other things.[865]

Ensuring equitable access to media

The EC has the responsibility to ensure that regular, free and fair elections are held, and additionally has the duty to organise, conduct and supervise elections in accordance with the Constitution.[866] The EC, therefore, has an important role in upholding the constitutional requirement that no candidate in the election should be denied reasonable access and use of state-owned communication media.[867] Indeed, the EC in April 2007 made recommendations for electoral reform by requiring national media to allocate sufficient time and space for registered political parties.[868] However, access to the media remains a challenge.

Conduct and management of electoral operations

The EC has a duty to organise, conduct and supervise elections. This includes the following duties:

- Appoint a polling day for any election;
- Design, print, distribute and control the use of ballot papers;
- Provide, distribute, and collect ballot boxes and establish and operate polling stations;[869]
- Take measures for ensuring that the entire electoral process is conducted under conditions of freedom and fairness;
- Take steps to ensure that there are secure conditions necessary for the conduct of any election;
- Promote and regulate through appropriate means, civic education of the citizens of Uganda on the purpose, and voting procedures, of any election, including where practicable, the use of sign language;[870]
- Ensure that the candidates campaign in an orderly and organised manner;
- Accredit any non-partisan individual, group of individuals or an institution or association, to carry out voter education subject to guidelines determined by the commission and published in the *Gazette*;
- Ensure compliance by all election officers and candidates with the provisions of the law; and
- Take necessary steps to ensure that people with disabilities are enabled to vote without any hindrance.[871]

---

865 Ibid., section 12.
866 Article 61(a) and (b) and Section 12 of the EC Act.
867 Ibid., Article 67(2).
868 Sekaggya (2010), *Uganda*, op. cit. p. 34.
869 Section 12(1)(a–d) of the EC Act.
870 Ibid., section 12(1)(e–g).
871 Ibid., section 12(1)(h–p).

Voter education

The Constitution gives the EC the responsibility to formulate and implement election-related voter education programmes.[872] The EC Act takes up and essentially re-delegates this responsibility by accrediting any non-partisan individual, group, institution or association to carry out voter education, subject to the commission's guidelines.[873] The UHRC likewise has the constitutional mandate of conducting general civic education to create and sustain within society the awareness of the provisions of the Constitution as the fundamental law of Uganda.[874] This includes human rights education as well as voter education.

Publication of results

The EC is required to produce and submit to Parliament, through the minister, a report on any election conducted by it within six months after the declaration of the results.[875] On Election Day, the EC is required to announce the results of voting at the polling station before communicating them to the returning officer.[876] It is required to publish results of the presidential election within 48 hours from the close of polling.[877]

Hearing and determination of complaints

The EC has powers to resolve complaints related to any irregularities in the electoral process.[878] Any complaint can be submitted in writing, alleging any irregularity on any aspect of the electoral process at any stage. Any complaint that has not been satisfactorily resolved at a lower level of authority can be examined and decided by the EC. If the irregularity is confirmed, the EC has a duty to take the necessary action to correct the irregularity and any effects it may have caused. If anyone is dissatisfied with the decision of the EC, they can appeal to the High Court and the decision of the High Court is final.[879]

Amendment of electoral laws

Amendment of electoral laws (and any other law) is generally the role of Parliament.[880] Nevertheless, the EC can make recommendations for the amendment of electoral laws. Although the EC recommendations are not binding, they are persuasive. In April 2007, the EC proposed 18 amendments concerning electoral laws to the Minister of Justice and Constitutional Affairs, including provisions relating to access to media, voter education, the management of local government elections, qualifications for election as

---

872 Article 61 of the Constitution.
873 Article 12 of the EC Act.
874 Article 52(1)(c, e, g) of the Constitution.
875 Section 12(1)(o) of the EC Act.
876 Section 48(4)(b) of the Presidential Elections Act.
877 Ibid., section 57(1).
878 Section 15(1) of the EC Act.
879 Ibid., section 15(2–4).
880 Article 76 of the Constitution.

an MP, and timeliness for the adoption of election laws.[881] Some of the recommendations, especially the adoption of election laws, were adopted. However, the laws were passed less than a year before the elections, contrary to the EC's recommendations. Other recommendations, such as those relating to access to media and voter education, are still pending.

Independence of the EC

According to the Constitution of Uganda, the EC is supposed to be independent and should, in the performance of its functions, not be subject to the direction or control of any person or authority.[882] The Constitution further requires that members of the EC should be persons of high moral character, proven integrity and possess considerable experience and demonstrated competence in the conduct of public affairs.[883]

Despite legal provisions relating to the appointment and independence of the EC, many political groups strongly believe that the commission is not independent and does not reflect diversity as expected in a multi-party system. In particular, there are concerns relating to the system for appointments to the EC,[884] credibility and security of tenure for commissioners,[885] among others.

During the 2011 presidential election campaigns, there were threats of withdrawal from the political process and calls for the disbandment of the EC by both CSOs and political parties. They claimed that the EC was not independent and impartial, and that it could not deliver free and fair elections.[886] The EC dismissed these calls[887] and refused to succumb to the pressure to disband. Instead, it went ahead to organise polls that were considered to have been better than the 2006 ones by some observers, despite anomalies such as the monetisation of elections, unequal access to media and problems with the national voters' register, to mention a few.[888]

The appointment of the current members of the EC by the President raised concerns about their ability to deliver a credible election. This was because the same team, with the exception of one member, had handled the 2006 elections. The 2006 elections had been marred by voter bribery, intimidation, multiple voting, ballot stuffing and disenfranchisement of voters, as well as inaccuracies in the counting and tallying of results.<?>

---

881 AfriMAP (2010) *Uganda: The Management of Elections*, OSIEA.

882 Article 62 of the Constitution.

883 Ibid., Article 60(2).

884 Okille, A et al. (2010) *Towards the Uganda 2011 Elections: An Assessment of Conflict Risks and Mitigating Mechanisms*, Deepening Democracy Programme, pp. 44–50.

885 Opiyo, N et al. (2013) *Breaking the Conflict Trap in Uganda: Proposals for Constitutional and Legal Reforms*, ACODE Policy Research Series No. 58.

886 Okille et al. (2010) *Towards the Uganda 2011 Elections*, op. cit.

887 'Uganda's Electoral Commission Chairman Promises Fair Elections', *Voice of America*, 15 February 2011, www.voanews.com/content/ugandas-electoral-commission-chairman-promises-fair-election-116326194/157442.html, accessed 15 October 2013.

888 EU Election Observation Mission (2011) *Uganda Final Report*, op. cit.; UHRC (2011) *Report on the 2011 Uganda Elections*, op. cit.

889 *Col. Rtd Kizza Besigye vs Yoweri Museveni and the Electoral Commission* (Election Petition No. 1 of 2007).

> ## The nomination of Kizza Besigye as presidential candidate
>
> A test of the independence of the EC in the 2006 presidential election was when Dr Kizza Besigye's nomination as a presidential candidate was challenged in the Constitutional Court because it had occurred in absentia. The Attorney-General, together with the petitioners, stated that by nominating Dr Besigye while he was in prison, the EC had disregarded the Attorney-General's advice not to do so, thus contravening Article 119(3) of the Constitution, which provides that the Attorney-General is the principal legal advisor of government. The EC argued, however, that it was an independent body and not subject to the authority of the Attorney-General. The EC further argued that the act of nominating Dr Besigye in absentia did not contravene the Constitution as alleged by the petitioners and that the Presidential Elections Act does not provide for physical presence of candidates during nomination. The Constitutional Court dismissed the petition.[890]

The African Peer Review Mechanism (APRM) panel of eminent persons, in noting the issues surrounding the EC in relation to independence and security of tenure, recommended that Uganda 'devise a system of appointing electoral commissioners so that only non-partisan, independent and professional people with a high reputation are selected'.[891] The UHRC likewise recommended reviewing the process of appointing members of the EC to establish greater consensus and acceptance of the members by the opposition, civil society and the public.[892] The EU Mission observers also noted the vague and subjective criteria for the selection of commissioners, concluding that they are not consultative and the qualifications are not the same as those of the UHRC and the Director of Public Prosecutions.[893]

There are proposals to amend the Constitution to provide for nomination, vetting and appointment of members through an open and competitive process to ensure an electoral process that is acceptable, transparent and credible. It has been recommended that the process of recruitment should be carried out in consultation with the registered political parties and organisations, as well as other interest groups, CSOs, professional bodies or associations, and the general public.[894]

Regarding security of tenure, the Constitution provides that the members of the EC can be removed from office by the President for physical or mental incapacity, misconduct or misbehaviour and incompetence.[895] It has been suggested that this affects their independence as their tenure is at the mercy of the President. Unlike other public

---

890 *Kabagambe Asol and Others vs Electoral Commission and Another* (Constitutional Petition No. 1 of 2006).
891 'Country Self-Assessment Report', as reported in APRM (2009) *Republic of Uganda, APRM Country Review Report, op. cit.*, paragraph 284.
892 UHRC (2011) *14th Annual Report*, p. xxviii.
893 EU Election Observation Mission (2011) *Uganda Final Report, op. cit.*, p. 16.
894 *NCF Proposals on Electoral Reform*, on file with the author.
895 Article 60(8)(a–c) of the Constitution.

officials, such as members of the judiciary<?> and the UHRC,<?> who cannot be removed without a tribunal hearing, the members of the EC can be removed from office by the President for any of the grounds listed without a hearing. This provision was applied in 2002 when President Museveni removed Aziz Kasujja from his position as the head of the EC, as well as five other commissioners, on the grounds of financial mismanagement and administrative incompetence on the recommendation of the Inspector-General of Government.[906]

It is important that the EC has security of tenure by protecting members from arbitrary removal. It has been recommended by the APRM panel that Uganda 'institutionalise security of tenure for members of the EC by ensuring that removal is dependent on recommendations of a tribunal'.[899] This has been echoed by other stakeholders such as CSOs.[900]

D. Management of electoral disputes

The Constitution and various laws provide for ways and means through which electoral disputes are dealt with by the EC and the courts of law such as tribunals.[901] The Constitution empowers the EC to hear and determine election complaints arising before and during polling.[902] Any aggrieved person may appeal to the High Court against a decision on an election complaint.[903] Any dispute relating to demarcation of electoral boundaries may be appealed to a tribunal and further appeals can be lodged in the High Court, whose decision is final.[904]

Electoral adjudication by the EC

The EC has powers to resolve complaints related to any irregularities in the electoral process.[905] Any complaint that has not been satisfactorily resolved at a lower level of authority can be examined and decided by the EC. If the irregularity is confirmed, the EC has a duty to take the necessary action to correct the irregularity and any effects it may have caused. If anyone is dissatisfied with the decision of the EC, that person can appeal to the High Court, whose decision is final.[906] The Constitution permits a person

896 Ibid., Article 144.
897 Ibid., Articles 56 and 144.
898 United States Department of State (2003) *US Department of State Country Report on Human Rights Practices 2002: Uganda*, www.refworld.org/docid/3e918c2f8.html, accessed 31 October 2013.
899 'Country Self-Assessment Report', as reported in APRM (2009) *Republic of Uganda, APRM Country Review Report*, op. cit., paragraph 284.
900 Opiyo, N et al. (2013) *Breaking the Conflict Trap in Uganda: Proposals for Constitutional and Legal Reforms*, ACODE Policy Research Series No. 58, p. 14.
901 Presidential Elections Act, 2005; Parliamentary Elections Act, 2005; EC Act, 1997.
902 Article 61(f) of the Constitution.
903 Ibid., Article 64(1).
904 Ibid., Article 64(4).
905 Section 15(1) of the EC Act.
906 Ibid., section 15(2–4).

aggrieved by a decision of the EC regarding the demarcation of a boundary to appeal to a tribunal consisting of three persons appointed by the Chief Justice, and the EC shall give effect to the decision of the tribunal.[907] The Constitution further stipulates that a person aggrieved by a decision of the tribunal may appeal to the High Court, and its decision shall be final.[908]

Appeals to the courts

Anyone aggrieved by the decision of the EC has the right to appeal it in court. The court chosen depends on the nature of the matter. If it concerns the election of the President, the Constitution provides that petitions be lodged with the Supreme Court for an order that a candidate declared by the EC to have been elected as President was not validly elected.[909] Regarding complaints relating to the electoral process in general, where complaints have been heard and determined by the EC, the High Court is the forum for appeal and its decision is final.[910]

Presidential elections

After the EC announces the presidential election results, any aggrieved candidate has ten days to file a petition in the Supreme Court to invalidate the election.[911] The court must then make an expeditious inquiry and make a determination within 30 days. The court may choose to dismiss the petition, declare which of the candidates was validly elected, or annul the election and order a new election within 20 days of the annulment.[912]

In the 2001 and 2006 elections, Dr Kizza Besigye petitioned the Supreme Court on the grounds that President Yoweri Museveni was not validly elected due to the various contraventions of the law during the electoral process.[913] Although the Supreme Court in both instances acknowledged that there were some malpractices that compromised democratic principles embedded in the law – such as voter bribery, intimidation, multiple voting, ballot stuffing, disenfranchisement of voters and inaccuracies in the counting and tallying of votes – it was not satisfied that these actions affected the results in a substantial manner. As such, the results of the elections were upheld.

Although opposition political parties rejected the outcome of the 2011 presidential election, they did not lodge any petitions because they did not trust the judiciary to make an appropriate decision, based on the decisions made in the 2001 and 2006 election petitions.[914]

---

907 Article 64(2) of the Constitution.
908 Ibid., Article 64(3).
909 Ibid., Article 104.
910 Article 61(f) of the Constitution and section 12 of the EC Act.
911 Article 104(1) of the Constitution.
912 Ibid., Articles 104(5)(a–c) and 104(6).
913 *Rtd Col. Dr Kizza Besigye vs Electoral Commission, Yoweri Kaguta Museveni* (Election Petition No. 1 of 2001) and *Rtd Col. Dr Kizza Besigye vs Electoral Commission, Yoweri Kaguta Museveni* (Election Petition No. 1 of 2006).
914 UHRC (2011) *14th Annual Report*, op. cit., p. 64.

Parliamentary elections

One of the functions of the EC is to hear and determine election complaints arising before and during polling at all levels.[915] Any person aggrieved by a decision of the commission may appeal to the High Court, whose decision is final.[916]

The Parliamentary Elections Act, 2005, also provides for election petitions to be filed within 30 days by a losing candidate or a registered voter in the concerned constituency.[917] Such election petitions are based on the grounds that:

- The law was not complied with during elections and that this affected the results in a substantial manner;
- A person other than the one elected won the election;
- An illegal practice or any other offence was personally committed by the candidate or with his or her knowledge and consent or approval; and
- The candidate was disqualified or unqualified.[918]

The High Court has a maximum of six months to make a decision on the election petitions.[919] Anyone dissatisfied with the decision of the High Court has the right to contest it in the Court of Appeal, and subsequently in the Supreme Court.[920]

After the 2006 elections, about 40 election petitions relating to parliamentary elections were lodged in the High Court.[921] Some of the petitions were successful, resulting in the annulment of results and fresh elections. For instance, in *Abdu Katuntu vs Ali Kirunda Kivenjinja and the Electoral Commission,*[922] the petitioner and first respondent contested the parliamentary seat in Bugweri County, Iganga District, in 2006. The petitioner filed a petition on the following grounds:

- That the electoral process was non-compliant with the provisions and principles of the Parliamentary Elections Act, 2005;
- That the failure to conduct the election in compliance with the provisions and principles in the electoral law benefitted the first respondent and affected the final result in a substantial manner; and
- That the first respondent personally or through his agents, with his knowledge, consent or approval, committed numerous election offences and illegal practices.

The court ruled that there was widespread intimidation, violence and torture by gangs

---

915   Article 61(f) of the Constitution. Also see sections 15, 16, 46, 48 and 59 of the Parliamentary Elections Act, 2005.
916   Article 64(1) of the Constitution.
917   Section 60 of the Parliamentary Elections Act, 2005.
918   Ibid., section 61.
919   Ibid., section 63(9).
920   Ibid., sections 60, 63 and 66.
921   EC (2006) *Report on the 2005/2006 General Election.*
922   Election Petition No. 7 of 2006.

trained and deployed by the first respondent, and furthermore that incidents of multiple voting occurred at a number of polling stations. The court concluded that there were instances of non-compliance with the provisions and principles established in the Parliamentary Elections Act, and that this affected the results of the election in a substantial manner.[923]

After the 2011 elections, there were about 110 election petitions challenging parliamentary election results. The judiciary developed a strategy to handle election petitions effectively. The Principal Judge appointed 25 judges and 43 magistrates to hear election petitions. These judicial officers would liaise with the civil division in making all the requisite arrangements for the efficient and expeditious disposal of all petitions.[924] Furthermore, the judiciary affirmed that the Court of Appeal would promptly dispose of appeals arising from the election petitions in six months.[925] The strategy is deemed to have been effective in yielding results. Judiciary Spokesperson Erias Kisawuzi said that out of the 110 election petitions filed, 105 were disposed of within the first four months after the 2011 elections.[926] This was a remarkable achievement for the judicial system, which still had a case backlog from the 2006 elections.[927]

E. Financing the EC

Legal framework for election funding

Parliament is required to ensure that adequate resources and facilities are provided to the EC to enable it to perform its functions effectively.[928] The EC is a self-accounting institution and deals directly with the ministry responsible for finance on matters relating to its finances.[929] The administrative expenses of the EC, including salaries, allowances and pensions payable to persons serving on it are charged to the Consolidated Fund.[930] Other funds may, with prior approval of the minister responsible for finance, include grants and donations from sources within or outside Uganda to enable the EC to discharge its functions.[931]

---

923 Ibid.
924 Justice, Law and Order Sector (JLOS) 'Judiciary Begins Hearing of Election Petitions', www.jlos.go.ug/index.php/document-centre/news-room/archives/item/199-judiciary-begins-hearing-of-election-petitions, accessed 17 October 2013.
925 JLOS 'Press Release on Handling Electoral Disputes', www.jlos.go.ug/index.php/document-centre/document-centre/doc_download/109-jlos-press-release-on-the-handling-of-election-petitions-2011, accessed 17 October 2013.
926 Mukiibi, S (2011) 'Election Petitions Observer', 15 November 2011, www.independent.co.ug/News/news-analysis/4869-election-petitions, accessed 17 October 2013.
927 'Judiciary to Conclude Election Petitions before Elections', *Uganda Radio Network*, 10 February 2011, ugandaradionetwork.com/a/story.php?s=31421, accessed 17 October 2013.
928 Article 66(1) of the Constitution.
929 Ibid., Article 66(2).
930 Ibid., Article 66(3).
931 Section 9(3) of the EC Act.

Funding of the IEC (1993–1996)

The Constituent Assembly and the 1996 electoral processes were products of a combined and concerted partnership involving the government, the election managers and the donor community. In the late 1980s and early 1990s, support by the donor community was predicated on a genuine effort by the government of Uganda towards establishing a democratic system of governance. Various donors were willing to give financial and technical support to the Constituent Assembly electoral process as part of the transition to democratic governance in Uganda.[932]

The UNDP provided direct financial and technical assistance through the National Execution Unit in the then Ministry of Finance and Economic Development. It also coordinated donor assistance from Austria, Sweden, Norway, the Netherlands, and to some extent, the United States Agency for International Development.[933] The UN Department for Development of Support Management Services sent a needs assessment mission to Uganda to determine electoral support requirements and thereafter some external donor assistance began.

Funding of elections since 1996

General elections in Uganda have been characterised by late enactment of enabling laws, late releases of funds and inadequate time to carry out activities as a result of inadequate planning and bureaucratic administrative systems, among others. In order to avoid problems previously witnessed, the EC developed a roadmap for the 2010–2011 general election, in which activities leading to the elections were regarded as a project funded over a period of three years, beginning with Phase I in 2008 and 2009 to Phase III in 2010 and 2011.[934]

General elections in Uganda are largely financed by the government, and on average cost UGX 280 billion (approximately USD 112 million) over a period of three years. The government funds about 95% of the election budget, while about 5% is funded by donors. For example, the EC received donor funds relating to specific projects by such donors as the EU and the Danish International Development Agency (Danida, under the Deepening Democracy Funding Project) in the form of information technology equipment and budgetary support. The 2011 general election was better funded than the previous elections in 2006 and 2001.

In 2011 and 2012, the EC received adequate funds to execute its mandate of organising presidential and parliamentary elections, as indicated in its own reports:

---

932 EC/UNDP (1997) *Election Funding: Report on the Support to the Electoral Process in Uganda: 1993–1996*.
933 Ibid.
934 EC (2011) *Report on the 2010/2011 General Elections*, http://www.ec.or.ug/docs/General%20election%20 Report%202010-2011.pdf, p. 7.

The commission was adequately funded and was able to procure all the equipment, vehicles and materials required for the conduct of the general elections and, therefore, the electoral activities were executed in accordance with the strategic plan and road map.[935]

Most donor support was channelled through the Democratic Governance Facility to the EC, and was aimed at or related to political party activities such as operationalising the political parties' desks, workshops involving the political parties, meetings of the NCF, and civic education.[936]

Table 6.2: Budget and source of funds for the 2011 general election

Period	Total Amount in UGX (USD)	Source of funds
2008/2009	6.2 billion (USD 2.5 million)	Government of Uganda
2009/2010	88.8 billion (USD 35.5 million)	Government of Uganda
2010/2011	185.3 billion (USD 74.1 million)	Government of Uganda
	921 million (USD 0.37 million)	EU
	4.5 billion (USD 1.8 million)	Danida, Deepening Democracy Funding Project

Source: EC (2011) *Report on the 2010/2011 General Elections*, op. cit.

The budget for elections is usually spread out over more than one year, as can be seen from Table 6.2. Even when it is not an election year, money is disbursed to the EC for preparations for the next elections, for elections that may arise following the death of some of the elected officials, or decisions from courts overturning the results of previous polls. The EC budget is mainly funded by the government of Uganda.

The EC's management of funds

The EC is accountable to Parliament[937] and is audited by the Auditor-General.[938] As such, the commission appears before the Parliamentary Accounts Committee to present its policy statement and budget, and to answer any queries from the Auditor-General. The EC, like most institutions funded by government, has raised queries, some of which have been related to delays in submitting accountability reports. For example, when the EC spent UGX 2.93 billion on security,[939] it claimed that the money had been given to the police and that the Ministry for Internal Affairs had been late in submitting accountability reports. Other complaints relate to failure to comply with procurement

935   Ibid.
936   Ibid., pp. 28–32.
937   Articles 60(1), 66(1) of the Constitution and Section 12(1)(o) of the EC Act.
938   Section 23 of the Public Finance Act, 1962.
939   'Electoral Commission Ordered to Account for UGX2.39B', *Uganda Radio Network*, ugandaradionetwork. com/a/story.php?s=14437, accessed 17 October 2013.

procedures, for example, the procurement of the road show blitz, where the Public Procurement and Disposal of Public Assets Authority found that in this instance the procedures did not comply with the law and that there was contract mismanagement, among other irregularities.[940]

F. A critical assessment of election management in Uganda

The Electoral Commission of Uganda has several duties, which include:

- Formulating and implementing civic education programmes relating to elections;
- Compiling, maintaining, revising and updating the voters' register;
- Demarcating constituencies;
- Conducting regular, free and fair elections in line with the Constitution and other laws of Uganda;
- Ascertaining, publishing and declaring results of the elections; and
- Hearing and determining election complaints arising before and during polling.

The EC has done well, especially in terms of declaring the results of the elections, particularly the presidential election in the requisite time of 48 hours. It has also done well in determining complaints regarding the nomination of candidates for elections. However, it has experienced challenges in implementing civic education, updating the national voters' register, demarcating constituencies, conducting elections in line with the law, and determining complaints at the local level.

Civic and voter education

Although there were some improvements in 2011 over the 2006 elections in terms of publicity, civic education was on the whole insufficient.[941] The Constitution provides that both the EC and the UHRC have a duty to provide civic education.[942] The EC mainly provides voter education while the UHRC provides civic and human rights education. The EC carried out voter education through radio, newspapers, television, booklets, leaflets and drama, but it did not reach all voters. The UHRC also carried out civic education, including human rights education for security agencies, and hosted national and regional dialogues to promote violence-free elections. However, civic and voter education was insufficient.

---

940 Public Procurement and Disposal of Public Assets (2006) *Investigation Report for the Procurement of Road Show Blitz by the Electoral Commission.*
941 EU Election Observation Mission (2011) *Uganda Final Report*, p. 18; also see UHRC (2011) *14th Annual Report*, op. cit., pp. 62–63.
942 Articles 61(g) and 52(1)(g) of the Constitution.

In order to address this deficit, the EC has prioritised effective and comprehensive voter education in its strategic plan for 2013–2017 and the UHRC is developing a National Civic Education Policy to guide the delivery of civic education. It is important for the EC and the UHRC to work in partnership to enhance civic education.

The voters' register

There were problems in 2011 with the national voters' register, just as there had been in the 2006 elections, despite efforts to update it. The EC updated the voters' register by registering voters from 3 May to 18 June 2010. The updated lists were displayed in August and the public invited to submit information relating to the accuracy of the rolls. The final updated voters' register had photographs for most of the voters and was relied upon heavily during elections. On Election Day, there were complaints by voters who were unable to find their names at the polling stations where they were supposed to vote. Some observers noted that there were inconsistencies between the online voters' register, or short text message information, and the hard copy at various polling stations, which led to the disenfranchisement of some voters.[943]

A credible, accurate and accessible national voters' register is high on the priority list of the EC in the upcoming elections.[944] The EC planned to obtain primary data for the compilation of the national voters' register from the National Security Information System Project by 1 September 2014.[945] There are high expectations that this system will work, but in the event that it does not, the EC will have to register voters in order to comply with the Constitution and other laws.

Demarcation of constituencies

The EC has had challenges in keeping up with the demarcation of constituencies whenever new districts are created. The district is a basic unit within which electoral areas are determined. Counties in a district are usually constituencies for elections of MPs. Each county has at least one MP. In the past 27 years, the districts have increased from 33 to 112. The EC faced challenges particularly when new districts were created close to the elections, as was the case in 2000, 2005 and 2010.[946] The EC usually organises elections according to a roadmap and it is on the basis of such a plan that the budget is prepared and disbursed. The EC's plans are affected when a new district is created, as it may require additional resources, which may times not be readily available outside the government budget cycle.

---

943 UHRC (2011) *14th Annual Report*, op. cit., p. 61.
944 *Strategic Plan*, op. cit.
945 Ibid., p. viii.
946 Leonard Mulekwah, Director of Operations, EC, interview, 3 October 2013.

Conduct of elections

Although the conduct of elections has improved over the years, it is still wanting; this has been confirmed by court rulings in various election petitions.[947] The EC has the duty to conduct regular, free and fair elections in line with the Constitution and other laws. This entails:

- Election administration;
- Registration of candidates and political parties;
- Ensuring a conducive electoral environment;
- Access to media;
- Participation of minorities and vulnerable groups;
- Participation of CSOs;
- Management of the Election Day;
- Announcement of results; and
- Managing the dispute resolution processes.

Electoral administration

Apart from implementing the roadmap for the 2011 general election, the EC faced the arduous task of trying to gain the trust of various stakeholders involved in the electoral process. Opposition political parties and CSOs raised concerns right from the start about the EC's ability to conduct a credible election. It was argued that the EC was largely composed of the same members who had conducted the 2006 elections, which were marred by voter bribery, intimidation, multiple voting, ballot stuffing, disenfranchisement of voters, and inaccuracies in the counting and tallying of results. Regardless of the fact that the court had ruled that these malpractices did not affect the results of the presidential election in a substantial manner, many stakeholders did not – and still do not – trust the members of the EC.[948]

In spite of its negative image, the EC conducted the 2011 elections better than it did those of 2006.[949] The EC followed the roadmap for elections, and improvements were noted in terms of its staffing and logistics, innovative use of technology and increased publicity and transparency with stakeholders.[950] However, there were issues of concern relating to the following:

- Errors in the national voters' register, resulting in the disenfranchisement of some voters;
- Inadequate implementation of electoral laws;

---

947   *Col. Dr Besigye Kizza vs Museveni Yoweri Kaguta, Electoral Commission* (Election Petition No. 1 of 2001) and *Rtd Col. Dr Kizza Besigye vs Electoral Commission, Yoweri Kaguta Museveni* (Election Petition No. 1 of 2006).

948   Liebowitz, J, Sentamu, R & Kibirige, F (2013) *Citizen Perceptions of Democracy in Uganda: The Growing Gap Between Expectations and Realities*, Afro Barometer Briefing Paper 111, p. 5.

949   EU Election Observation Mission (2011) *Uganda Final Report*, op. cit.

950   UHRC (2011) *14th Annual Report*, op. cit., p. 60.

- Unequal access to the media;
- Insufficient civic education;
- Limited participation of minorities and vulnerable groups in the elections;
- Lack of a level playing field;
- Commercialisation of elections; and
- Electoral violence.[951]

Registration of parties and candidates

The EC has attempted to fulfil its role in the registration of parties and ensuring that these parties submit financial and other records by threatening to de-register those that fail to submit records of accountability.[952] In July 2013, the EC filed an application to de-register ten political parties that had not declared their sources of funds, audited accounts and other assets and liabilities. Notably, most parties are lackadaisical in filing declarations with the EC. By and large, the EC has been lenient with political parties and organisations, but it has had to step up its efforts in order to ensure compliance with the law.[953]

The EC has done well in the registration of candidates – both party and independent candidates – for parliamentary and presidential elections, as well as in handling complaints relating to the candidates who have been nominated to contest. In the 2011 general election, the EC deregistered or reversed nominations for 21 candidates and only two of its decisions were overturned by the High Court.[954]

Election campaign and pre-election environment

The EC's role in campaigns and making the environment more conducive for free and fair elections has been limited by its inadequate civic education programme, among other factors. The election campaign and pre-election environment is largely determined by civic education, which ensures that citizens know and can claim their rights and perform their civic duties. It is also dependent on the rule of law, democracy and good governance.

Violence during election campaign periods was a cause for concern. Violence in the 2006 elections took the following forms:
- Intimidation of opponent supporters;
- Threats through agents, phone calls and public and radio statements;
- Assaults;
- Intimidation, arrests and beatings by security personnel; and
- Destruction of property.[955]

---

951 Commonwealth Secretariat (2011) *Report of the Commonwealth Observer Group, Uganda Presidential and Parliamentary Elections 18 February 2011*; EU Election Observation Mission (2011) *Uganda Final Report*, op. cit.
952 Patrick Byakagaba, Head Political Parties Desk, EC, interview, 3 October 2013.
953 Ibid.
954 EC (2011) *Report on the 2010/2011 General Elections*, op. cit., p. 55.
955 Okille (2011) *Towards the Uganda 2011 Elections*, op. cit., p. 42.

In the 2011 election campaign, basic rights such as freedom of association, movement and assembly were generally respected. Most political parties and candidates held campaign rallies that attracted large crowds. The EC coordinated campaign schedules to prevent party rallies from overlapping and thereby ensured the peaceful conduct of campaigns.[956] By and large, the candidates complied with the requirements of the law and EC directions in relation to the campaign schedules. However, there were complaints relating to the following:

- Denied access to media;
- Meddling by the Resident District Commissioners, who disrupted rallies (especially opposition candidate rallies);
- Use of excessive force by security agencies, especially against opposition party members; and
- Buying of votes.[957]

Moreover, some political parties and candidates were reported to have formed vigilante groups to allegedly protect their votes. This was a source of concern as stakeholders feared that these groups could become violent during elections; the EC and the Inspector-General of Police, however, warned against interfering with the electoral process.[958] Further, the recruitment of crime preventers by the Uganda Police Force sparked a lot of suspicion and disquiet because the recruits were allegedly mainly NRM supporters.[959]

Another issue of concern for the opposition, CSOs and observers during the campaign period was the use and misuse of state resources.[960] Use of state resources for election campaigns is prohibited except for a candidate who is holding the office of President. The President is allowed to use those resources that are ordinarily attached and utilised by the President.[961] It was alleged that this was abused especially by the NRM party candidates.[962] It is believed that the law, which has no restrictions on term limits, enables the President to stay in power and makes the electoral field uneven.[963]

Access to media

The right to media access has continuously been abused in the country's recent elections – opposition candidates do not receive the same space as the ruling party to canvass support.[964] As mentioned before, the EC has a responsibility to ensure that regular, free and

---

956 EU Election Observation Mission (2011) *Uganda Final Report*, op. cit., p. 22.
957 UHRC (2011) *14th Annual Report*, op. cit., p. 61.
958 Ibid., p. 64.
959 Ibid.
960 Commonwealth Secretariat (2011) *Report of the Commonwealth Observer Group*, op. cit., p. 14–15.
961 Section 27 of the Presidential Elections Act.
962 EU Election Observation Mission, 2011 general election, op. cit., p. 24.
963 Citizens' Coalition for Electoral Democracy (2011) *The Citizen's Electoral Reform Agenda: Beyond 2011*, p. 2.
964 EU Election Observation Mission (2006) *Final Report on the Uganda General Election 2006*, p. 29; EU Election Observation Mission (2011) *Uganda Final Report*, op. cit., p. 28; Commonwealth Secretariat (2011) *Report of the Commonwealth Observer Group*, op. cit., pp. 4–5, 23–24.

fair elections are held. It also has a duty to organise, conduct and supervise elections in accordance with the Constitution.[965] The EC should, therefore, play an important role in ensuring the constitutional requirement that no candidate in the election is denied reasonable access and use of state-owned communication media.[966] Indeed, in April 2007, the EC made recommendations for electoral reforms requiring national media to allocate sufficient time and space for registered political parties.[967] However, this recommendation has not yet been implemented and access to the media by the opposition political parties, especially during campaign time, remains a challenge. Although state media reported all candidates, there were complaints of unequal coverage, which the EC also acknowledged and highlighted as an area in need of improvement.[968] The Code of Conduct for the media covering elections was also issued very late – only a few days before the 2011 elections, and just before the end of the campaign period. Perhaps, if the Code of Conduct had been issued and disseminated earlier, the situation would have abated. The EC has provided for the establishment of a mechanism to ensure that media adhere to the Code of Conduct on Elections in its strategic plan. In addition to this mechanism, the EC should follow up on its recommendation on amending the law and ensure that it is passed and enforced.

Management of polling on Election Day

Most election days have been uneventful, save for a few incidents. The EC is supposed to ensure the prompt delivery of election materials such as kits for the registration process, sufficient equipment such as cameras and computers, staff professionalism in the administration of the process, and adequate resources to pay officials manning electoral activities. Polling stations open at 7am and voting can only start in the presence of a minimum of five registered voters. At every polling station, there must be a presiding officer, four polling assistants and an election constable (police officer). Where there are more than 1,000 voters at a polling station, two constables should be deployed. Transparent ballot boxes are used, which increases accountability and electoral security.

In the 2006 elections, voting procedures were generally followed in most polling stations. Party and candidate agents were present in most polling stations, except in some upcountry ones. The presidential election results were declared within 48 hours. Nevertheless, the 2006 elections were also characterised by the following:

- Acts of intimidation;
- Lack of freedom and transparency;
- Unfairness and violence;
- Disenfranchisement of voters by deleting their names;
- Bribery and intimidation;

---

965 Article 61(a&b) and Section 12 of the EC Act.
966 Ibid., Article 67(2).
967 Sekaggya (2010), op. cit., p. 34.
968 EC (2011) *Report on the 2010/2011 General Elections*, op. cit., p. 67.

- Allowing multiple voting and ballot stuffing;
- Failure to cancel results at polling stations where gross malpractices took place;
- Failure to declare results in accordance with the law; and
- Failure to take measures to ensure that the entire electoral process was conducted under conditions of freedom and fairness.[969]

During the 2011 elections, most polling stations opened slightly after 7am. However, it was reported that a few polling stations opened much earlier, while others started hours later than 7am because of the late arrival of electoral materials, polling officials and voters. Concerns raised on polling day included disenfranchisement of registered voters who could not find their names on the national voters' register and inadequate training of the polling station officials.[970] There were unfortunate incidents of clashes between political parties on Election Day, as was the case in Serere and Iganga, and there was violence in Budadiri West and unlawful interruption of the voting in Mbale by armed gangs.[971]

In future elections, the EC and the Uganda Police Force should ensure that security is maintained and that any incidents on polling day are managed to prevent disruptions to the electoral process.

Access for disabled persons

During the 2011 elections, the EC delegated the role of support for the participation of disabled persons to NUDIPU. However, there were complaints that the EC did not provide adequate resources and assistance to NUDIPU. The delegation of its authority to the union allegedly affected the participation of persons with disabilities who were not NUDIPU members. Furthermore, the participation of persons with disabilities was compromised by a lack of sign interpreters and Braille, among others.[972]

Publication of results

The EC must ascertain, publish and declare results of all elections. It has, by and large, carried out this duty satisfactorily although there have been some problems.

Counting, transmitting and tallying results

After polling closes, ballot boxes are opened, votes counted, and the declaration of results filed and signed by the presiding officers and candidates' agents. The results are then publicly announced at the polling station. The announced results are delivered to sub-county headquarters with a sealed Declaration of Results form, routed to the districts for tallying, and thereafter the returning officer declares the winner. In 2006,

---

969 Rtd Col. Dr Kizza Besigye vs Electoral Commission, Yoweri Kaguta Museveni (Election Petition No. 1 of 2006).
970 EU Election Observation Mission (2011) Uganda Final Report, op. cit., p. 20.
971 UHRC (2011) 14th Annual Report, op. cit., p. 64.
972 UHRC (2011) Report on the 2011 Uganda Elections, op. cit., p. 27.

the court found that there had been some inaccuracies in the counting and tallying of results in some polling stations.[973] In 2011, the EC used a new electronic results transmission and dissemination system for tallying. Data relating to the results, in particular the Declaration of Results form, was entered at the District Tally Centre from the polling stations and transmitted to the National Tally Centre. However, there were some glitches as the system was sometimes slow.

Declaring of election results

The EC has a duty to declare the results of elections and referenda. The EC declared presidential results within the constitutional timeframe of 48 hours after the closure of polling stations. Results were also published for each polling station on the EC website. This was not the case for parliamentary election results, which were published over two weeks after the closure of polling. This is probably because there is no time limit for declaring the results for parliamentary elections as is the case for presidential elections.

Hearing and resolving complaints

The EC has competently handled dispute resolution during and after polling with fairly good results. For example, in the year 2005/2006 the EC handled a total of 856 complaints, which included:

- Presentation of questionable academic papers during nominations;
- Failure to resign from public office before contesting elections;
- Intimidation during campaigns/polling;
- Missing/misallocation of symbols and names of candidates;
- Underage persons in the voters' register;
- Double registration;
- Requests to nullify declared results;
- Voter bribery;
- Ballot stuffing;
- Defacing of posters;
- Disrupting rallies; and
- The use of abusive language.

The courts also determine or resolve electoral disputes. In 2006, the courts received 122 post-election petitions, some of which have been resolved while others are still pending. There has been a general complaint over delays in disposing of election petitions, especially those regarding parliamentary and local government elections. Another concern is the high awards made, which discourage potential litigants from petitioning courts whenever they are dissatisfied with the results of an election.

---

973 *Col. Dr Besigye Kizza vs Museveni Yoweri Kaguta, Electoral Commission* (Presidential Election Petition No. 1 of 2006).

As part of the electoral reforms, the EC stated that in 2011, it established complaints desks at the district level in addition to the national desk to handle election-related complaints.[974] The EC also established Election Liaison Committees at the national and district level, consisting of a representative of the police, the EC and contesting political parties,[975] which were to support the operations of the complaints desk, although it is reported that only a few of them were established.[976]

From 12 February 2011 to 13 March 2011, the EC conducted elections countrywide for the presidential and parliamentary offices, Local Council 3 and 5 representatives, municipal leaders and special interest groups – the second of its kind under the multi-party system. As of 1 April 2011, the EC had filled more than 18,650 elective positions, including that of the president, MPs, local government councils and representatives of special interest groups.[977] The EC received up to 358 pre-electoral complaints. A vast majority of the cases were about nomination requirements and eligibility.[978] The EC reported that it reversed 21 nominations of candidates in the parliamentary, district, municipality and sub-county elections; the High Court overturned two of its decisions.[979]

Relationship with security agencies, political parties and civil society

Security services
The EC relies heavily on the Uganda Police Force and other security agencies to maintain law and order during elections; however, it does not seem to have any control over errant security personnel. For example, when some opposition party candidate rallies were unlawfully disrupted by security agencies and Resident District Commissioners, the EC could not address these transgressions.

The EC should have quasi-judicial powers to provide redress for complainants in such cases. Although the Uganda Police Force is constitutionally mandated to preserve law and order in the country,[980] the overall supervisory role on the security of elections lies with the EC, which is in charge of all its aspects. The EC should be able to assert its constitutional mandate, which gives it authority over all election-related matters in Uganda.[981]

---

974 EC (2011) *Report on the 2010/2011 General Elections*, op. cit., p. 58.
975 Ibid., p. 65.
976 Commonwealth Secretariat (2011) *Report of the Commonwealth Observer Group*, op. cit., p. 13.
977 'Press Statement on Implementation of the Road Map for 2011 General Elections', EC, 1 April 2011.
978 EC (2011) *Report on the 2010/2011 General Elections*, op. cit., pp. 54–55.
979 Ibid.
980 Article 212(b) of the Constitution.
981 EC Act (as amended) and Articles 60–68 of the Constitution.

Political parties and agents

Political party agents usually work with EC officials to ensure that the elections are conducted in compliance with the law. In order to curb the incidence of pre-ticked ballots, the EC allowed political parties to have their agents present at all polling stations during the 2011 elections. Parties were, therefore, able to monitor the process from the beginning. Where malpractices were detected, steps were taken to address them depending on the situation. Where necessary, elections could be postponed. For example, the EC reported that the Kampala mayoral and councillors' elections were called off owing to failure by polling officials to observe opening procedures, as well as ballot stuffing and connivance by some polling officials with candidates, which had been observed by party agents. These failures resulted in violence in some parts of Kampala and forced the EC to postpone the elections.[982]

CSOs

Ugandan elections have had observers since 1980. Both international and domestic observers must apply for accreditation from the EC. The EC may, at any election, accredit any individual, group or institution to act as election observer. It also issues guidelines for them. Anyone who observes elections without accreditation or does not write a report within six months after the declaration of results (or earlier as the EC may require), is liable on conviction to a fine or imprisonment not exceeding six months.[983] Although this law has not been put into practice, it can act as a deterrent for election observers.

In 2011, regional observers such as the Inter-Government Authority on Development and international missions from the East African Community, African Union, the EU and the Commonwealth were also present. Local observers came from CSOs such as the Citizen's Coalition for Electoral Democracy in Uganda (CCEDU), Human Rights Network (HURINET), Democracy Monitoring Group and the Inter-Religious Council of Uganda, among others. The EC reported that a total of 3,497 observers were accredited to observe the general election:

- 706 international observers;
- 1,232 national observers;
- 369 political parties/organisations;
- 116 international journalists; and
- 533 national journalists.

The national tallying process was observed by 541 observers.

CSOs used innovative ways to observe and monitor the elections. In the 2011 elections, observers were drawn from their local communities due to their understanding

---

982 'Why Kampala Mayoral Poll Was Postponed', *New Vision*, 24 February 2011, www.newvision. co.ug/D/8/12/747439, accessed 31 October 2013.
983 Section 16 of the EC Act.

of the local terrain. This innovation increased the people's alertness on electoral mal-practices. For instance, in Kasese, the local observers were able to alert the CCEDU on the polling stations that had not been gazetted, since they were aware that the places being used as polling stations were not legally designated as such.

The other innovative method was to set up parallel vote tallying. This has mainly been used during the by-elections and could be used to challenge the results the EC announces. The CCEDU used the Kodeo Vote Tallying Centre in the by-elections. The CCEDU has also built a network of voter observers who conduct voter education from door to door. This approach was used for the Butaleja by-elections. In 2016 elections, the CCEDU intends to rely on these observers, who are already trained, and will also have an observation centre that will collect information from the public and be a central reporting unit for observers.

Technology has played a critical role in the monitoring and observation of results. CSOs have used short text messages and websites. In 2011, they were able to identify hotspots and alert the responsible people in the EC of malpractices. They formed the 'Uchaguzi Platform', which was used to obtain information and plan for hotspots. Vote mobilisation and 'honour your vote' campaigns were carried out through social media using Facebook pages and through websites. There is evidence that mobilisation, detec-tion of malpractices and tallying of results is possible because of technological innova-tions. CSOs opened platforms on Twitter and other social network websites and posted voter education messages, so there is more use of the electronic media in campaigns.

Notably, most observers concentrated on polling day and did not monitor the pre-election and post-election periods, which are equally important in the electoral process. Furthermore, the advanced electronic technology that was introduced in the 2011 elec-tions requires expertise. Observers without the requisite knowledge were limited in their ability to observe the elections.

G. Conclusion

The Electoral Commission of Uganda has come a long way. It has laboured under the weight of negative public perception and a lack of trust from most stakeholders, but to its credit, it has taken steps to address most of the issues raised by observers and critics. In its report on the 2011 general election, the commission acknowledged areas in need of improvement, which included:

- Delays in the delivery of election materials in some polling stations;
- Imbalances in media reporting and coverage;
- The use of basins as voting booths;
- Bribery and commercialisation of elections;
- Inadequate voter education;

- Issues with the national voters' register such as missing names and mix-ups in some voter locations;
- An uneven electoral ground for presidential candidates;
- Election violence and voter intimidation;
- Violation of electoral guidelines;
- Absence of legal ceilings for campaign expenditure; and
- Separation of elections to reduce voter fatigue and congestion.[984]

After the 2011 general election, there were extensive consultations, including discussions on the recommendations of observer missions. The EC has internally evaluated the 2011 general election through an analysis of internal reports, observer reports, political party criticisms, petitions and court rulings, assessment surveys and a series of regional and national workshops for stakeholders.[985] These assessments have been taken into account in the formulation of a new strategic plan for 2013–2017, whose purpose is to address shortfalls, weaknesses and challenges, as well as build on the strengths identified during the 2011 elections. The plan seeks to leverage the positive reforms introduced during the preparations for the previous elections and address the gaps and weaknesses that manifested themselves. It seeks to enhance the organisational and individual capacity of EC employees in administering the electoral process in partnership with external stakeholders.

Specifically, the EC strategic plan has five major areas of focus, which address some of the concerns raised by various stakeholders. The plan is based on five pillars:
- An institutionally strengthened election management body;
- Free, fair and transparent elections;
- A credible, accurate and accessible national voters' register;
- Effective and comprehensive voter education; and
- A more service-oriented EMB.

However, the EC's strategic plan does not address all the issues surrounding the electoral process, such as its own independence, restoration of term limits for the office of President, strict implementation of all electoral laws, as well as review and amendment of current laws that have an impact on elections, among other issues. The EC is one of the many key players in the electoral process. The following recommendations are made to deepen reforms of the electoral process in Uganda.

---

984 EC (2011) *Report on the 2010/2011 General Elections*, op. cit., pp. 67–68.
985 *Strategic Plan*, op. cit., p. vii.

H. Recommendations

In order to improve the electoral process and the work of the Electoral Commission, the following recommendations are made to Parliament, the EC and other stakeholders.

Parliament

- Pass laws relevant to elections relating to the appointment and removal of the members of the EC, access to media, use of state resources, term limits for the office of President, and time limits for the declaration of parliamentary election results. Recommendations from the EC for amendment of laws to provide for provisions relating to access to media, voter education and timely adoption of election laws should be heeded.
- Increase the funding allocated to the EC to enable it to perform its functions effectively. The EC should not be subjected to the Medium Term Expenditure Framework for critical areas such as the national voters' register and obtaining election materials. The phased funding approach that was applied in the 2011 election cycle should be maintained.
- Ensure that the creation of districts and the subsequent demarcation of constituencies is being carried out in a planned, coordinated and efficient manner before the elections.
- Ensure that the National Consultative Forum is strengthened to secure the multi-party system.
- Pass the Code of Conduct for political parties.

Electoral Commission

- Ensure the maintenance of an accurate, credible and accessible national voters' register.
- Enhance the conduct of elections by training all polling officials and ensuring compliance with the electoral law.
- Enhance dispute adjudication mechanisms by strengthening and establishing complaints desks in all districts and at the national level to handle election-related complaints.

- Establish and strengthen Election Liaison Committees comprising a representative of the police, the EC and contesting political parties, at the national and district levels.
- Work with the Uganda Police Force to ensure that elections are secure and are not unlawfully interrupted by anyone.
- The EC should comprehensively perform its role and use its constitutional powers to ensure that the elections are conducted in accordance with the law.

Electoral Commission and other stakeholders

- The EC and the Uganda Human Rights Commission should work in partnership with CSOs to enhance civic education efforts to fulfil its constitutional obligations. Civic education should be comprehensive and provided in a continuous manner.
- The EC and the Communications Commission should ensure that media houses adhere to their code of conduct on elections.

CSOs

- CSOs need to build their capacity to observe elections, including electronically, and to be able to observe the whole electoral process, including the pre-election and post-election period, and not just polling day.
- It may be necessary to consider establishing an independent monitoring system to audit the whole electoral process from beginning to end.

www.ingramcontent.com/pod-product-compliance
Lightning Source LLC
Chambersburg PA
CBHW080356030426
42334CB00024B/2889